VIRGINS WEEDERS AND QUEENS

A History of Women in the Garden

TWIGS WAY

SUTTON PUBLISHING

First published in the United Kingdom in 2006 by
Sutton Publishing Limited · Phoenix Mill · Thrupp · Stroud
Gloucestershire · GL5 2BU

British Library Cataloguing in Publication Data
A catalogue for this book is available from the British Library.

Hardback ISBN 0-7509-4106-5
Paperback ISBN 0-7509-4107-3

While every effort has been made by the author and publisher to obtain permission from copyright holders, if any credits have been omitted please contact the publisher and the correct acknowledgements will be made in future editions.

Typeset in 10½/14pt Sabon
Typesetting and origination by
Sutton Publishing Limited.
Printed and bound in England by
J.H. Haynes & Co. Ltd, Sparkford.

Contents

Dedication

This book is dedicated to my mother,
Beryl Margery Clarke (née Woods)
1935–2005

and to
Sweet Pea, Bramble, Parsnip, Quince, Damson, Sage,
Mulberry, Teasel and Florence

The greatest love may be found in the garden

Preface

'Tis Flora calls, bright Beauty come
Walk forth and view Elizium,
Where happy Lovers, crown'd with Flow'rs,
Do sit and sing, in still-green Bow'rs;
And many smiling Virgins stand,
Humbly expecting your Command.

John Rea, *Flora*, dedication addressed
to Lady Gerrard (1665)

'Gardening', claimed Viscountess Frances Wolseley in 1908, 'offers a considerable amount of freedom, the refining influences of poetry and beauty, contact with intelligent, interesting people, and health and happiness to mind and body.'[1] Little wonder then that throughout the ages women have been drawn to the garden as a source of both physical and spiritual sustenance. Weeders, artists, housewives, designers, society refugees, plant lovers, and even just plain 'gardeners'; the history of the garden is a history of women. However, it is a history from which we are all too often shut out. With its emphasis on famous landscape designers, intrepid plant hunters and grand estate owners, traditional garden history has all too often served to exclude women, whose contributions to these grandiose themes have been seen as marginal. Like Eve catching at the Tulip Tree leaf as she passes forever from the Garden of Eden, we are rewarded with only the smallest fragment, although our efforts have been great. Looking back over six centuries of garden writing, Eleanour Sinclair Rohde was driven to exclaim over the paucity of books written for the woman gardener, a paucity that she felt 'all the more remarkable because since medieval days the garden has been regarded as the special province of the housewife'.[2] Eighty years on, the paucity of books on the history of women gardeners is remarkable still.[3]

An argument might be made that the history of the garden, in common with the fern beloved of Victorian female plant collectors, is genderless. Yet, for the medieval weeding woman paid exactly half the wage of the men working alongside her, or the Victorian spinster struggling to dig in constricting corsetry, the garden experience was indeed distinct from that of the men around her. But much as it was different from that of men, the experience was not the same for all women. Conditioned by cultural context or social class, they might languish virginal on daisied lawns or hunt plants through the Himalayas, design gardens for Edwardian villas or cultivate Carolingian auriculas. The role of women has been as various as it has been neglected. For women such as Lady Luxborough or Louisa Johnson the garden was a very personal world, a retreat from the disappointments of life: ill-matched marriages, debts, scandals or spinsterhood. For others it was an arena of public achievement in a man's world. Eleanor Coade ran her own factory creating statues and urns that still inhabit thousands of gardens, while Ellen Willmott and Gertrude Jekyll were the first women to be honoured with the Royal Horticultural Society Victoria Medal. Ales Brewer, selling strawberry plants for Henry VIII's garden at Hampton Court, represents the many who sought neither consolation nor fame, but merely the opportunity to make a living. Housewives, whose skills in the garden supported the family with herbs for the pot and medicines in the cupboard, must form a silent majority. Writers, artists and needlewomen from the medieval period onward have also found inspiration, and sometimes consolation, in the garden: publishing against the wishes of husbands or painting despite the conventions of society, they recorded their experiences for future generations to share.

To write a history of women and the garden is to enter a world of toil and struggle, hopes and cares, successes and failures. Plants that flowered, careers that blossomed, weeds that grew, marriages that failed; all of life played out within the garden fence. As society defined and redefined women's roles, so their relationships with the garden changed. As Elizabeth von Arnim so perceptively commented, 'If Eve had had a spade in Paradise and known what to do with it, we should not have had all that sad business of the apple.'[4] A history of women in the garden thus also becomes a history of women's lives beyond the garden gate. As Tudor weeding women gave way to horticultural students, and aristocratic plant collectors to Amazonian plant hunters, so history moved on and women's roles with it. Few people can name more than two or three women in the history of the garden, and yet hidden below the surface are literally thousands waiting for recognition and rediscovery. Unappreciated, unacknowledged and often unremembered, women have strived to bring life and colour to the most barren of seedbeds only to be consigned to the deserts of history. This book celebrates the lives of many of those who have trodden the garden path before us: the named and the unnamed, the rich and the poor, virgins, weeders and queens.

Acknowledgements

When I was first commissioned by Sutton to write this book I had two fears. The first was that there would not be enough material (a fear I can hardly comprehend in retrospect), the second that I would in some way fall by the wayside and fail to complete the work. That there has been more than enough material I owe to the vast legions of women who have gone before me into the garden: the weeders, collectors, designers, artists, needlewomen and lovers. That I have not fallen by the wayside I owe to the interest, enthusiasm, patience and knowledge of similar legions of friends, colleagues and experts.

My interest in the history of women and the garden arose, rather contrarily, from the paucity of their appearance in studies in garden history. Lecturing on all aspects of garden history, I was struck by the contrast between the high percentage of women students and researchers, and the very low representation of them in the subject we were exploring. Thus was born the idea of a course on *Women in Garden History* for the University of Cambridge, Institute of Continuing Education. My first acknowledgement therefore belongs to the programme co-ordinators and staff tutors for their support for this programme. Enthusiastic research among the students led to a much greater appreciation on all our parts of the role played by women in all walks of the garden. This has continued as new students have joined the courses, often bringing with them information on little-known female garden owners, distant female ancestors, grandmothers and mothers, for whom the garden played a vital role. Each wave of students has brought with it a renewed commitment to the subject and growing confidence in its validity, and for this I thank them.

Colleagues in garden history have also been of enormous assistance. I would particularly like to thank Dr Stephen Bending for taking time to discuss his work on eighteenth-century women and 'garden retirement', and for allowing me to see drafts of his research papers. Dr Anne

Meredith shared with me her expertise on horticultural schools for women, and ensured that my early enthusiasm for Viscountess Frances Wolseley did not go entirely unchecked. Steffie Shields provided information on Lady Elizabeth Pope (an ancestor), and Joanna Martin brought to my attention her research on her ancestors, the Fox Strangways family. Anne Shellim shared information on the destination of female pupils from a larger project she was undertaking, while other colleagues brought to my attention women who had slipped through my net. Cassandra Phillips was also kind enough to allow me to quote from her grandmother's war journals, despite being in the process of publishing them herself.

Caroline Holmes deserves particular thanks for her support, both as a fellow lecturer and experienced author. Despite working to deadlines for her own book (on the history of dung) during the last year, she has always given advice and assistance freely, and passed on information of interest from her own research. Kristin Hollis has proved yet again to be an invaluable friend, colleague and student simultaneously, and did me the huge favour of reading the manuscript in draft to help spot repeats, typos and spelling errors, etc. Without Kristin there would be a lot less plants in the garden and considerably more pants. Every non-speller needs such a friend.

Research has been made possible primarily by the collections and facilities of the Cambridge University Library, the University of Cambridge Botanic Garden Library (a superb and much underused resource), and the British Library. Information has also been provided by the Royal Horticultural Society Lindley Library (and in particular Brent Elliott), the National Portrait Gallery Archives and Collections, The National Trust, and the Royal Botanic Gardens, Kew. In addition, the many excellent authors of websites including, notably, the *Oxford Dictionary of National Biography* made my task much easier. Where these have been used they have been acknowledged.

Jaqueline Mitchell at Sutton Publishing responded to my enthusiasm by commissioning this book, while the supporting cast of copy editors, designers, marketing, etc. at Sutton guided it to fruition. To whom many thanks.

Finally I would like to thank Stephen Kemp and Steve Ouditt for sharing the last year with more women than they ever bargained for.

ONE

Weeders and Breeders

EARLY WOMEN IN THE GARDEN

> Eve . . .
> Rose, and went forth among her Fruits and Flowers,
> To visit how they prosper'd, bud and bloom,
> Her Nurserie; they at her coming sprung
> And touch't by her fair tendance gladlier grew.
> Yet went she not, as not with such discourse
> Delighted, or not capable her eare
> Of what was high . . .
>
> John Milton, *Paradise Lost* (1667)

Eden, that illusory and much-sought paradise, forms a dual origin in Western culture for both the history of women and the history of the garden. Adam was created to till the ground and tend the trees of the garden, while Eve was his helpmate and, according to Milton's *Paradise Lost*, his equal in the tending of the sweet fruits and blossoms. The buds and blossoms 'gladlier grew' at her touch, and the nectarines and peaches refreshed her after her gardening labours. Eve named the plants, and knew each one. Every tree pleasant to the sight, every plant good for food and every herb that brings forth seed was in that garden, including (rather inadvisably on the part of the garden designer) the tree of knowledge of good and evil. Like a poisonous laburnum, swaying golden showers and nut-brown podded seeds over a children's playground, the tree of knowledge proved too much of a temptation. For as Eve pointed out, surely the gaining of wisdom is a good thing. Alas, as many women have subsequently discovered, a little wisdom can lead you astray from the paths of social acceptance, and it is but a short distance from the tree of knowledge to the gate out of the garden. To compound the misery of this earliest gardening couple, the goodly fruits and herbs were henceforth to be joined by thistles and thorns, and weeding was to join tending as their labours on earth. This ancient tale of the enclosed garden of paradise has echoed down the centuries, influencing our love of gardens. Rather more subtly it has influenced the history of women's relationship with the garden.

Restored as the original Eve into the Garden of Paradise, transfigured and transformed through the Virgin Mary, medieval women feature in endless illuminated manuscripts. Framed by rose arbours and turf benches, they are captured forever behind the locked gates of an enclosed virginal world. The Song of Solomon gives voice to this mix of passion and seclusion with its well-known verse: 'A garden enclosed is my sister, my spouse; A spring shut up, a fountain sealed. Thy plants are an orchard of pomegranates, with pleasant fruits.'

More worldly Eves also found themselves banished from the orchards, lest further untoward incidents led to a second fall for humankind. The flower garden with its scented blossoms, the hothouses with their childlike tender exotics, and even the weeds of the vegetable plots, all called for their attention; fruit trees, however, were strictly out of bounds. The Roman author Pliny, combining agricultural advice with rural myth, claimed that 'On the approach of a woman in this state [menstrual], must will become sour, seeds . . . sterile, grafts wither away, garden plants are parched up, and the fruit will fall from the tree.'[1] William Lawson, perhaps mindful of Pliny's advice, was still separating out the gardens of flowers and vegetables from the orchard. Lawson's *The Country Housewifes Garden* contained instructions on all types of herbs and flowers mete for her garden, but fruit trees were firmly dealt with in a separate part when he published the whole as *A New Orchard and Garden* in 1618. Referring throughout to the gardener as 'he' in the main part of his writings, Lawson eschews any reference to the goodly housewife in the orchard, although, rather perversely, the instructions within *The Country Housewifes Garden* do assume that she has read the rest of the book. One can only hope for the sake of the fruit that she has avoided actually visiting the trees.

Horticultural writers of the seventeenth-century Commonwealth, such as Samuel Hartlib, Ralph Austen and John Beale, concentrated much of their writings on the necessity for new orchards to be planted throughout the country. Encouraging both the material fruits of shared labour and the spiritual fruits of a paradise on earth, Austen's *Treatise on Fruit Trees Together with The Spiritual Use of the Orchard*[2] does not, however, go as far as to extend its commonwealth zeal to allowing women back among the fruit trees. Even in the nineteenth century most women writers confined themselves to the flower garden and greenhouse as Eve's unfortunate error echoed down the millennia.[3] The flower garden was long regarded as the especial domain of the woman, a domain which in the medieval period both symbolised her virtues and echoed her virginity.

The *hortus conclusus* (literally enclosed garden) beloved of the medieval and Tudor periods appears in thousands of brightly coloured illustrations in Books of Hours, romantic texts and even the odd gardening manual. Reflecting the circumscribed lives of the women at whom the texts were often aimed, the garden appears walled or paled in, often set within a castle beyond whose boundaries we glimpse an idyllic yet unobtainable landscape. A turf seat, often with meadow flowers, is occupied by the central character of the text. Whether holy virgin, queen or courtly lover, they are shown seated demurely within their gilded and petalled cages. A fountain representing life and love springing eternal occupies part of the picture, perhaps flowing beyond the walls recalling the rivers running from Eden. Tables hold delicacies and fruits, representing the Last Supper or the unobtainable delights of lust depending on setting and symbol, while flowers hold further clues to the meaning of the picture. Lily for purity, violet for humility, wild strawberry for the Passion, and the iris of the Trinity. A garden or flower picture could be read as a book and did indeed 'illuminate' the text. An astoundingly wide range of plants symbolised virginity, from the obvious pure white of the lily to the rather more obscure foxglove where only the shape of the flower (sealed at one end) gives away the source of the symbolism. That all these might be grown within the *hortus conclusus* gave added emphasis to its sealed and enclosed nature. Lilies of course also remind us of Eve's departure from Eden, as they were believed to have grown from the tears that she shed on leaving that gardeners' paradise.

Books of Hours, used to remind their owners of the religious lessons of the days and the seasons, also indicate the crossover between religious and sexual symbolism. Noblewomen are portrayed sitting in enclosed gardens studying an illustration of the Virgin Mary, herself seated in an enclosed garden. This peaceful image, encouraged and promulgated by social and religious morality of the period, has long influenced our view of women's relationship with gardens in the

Blessed Milk Thistle *(Silybum marianum)*

Originating in the Mediterranean but long naturalised throughout Europe, the blessed (or holy) milk thistle was named for its association with the Virgin Mary. Drops of the milk of Christ's mother having fallen onto the thistle while she was breast feeding, the plants have born the mark ever since as white veins on their dark green leaves. The plant was one of many associated with the Virgin Mary by the medieval period, the most famous of the others being the madonna lily, frequently used in pictures of the annunciation to symbolise purity. Mar[y]golds were also associated with the Virgin, as were foxgloves, commonly known as 'Our Lady's Gloves', and *Alchemilla mollis* which is still known today as 'Our Lady's Mantle'. In Germany the milk thistle was actually used as a symbol for the Virgin. Known since the Roman period as beneficial for the cleansing and healing of the liver, Hildegard von Bingen refers to the milk thistle in her *Physica* (*c.* 1150), extolling the benefits of the roots and leaves. It was still in use in the eighteenth century when Culpeper noted that it was good against jaundice and other diseases of the liver. In the last few decades intensive research has been carried out on the chemical constituents of the milk thistle and the protective properties of silymarin analysed and tested.

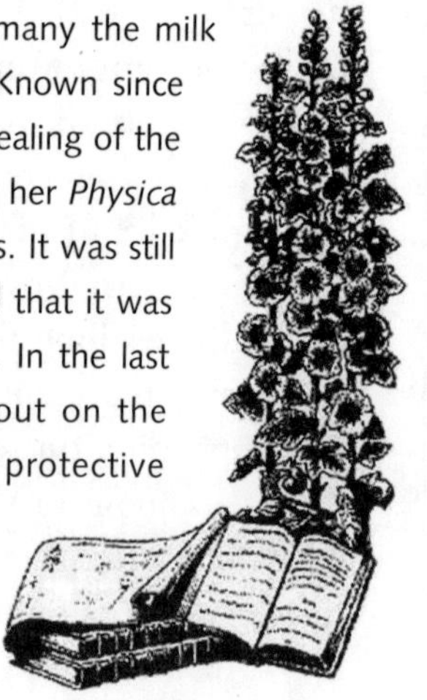

medieval period. Closely connected with the cult of the Virgin, women in gardens (and women as garden plants) are also portrayed in the courtly love literature and illuminations of the court of the Middle Ages. Perhaps the most famous of these is the thirteenth-century *Roman de la Rose*. One of the medieval world's 'bestsellers', this allegorical poem by Guillaume de Lorris expounded the whole art of courtly love. In the poem the lover is searching for his true love, which takes the form of a rose. He enters first an orchard and then a walled garden, the door of which is opened by Idleness in the form of a yellow-haired lady in a green dress. Inside the garden allegorical characters discuss with him the art of love as he continues his search for the elusive rose of perfection, a rose eventually found among the pricks of thorns and stings of nettles. Continually retold (not least by Chaucer), translated, and reproduced in a series of richly illustrated manuscripts, the *Roman de la Rose* offers us yet another vision of the link between the female and the garden. A French manuscript *c.* 1500 also tells the tale of a lover. Let into a walled garden by Dame Nature his task is to choose between three ladies in the shape of fleshy love, wisdom or courtly womanhood, each ensconced in towers within the walls of the garden.

Other tales of love and romance took up the theme of the garden as an arena for dalliance within the safety of the castle walls and soon the walled garden took on the same shades of meaning, as the shrubbery was to do in the Victorian period. A retreat in which the bounds of convention might perhaps be loosened or exchanged, where romance and reality merged. This romantic vision may be glimpsed through 'cut-away' walls and between rose-entwined trellises, as we peer into the private retreats of noblewomen of the period.[4] Tranquil and pale as befits their status, they spend their hours in the garden in religious devotion, contemplation and needlework; at least that's how the illustrators of the period would have them appear. Idealised settings include flowery meads, turf seats backed with roses, pinks and hollyhocks gay in borders. Picnic tables, water rills, and the odd troubadour added sound and sustenance to the scent and colour of their caged world. We know from Master Jon Gardener's 'The Feate of Gardening' that real English gardens contained foxgloves, hollyhocks, lilies, lavender, roses and rue alongside the rather less symbolic thyme, chamomile and garlic.[5]

Although both the plants and the gardens seen in the jewel-like manuscripts contained a strong element of symbolism this does not mean that they did not also represent a more earthly reality. Enclosed gardens of castle and manor house were also recorded in descriptions and, less poetically, financial accounts of the period. At Woodstock in 1250 the Queen's garden was ordered to be enclosed by two walls 'well built and high' by command of King Henry III.[6] The Book of Hours owned by Anne of Brittany, and now in the Bibliothèque nationale de France, shows Anne in her own garden, with its crenellated walls, turf seats and trellis. James I of Scotland first spied his future wife Jane Beaufort while she was walking in her garden within the walls of Windsor Castle. Looking down from the tower in which he had been imprisoned, the young James saw a fair garden, made fast within the tower's walls. Hawthorn hedges and green arbours protected the complexion of his lovely Jane, who walked as 'Cupides own princess' in her garden of flowers. James recorded the garden, and his love, in a poem which gives us a wonderful picture of these enclosed gardens at the beginning of the fifteenth century.

Some gardens were more extensive than could easily be shown on an illuminated miniature. At her castle in Clare, Suffolk, Elizabeth de Burgh, Lady Clare (endower of Clare College, Cambridge in 1338), had a private garden securely placed within the castle walls. The garden was crossed by paths of flint, perhaps leading to and from the fountain that is clearly recorded in her accounts. In addition she had an 'aviary' in the form of a pheasant house containing a glass chamber, a house for deer, and a model sepulchre or tomb, perhaps modelled on the Holy Sepulchre in Jerusalem.[7] Depending on one's viewpoint, Lady Clare was either an extraordinarily unfortunate or fortunate woman. Granddaughter of Edward I, she was married three times, but all of her husbands pre-deceased her, leaving her an extremely wealthy widow at the age of 28. Taking a vow of chastity she devoted herself to her estate and her family, although she gave generous gifts to religious houses and Clare College. Undoubtedly she would have appreciated the fine gardens that now exist at the college with their smooth grass, year-round colourful borders and enclosed tranquil pool.[8] Her castle at Clare was recorded as having its gardens increased by a 'new paling about le Maydengardeyn' in the mid-fifteenth century by its then occupant Richard, Duke of York. Whether this was truly a garden for maidens, or perhaps a maiden (new) garden, must be speculation.

Undoubtedly for some women, in particular the nobility, the garden was a place to languish rather than labour; however, for others the reality of the garden involved less purity and more earthiness. A life at court was not the agreeable fate of the majority in the Middle Ages, or indeed at any subsequent time. Rather than having their hearts swelled among jewel-like flowers, the responsibilities of most women were rather the swelling of the stomach. Housewives were busy with sowing and raising in kitchen, herb and physic plots; weeding women laboured earning a poor but honest wage. These are the women who were not merely in the garden but were part of the garden, for whom the garden was a place of engagement and activity, rather than isolation and repose. Neglected in the sparkling books of romance, their story may be found in more prosaic books of instruction and accounts recording the day-to-day dealings of working women or worried housewives. Without them the medieval garden would have been a much poorer, and weedier, place.

Following her expulsion from the paradise of the weedless Eden, and subsequent heartless imposition of thorns and thistles on the world, Eve would have found herself carrying out that most basic of gardening duties – weeding. Equipped 'with such gardening tools as art, yet rude, guiltless of fire, had form'd, and angels brought'.[9] It comes as no surprise to discover that the deity associated with weeding is, in fact, Runciana, a goddess.

Although this vital duty often fails to merit a specific mention among the numerous exhortations to the housewife to 'plant and tend', this may be regarded more as an oversight than an indication of lack of weeds. Fitzherbert in his sixteenth-century *Book of Husbandry*, stated that the housewife's garden should be weeded 'as often as need shall require . . . for else the weeds will overgrow the herbs'.[10] Almost 100 years later, in 1618, William Lawson extolled the seventeenth-century 'Eve' to take 'skills and pains with weeding the garden, with weeding knives or fingers'. William Coles also observed that even Gentlewomoen, if the ground be not too wet may doe themselves much goode by kneeling upon a cushion and weeding.'[11]

Weeding was not only the duty of the meritorious housewife, but was one of the relatively few ways in which 'respectable' women, including undoubtedly the spinster and the widow, might earn a small income. The sturdy figure of the weeding woman plods through the history of the garden from the Tudor court to the Victorian kitchen garden. Consistently poorly paid and little regarded, these women had the merit (from an employer's point of view) of being able to carry out monotonous but intricate work for remarkably little reward. The restricted social position and financial precariousness of the single woman made them ideal for such positions. As early as 1354 women were employed among the gardening workforce at Rotherhithe (Surrey).[12] Perhaps the most famous women weeders are those listed in the Royal Accounts of Hampton Court in the first decades of the sixteenth century. Here we learn of women such as Agnes March, Alice and Elizabeth Alen, Elizabeth Anmun, Joan Smeton, Annes Lewes, Jone Abraham, Margaret Cookstole, Katherine Wite and Agnes Norton. Their duties, paid at the rate of 3*d* a day, were the removal of charlock, cockles, convolvulus, dandelions, docks, dodder, groundsel and nettles. In addition they were to attempt to eradicate that very weed that Eve had been the cause of, the thistle. A further two women, Ales Brewer and Margaret Rogers, appear to have expanded their role beyond their weeding duties by selling strawberry roots, primroses and violets. These were collected by the bushel load (at 3*d* a bushel) and presumably indicate plants being collected from the wild to be planted in the gardens.

In the early fifteenth century the wife of William Bishop, gardener at Winchester College, had earned 4*s* by weeding, a considerable amount, although how many days she spent on her knees we do not know.[13] A hundred years later, in 1515, twenty-two women were employed at York Place (later Whitehall), each earning what appears to have been the standard wage for the period of 3*d*. More weeding women appear in the accounts of Cardinal's College (later Christ Church), Oxford. In the spring and summer of 1530 Margaret Hall, Joan Fery and Agnes Stringer were all paid 3*d* a day, plus free bread, ale and herrings, for 'cleansing the garden' and 'rooting up unprofitable herbs'. Rather disturbingly, wages of weeders were still 3*d* a day at Knole (Kent) in the time of Charles I, although they could earn 5*d* a day for picking hops in the grounds. By the reign of William III wages at Hampton Court had increased to some 8*d* a day – although with a maintenance budget of £4,800 a year either there were an awful lot of weeders or some gardeners were getting rather more than their fair share. Picking light or difficult crops such as hops or peas was another task commonly allotted to women through the centuries. Women pea-pickers were recorded in a photograph in *Country Life* in the early twentieth century, and hop-pickers still worked in the Kentish hop fields after the Second World War.

Actual weeding women were one thing in the garden, but at Woburn they went one step further in their commitment to the working woman. In 1697 the intrepid garden visitor Celia Fiennes recorded that 'you pass under an arch into a Cherry garden in the midst of which stands a figure of stone resembling an old weeder woman used in the garden, and my Lord would have her effigy which is done so like and her clothes so well that at first I took it to be a real living body'.[14] To modern minds it may seem unusual to celebrate one's employees in such a public way, but in the first century AD Pliny also suggested that one might place the initials of the 'gardener' in topiary about the garden. Much as such a permanent monument might serve to please, the small matter of remuneration was undoubtedly foremost in the minds of most of the women gardeners and harvesters. To place the wages of weeding women in perspective, a sixteenth-century wheelbarrow might cost 1*s* 3*d*, a shovel 4*d*, and a ceramic watering pot 1*d*. After a hard day's weeding a woman might thus earn almost enough to purchase a shovel with which to cultivate her own garden – if she had energy left to do so – or perhaps a choice variety of apple tree for 6*d* under which to contemplate the turn of fortune's wheel since the Garden of Eden.[15]

Although it looms large in the accounts of the Middle Ages and Tudor periods, weeding was not the only task that working women gardeners might carry out. At Little Downham, the Bishop of Ely's manor in Cambridgeshire, 'Juliana' was in charge of the labourers in the kitchen gardens, keeping the kitchens provided with peas, beans and orchard fruits.[16] Illustrations in estate management books of the fifteenth and sixteenth centuries give us further clues to the varied role of women in the garden. Although of wider European origin, these manuscripts perhaps give us an insight that may well be of relevance to the English experience.

One of the most popular, and frequently copied, of these texts is *Liber Ruraliam Commodorum* by Pietro de' Crescenzi. Written in the first years of the fourteenth century, it repeated much information on estate management, agriculture and horticulture from the classical texts. It became extremely popular across Europe and was translated from the original Latin into four languages including Italian, French and English (the last as *Treatise on the Advantages of Country Life*). Each of the translations was accompanied by a series of illustrations illuminating the text and often showing Crescenzi himself in the act of pointing out particular tasks to the landowner. Also illustrated are the labourers carrying out these gardening tasks, among them many working women. Women are shown planting seedlings, raking and preparing ground for seed, and also tending to the training of plants into the particular shapes (known as *estrades*) favoured in this period. Often distinguished by their practical brown clothing, some appear to wear gloves or gauntlets, similar to those that would be recommended by Jane Loudon some 500 years later. Some wear practical white headgear, while others are shown balancing a wimple while coaxing recalcitrant herbs into anguished positions.

Unsurprisingly, the illuminations in Christine de Pizan's fifteenth-century *Le Livre de la Cité des Dames* also include women involved in manual labour. In a hurdle-bound field or garden a woman turns the earth with a spade while another watches. Both in the same practical grey clothing, the one watching wears a wimple – one wonders is she mistress or work colleague? Are the women real or imaginary in this world of exceptional women that also includes artists, stone masons, and writers. Christine de Pizan was herself a professional woman writer. Born in 1363, she was married at 15 and widowed at 25. She combined a career in epics and verse with bringing up three children and caring for her own mother; unsurprising then that she should extol the virtues of the working woman in all fields.

Books of Hours of this period also portray women in horticultural tasks, either as the main picture or more often in the decorative borders surrounding the text. An early sixteenth-century Flemish example includes a lady of the manor supervising her female gardener, who is on her knees tending to one of the small boarded beds in a railed garden.[17] The scene reminds us immediately of the instructions given by the contemporary gardening author William Lawson that the lady of the house should always superintend her weeding women to avoid costly and unfortunate errors of identification; an admonition repeated in the nineteenth century by Louisa Johnson.

A wheelbarrow is pushed by a woman in another Flemish Book of Hours of *c.* 1500.[18] Her colleague or husband helps support one end of an unfeasibly enlarged and extended carnation that grows from the wheelbarrow and continues around the page border. They are both dressed in plain working clothes and she has tucked up her aprons as she lifts the burden. Another border has the tables turned as a man wheels a barrow loaded with potted plants, while two women carry further flowers and pots – whether from their own home or a nursery we do not know. A fourteenth-century guide to the healthy life, *Tacuinum Sanitatis*, shows women working in small fields or gardens collecting spinach leaves and cabbages or coleworts (a non-heading brassica) of some kind. Most of these women appear to be workers in the gardens they inhabit, toilers for money rather than love, but many more must have taken on the burden of the garden as part of their wider duties to home, hearth and husband.

Between the working women and the leisured noblewomen lay the 'gentle housewives' who worked in their own kitchen gardens, laying siege to the labouring man's heart with their concoctions of herbs and simples, or perhaps with their melons and parsnips. Barnaby Googe, in his *Foure Books of Husbandry* (1577) claimed that an out of order garden was the sure sign of a 'no goode huswyfe' for unto her was the charge of the garden.[19] Although books of gardening advice were rare until the seventeenth century, the few that we do have emphasise the vital role of the housewife in both the flower garden and, especially, the productive garden. Divisions between the several types of garden were not so strong in the medieval period as they were to become by the eighteenth and nineteenth centuries, and so the idea of a housewife being responsible only for flowers, while her husband grew the vegetables and herbs in a separate area, would not have been appropriate. Within the productive gardens would be grown not only the vegetables for cooking and for salads but also the herbs for physic and flavouring. Intermingled with these might be the scented plants, whether for decoration, cooking or strewing. Not only did these scented herbs act as 'companions' at the dinner table, but their properties were believed to keep away the harmful pests and insects in this pre-chemical age.

The skills needed to understand the growing and tending of these plants were as vital to the housewife as the knowledge of how to eventually use them. Distillations and decoctions of herbs would keep her household healthy and fed during the coming months, but only if she could provide the plants needed for them. Gardening was not merely a leisure activity but an occupation vital to the success and survival of a woman's household and her family. Gardening and medicinal skills would be handed down from mother to daughter in an age when female literacy was low and patent medicines unknown. Concerned by the inexperience of his youthful wife, 'Le Ménagier de Paris' prepared detailed instructions on her household, cookery and garden duties. His 1393 script included such tasks as setting rosemary cuttings and preparing them for sending to 'distant parts'. One wonders whether the rosemary cuttings supposedly brought into England by Queen Philippa at the start of the fourteenth century had themselves been prepared with the waxen cloth, smeared honey and wheaten flour Le Ménagier recommended.

The *Book Of Husbandry* by Sir Anthony Fitzherbert is one of the first books in England to acknowledge the vital role that the housewife has to play as gardener and producer. First published in 1523, and marketed as a general book of instruction to the husbandman, the book also addresses the good housewife of the day. Although he admits himself ignorant of many of the tasks undertaken by women, Fitzherbert acknowledges the multiplicity of their tasks and proffers advice on time management to help them through the day. A task he refers to as essential for the housewife is the obtaining of as many seeds and herbs as she can, especially those that are good for the pot and to eat. One can imagine the relevant parts of Fitzherbert's book being read to the conscientious housewife by her more literate husband, in an age when reading aloud was a common practice. A less conscientious housewife might have preferred the more satirical *Ballad of the Tyrannical Husband*, published anonymously a few decades earlier and recording a lively debate as to whether it was the husband or wife who contributed more to the household. But choice was not on the housewife's side. The paucity of household books in general prior to this period, and more specifically those aimed at women, can be blamed on both lack of printing and also lack of general literacy. As the century progressed, bringing with it a Protestant emphasis on Bible reading, the number of literate women grew, particularly among the gentry. By the end of the century texts addressed to the housewife might actually have been read by them, although book buying would still be seen as a male pursuit.

Thomas Tusser was one of the most successful writers, catering for both the rise in literacy and the desire to understand estate management. His book *A Hundrethe Pointes of Goode Husbandrie* was first printed in 1557 and became an instant success. Having married shortly before this, he was able in later editions to append *A Hundrethe Pointes of Goode Huswifery.* Not content with having amassed by then over 200 bestselling 'good points', 1573 saw the good husbandman and his wife bombarded with *Five Hundred Pointes of Good Husbandrie*, of which some were specifically aimed at the education of the gardening housewife. Written in excruciating but memorable doggerel, these five hundred points went well beyond estate husbandry. Drawing on his own by then considerable experience, Tusser gave advice on farming, animal management, religion, marriage, life and just about everything. He even included a short autobiography by way of proving his authority. To avoid information overload (not to mention doggerel indigestion) Tusser helpfully divided his 'Hints' into seasons, with jobs for each of the months. In January, for example, the housewife should be busy planting peas and beans and setting young rose roots; during March and April she will work 'from morning to night, sowing and setting her garden or plot', to produce the crops of parsnip, beans and melons which will 'winnest the heart of a labouring man' for her later in the year. Her strawberry plants will be obtained from the best roots which she has gathered from the woods, and these are to be set in a plot in the garden. Berries from these plants will be harvested later the same year, perhaps a useful back-up if the parsnips have failed to win the man of her dreams. July will see the good wife 'cut off . . . ripe bean with a knife' as well as harvesting the hemp and flax which it will be her responsibility to spin later in the year.

As the seasons turn so does the weather, and by December the strawberry plants will need covering with straw (hopefully having accomplished their aims): 'Laid overly trim upon crotchis and bows, and after uncovered as weather allows'. Also susceptible to the hard frosts and winters of the sixteenth century were the small pinks or gilleflowers and Tusser notes that, 'The gilleflower also, the skilful doe knowe, doe look to be covered, in frost and in snowe. The knot, and the border, and rosmarie gaie, do crave the like succour for dieng awaie.'[20] Small wonder, perhaps, that Fitzherbert had noted that the housewife's duties were never at an end.

Tusser lists the plants that would provide the colours and scents to uplift the soul, as well as those used more practically to lift the body from illness and affliction. Those that he expects the country housewife to be familiar with include Bachelor's Buttons (the double buttercup), Campions, Columbines, Daffadowndillies, Gilleflowers, Hollyhocks, Lark's Foot, Rosmarie, Snapdragons and Sops in Wine. This last was the charming name for the pinks that are white or pink with red edgings and markings. They could be dropped into wine to give a subtle flavouring as well as looking pretty. Most of this array of country flowers would either be planted as sets from existing plants or produced from sowings. Unsurprisingly, among other tasks the good housewife is admonished to save her own seeds for next year's planting, and swap with neighbours as needs be to supplement her own stores. The obtaining and the propagation of plants was, of course, one of the main concerns of the housewife, and something which in the age of the catalogue and seed packet we are prone to neglect – if not forget altogether.

Another essential of the good housewife, according to Tusser, was the ability to rise early. This is mentioned with a suspicious frequency within his 'points', perhaps suggesting that rising on a cold March morning to collect and set strawberry roots was not a task relished by many. Rising late, we are told, would betoken a bad housewife or one of ill repute. Magdalene Herbert is a shining example of one of the many women who undoubtedly took Tusser's advice to heart. Born and brought up in a proud border family at Eyton-on-Severn in Shropshire, she was married to Richard Herbert. Her son George (born in 1593) immortalised his mother with the poem '*Memoria Matris Sacris*', in which he recalls how she began every day early, with prayers and simple braiding of her hair. Then 'on her family forth she shone, and spent on kitchen, garden, house, due management'.[21] Perhaps reflecting as she went on Fitzherbert's hints on multi-tasking.

At the beginning of the seventeenth century, the newly literate country housewife was rewarded for her studies with the first book specifically addressed to her gardening duties, William Lawson's 1618 publication, *The Country Housewifes Garden*. A practical gardener himself, with over forty years' experience in his own gardens in Yorkshire, Lawson outlines both the design and planting of the housewife's garden, before then leading her through the monthly tasks to be carried out in both the productive and flower gardens. Lawson's division of gardens into the kitchen garden and the summer garden reminds us of the very restricted number of plants available to gardeners of the period. Extending the flowering season beyond late spring to autumn was almost impossible without recourse to the new and expensive 'exotics'. To make up for the lack of these Lawson recommends the country housewife to make 'those herbs and flowers comely and durable in squares and knots' to provide pattern in the garden in the autumn and winter period. No doubt some of these were to be raised from the seeds and division the goodly housewife had stored up, while others might be swapped with neighbours.

The kitchen garden was to contain the standard mix of herbs, fennel, onions, skirrets and worts, which seem to have dominated the medieval and Tudor diet. In case of a 'cloyed' stomach, rather than a warmed heart, wifely ministrations might include radish sauce, capers and cucumbers. Cucumbers might be had 'young and fresh' by casting the seeds all summer long 'here and there'. Rue, set from slips along with rosemary, was used in physic only, being 'too strong for my housewife's pot, unless she will brew Ale'. Turnips, thyme, parsnips and pennyroyal were among the simple 'herbs' Lawson recommended because, as he said, 'I teach my Country-Housewife, not skilful artists . . . Let her first grow cunning in these and then she may enlarge her garden as her skill and abilities increaseth.'[22]

During the English Civil War, Goodwife Cantry was one of those who seem to have enlarged their gardens and their skills. Her Northamptonshire garden might appropriately be described as a riot of colour, with larkspur, single and double, three kinds of spiderworts, and lupins in four different colours vying with each other for attention, while chamomile provided a calming sedative in those troubled times. With herbs from the garden this Goodwife brewed a potion against plague which no doubt was as effective as any other of the medicines available for this scourge of the times.[23] To help the budding housewife gardener achieve the skills attained by Goodwife Cantry, Lawson closes with a list of sixteen good gardening rules, many of which have stood the test of time: set moist and sew dry; gather herbs for pot when tender and true; gather seeds ripe and dry; thin out settings and sowings; and the somewhat rueful reflection that Yorkshire, Lawson's home, is colder and less timely for gardening than more southern parts. His parting shot (an unnumbered seventeenth 'rule') brings us firmly back to that other role that women were thought to excel at in the garden, weeding: 'The skills and pains of weeding the Garden with weeding knives or fingers, I refer to themselves and their maids, willing them to take the opportunity after a shower of rain, withal, I advise the Mistress either to be present herself, or to teach her maids to know herbs from weeds.' No wonder the diligent but indigent old maid or widow might turn to weeding as a way to keep the wolf from the door when the skills of weeding had been instilled from an early age.

Preparation of physic (medicine) was another female duty that most of us have abandoned, but the relationship between the garden and the physic chest was a very close one in the days before patent medicines. Tusser tells us that the sixteenth-century housewife should keep, among many others, 'cold herbes in her garden for agues that burne, that over strong heat to good temper may turne. While endive and Suckerie, with spinach enough, all such with good pot herbes should follow the plough.'[24] Mystic visionary and saint, Hildegard von Bingen compiled one of the earliest medicinal herbals in *c.* 1151. The tenth child of a German noble family, Hildegard von Bingen became an anchorite at the age of 14. Visions of salvation came to her over the following years and were recorded in a book entitled *Scivias* which appeared in 1151. The following years saw her writing on health and healing (the *Liber simplicis medicinae*, later called *Physica*), and notes for a medical handbook (*Liber compositae medicinae*, later called *Causae et Curae*). With the protection of her position as head of a nunnery, and the blessing of her archbishop, Hildegard von Bingen did not run the risks faced by most wisewomen and was able to explore fully the use of herbs and plants. Describing 230 plants, 63 trees, and 45 animals under nine general headings, she tells of the basic qualities, the medicinal value, and the proper application of each. From the *Liber compositae medicinae* comes this recipe: if a depression conditioned by various fever attacks should cause a person headaches, they should take some mallow and twice that amount of sage, crush these into a pulp in a mortar and pour a bit of olive oil on it. If there is no oil, a little vinegar will do. They should then apply it over the skull from the forehead to the neck and cover with a cloth, repeating this for three days. Sage was known as a cure-all in the medieval period, and mallow drew the bile of black humours.

Teresa McLean in her study *Medieval English Gardens* draws attention to the numerous references to women herbalists in medieval literature, many growing medicinal and pot herbs in the same small plots, others with separate infirmary gardens based on those of the Benedictine infirmerers, or perhaps inspired by von Bingen.[25] William Turner's three-volume herbal (1568) was written in English to enable those not schooled in Latin to have access to the knowledge of herbs and physics which he takes from the classical scholars. Most women of course would have been 'unschooled' and Turner thus made the works of Pliny and Dioscorides available to them for the first time. Although, perversely, the dedication to Queen Elizabeth draws attention to a conversation she had with Turner in which he states her Latin was far above that he had encountered in any other gentlewomen.

John Gerard's famous *Herball or General Historie of Plants* (1597) was addressed to the 'Courteous and the well-willing' as an introduction to the gentle art of 'simpling' or herb knowledge. Written in English and including plant identification, cookery and physic, it has been argued that it might have been intended for the use of the gentlewoman,[26] freeing her from the need to resort to the wise woman or the witch. Frowned on by apothecaries and herbalists, the lower class herb-wise woman always flirted with danger. There was a fine line between the goodly housewife curing the ague and the witch who was accused of creating potions for less worthy purposes. Gerard relates how the Small Moone-Wort [*sic.*] (Lunaria) might be used by both apothecaries and witches, and urges caution in resorting to the wiles of the latter. Mandrake was a popular herbal cure among women, causing them to be fruitful and bear forth children, but again caution is urged and the words of the 'unschooled' doubted. Certainly the long-held belief in the ability of the mandrake root to scream as it was dug up, and cause insanity and death in those who overheard, deserved debunking as it was based largely on a desire to artificially inflate prices rather than any reality.

The cautious housewife might be safer sticking to Gerard's recommendations for nosegays and posies or flowers for decking the house, advocated by him for their sight and smell and their ability to make the heart merry and joyful. House decorations included pinks, columbine and meadowsweet, which used as garlands and nosegays might keep away not only the pervasive noxious smells of the sixteenth century, but also ward off the plagues and diseases that periodically swept through both urban and rural areas.[27] Gerard does, however, relent in recording the common names given by the 'English women' to herbs and plants; cotton-weed, for example, being known by countrywomen as 'Live Long', due to its long-lasting flowerhead.

Thomas Johnson, a seventeenth-century apothecary, was so concerned about the dependence of the medical profession on women who dealt in roots and herbs that he instituted the idea of the botanical outing among his profession. Until that time his fellow apothecaries had relied on purchasing the ingredients for their remedies from the market place, a market place they shared with the very women healers and collectors that they despised. 'Almost every day in the herb market', he claims, 'one or other of the druggists, to the great peril of their patients, lays himself open to the mockery of the women who deal in roots. These women know only too well the unskilled and thrust upon them brazenly what they please for what they will.' One wonders whether he himself has been the subject of such mockery as he continues in uncomplimentary terms, 'the doctor relies on the druggist and the druggist on a greedy and dirty old woman with the audacity and the capacity to impose anything on him. So it often happens that the patients' safety depends on the herbal knowledge of an ignorant and crafty old woman.'[28] This description of old, crafty and ignorant is one that would be levelled by men at women collectors and gardeners through the centuries.

In his work of 1629, *Paradisi in sole Paradisus Terrestris, or A Garden of all sorts of pleasant flowers which our English ayre permitt to be noursed up*, John Parkinson is more complimentary about some of the women who had helped him in his quest for plants, either by exchange of knowledge or with specimens. Tomazin Tunstall, a gentlewomen from the north of England, was one such. She provided material for Parkinson from her collection of rare plants. Parkinson dedicated his work to Queen Henrietta Maria (herself a plant lover and known as the 'rose and lily queen') but he also had care to address himself to the lesser gentlewomen. To these he devoted his discussions on the planting and ordering of 'The Garden of Pleasant Flowers', and in particular the tulip, a flower which he says owes its popularity to the love and liking that women bear to them.[29] Parkinson's combination of plants for physic and plants for the aesthetic captured the dual concerns of the seventeenth century. As Jonathan Goddard (erstwhile physician to Cromwell) stated in 1670, both 'worthy ladies and gentlewomen of quality, do employ themselves in making confections, and medicines both internal and external',[30] while the influx of new plants and flowering bulbs made the creation of a garden a thing of delight. Parkinson was also happy to find among these new delights a place for 'those that are usually called English Flowers' and grow in 'every woman's garden' such as gilleflowers and wallflowers.[31]

By the early seventeenth century there was an increased emphasis on the active role of upper-class women in the creation of the decorative or pleasure garden. Lucy Harington, Countess of Bedford (1581–1627), was not a woman to languish on a scented chamomile seat. Although her husband, Lord Edward Russell, had been forced by ill health to retire from court, Lucy remained socially and culturally active, perhaps relieved by the absence of a man she had been married to since the early age of 13. A close friend of Anne of Denmark and a wealthy heiress in her own right, Lucy created two spectacular gardens to rival Anne's own. At Twickenham she created a garden laid out in the design of the pre-Copernicum universe, where trees and shrubs took the place of planets in their orbits. Granted her second garden of Moor Park (Hertfordshire) by James I, she used the court designer Isaac de Caus to lay out terraces and parterres in the latest fashions. Summerhouses, statues and grottoes added to the early Renaissance feel of this garden, which eventually gave its name to the 'Moor Park' apricot. The gardens can barely have matured when she died tragically at the age of 46, scarcely into her gardening stride. A patron of Ben Jonson, she was commemorated by him in 1616 in an ode that delights in her being 'fair, free and wise' as well as learned as a man. In reference to her gardening skills he envisages her with powers, 'The rock, the spindle, and the shears [to] control'. Multi-tasking among the noblest of women.

John Rea, whose *Flora; seu de Florum Cultura* was published in 1665, also targeted the various 'gentle ladies' of his aquaintance in his dedications. Lady Gerrard of Gerrards Bromley, wife of Rea's patron, was duly extolled to 'walk forth and view Elysium,'[32] although little more than viewing was envisaged for this noble lady. The wife of Rea's fellow florist and plant lover, Thomas (or Trevor) Hanmer, was given a similarly inspirational role as 'genius of the plants and flowers', but also noted for being herself a born florist and plant lover, a role that she apparently continued even after widowhood and remarriage. In his final dedication (the first eighteen pages of Rea's *Flora* are made up of rather florid poetic dedications) Rea extols the virtues of the flower garden to 'The Ladies' who will read his work and nurture the new exotics which he lists within it, the newly bred 'Orient Virgin' and 'Grand Purpur' tulips, the damask roses, and the auriculas. Mistress Buggs raised her own fine purple auricula in her Battersea home, rating a special mention by Rea, as well as a purple and lemon striped version. With white eyes, stiff and erect, both plants were held 'in good esteem'. A trip to Mistress Buggs was a delight for any dedicated florist.

At Swallowfield, Berkshire, the garden of Lady Clarendon was described by the diarist John Evelyn during his visit in October 1685. Despite the unpropitious time of year the gardens obviously impressed Evelyn and he gushes forth with admiration:

> I have hardly seen a seat which shows more tokens of [elegance] than what is to be found here, not only in the delicious and rarest fruits of a garden, but in those innumerable timber trees in the ground about the seat, to the greatest ornament and benefit of the place. There is one orchard of a thousand golden, and other cider pippins; walks and groves of elms, limes, oaks, and other trees. The garden is so beset with all manner of sweet shrubs, that it perfumes the air. The distribution also of the quarters, walks, and parterres, is excellent. The nurseries, kitchen-garden full of the most desirable plants; two very noble orangeries well furnished; but, above all, the canal and fish ponds, the one fed with a white, the other with a black running water, fed by a quick and swift river, so well and plentifully stored with fish, that for pike, carp, bream, and tench, I never saw anything approaching it.[33]

The seventeenth-century preoccupation with the scents of the garden, and the house, appear again here. Lady Clarendon has flagged the waters with *Acorus calamus* (sweet flag) and other exotics we are told, and the sweet scent not only pervades the ornamental waters but also an indoor closet, in which she has placed the scented reed. In all his praise Evelyn makes an especial point of complimenting Lady Clarendon who he says is so extraordinarily 'skilled in the flowery part'.

While Lucy Harington inspired an ode, and Lady Clarendon inspired a diary entry, their horticultural rival the Duchess of Beaufort inspired a whole book. When Charles Evelyn published *The Lady's Recreation* (1717, republished as *Being a Third Part of The Art of Gardening Improv'd* in 1718) he chose to devote the first page to proclaiming the talents of the lately deceased Mary Somerset, Duchess of Beaufort (*c.* 1630–1715). Referring to Mary as 'a certain Lady of the first quality who had a soul above her title, and sense above what is common in her sex', Evelyn praised her in particular for her knowledge and management of her greenhouses and parterres. Overflowing with exotics and newly introduced plants, these had, according to Evelyn, 'arrived at so great a perfection that she could challenge any foreign gardens to produce greater curiosities'.

The Duchess had started life as Mary Capel, born into a royalist gardening family at Hadham in Hertfordshire. A family portrait with the gardens at Hadham in the background shows her with her sister Elizabeth, who was to become a famous flower painter. In 1657 Mary had made a second marriage to Henry Somerset which resulted not only in nine children, but also two gardens. Based at Badminton and Chelsea the Duchess amassed a collection of thousands of exotics, under the supervision of famous botanists of the day (including William Sherard). Arranged in her 'infermeries' these exotics came from as far afield as Virginia and the Cape of Good Hope. Stephen Switzer eulogised the care she lavished on each of her charges which, he said, 'kept them in a wonderful deal of health, order and decency'.[34] Corresponding with John Ray, the Essex collector, and visited by Hans Sloane (plant collector, founder of the British Museum and closely involved in the re-founding of the Chelsea Physic Garden), the Duchess amassed a collection of thousands, many unknown elsewhere in England. Some of the earliest pelargoniums in the country were to be found here, including *Pelargonium peltatum*, or the ivy-leaved geranium. Introduced in 1701 this was a star set to rise, as the craze for pelargoniums lasted into the Victorian period. Widowhood in 1700, and a rather religious fervour, resulted in an increase in her collections as reflected in an illustrated catalogue, the latter largely accomplished by an underfootman (Daniel Frankcom) trained by the Dutch artist Everard Kickius (or Kik).

Combining the study of insects with botany, the Duchess was also patron of one of the most famous male entomologists of the day (Eleazar Albin, a professional painter). It was the Duchess who was the first person to suggest that each species of butterfly and moth had its own favoured food plant. A butterfly visiting the gardens and stovehouses of the Duchess would certainly have had an extensive menu to choose from. In addition to the butterflies, visitors to this large herbarium included Mary Delany in her never-ending quest for subjects to collage (see page 82), and Mary's sister, Elizabeth Countess of Carnarvon, who illustrated some of the collection.

Seeking to promote the flower garden as suitable for the 'fair sex', Charles Evelyn suggested that inspection of the gardens need not take up too much time. However, he might have thought twice before using the

Duchess as his exemplar, as she was rumoured to spend a third of each day with her plants, the rest of the day being divided between her household and her religious devotions. By the time of her death in 1715 a twelve-album herbarium had been produced, now in the care of the Natural History Museum, London.[35] The album demonstrates both the extent of her collections and her own inquisitive approach. A Chinese plant, recorded as tehima, is noted as making a very good oil which the Chinese use in cakes and call mayeou; while petsai, according to the Duchess, eats like a cabbage,[36] but much more tender – an adventurous contrast to the scented orange trees and tulips usually recommended by Evelyn for the lady's garden.

Beds 'filled with the most beauteous [ever]greens and borders set off with the most delightful flowers' were for Charles Evelyn the delights of the lady of leisure, but for others the orange tree and the evergreen represented a career. In common with most other trades, that of nurseryman was almost exclusively a male preserve into the twentieth century. However, death, infirmity or absence of the male head of the household could frequently lead to businesses coming into the hands of the females of the family, and the plant trade was no exception. As widows, women could carry on trading after their husband's death, thus sidestepping the undoubted discouragement of both the early guilds and the later married woman's property regulations whereby the profits of one's endeavours were not one's own.[37] Where the name of the nursery or business was not changed to reflect the change in manager or owner, it can be difficult to trace these women. Even where records and accounts exist (which in itself is unusual before the eighteenth century), they rarely specify the sex of the retailer. Fortunately a great deal of work has been carried out by the garden historian John Harvey on early nurserymen/women and their clients, and this has served to open up a previously hidden world of women on both sides of the counter.[38] Positions for women in the nurseries might include more than proprietorship, whether inherited or not. Women might also work in accounting, illustrating new arrivals, potting on and pricking out, cleaning, tidying and of course . . . weeding!

Nurseries, as a phenomena, first appear to emerge in the mid-sixteenth century, suggesting that they perhaps evolved to fill the vacuum left by the dissolution of the monasteries and priories with their specialist knowledge and skills in plants. The first record of the term 'nuseryman' appears in 1672, although of course a brisk trade in plants collected from the wild for resale or propagation existed prior to this. It would be underestimating the wiles of women to think that the weeding women at Hampton Court, who are recorded as supplementing their income by the sale of wild strawberry plants, did not go one step further and plant out runners, slips and seeds in their own gardens to provide a more assured income. The early nursery trade and suppliers were based almost exclusively in London until the mid-eighteenth century and provincial markets relied on many small or seasonal providers, especially for smaller gardens. Thus nursery gardening was often regarded as a second, or subsidiary, profession even by men. In the late seventeenth century William Lucas traded in seeds, trees and plants, but described himself in his will as a 'milliner'. How much more likely then that a woman might see it as a useful supplementary income, rather than a career?

One of the earliest known London nurserymen, a John Banbury of St Margaret's, Westminster, appears to have run a family business. At his death he directed that his son should continue to plant and graft for his mother, Margery. Although this might mean nothing more than an intention to support her, the wording implies that she was to continue to run the nursery, as was to become the common practice of widows in later centuries. Catherine Tuggie, despite having nine children born between 1621 and 1632, continued the nursery business of her husband Ralph after his death in 1632. Ralph Tuggie had specialised in some of the 'rarities' and florists' flowers that so delighted men such as John Gerard and John Parkinson, and his wife continued to raise some of the best examples of these plants. A later version of Gerard's *Herball*, edited by Thomas Johnson, recommends that any aspiring plantsmen obtain their Gilleflowers, Colchiums and Auriculas at the garden of 'Mistress Tuggy' of Westminster 'which in the excellence and varietie of these delights exceedeth all that I have seen'. The nursery retained its good name throughout the life of Catherine, who was able to contentedly pass the business to her son, Richard, on her own death in 1651.[39]

Not all of the nurseries and seed suppliers associated with women were of small or middling size. One of the greatest nurseries of the seventeenth century was that established by Moses Cook,[40] Roger Looker, George London and (later) Henry Wise (master gardener to Queen Anne). At its height the Brompton Park Nursery covered over 100 acres. Kensington and Chelsea had been famed for their small market gardens and nurseries since the sixteenth century, but that of London and Wise overshadowed them all. George London built up the business, supplying plants for his own great formal designs at sites such as Hampton Court. Royal gardener to George III, he had taken on Henry Wise as an apprentice at the nurseries, although Wise was destined to outlive his master. The nurseries were also to supply Sarah, Duchess of Marlborough with polyanthus, ranunculus, tulips, hyacinths, violets, carnations and other flowers at the end of the century. With commissions across the country the two partners were on the road for much of the time, and the work of keeping the financial side of the nursery going fell to Henry's wife, Patience. Patience Wise was the daughter of the royal master carpenter Matthew Banckes, and may well have learnt her skills from his business. For the Brompton Park Nursery Patience answered letters, directed work, and generally ran the business during the long and protracted absences of her husband. We know she had neat handwriting as she also kept a receipt ('recipe') book, which survives to this day. Patience had married Henry in 1695 when he was still on the way up in his career, and she was still with him when he retired in 1728. A portrait of Patience Wise also survives, and author Jane Brown describes her as looking out with dignity, dark eyes, a longish nose and a determined chin. The latter doubtless of use when dealing with recalcitrant customers.

Working alongside Patience Wise was Henrietta London, the daughter of her husband's partner George London. Henrietta married John Peachy in 1705, and it was as Henrietta Peachy that she became famed for her botanical drawings. In the year of her marriage she completed work on the additional illustrations for Maria Merian's *Metamorphosis Insectorum Surinamensium* (we will meet Maria Merian again in a later chapter as she lived a remarkable life dedicated to her own botanical illustrations). By the time of her father's death in 1713 Henrietta had worked for years illustrating and recording many of the fruits and flowers that came through the Brompton Park Nursery. Her father left her a leather-bound book of her own pictures of fruits in his will. Illustrations by Henrietta of plants newly arrived from South Africa still survive at Badminton House as part of the collections of the Duke of Beaufort. Among these are undoubtedly records of plants that would have been in the collections of Mary, Duchess of Beaufort as it was in this very period (1705–20) that her own collecting was at its height.[41] Nurserywomen were by no means confined to the Brompton Park Nursery. In another part of the country Elizabeth Clark, wife of Henry, was dealing with the accounts and correspondence of her husband's nursery and land agent business. Less prestigious, and less profitable, than that of the royal gardener, Elizabeth had to deal with

Swamp Bottlebrush (*Beaufortia sparsa*)

When the Duchess of Beaufort was busy tending her collection of exotics in the late seventeenth century, the Australian continent had only been known for a few decades and the first English colonies were almost a century away. Strange then that the Duchess should be commemorated by a genus of twenty species all of which occur naturally only in South Western Australia. The best known of the species is the *Beaufortia sparsa*, or swamp bottlebrush, a shrub of some 2–3m in height with bright green oval leaves. It is the flowers that catch the eye, orange-red clusters forming a cylindrical 'brush' on the ends of the branches. The plants can be difficult to rear in cultivation, needing extremely well-drained soil and warm conditions, and would have presented exactly the sort of challenge that the Duchess enjoyed. However, the seeds are difficult to remove from the capsules, which do not open of their own accord after collection. A method of extraction used by modern plant collectors is to break up the capsules in an electric coffee grinder and then sow all of the resulting debris, not a technique available to the seventeenth-century collector. The commemoration of the Duchess after so many centuries demonstrates clearly her importance as an early plant collector and her lasting fame.

wood stealers and thieves in addition to all the day-to-day difficulties caused by poor roads, bad weather and unreliable carriers which bedevilled their attempts to create a profitable business.

By 1786 nurseries and seedsmen in London were numerous enough to merit a list being produced by John Abercrombie for the use of fellow gardeners. Published in *The Gardener's Daily Assistant* it gives details of almost sixty nurseries and some thirty-four seedsmen.[42] Many are only identified by a surname, but we do see the first appearance of the Bailey seeds suppliers, which would pass to Elizabeth Bailey by 1794. Elizabeth continued to trade at the Rose and Crown, Bishopsgate, until 1813, presumably inheriting the business from her husband. Eleanor Compton was another business widow. Eleanor had married Henry Woodman in 1728 in St Paul's Cathedral, and on his death thirty years later he willed to her 6 acres of nursery and the stock of the nursery in Chiswick. She continued to trade from the premises, using her own name and managing the business. The Exeter nursery originally established by William Ford, was in turn run by his widow Ann following his death in *c.* 1829. She must have made a success of the business as it was still trading in 1850, having introduced the Exeter elm (*Ulmus glabra* 'Exoniensis'). Elizabeth Wheeler, recorded as a 'nursery and seedswoman', was trading in Gloucester from 1814 to 1820, taking our story into the nineteenth century and providing continuity from the earliest weeder woman who plied her wares of wild strawberry plants at the gates of a Tudor palace to the successful Victorian widow managing her own nursery.

TWO

Queen Bees

ROYALS IN THE GARDEN

E mpresse of flowers, tell me where away
L ies your sweet Court this merry May,
I n Greenewich garden allies?
S ince there the heauenly powers do play
A nd haunt no other vallies. . . .

R oses and lillies did them draw,
E re they diuine Astraea saw;
G ay flowers they sought for pleasure:
I nstead of gathering crownes of flowers,
N ow gather they Astraea's dowers,
A nd beare to heauen their treasure.

John Davies, *Hymnes to Astraea*, extract from Hymn No. IX (*c.* 1600). The first letter of each line spells Elisa(Betha) Regina[1]

Whether nurturing plants from every corner of their empires or occupying their empty hours by embellishing the royal grounds, Queens of England were rarely out of sight of a garden. For some the flower garden was a cult, for others it was a retreat. Arriving on England's plant-impoverished shores many a foreign princess saw her immediate mission in life not to provide heirs and princes, but to improve the island with new plants and gardens. From Eleanor of Aquitaine to Princess Augusta, none could resist the temptation to add to Britain's native flora. In a country always open to changing fashions, the arrival of French, Dutch, Danish and German royals meant constant changes. These were played out not only in royal gardens but also in those of the court and the country, as they 'followed the leaders'. A monarch interested in gardens could influence a whole nation; witness the mania for kitchen gardens during the reign of Queen Victoria, whose own 22-acre walled plot was laid out by her beloved Albert.

Even those who showed little interest in the creation of their own gardens might inspire the efforts of those around them, as did Elizabeth I on her courtly progressions. Leaving a trail of impoverished courtiers and splendid landscapes she led her court from the crescent lakes of Elvetham (Hampshire) to the fountain at Kenilworth (Warwickshire). Contentment in the gardens of others has not, however, been a hallmark of queenly virtue, and the royal palaces and homes of England are surrounded by remnants of hothouses, grottoes and terraces, where each consort or monarch has in turn made their imprint. Kew alone bears witness to at least three gardening queens as Caroline, Augusta and Charlotte each out-fashioned and out-gardened their royal mothers-in-law. Henrietta Maria went one better than most when she took on the mantle of the 'rose and lily queen' bringing a summer to follow on from Elizabeth's everlasting spring, but few have rested content without enriching the garden of England.

Three Eleanors commence our story, each from warmer shores and each making her own contribution to an island just setting out on its gardening career: Eleanor of Aquitaine, Eleanor of Provence and Eleanor of Castile. Eleanor of Aquitaine (1122–1204) had the dubious pleasure of being married both to a king of France (Louis VII from 1137 to 1152) and then to a king of England (Henry II from 1152), as well as being rumoured to having a long-standing affair with her uncle, Raymond, Prince of Antioch. Educated in the manners and ways of the French courts, Eleanor had created a garden at her Cité palace in Paris, while married to Louis. In the warm air of Paris, acanthus, poppies, lilies and roses grew in beds shaded by pear, fig, cypress and willow: a haven of colour and scent in a crowded city. She had followed her husband to the Crusades in the 1140s and would have seen the gardens of the Near East, which she was to visit again with her son. Her arrival in England, following the annulment of her French marriage, heralded the creation of an enclosed garden at Winchester (then the principal royal seat). Known as the Queen's Garden, this small courtyard garden was enclosed within the high castle walls. Rose-covered trellis and perhaps a raised turf seat and a bubbling water feature would have distinguished it from the more functional courtyards of the castle. Many of the plants that grew in the Cité may have flowered again under English skies. Whether they kept Eleanor's mind from straying to the courts of Paris and Poitiers we cannot know, but perhaps they were some consolation for the grey skies of England and Henry's affair with Fair Rosamund Clifford. Eleanor's life was not destined to be one of garden repose and she joined the cut and thrust of European court politics, some might say with a vengeance. The years 1174–82 saw this formidable woman first imprisoned by her husband and then reinstated to court life as Queen Mother. Patron of literature and familiar with the texts of courtly love, Eleanor outlived her husband and her son Richard, dying at the grand age of 82. Her tomb in Fontevrault Abbey depicts her clasping a book, an unusual addition for a woman of this period.

Eleanor of Provence (1223–91) led a slightly less turbulent life, being married to Henry III from 1236 (at the tender age of 13) until his death in 1272. Of legendary beauty and religious inclination, she, too, was to become involved in the rule of the country first through her husband and then her son. As with Eleanor of Aquitaine, Eleanor of Provence came from the background of courtly love and courtly gardens of continental Europe and spent lavishly on developing the arts in England. It is no surprise that in 1250 we find a reference to the Queen's Garden at the royal palace of Woodstock. The bailiff of the palace was instructed to encircle the Queen's Garden with two walls, 'well built and high with a good herbary in which the same Queen may be able to disport herself; and a gate from the herbary next the chapel of Edward our son, into the aforesaid garden'.[2] The herbary would have been a private garden for the use of the Queen and her attendants only, full of sweet-smelling flowers. Two years later the 'great herbary' was being returfed, perhaps with the sweet close-cropped turf of sheep downlands. In 1277 Eleanor, by then Queen Mother, petitioned the priory of Llanthony (Gloucestershire) that she and her ladies-in-waiting should be allowed to enter the priory gardens for their delight and exercise. They were to enter via a bridge between the castle and the priory that was to be newly made for the Queen, no doubt adding further pleasures to the outings. After Henry's death Eleanor took the veil and joined the prestigious priory at Almesbury (Wiltshire), perhaps encouraged by the gardens we know existed there.

Eleanor of Castile (1241–90) might have been presumed to have matters other than gardening on her mind when she arrived at the court of Henry III in 1255, again only 13 years of age. Her recent marriage to Henry's son, Edward, does not however appear to have taken up all her thoughts, for she is said to have brought with her quinces with which to make the Spanish confection of *mermelada*, or quince jam. Quince (*Cydonia oblonga*) was a luxury fruit in the thirteenth century, being priced as much as 4*s* a hundred (as opposed to 3*d* a hundred for apples and pears), while quince tree saplings were 2*s* for four in 1292. An orchard of quinces was planted in the royal garden at Westminster in the 1280s, supplying one hopes enough *mermelada* for the entire court.[3] There may have been more to the introduction of the quince than merely a sweet tooth. The Castilian court would have known that the quince was also regarded as the golden love apple of Aphrodite[4] and Eleanor

Hollyhock *(Alcea rosea syn. Althaea rosea)*

Also known by its common name 'Rose of Spain', this stately summer flower is supposed to have been introduced to England by Queen Eleanor of Castile. Reaching 3 metres in height, the prolifically seeding biennial has long been a firm favourite of cottage gardens. Originally found in pale pinks, it has been bred to encompass all shades from white and cream, through to gothic blacks (var. nigra). Despite its traditional English name its origins lie in the Near East, as indicated by its popular French name *ros d'outremer* and lesser-known English version rose ultramarina or outlandish rose. Queen Eleanor is popularly thought to have encountered it while accompanying Edward I on his crusade to the Holy Land, giving rise to its common name hollyhock or the holy mallow (*hoc* being the Anglo-Saxon for mallow). In addition to its statuesque proportions and long-lasting spires of colour, the pigment found in the flowers is supposed to have healing qualities, while the leaves were recommended by John Evelyn as a pot-herb. Its synonymous family name 'Althaea' comes from the Greek for healing and indicates an ancient origin for the use of its flowers in physic. Much hybridised in the Victorian period by the nurseryman William Chater, it was the traditional pink spire that figured so prominently in Victorian watercolours by painters such as Helen Allingham. One of its earliest appearances in a garden painting is in the mid-fifteenth century, when its tall spires can be seen above a low border of carnations and pinks, in the French translation of Boccaccio's *La Teseida* in the enclosed garden of Amelia.

was perhaps intimating at more than breakfast when she arrived as a teenage bride. When Edward departed for the Crusades, Eleanor elected to travel with him, following in the footsteps of Eleanor of Aquitaine. From her travels in the Middle East she is supposed to have brought back the hollyhock (from –hoc meaning mallow, literally the holy mallow), while from her native Castile came the sweet rocket or summer lilac (*Hesperis matronalis*). Other sources also credit her with the introduction of wallflowers and lavenders.[5]

Like Eleanor of Aquitaine, this Eleanor also had enclosed gardens tight within the castle keep. At Rhuddlan Castle, Wales, records describe a garden with a small fishpond, a well, seats and turfed lawn. In 1280 Eleanor obtained grafts of the Blandurel apple for her orchards at King's Langley.[6] The gardens at King's Langley survived until the time of Anne of Bohemia (wife of Richard II), although Anne does not appear to have had the same dedication to fruit growing as her predecessor. In 1289 Eleanor had several gardeners from Aragon working in the gardens, to which they must have brought both skill and exoticism. Aragon at that time was still heavily influenced by Moorish architecture and style, and the gardeners would have been well acquainted with the courtyard garden full of exotic foliage, skilfully propagated fruits and trickling waters over smooth stone. What they felt about their fate, to garden in the backwaters of Hertfordshire, is unrecorded. After Eleanor's death in 1290, a 'King's Garden' was created, hedged around and with an artificial swan's nest in the pool. Eleanor appears to have had a liking for property alongside her liking gardens. By 1290 her lands were worth £2,500 yearly, an unprecedented amount for a queen. Contemporary descriptions of Eleanor include the comment that she 'acquired many fine manors', giving rise to a verse by Guisborough: 'The king would like to get our gold, The queen, our manors fair to hold'.[7]

Eleanor of Provence and her daughter-in-law Eleanor of Castile are both commemorated in the re-creation of Queen Eleanor's Garden at Winchester. Little is known of the original Winchester Castle gardens and so this garden reflects fragmentary descriptions of several royal residences in the last part of the thirteenth century. Planting includes the hollyhock, wallflower, wild strawberry, violets, roses and gillyflowers. A trickle fountain of water adds sound to the scents of the herbs and roses, and the chamomile lawn. A tunnel arbour allows one to walk in the garden without fear of browning one's milk-pure complexion, a garden feature essential in Spain but perhaps less necessary in the

English climate. To complete the regal connection, this re-creation of a medieval herber was opened by the late Queen Mother in 1986.

The fourteenth and fifteenth centuries did not enjoy those periods of peace which are so conducive to garden making. It is perhaps telling that the plant gifted to Queen Philippa by her mother the Countess of Hainault in 1338 was not another breakfast fruit but instead the rosemary (or *ros marinus*), held in esteem throughout Europe for its medicinal virtues and its ability to be a 'great help and comfort'.[8] The Queen is said to have brought it back from Antwerp in her baggage with her new born son, the Duke of Clarence, along with instructions on its propagation. An early sixteenth century translator of this text stated that rosemary was not known in England prior to Philippa's introduction, although it had made an initial entry with the Romans.

Although Henry VIII certainly spent considerable sums on gardens, particularly those at Hampton Court, few of his wives had the opportunity to enjoy these in ease and quietude. Henry, one suspects, was not a man to be gainsaid over a planting plan. Hever Castle, the childhood home of Anne Boleyn, contains orchards and walks named after its famous occupant, but these were created at the beginning of the twentieth century by William Waldorf Astor as part of his re-creation. Queen Mary and Philip also appear to have been otherwise engaged. A single record of the Queen's Garden at Richmond, looked after by John Lovell, records only the location and the presence of a lodge there. Fortunately for the weeding women, however, 'weeding, sanding and sayling' was still necessary throughout the gardens and orchards of the old Richmond Castle, and so their meagre income remained assured.

It is thus with Elizabeth I, the fair virgin queen, that we retread the path to the royal garden. Her own childhood was largely spent at Hatfield House, where a re-created garden in the Tudor style commemorates her presence, thanks to the inspiration of Lady Salisbury. Elizabeth's rather fraught assumption of the throne brought into her care the royal palaces and gardens of her father, Henry VIII. Although she did not throw off these horticultural responsibilities entirely (in her privy garden at Whitehall, for example, she retained thirty-four heraldic beasts clasping vanes painted with royal arms and symbols[9]), she was no spendthrift. Unlike Henry, who had spent £62,000 on the buildings and gardens of Hampton Court alone, Elizabeth nurtured her finances perhaps more than her gardens. Not for her the extravagances of a reign based on the royal purse; instead it was to be her courtiers who vied to outdo and outspend in courtly entertainments and royal spectacles.

Sir William Cecil at Theobalds (Hertfordshire), Robert Cecil at Pymms (Middlesex), Thomas Cecil at Wimbledon (Surrey), Robert Dudley at Kenilworth (Warwickshire), Lord Lumley at Nonsuch (Surrey), Sir Christopher Hatton at Kirby Hall (Northamptonshire) and Lord Hertford at Elvetham (Hampshire); all courtiers turned gardeners in their desire to catch the eye, and the heart, of that most hard-hearted of queens. Easy to delight and yet difficult to pleasure, Elizabeth's court evolved an ever more complex code to symbolise the mythology of her unique reign. Specific plants and flowers, statues of deities, water features and secret enclosed gardens all symbolised the mystery and power of the virgin queen.

Meaning and symbol in the flower beds was of course nothing new in the Elizabethan age, and it comes as no surprise to find that many of the flowers that symbolise Elizabeth had previously been associated with the cult of Mary. Lilies of purity, the violet of humility, and the five-petalled eglantine rose, all were shared between the eternal and the mortal queens. Pictures of Elizabeth display the symbolic flowers, both embroidered on her clothes and entwining themselves around her portrait. An engraving by William Rogers (*c.* 1590–1600) shows Elizabeth as *Rosa Electa* flanked on the left by the red and white Tudor rose, and on the right by the virgin eglantine.[10] The *Phoenix Jewel* portrait also contains the same symbols, but using enamelled gold.[11] Virginal, deep-rooted, and 'so green that the sun of Spain at its hottest cannot parch it',[12] the eglantine was Elizabeth's very own rose, while the Tudor rose linked her to her father, to the roots of her inheritance, and to the peace of England. 'Wear eglantine, and wreaths of roses red and white put on in honour of that day' ran the verses of George Peele on the thirty-fifth anniversary of Elizabeth's coronation, celebrating peace and purity. Peace was also a factor in the transfer of many of the old Catholic flowers from the cult of Mary to that of Elizabeth, although some recusants still designed gardens designed to celebrate the Trinity rather than the earthly Virgin. Revealing the passionate side of the virgin queen was the pansy 'love-in-idleness' which, in Shakespeare's allegorical *A Midsummer Night's Dream*, released the potion of love to cause chaos in the fairy world. Elizabeth was also present as Shakespeare's 'fair vestal in the west' at which Cupid had aimed his bow only for it to glance off its mark and loose instead the pansies' power.[13] Thus in one scene Elizabeth was both purity and passion – a neat trick if you can pull it off.

'Daffadillies', primroses, pinks, 'cullambine', cowslips, kingcups and the sweet violet celebrated Elizabeth in verse and in embroidery throughout her reign. Crowned in the springtime of her life, she was to remain forever associated with the spring flowers and the 'grassie greene' of pastoral tradition as celebrated by Edmund Spenser in *The Shepherds Calendar* (1579).[14] Twenty-one years later spring was becoming eternal, as John Davies's *Hymnes to Astraea* celebrated 'Green garlands never wasting; In her shall our State's fair Spring, Now and forever flourishing'. Year-round spring is perhaps easier achieved in verse than in the garden, but statues helped to extend the seasons of praise. Astraea, the Just Virgin in Virgil's IVth Eclogue, was one of many identities that Elizabeth partook of. Astraea had returned to earth from the heavens, bringing with her a Golden Age, and was thus an ideal allegorical character to decorate a courtier's garden. Diana, chaste hunter and killer of the upstart Actaeon, was another favourite, as was the moon goddess Cynthia. Easily identified by her crescent moon headdress, she was most prominent at Nonsuch. Here Lord Lumley begged symbolic forgiveness for his own youth, when under Catholic influence he had supported the Ridolfi Plot to assassinate Elizabeth. Allegorical gardens such as Lumley's were the culmination of Elizabeth's long reign. They built on a long history of heraldry and display, which had been present in Henry VIII's gardens as knots, heraldic beasts and topiary. Elizabeth's courtiers took this one step further as poetry gave way to real flowers, prose to statuary, and myth to reality in the form of new and more splendid gardens.

An examination of some of the gardening efforts of Elizabeth's most favoured courtiers gives us a clear insight into this shifting relationship between setting and symbol. A firm favourite of the Queen, and one who was rumoured to have been rewarded with the cherry-ripe rather than the lily, was Robert Dudley, Earl of Leicester. Dudley entertained the Queen and her court at his castle at Kenilworth in 1565 and 1575. In preparation for her visit in 1575 Dudley laid out what was probably an extensive new garden, providing that surprise and variety which was an essential for any successful royal visit. These new gardens were described by Robert Laneham in a gushing style that would do justice to any celebrity magazine today. The goddess Diana herself, we are told, would have enjoyed the bowers, arbours, seats, walks and fragrant trees within the garden. A terrace walk gave views over a sunken area bordered by obelisks and spheres. This sunken garden contained quarters of herbs and fruit trees, divided by grass walks that met at an 8ft-high fountain of white marble. The fountain consisted of athletes and a bear with staff, emblematic of Dudley himself, rather than

Elizabeth, perhaps giving us an insight into what it was about their relationship that didn't quite suit her.

Lord Lumley, at Nonsuch, was a little more prescient. We have already encountered his statues of Diana and Cynthia at Nonsuch, but these were a small part of the Elizabethan whole. Heavily influenced by Italian symbolic landscapes, Lumley planned a garden not in patterned parts but as an emblematic whole. Formal gardens close to the old royal palace contained the queen in various guises, including the pelican (as nursing mother of *Ecclesia Anglicana*) and the chaste huntress, all set within knots, mazes and labyrinth, and viewed from a mound. Unlike Kenilworth's formal gardens contained within the walls, those at Nonsuch led on to informal gardens where the imagination ran riot. Between groves of shady trees a series of tableaux were created that preface in many ways the theatrical visions of the eighteenth century. A Grove of Diana contained a spring and grotto round whose mouth the figures of Diana and Actaeon stood, Actaeon's antlers already forming. Also at the mouth a motto (in Latin) described the fate of lust in the face of purity – a theme, perhaps unsurprisingly, absent from Dudley's garden setting at Kenilworth. A further grove contained a Temple or Bower of Diana, overhung with praises to the goddess of the chaste. In yet another stood pillars topped with phoenix and pelicans. Surely even the most untrained English eye would be able to identify the myth of the sacred Diana from Ovid's *Metamorphoses*?

The crescent moon of Cynthia appeared again at the gardens of Elvetham, although on a vastly different scale. Playing host to Elizabeth's court in 1591, Lord Hertford created one of the most memorable entertainments of the age. A lake, in the shape of a crescent moon, was excavated within the park, and three islands created within it. On one of these islands were placed trees in the shape of ships' masts, on another a fort of Neptune, and on the last a huge mount, with a spiral walk of privet representing the 'monster of Spain'. Within this setting, watched by Elizabeth from within a specially created bower, the battle of the Armada was replayed over two nights, culminating, as at Kenilworth, with fireworks.

Even without the fair Elizabeth, one wonders if the Cecil family might have been notable gardeners. William and his sons Robert and Thomas all chose to entertain Elizabeth with gardens. Theobalds, home of William Cecil, was visited frequently by Elizabeth, so much so that it was regarded by some almost as an additional royal palace.[15] A Privy (or private) Garden contained knots, fruit trees and corner arbours, all set within an enclosing hedge. The Great Garden also contained patterns and knots but on a much vaster scale, being over 7 acres in area. Here, nine knots each contained different features: one a marble fountain, another heraldic symbols, a further flowers, while wooden columns or obelisks and a summerhouse also added decoration. A decorative canal or moat provided an area for bathing and fishing, while it was said one could walk for 2 miles in the allées. Elizabeth, unusually in the guise of Venus, was to be found at the centre of a maze, raised on a mound, which we presume gave views over the rest of the garden. Thomas Cecil, eldest son of William, learnt by his father's success and also created a house and Garden to accommodate the Queen and court. Wimbledon was a late Elizabethan house but again included the typical Privy and Great Gardens, with walks, knots, fountains and fruit trees. A pillar, perhaps crowned, was the focal point of the Great Garden. The pillar was a symbol used by Emperor Charles which Elizabeth took as hers after the defeat of the Spanish Armada in 1588, just as the gardens at Wimbledon were being created. The gardens at Wimbledon were much altered by Henrietta Maria but we do not know whether she symbolically overthrew the pillar.[16]

Finally, in our horticultural search for Elizabeth, we see her not as a statue or pillar, but as an emblem for an entire garden. Pymms, Middlesex, was purchased by William Cecil in 1582 for £250 and given by him to his second son, Robert. A relatively small manor, the gardens lay some distance away from the house and were being created afresh by Robert, one suspects with assistance from his father. A description of the work in progress was given to Elizabeth as an allegorical speech by a 'gardener' on her visit to Theobalds in 1591. From this we learn that the garden was to have four quarters and within each was to be set a knot. Tradition ends there however, for the first knot (the only one we have a description of) was to be set not with herbs but with a selection of flowers each emblematic of her majesty. These were to include the twelve Virtues set out in roses, the three Graces in pansies, and the nine Muses in different flowers. At the centre was to be placed an arbour of eglantine for, as the gardener said, it is so deep-rooted and so green that 'the sun of Spain at its hottest cannot parch it'.[17] Thus not just part but the whole of this quarter, and one may presume the other three, was to be a complex representation of the virtues of Elizabeth. Not just the Queen in a garden but the garden as Queen.

For Anne of Denmark, wife of James I of England, gardens were a diversion from disappointment in much the way as was later to be recommended by Louisa Johnson.[18] James's open homosexuality and distaste for women led to a divided marriage, despite the seeming evidence of eight children. Anne had married James (then James VI of Scotland) by proxy in Oslo, and one cannot help feel that the reality might have been purposely hidden from her for as long as possible. Anne, a devout Catholic, was from a cultured and artistic background at odds with that of the Scottish James. Once jointly crowned on the death of Elizabeth in 1603, Anne took on responsibility for the redesign of the gardens at both Greenwich and Somerset House. She probably chose the newly created gardens at Somerset House to be the backdrop to her portrait by Marcus Gheeraerts the Younger. The painting shows patterned squares of turf and gravel with paths leading between them, and demonstrates the importance that Anne gave to the connection between royalty and gardens. Much of the new Upper and Lower Court buildings were to the designs of Inigo Jones, whom Anne also commissioned to design and build the five gateways at her other residence at Oatlands, Surrey. The building works at Somerset House (temporarily renamed Denmark House) cost some £34,000 and included rendering the river/garden front to imitate stone.

Anne had one of the most famous garden designers of the Renaissance in her employ: Salomon de Caus. De Caus's speciality was water features, fountains and grottos – often combined to spectacular effect using hydraulics. He was in England from 1607/8 until 1613 and was involved in the creation of gardens for Anne at Somerset House and for her son Henry, Prince of Wales, at Richmond. At Somerset House de Caus incorporated a huge grotto fountain depicting Mount Parnassus, around which reclined four river gods representing the principal rivers of Great Britain, while on the mount itself sat the nine Muses, with a golden Pegasus on the top. A contemporary plan of the gardens reveals symmetrical parterres bordering on the River Thames with the grotto fountain in the east garden. With its fountains, grottos, parterres, walks and hydraulics, Somerset House must have been one of the most striking gardens in England at the time, incorporating much of the new European Mannerist style of garden. Its only rivals were the gardens of Lucy, Countess of Bedford (see page 18), and Anne's other house, at Greenwich. De Caus was again employed at Greenwich, and here again water, automata, hydraulics and grottos were the hallmark of his design. A grotto-aviary, with shells, stones and plants encrusted on its walls and real birds flying through it, formed a living feature. Huge statues spouted fountains from cornucopia, and a female centaur cavorted in spray, while a ball was held aloft by a jet of water.[19] Only Italy and France had seen gardens of this style before, and it was Anne who formed the vital link to European Courts via her Catholic leanings. Her son Henry, Prince of Wales, would perhaps have been England's Renaissance Prince, had it not been for his untimely death in 1612, leaving his mother bereft and his gardens unfinished. With Lucy, Countess of Bedford, dying in 1627, and Anne in 1619, the gardening world also lost two of its great female patrons.

Treading a similar path to that of Eleanor of Castile, Henrietta Maria of France arrived in England in 1625 bearing orange trees. While the quince had represented love, the orange represented purity and chastity. Rather than smelling of the 'loved woman' it gave off the sweet smell of paradise, rather than the hard centre, a sweet juice. Its ability to bear flowers and fruits at the same time symbolised the transience of worldly pleasures; that both the quince and the orange are used to make breakfast spreads seems a strange coincidence in the history of queenly horticulture. Henrietta Maria married Charles I by proxy at the age of 15, and the marriage was initially undermined by Charles's favourites and infidelities. The relationship was eventually to blossom and attain mutual respect, genuine regard and eventually strength in adversity. In 1637 they were portrayed as the 'ideal couple' posing against a backdrop of gardens taken from Crispin de Passe's *Hortus Floridus*, little knowing what lay in store. On her initial arrival in England, accompanied by a retinue of French Catholic attendants, Henrietta Maria had brought with her a love of gardens which she had imbibed at the court of her mother, Marie de' Medici. Henrietta introduced to England not only French style and French plants but also French gardeners and garden designers. André Mollet, son of Claude Mollet who designed gardens at the Tuileries and Versailles, was brought to England by the Queen to design her greatest garden, at Wimbledon House. André was to divide his time and his attentions between pleasure grounds for Henrietta Maria, designs for Prince Frederik Hendrik of Orange and, from 1648, Queen Christina of Sweden, also an avid gardener and plant collector.

Henrietta Maria took over the gardens at Denmark House after the death of Anne. Happy to transfer employers, Inigo Jones returned to work there adding an ornamental seat in the bowling alley, a cistern house and an arbour for Henrietta. A less successful addition was the Catholic chapel, of such magnificence as to cause extreme anxiety and hostility in the Protestant court. A new river landing was created from Portland Stone, while fountains and grottos elaborated the gardens still further, including the splendid Arethusa fountain, now to be found at Bushy Park,[20] and another of Mercury (both by Hubert le Sueur). Henrietta Maria also 'inherited' the palace at Oatlands, Surrey, from Anne, and kept some of her large collections of orange trees there under the care of John Tradescant. In 1649, after the execution of Charles, Parliament recorded a large garden house at the palace at Oatlands for the keeping of forty-two orange trees. Surprisingly, these were bearing 'fair and large' oranges[21] despite, one presumes, some neglect in the previous months as Henrietta abandoned her English palaces for the courts of France. At Wimbledon House, purchased from the Cecils and given by Charles I to Henrietta Maria, the Elizabethan garden was still in the process of being redesigned and replanted under the direction of André Mollet when Henrietta was forced to flee the country. Embroidered parterres, fountains, and summer-houses were abandoned, some half-finished, others never seen. In 1649 the Commonwealth beheaded not only the king but avenues, fruit trees and statues, destroying for ever the gardens of the Elizabethan and Caroline queens.

What the Commonwealth could not destroy, or not for long, was the link forged by Elizabeth, Anne and Henrietta Maria, between garden imagery and the royal court. Masques, poetry and portraiture portray royalist gardens, many soon to be destroyed, some only imagined. Inigo Jones had created plays for Anne of Denmark and moved effortlessly from one queen to the next as patronage dictated. When William Cavendish, Earl of Newcastle, welcomed Charles and Henrietta to his new gardens at Bolsover Castle in 1634 he welcomed them not just to an earthly paradise but to a symbolic Garden of Love, containing statues of Eros and Venus, fact mingled with fiction in a design of Inigo Jones's creation. In Ben Jonson's *Chloridia*, Henrietta Maria was enthroned as Chloris, transformed to Flora, goddess of the flowers, sitting within a golden arbour; while the 'Gardens of the Britanides' in Jonson's *Luminalia* represented the rule of Charles and Henrietta as heaven come momentarily to earth. Heaven is a tall order even for monarchy, but a garden is after all paradise on earth, and a paradise that was to see a revival with the restoration.

Charles II himself was rather too short of finance and power to implement the paradise that he envisaged, although St James's Park, London owes its water features and avenues to his ambitions (now greatly informalised). His wife, Catherine of Braganza, was similarly handicapped in her creativity, although she did popularise the drinking of tea and the establishment of trade with Tangiers, which assisted the trade in plants.

A mutual interest in gardens can often seem to cement even the most unlikely marriage, and so it was for Queen Mary (1662–94) and William III (William of Orange). A lively and attractive girl of 15, Mary, daughter of James II, was devastated at the prospect of her politically arranged marriage to the older, more reserved, William. Compensations and shared interests soon emerged, however, with the opportunity to redesign the palaces, first at Het Loo and then at Hampton Court. Originally a hunting palace, the buildings and gardens at Het Loo were enlarged on William's unexpected ascension, first to the throne of the Netherlands and then (via Mary) the throne of England. The designs at both palaces were heavily influenced by both Mary and William, Mary in particular being concerned with the flower gardens and collections. At Het Loo Mary had an indoor chamber for flowers complete with a small grotto; a door from this apartment led directly out to Mary's own private garden, while a staircase led to her upper chambers. Although undoubtedly of the highest status, the garden abandoned the infinite perspectives of contemporary French gardens and concentrated on the creation of harmony between man and nature, rather than triumph over it. The design of the main gardens not only reflected the couple's career, but also expressed strong Protestant beliefs, eschewing displays of divine right such as had been created at Versailles. Statues, urns and celestial globes all proclaimed the couple's belief that creation of the perfect garden state on earth reflected the equally ordered heavenly state. The obvious connection between the moniker 'William of Orange' and love of the orange tree was also fully exploited during their reign, with a renewed interest in the cultivation of this sweet-smelling shrub. Their display, both within special buildings and during the summer months within pots (or 'boxes') in the garden, became a hallmark of Dutch-style gardens throughout England, along with canals and topiary.

On their coronation in England, new gardens were created at Hampton Court to complement the new frontage designed by Wren. Alongside designers such as Hans Willem Bentinck (brought from Apeldoorn), and Daniel Marot, William and Mary employed a mix of English and French designers to create a formal 'privy' garden that was of international importance. The royal couple were recorded as personally superintending the work in the gardens, taking great interest in their development and planning. Daniel Defoe commented that 'the amendments and alterations were made by the King or the Queen's particular special command, or by both, for the majesties agreed so well in their fancy, and had both so good judgement in the just proportion of things, which are the principal beauties of a garden, that it may be said they both ordered everything that was done'.[22]

An important element of the gardens was the new 'glass case' created for Mary's outstanding plant collection and transported from its original site at Honselaarsdijk. The Netherlands was already well known for the collection and breeding of new plants, and Mary collected both plants and ceramics for the display of flowers indoors and out. The fabulous *Codex Honselaerdicensis* records part of a plant collection acquired while the couple were still in the Netherlands and later transported to Hampton Court. Mary had taken advantage of the Dutch trade with the East Indies to commence a collection of what were then known as 'exotics' – a general term for plants from overseas and tender plants. However, she did not remain content with her East Indian and Cape of Good Hope sources, sending additional plant collectors to Virginia and the Canary Isles to add to this important collection. She employed a personal botanist, a Dr Leonard Plukenet, to oversee her growing collections and the growing number of 'stoves' in which they were housed. These hothouses sheltered the exotics from the mists and fogs of London and the River Thames which crept up the gardens and lawns at Hampton Court.[23] Her collections became a focus for other botanists and collectors, with visitors including the Duchess of Beaufort and Charles Hatton. On his visit in 1690, Hatton recorded that he saw 'about four rare Indian plantes which were never seen in England'. Hatton also noted the finest collection of 'amaranths and hollyoke' at Hampton Court, reminding us of the colourful nature of some of these formal gardens.[24]

Mary's stoves overlooked the old Pond Yards, which were planted with an extensive selection of florists' flowers. Florists' flowers at this period referred not to flowers used in arrangements, but those which were considered appropriate for collection and improvement by botanical collectors. These were to form the basis for the florists' clubs and shows, which have their modern expression in the numerous county and village flower shows. Auriculas, one of the most popular of these flowers, had an entire garden to themselves in the area known in Mary's time as the Glass Case Gardens. Mary also had the old Water Gallery of Henry VIII refitted for her own personal use, and this was exquisitely furnished with the ceramics and still-life paintings which she had collected, including the famous Delftware flower pyramids which still remain in the Palace today. Fresh flowers would be placed in these every day for the enjoyment of Mary and her ladies-in-waiting, while in finer weather the ladies would take their embroidering ('knotting') and sewing to the outdoors and sit in the long tunnel arbour or shelter that was planted overlooking the Privy Garden.[25]

Unfortunately Mary had only five years in which to enjoy her new gardens and exotics, dying of that seventeenth-century scourge smallpox in 1694. With her death William III abandoned the site for some five years as their shared gardens brought back memories too painful to bear. Although work recommenced with his return in 1699, in the absence of Mary he was said to be gripped by indecision, making work on the gardens painfully slow. Following a further re-levelling of the entire garden to balance the new garden front, the parterres and avenues were almost completed when William himself died unexpectedly in 1702, putting an end to the magnificent garden plan. Mary's Water Gallery had already been demolished following her death and much of the rest of the gardens must have been immature and even incomplete when they passed to William's sister, Queen Anne.

Anne famously disliked anything to do with her brother and took an early opportunity to sweep away his painfully considered gardens at Hampton Court. Reviling the smell of box and what she felt was the unpatriotic nature of the complex parterres de broderie, she replaced the grand fountains and abundant exotics with plain turf and narrow flower beds. Slashing the royal gardening budget from £4,800 to £1,600 she employed Henry Wise as royal gardener, a man who should have had more respect for his own profession than to comply with such swingeing cuts. In her favour horticulturally, Anne did spend £6,000 on an orangery at Kensington Palace, and turned a natural hollow into a sunken garden with viewing galleries. She also acquired 30 acres of Hyde Park in order to create one of the first wooded 'wildernesses' of the eighteenth century. It must have been a damp part of the park as she also created ten ponds within the area. Anne was also, rather surprisingly, responsible for the earliest version of the maze at Hampton Court, located in an area that had been a planted formal 'wilderness' in the time of William and Mary. Nowhere is the contrast in styles between Mary and Anne plainer than in their two portraits, now in the National Portrait Gallery. That of Mary (by William Wissing) portrays her with white flowers in her hand, and a half-glimpsed background of a garden adorned with roses and fountains and a probable orangery; that of Anne (by Godfrey Kneller) portrays instead a stone statue gazing out on to dark trees and shrubs, a rotunda temple being the only embellishment.[26]

Just as Hampton Court and Somerset House had been the centre of the gardening world for Tudor and Stuart monarchs and consorts, so the twin estates of Richmond and Kew were to become the focus of attention through the eighteenth century. As London expanded, country villas began to spread westwards down the flowing Thames. Twickenham and Richmond became marked by 'beautiful buildings, charming gardens, and rich habitations of gentlemen of quality' to such an extent that views from the river were claimed to rival those from the Seine, the Danube or the Po.[27] Landscape gurus including Alexander Pope and Horace Walpole, as well as poets, painters and politicians, adorned their riverside gardens in ever increasing 'taste', with Dame Nature as their guiding hand and their neighbours as their critics. Elsewhere in the country Charles Bridgeman, Stephen Switzer, William Kent and the delightfully named Batty Langley were intent on creating that 'indefinable somewhat'[28] that would distinguish natural art from artful nature. Political landscapes reflecting divisions between libertarian Whigs and interventionist Tories were sprouting temples to virtues antique and modern, while headless statues vied with philosophers' busts to express the politics of garden owners. At Stowe, Buckinghamshire, Lord Cobham employed each of the most famous landscape gardeners of the period in turn to ensure this most visited of landscapes proclaimed its owner's innermost thoughts. The Queen's Temple at Stowe (built *c.* 1742–50) included murals of 'Ladies employing themselves in needle and shell-work' and 'diverting themselves with Painting and Musick', to emphasise the true domestic sphere of womanhood. Lord Cobham may have wished to keep women out of the political landscape, but this did not deter Queen Caroline from her own landscaping enterprises at Richmond.[29]

The classic tale of the mismatched royal couple applies again to Caroline, Princess of Brandenburg-Anspach and George, Prince of Wales (later George II), but with the added complication of a hostile and belligerent father. Married in their homeland of Germany, and united by their Protestant views, the couple appear to have had little else in common. Caroline had grown up in the cultured surroundings of the Charlottenburg Palace, Berlin (laid out under the directions of Sophie Charlotte, wife of Friedrich I), and the superb Baroque gardens at Herrenhausen, Hanover (laid out by Sophie of Hanover, mother of Sophie Charlotte). She was a charming and lively figure who combined social wit with philosophy and intellectual studies. He, on the other hand, devoted himself to hunting, shooting and infidelity, with any spare time spent studying the genealogy of Europe's royal families, in particular his own. Gardening and spending became Caroline's linked preoccupations when the couple arrived in England as Prince and Princess of Wales in 1714. Taking on Richmond Lodge from the disgraced Duke of Ormonde, the couple moved in after a more than usual acrimonious row with George I led to their banishment from the royal court. Almost immediately, Caroline took advice on garden layout from the foremost designers and garden critics of the day, convening a meeting at Richmond Lodge. At a period when the profession was undergoing a major upheaval this was unlikely to result in any agreements and the predictable outcome was amusingly described by the cynical Alexander Pope in a letter to his friend Lord Bathurst:

> Several Criticks were of several opinions: One declar'd he would not have too much Art in it, for my notion (said he) of gardening is, that it is only sweeping nature; Another told them that Gravel walks were not of good taste, for all the finest abroad were those of loose sand; A third advis'd peremptorily there should not be one Lyme-tree in the whole plantation; a fourth made the same exclusive clause extend to Horse-chestnuts, which he affirmed not to be Trees, but Weeds; Dutch Elms were condemn'd by a fifth; and thus about half the Trees were proscribed . . . There were some who cou'd not bear Ever-greens, and call'd them never-greens; some who were angry at them only when cut into shapes . . . some who had no dislike to Cones and Cubes, but would have 'em cut in Forest-trees.[30]

Lack of available funds, perhaps fortunately, prevented an immediate start being made on the gardens, and it was not until the death of George I that Caroline had sufficient money to implement her own improvements. A very substantial annual allowance of £100,000 was granted to her by Robert Walpole's Parliament as reward for her support in a power struggle that had threatened to unseat Walpole's government, and political gains were used to serve the purpose of paradise. Caroline's first foray into serious landscaping was not in fact at Richmond (perhaps the squabbling critics had cooled her enthusiasm?), but at the royal gardens at Hyde Park and Kensington. Employing the designer Charles Bridgeman as Royal Gardener, she eschewed the formal style to create a naturalistic *jardin anglais* with winding walks, serpentine lakes and open glades. A revolving summerhouse (created by William Kent) and a temple added focal points and presaged greater things to come. Turning her attentions to Richmond Lodge, Caroline's first move was to expand her estate to over 400 acres by the purchase and demolition of adjoining houses. Employing again the Kensington 'team' of Bridgeman and Kent, the enlarged gardens were to include a wilderness, winding walks, a raised mount, open fields, the Great Terrace and menagerie, as well as the walled potager and river walks. It was William Kent, however, who introduced the most fashionable, and most controversial, aspects of the gardens. Undoubtedly under instructions from the Queen, Kent designed a series of unusual and eventually politically motivated buildings within the gardens. Illustrated in many subsequent descriptions, these included the Queen's Building, the Summerhouse on the Terrace, the Duke's Summerhouse, the Dairy, Merlin's Cave and the Hermitage.

It was the last two, the cave and hermitage, that marked Caroline's attempted entry into the world of political landscape gardening. Described in the *Gentleman's Magazine* as 'Her Majesty's Grotto', the hermitage was a typical Kent construction: triple-arched, with central pediment, entirely faced with rusticated blocks. On the interior two symmetrical wings flanked an octagonal room containing an altar and niches. Resting on the altar was a bust of Robert Boyle, while in the flanking niches further busts commemorated the achievements of Isaac Newton, John Locke, Samuel Clarke and William Wollaston. The meaning of this collection, although obscure to modern understanding, would have been obvious to the contemporary eighteenth-century visitor. Isaac Newton was the discoverer of the laws of the universe, Locke a Christian rationalist, Clarke a philosopher on metaphysics and theology, and Wollaston the author of *The Religion of Nature Delineated* (1724). Robert Boyle was also a participant in theological debate and founder of the Royal Society.[31] Together these British philosophers and scientists represented Caroline's public identification of her court with the intellectual life of England, and her distancing from her unpopular German background. This celebration of the rational philosophy above natural laws and passions was further alluded to in the sharp contrast between the rusticated exterior of the hermitage and the classical interior.

Merlin's Cave was similarly iconographic. Placed on the south side of the rectangular Duck Pond this was again a tripartite building. Composed of a central circular pavilion with octagonal wings, this extraordinary building, perhaps Kent's most unusual in terms of its rustication, was topped by three conical thatched roofs. A gothic door with ogee arch in the central pavilion led directly to the central chamber. This chamber contained three further gothic arches, and under each arch a tableau of wax figures told a 'story' or political message. The figures have been variously identified but there is general agreement on the main tableau and its import. Merlin and his 'secretary' formed the central stage, with Queen Elizabeth and the consort of Henry VII. Two remaining figures appear to have represented Minerva, Britannia or Britomart (from Spenser's *Faerie Queene*) accompanied variously by Mother Shipton, Queen Elizabeth's nursemaid, or Melissa (a rather obscure prophetess). In addition to this rather bizarre collection of waxworks, a live hermit, Stephen Duck, inhabited the cave for over seven years, until the eventual death of Queen Caroline and his retirement and subsequent death from alcoholism.

Discerning a theme or meaning in this disparate collection of figures proved to be a considerable challenge to contemporary visitors. It was suggested by some that Caroline might be claiming that the coming of the Hanoverians had been predicted by Merlin, or that she herself identified with Elizabeth I in her role as Britomart (although that still left the small matter of the nursemaid and consort). *Fog's Weekly Journal* claimed that it was 'Hieorglyphical [*sic*], Emblematical, Typical and Symbolical, conveying lessons of Policy to Princes and Ministers of State',[32] which although all-encompassing was not especially enlightening. Other critics were more forthright in their dismissal of the waxworks and Caroline's rather bizarre gothic hermitage. Horace Walpole, son of the Prime Minister, said that 'Queen Caroline made pretensions to Learning and Taste, with not much of the former and none of the latter'.[33] Although it is tempting to empathise with George II when he dismissed Caroline's complaints with the unsympathetic comment, 'you deserve to be abused for such childish silly stuff', there is also a serious aspect to the mockery that she met with. By 1735 (the date of the review in *Fog's Weekly Journal*) Viscount Cobham's landscape gardens at Stowe were in full swing. Started at the beginning of the century, by 1730–40 these gardens were full of temples and monuments inspired by political machinations and sympathies. Statues and busts of philosophers, politicians and monarchs rubbed shoulders with Roman emperors and Saxon deities. Newton, Locke, Boyle and Elizabeth I were present at Stowe as at Richmond, and yet Lord Cobham was met not with ribaldry but with admiration. Women, it seemed, were not welcome in the world of political landscaping.

Princess Amelia was rather more lighthearted in her landscaping designs. Favourite daughter of George II she was given Gunnersbury Park in 1761, perhaps as consolation for a failed match with a German prince. She too probably used William Kent, to design a temple disguised as a dairy (or is it a dairy disguised as a temple?). Amelia and her ladies played at milkmaids in the style of Marie Antoinette at Versailles, with picnics and gowns far beyond the wildest dreams of the average cowhand. A bathhouse was built in the 1770s–80s, with a grotto chamber and cold plunge pool for any overheated dairymaids.

Mutual dislike between father and son appeared to dog the Hanoverian line, and George II disliked his son Frederick as much as his own father had disliked him. When the royal couple chose a bride for their son it was therefore based not on a sympathetic judgement of suitability of character, but on political and religious factors. Princess Augusta (1719–72), aged 17, entered a family where mutual antagonism was the norm. Fortunately for her, her husband Frederick was a cultured man and could console her for the loss of civil in-laws. A collector of art and supporter of painters, Frederick played the cello and had in his close circle poets and painters, as well as politicians. When the newly wed couple purchased the Capel family's old estate at Kew it was primarily Frederick, rather than Augusta, who took the lead in landscaping the garden. William Kent, the same designer hired by his mother at Richmond and sister at Gunnersbury, was to redesign both Kew House and the 12-acre gardens, adding another instance of royal patronage to his meteoric career from coach-painter in Bridlington to landscape genius. Considerable further work was carried out in the twenty years between Frederick's purchase of Kew and his unexpected death in 1751. It was while supervising his gardeners at Kew that he was caught in the rain shower that was to prove fatal. Rain to gardeners is like water off a duck's back, but in this instance it progressed from a drenching to a cold, from a cold to pleurisy, eventually precipitating the bursting of an abscess that had formed on his sternum some years previously. Plantsmen (and women) mourned his passing with genuine feeling as a man who had proved a 'best friend and encourager', but fortunately for the gardening world Augusta was to take up where he had left off.

Also rumoured to be taking up where the Prince had left off was John Stuart, Earl of Bute. A trained botanist and experienced landscaper, Bute had become close friends with Frederick, before being promoted to First Lord of the Bedchamber. He had given advice and expertise when gardening matters arose and so it was natural that he should continue to do so when the unfinished garden projects fell into the hands of Augusta. Rumours, however, abounded that the relationship between widow and earl was one based more on physical attractions than that provided by botanical registers. Augusta and Bute were to spend the next ten years expanding and embellishing Kew until it became one of the most famous gardens in Europe. Its fame rested on two strands: the extraordinary collection of buildings designed to celebrate England's role in the world, and the well-stocked physic or botanic garden. Under the direction of Augusta, the architect William Chambers designed a series of buildings for Kew that reflected fashionable preoccupations with the world beyond Europe. In 1757 Chambers published *Designs of Chinese Buildings, Furniture, Dresses, Machines and Utensils* (dedicated to the Prince of Wales, later George III). Many years later, in 1772, he was to publish his more famous *Dissertation On Oriental Gardening*, but in the years between he was occupied with Augusta's plans (and, coincidentally, plans for the reconstruction of Somerset House).

Starting in 1757, Chambers's work at Kew included a wooden aviary, an octagonal chinoiserie, the open-air Colonnade Theatre, a mosque, a Moorish building, temples to Arethusa, Peace and Victory, temples of Bellona and Pan, the Ruined Arch and House of Confucius. As a special surprise for Augusta a Palladian bridge was constructed overnight, although whether she noticed it among the vast array of other buildings is another matter. Made largely of impermanent materials, and built on a whim of fashion, few of the buildings constructed for Augusta now remain. One famous exception is the Chinese Pagoda, although sadly roped off to prevent the lovelorn from ending it all from the top of its ten octagonal storeys. The Temple of the Sun, the Ruined Arch and the Temple of Bellona also survive, although mostly moved from their original locations in a flurry of later landscaping. In a strange coincidence another of Chambers's Chinese buildings, the Pagoda at Blackheath for the Duke and Duchess of Buccleugh, later housed Caroline of Brunswick after her separation from her husband the Prince Regent in 1799. Queens and consorts have a way of getting into the garden story even when not famous for their planting.

While Chambers decorated the gardens with buildings, Augusta turned her attention to putting gardens and plants within buildings. Bitten by the plant-collecting bug, and primed with exotics from Bute's contacts in the horticultural world across Europe, Asia and Africa, Augusta decided to create a botanical garden at Kew. Setting aside

9 acres she built up a collection of both tender and hardy exotics of all kinds, each labelled according to the new Linnaean system, and each with their origin recorded. In addition to the herbaceous beds there were greenhouses and hothouses, including a 'Great Stove' of some 114 feet in length, larger than any other of the period. To give the gardens a more scientific basis, and the plants a greater hope of survival, she 'requested' the services of the botanist William Aiton, who had been working at Chelsea Physic Garden. A royal request is rarely denied, and Aiton came, for a salary of £120 a year, staying until his death in 1793. Also superintending the gardens was John Hill, publisher of a twenty-six volume, sixteen-year work on *The Vegetable System* (1759). With such men in charge it is little wonder that the idea of the botanical garden grew to become one for 'a garden which was to contain all the plants known on earth'.[34] Currently a café, the orangery at Kew is the only survivor of Augusta's plant houses, with her armorial bearings placed in the centre of its façade. In 1987 the new Princess of Wales Conservatory was opened in commemoration of the work of Princess Augusta in the founding of one of the world's most important botanical collections. An ironic twist of fate, in the shape of the early death of Diana, Princess of Wales within a few years of her inauguration of the conservatory, has led to many visitors to Kew assuming that the conservatory is in fact a memorial to this popular Princess. Augusta thus remains a shadowy and obscure figure for most visitors to Kew, although they are often grateful for the reviving refreshments to be found within her splendid orangery.

Back at Richmond, the adjoining site of Queen Caroline's gardens, changes were afoot. In 1760 George III had ascended the throne and within a year had married (on the advice of Lord Bute) Princess Charlotte Sophia of Mecklenberg-Strelitz (1744–1818). The fashion for landscape gardening was in full swing and soon Caroline's treasured, if foolish, garden buildings were swept away as the perfect Brownian formula was imposed. Clumps, lakes and lawns replaced terraces and temples. Anxious to provide accommodation for a rapidly growing family (Charlotte was to have fifteen children in all), George III threw himself into building. A contemporary plantsman noted that 'I wish the King had any taste in flowers or plants but he has none, there are no hopes of encouragement from him, for his talent is in architecture.'[35] With the death of Augusta in 1772, it was Charlotte rather than George who was to be the saviour of English botany. Charlotte took an academic as well as artistic interest in plants, as did her four daughters.

A herbarium was purchased in 1788 for the price of 100 guineas and used to assist their studies, which took place under the President of the Linnean Society. Joseph Banks rather patronisingly recorded that the Queen was studying botany intensively and 'really reads with perseverance elementary books'.[36] The Queen, Princess Royal and Princess Elizabeth also studied botanical art under the artist Margaret Meen,

Bird of Paradise (*Strelitzia reginae*)

A South African plant, named after an English queen and an Austrian province, the Bird of Paradise flower rightly deserves its international reputation. This superb orange and mauve/blue flower rises from a forest of tall green spikes, its smooth aerodynamic lines echoing the shape of a bird in darting flight. Reaching over a metre in height the strikingly colourful flower heads can be up to 10cm long and pierce the dark green foliage like flocks of exotic birds. Discovered by plant hunters in the Kwa-Zulu-Natal region of South Africa, it was sent back to England to join the collections of Joseph Banks at the Royal Botanic Gardens at Kew. Arriving in 1773 it caused a sensation and was named in honour of Charlotte Sophia of Mecklenburg-Strelitz, wife of George III. Charlotte was a keen plantswoman herself, having studied botany with the then president of the Linnean Society. Her rustic-style cottage at Kew, which served as a summer picnic spot for the family, was decorated by the Queen and her daughters with botanically correct wall paintings of nasturtiums and ipomoea. The Bird of Paradise flower, meanwhile, took on a more international life of its own, arriving in America in 1853 and becoming the city flower of Los Angeles in 1952. In 1932 a film set on the island of Waikiki and starring the sex symbols of the day was to be called 'The Bird of Paradise', extending its world domination to the South Seas. Its resemblance to a complex but brilliant piece of origami led to its adoption by the Japanese flower farmers of Southern California who grew acres of the plants for the flower trade. Over-popularity and readiness to grow has led to a decline in its fortunes in America, where it is now regarded as a rather common plant. At Kew, however the *Strelitzia reginae* still draws the gasps of admiration and delight that it has done for over 200 years.

who recorded much of the Kew collection. Princess Elizabeth and Mary Moser[37] worked together on the floral paintings that decorated Frogmore House, the site of the royal botanising, as well as on floral embroidery and botanical painting. Following the fashion for rustic, Queen Charlotte had a thatched cottage erected as a summerhouse and menagerie in the grounds of Kew. Taking tea there might be interrupted by the surprise appearance of one of the twenty-strong kangaroo population; although not half as likely to cause upset teacups as the tiger that Queen Caroline had kept in her menagerie. Set among bluebells and meadow the botanically decorated cottage now belongs to English Heritage and is open only on special occasions. From her bolt-hole in the Pagoda at Blackheath (and numerous other retreats) Caroline of Brunswick was in no position to embark on a career in gardening at Kew or elsewhere, and with Charlotte we lose for a while the trail of queenly gardens.

THREE

Gardening in the Wilderness
THE LONG EIGHTEENTH CENTURY

> As to myself, I have strayed three days of last week in the woods; or to be less poetical, I have stood from Eleven to Five each day, in the lower part of my Long Walk, planting and displanting, opening views &c. I wish it may be for the better.
>
> Lady Luxborough, Letter to William Shenstone (1 November 1749)[1]

The traditional roll-call of the eighteenth-century English landscape trips off the tongue of the garden historian like the class register of a distinguished boys' preparatory school: Bridgeman, Charles; Brown, Lancelot; Kent, William; Switzer, Stephen; Vanbrugh, John. No female names appear in the litany of designers. Even the influential garden and landscape philosophers and essayists such as Addison, Walpole or Pope, were exclusively male. More than any other century, the years that saw the seed and flowering of the English landscape have been declared the Age of Man. But if one steps off the well-worn path of garden history, and ventures instead into the shrubberies and wildernesses flanking the smooth elysian fields, one encounters women involved in the full range of garden life. From planting to 'displanting', picturesque to painting and manufactory to management, women were there.

The very nature of society in the eighteenth century meant that women were unlikely to become active designers, either professional or dilettante. However, the care and creation of their own gardens was something deemed an appropriate arena of action in a country increasingly dominated by the mores of the 'polite society'. The garden could thus bring both cultural and artistic fulfilment to complement the more traditional releases of embroidery, drawing, music and conversation. For some women, such as Henrietta Knight, or Eleanor Butler and Sarah Ponsonby, the garden could also act as a release or retreat from the dictates of a society with which they had become frustrated or with which they found themselves in opposition. Other women saw the garden as part of their intellectual spheres, connecting them with cultural coteries revolving around the influential literati of the day. In the case of Jemima, Marchioness Grey, the intellectual and the domestic combined, as she developed the gardens at her family seat of Wrest Park in the fashions of the day, taking responsibility for designers, workmen and gardeners. Whatever their motive for embracing the world of the garden, or their involvement within it, a common thread runs through the gardening lives of almost all these women. For them the garden is not a place in which to parade the accomplishments of polite society but instead a place in which that society might be challenged or evaded.[2]

For Lady Mary Coke (1726–1811) the garden served as both a retreat from one society and an entry into another. Victim of one of the most embarrassing and inconclusive divorce cases of the eighteenth century, in 1767 Lady Mary purchased the lease of Notting Hill House, a large villa and grounds in the then rural area of Kensington. Married to Lord Coke in 1747, at the age of 21, Lady Coke had been finally freed into widowhood in 1753. She never remarried and instead gradually transformed into a somewhat eccentric grande dame, confidante of cultural icons of the period and a familiar figure at court.[3] Notting Hill House was well situated for a woman in Lady Mary's position. Retired from the centre of London, and yet in proximity both to London and also to Gunnersbury, the country house of Princess Amelia, sister to the King and a great friend of Lady Mary. Edward Lloyd, George II's Secretary of War, had been the previous owner, himself in need of a retreat. In addition, the house itself was superbly located. It was built on an eminence rising 130ft above the Thames, and the potential views and prospects into the countryside were to attract Lady Mary's immediate attention. Before the year of purchase was out, Lady Mary's journal and letters record her approaches to the neighbouring landowners concerning the possibilities of extending both the views (by negotiating for the felling of trees on adjoining land) and also the actual grounds themselves.

The house appears always to have been surrounded by gardens.[4] To the south was a lawn terminated by a rectangular sheet of water, to the west rows of trees or hedges denoted garden boundaries, while to the east was a larger productive garden. These, however, were said by Lady Mary to be in 'the most terrible disorder' when she moved in, with grass and weeds in the gravel walks, and 'nothing in my kitchen garden but cabbages and onions'. As this was September, that most productive and fruitful of English months, one can only sympathise. One of Lady Mary's first moves that September of 1767 was to 'hire a woman to come tomorrow that it may not look like an uninhabitable place', as it appeared 'the gardener will do nothing'. A woman, Lady Mary felt, was far more likely to whip the place into order than the long-standing (male) gardener. This poor opinion of the gardener, who was inherited from Mr Lloyd, unfortunately continued. In 1768 she records that she was 'grown a great weeder. I am glad I like it better than my gardener. My garden would otherwise be in great disorder', while in 1769 she was obliged to again take a hands-on approach (this time transplanting stocks) as the gardener had been found 'drunk and incapable of doing anything'. In 1775, after spending the summer in Paris, she returned to find the garden (and house) a practical wasteland. The grass grown wild as meadow, crops in the kitchen gardens choked with weeds, and the pear trees cropped too early for keeping. One would like to believe that Lady Mary was particularly unfortunate in her choice of gardeners (and indeed most of her menials) rather than believe that this was the standard of most private house gardeners of the period. But the fact that the gardener escaped being turned away by virtue of merely promising 'to do better in the future' seems to indicate that there was not much choice available.[5]

Even more astounding perhaps than her forbearance with her staff, was the range of Lady Mary's practical involvement with her gardens. Although she appointed James Lee as her garden adviser (a noted horticulturalist and proprietor of a nursery on Hammersmith Lane) her journals and letters make clear her own enthusiastic and practical role. She was involved at all stages of design and implementation. Visits to nurseries, purchase of tools, and even tree and shrub planting are all clearly documented as being of her own doing or directing. A letter to her sister records not only a meeting with her adviser but also her own ideas for the walks and vistas that she intends on creating. Horace Walpole one day found her at 'work in my North Walk . . . in my garden Equipage, a paddle and a great basket', while she further scandalised the neighbourhood by watering the sweet-smelling plants along her boundary walk on the Sabbath. Demonstrating a more eccentric approach to the hazards of gardening, she consulted with a famous gynaecological surgeon of the day over the removal of thorns from her fingers, gained when pruning roses. Lady Sackville,[6] Princess Amelia (of Gunnersbury) and Lady Temple (of Stowe) all visited the gardens thus securely placing Lady Mary within the heart of polite society and court circles. Additional gifts of plants came from the Duchess of Norfolk, and Lord and Lady Strafford (her sister). The garden undoubtedly also formed one of the shared interests between herself and the influential Horace Walpole, essayist, critic and gardener, who published *An Essay on Modern Gardening* in 1780, after first printing it privately in 1771. Lady Mary's practical involvement and enthusiasm were looked on with a mixture of indulgence and bemusement by many of her social circle. However, an active involvement in the 'improvement' of one's garden and grounds was in the spirit of the age. Adornment of a small *ferme ornée*[7] acted as a socially acceptable divertissement for a woman touched by a scandal but (in this instance) saved by a death.

Henrietta Knight, Lady Luxborough (1699–56),[8] was not so fortunate. In common with Lady Mary Coke, she too found that marriage was followed within a few years by misery, scandal and public denouncement, but her estranged husband failed to oblige with an early death. Lord Luxborough banished his wife to a 'remote cottage' in Warwickshire, forbidding her ever to see himself or her children again. Although we may still concede to the rurality of Barrells Hall, there are few who would now apply the term 'cottage' to the family house and 400-acre estate to which Henrietta (and her seven servants) retired in 1736. The house had been neglected since her husband had purchased it six years earlier, and Henrietta's first task was to put the gaping windows and damp rooms in order, before concentrating on the gardens. Barrells appears to have had the remnants of a formal garden in the immediate vicinity of the house (described by Jane Brown as 'dishevelled'), and it was to this area that Henrietta turned her attention. Although much of the estate was tenanted, Henrietta retained some 56 acres of woods, meadows and gardens.

In 1738 we learn from her brother's letters that Henrietta occupied her solitude with her 'books and her gardens'. The following year was to see the sharing of those interests with a group of like-minded neighbours who were to form the 'Warwickshire coterie'. Loosely composed of poets and writers, such as William Somerville, William Perks and the Revd Richard Jago, the group was later to include the poet and landscape gardener William Shenstone who became the major influence on Henrietta after Somerville's death. Shenstone's own small estate of The Leasowes was situated 12 miles from Barrells Hall. The Leasowes was famous in the mid-eighteenth century for its owner's poetic rural style, which attempted to combine practicality with aesthetics, classical with rural, and pleasure with melancholia. That it was not only visited but also widely copied, is a tribute to the influence of William Shenstone and also to the very particular tastes of the time. Shenstone had promulgated his own picturesque ideas on garden design in his *Unconnected Thoughts on Gardening*. Published posthumously by his friend Dodsley in 1764, this had proved an enormous success with the romantic movement in landscape and gardens. Shenstone was to become both a frequent correspondent with Henrietta and one of the few visitors to Barrells. Although neither the letters nor the visits were as frequent as Henrietta desired, it is through their correspondence that we learn of her increasing fascination with improving her own grounds, and her enthusiasm for 'planting and displanting'.

Within a year of her meeting Shenstone, Henrietta was declaring that Barrells had become 'very habitable'. More importantly it had also acquired all the attributes necessary to declare it, if not a *ferme ornée* certainly a *ferme negligée*. In a rare letter to Lady Hertford during this period (Henrietta was actually banned from correspondence with her friend until 1743) she describes the rural idyll that she had created on the estate: 'I have made a garden which I am filling with all the flowering shrubs I can get. I have also made an aviary, and filled it with a variety of singing birds, and am now making a fountain in the middle of it, and a grotto to sit and hear them sing in, contiguous to it . . . and in a coppice a little farther I have made a very lovely cave shaded by trees.' The pastoral aspect is further enhanced by the inclusion of 'some few cows, sheep etc near me'. Reminiscent of Queen Caroline's ill-fated gardens at Richmond, we also learn from her own letters that Lady Luxborough had 'made a little summer house that is stuccoed and adorned with the busts of my Brother Bolingbroke, Pope, Dryden, Milton, Shakespeare, Newton and Locke'. Her strictly enforced isolation hopefully kept her safe from the ridicule of society over such political allusions.

Henrietta's letters to Shenstone are full of anxious concerns over the designs and layout of the gardens and their contents. The building of a small pavilion with a shrine for a statue of Venus takes up many pages, as first the placement, then the pediment, and finally the inscriptions, are discussed. The poet, philosopher and friend William Somerville wrote 'Song to Asteria' to record the bucolic pleasures of Barrells and dedicated it to Henrietta. The commission and decoration of a memorial urn to Somerville, to be placed in Henrietta's garden, forms a melancholic (although not less hotly debated) subject matter that trails on for what seems like years. The laying out of the garden walks literally winds and diverts through their correspondence. To read these personal letters is to enter into the breathless and somewhat erratic concerns of Henrietta's life. They display a wit and intelligence that belies their 'polite' self-deprecation. Dutiful requests for guidance and clarification vie with a lively awareness of the weaknesses of others within their social circle. Listings of the numerous features within the garden, and work to be carried out, allows at least an outline layout of the garden to be reconstructed; although one is left with the impression that both plants and paths were rarely left for long in any one place.

Activity was Henrietta's constant companion. In 1749, in reply to the usual abundant landscaping advice from Shenstone, Henrietta writes (slightly impatiently):

> I doubt whether I rightly understand in what manner you would have the Hermitage become part of the shrubbery, by means of about three yards of shrubbery on the outside of my lime-walk? I should be glad to make this connection, but will it not lay my garden open to the field through which passes a foot-road to Henley? And yet, according to your advice, might I not plant that straight walk, which is now gravelled, full of shrubs, and not let it lead to the Hermitage but return in a serpentine manner one of my crooked sand-walks beyond the Ha! Ha! So as to meet the walk which is bordered by service-trees and fenced with rails, and does lead in a curve to the Hermitage; in which walk might also be shrubs and a serpentine sand-passage? This could be done, but I question it is your meaning.[9]

We learn later that a sketch from Shenstone has resolved the queries and that 'I have begun by taking down the styles, that no foot-road may prevent the execution of what we propose', although as she says plaintively, 'I still do not know if you would have the little gates left or no at each end of the Service Walk'! Visits from Shenstone provoked a similar flurry of activity. After one such we hear that:

> The first thing I did on Monday was to order the Ha! Ha! To be lowered two bricks, but found it not necessary to lower it even one;

> for the paper you stuck up is seen from the Hall-Door by lowering the earth a considerable length of the way. . . . I also staked out the ground for the sweep of pallisadoes and trees at the hither end of the Long Walk, and I banished the auricula pots from the Library-window; and yesterday I wrote to bespeak the pediment for the Pavilion.[10]

It is with heartfelt sympathy that we read, 'More I could not do in this short time; but will have regard to your advice about the shrubbery.'

Although these letters appear to suggest a reliance on the advice of Shenstone, others portray a woman who designed, oversaw and implemented improvements herself. She notes, for example, that she has stood 'from eleven to five each day, in the lower part of my long walk, planting and displanting, opening views etc'.

Subject to fits of depression (probably brought on by her isolation) Henrietta revelled in the outdoors, despite developing rheumatic pains in her hands. Throughout her letters she frequently commends her garden at all seasons and in all weathers with the enthusiasm of a real garden lover. A particular letter to Shenstone argues strongly for the joys of the garden in autumn, when summer suns do not scorch nor the unpredictable rains of spring spoil all. It is an argument that one feels echoes the realisation of the passing years. A plea for maturity above youth, made by a woman for whom life had been blighted. On her death in 1756, Henrietta left a garden adorned and a farm 'ornamented' where pleasure mingled with surprise 'by nature blest in every part, adorn'd with every grace of art' (as Somerville recorded in his 'Song to Asteria'). When her letters were published the frontispiece read: 'Letters from the Lady Luxborough, written with abundant ease, politeness and vivacity in which she was scarce equalled by any woman of her time.' Neither was her gardening.

For Henrietta, the garden had proved a rather too solitary retreat, for others it proved positively crowded. Eleanor Butler (1745?–1829) and Sarah Ponsonby (1755?–1831) created a rural retreat for their own retirement from the world, only to find that world beating a path to their doors. Celebrated in late eighteenth-century society for their 'perfect friendship' they were known as the Ladies of Llangollen.[11] The attractions of their Welsh retreat included both the gothic witticisms of their cottage and the charms of their picturesque garden. Visitors to the cottage, from which they themselves had sworn never to spend a night away, included the likes of the Duke of Somerset, Duke of Gloucester (the king's nephew), Madame de Genlis, De Quincey, Anna Seward, Lady Lonsdale, William Wordsworth, Walter Scott, and that indefatigable garden visitor and writer Prince Pückler-Muskau; while an even wider circle of correspondence was kept up on matters appertaining to lifestyle and gardening.

'The most celebrated virgins in Europe', as Prince Pückler-Muskau called them, had entered into their Welsh retreat following an elopement from their native Ireland. Probably in her mid-thirties and unlikely to marry, Eleanor Butler was being pressed by her stepmother into joining a convent; while her younger friend Sarah Ponsonby was the subject of unwanted marriage proposals, enthusiastically encouraged by her family. On 3 April 1778 Sarah followed romantic tradition in one aspect at least, leaping out of a window at night to join her lover in flight. Alas for her family's hopes and her own reputation, her 'lover'[12] was Eleanor. Captured, they fled again a month later, this time with the unwilling agreement of their families. A tour of Wales revealed to them the picturesque qualities of the landscape and by the next spring they were settled in the village that was to be their home for the rest of their lives.

The regime by which they were to live was also established at an early stage in the relationship. Eleanor recorded all the details of their lives in a day book, neatly ruled into hours from their rising at six (eight in winter), to their evening retirement. Most days were divided between indoor activities (writing, drawing, reading to each other, etc.) and the outdoor 'projects', as they called them, many of which occupied a separate project book. Visitors recorded that it was Eleanor who oversaw the outside projects and who appears to have taken the lead in much of the relationship. Eleanor, the taller of the two, was described by a critic as wearing a top hat and man's coat, with the implication that she played the male part of the relationship. However, in their most famous portrait the two are in matching top hats and voluminous overcoats, and Mavor argues that although they were of different humours, Eleanor's was a strong rather than essentially male character.

Their retreat at Plas Newydd had begun life as a standard farmhouse and pictures reveal its plain frontage, set within sheep fields and overlooked by the towering hills beyond. Subsequent engravings by their numerous visitors reveal a steady move towards the romantic gothic, very much in the style of Strawberry Hill. By 1794 a hexagonal extension had been built, with gothic arched windows. By 1810 triple gothic arches, complete with pinnacles and internal relief decoration,

Tankerville Orchid (*Phaius tankervilleae* (was *Bletia tankervilleae*))

This tropical orchid was first brought to England from China in 1778. Nurtured into flower by the famous plantsmen Peter Collinson and Dr John Fothergill, it was one of very few orchids available at that time. With red-brown flowers, a yellow throat and red lips, Lady Tankerville's orchid is also known as the Swamp Orchid. The plant prefers damp depressions and black peaty soils, altogether an odd choice perhaps for a namesake to flatter a cultured lady. Lady Emma Tankerville (1752–1836) herself might have thought twice before accepting the honour had she realised that the meaning of the word 'orchid' derives from the Greek for testicle. During the Victorian period the acquisition and hybridisation of orchids was to become big business as wealthy orchid collectors vied to obtain the latest varieties. Women were largely excluded from this particular race, as the overtly sexual nature of the orchid flower made them unsuitable for women to collect. Lady Tankerville's husband (the 4th Earl 1743–1822) appears to have been famous solely for his ability to play cricket, his shell collection, and his association with 'low life' of the non-marine kind and it is a slight mystery as to why the orchid was named after Lady Tankerville. However, either Lady Tankerville or her husband must have had botanising interests as also connected with the Tankerville name is a vast collection of almost 700 botanical drawings. These were acquired by the Earl from the collections of Lord Bute and Princess Augusta in 1794 and included works by the female botanical artist Margaret Meen. The collection is now back at Kew having been repurchased in 1932.

greeted the weary visitor. By 1815 any hint of the former plain farmhouse had been lost under a welter of external relief decoration, with the unwelcome visitor kept at arm's length by decorated iron railings. Even the bird table, sketched by Lady Leighton on a visit, had been given gothic pinnacles and ogee arches. The house was surrounded by

2½ acres of land and this, too, was to be supplemented over time, with additional land being rented so that the famous gardens might be expanded. To the south-eastern side of the cottage, approached through a suitably gothic arch, were four enclosures for fruit, vegetables and flowers. This walled area was complete with a bell for summoning the gardener,[13] for even these unusual ladies did not do their own vegetable gardening. Behind the cottage a small lawn sloped away from the libraries to a shrubbery of lilac, syringas and laburnum, while the lawn itself was allowed to grow wild with daisies and primroses. This jewelled mead was in complete accordance with the work of Henry Phillips (the fashionable Regency plant collector and writer of *Sylva Florifera*), whose books were placed in the gardening library. A 'Home Circuit' led its winding way to the Model Dairy, the fowl yard and the drying green, echoing the layout of the *ferme ornée* at Barrells Hall. The final decades of the eighteenth century, the period when Plas Newydd was being developed, were to see an increasingly acrimonious clash between the lovers of the wild romantic (championed by Uvedale Price and Richard Payne Knight in the nearby Herefordshire hills), and those who favoured the easy, gentle and, occasionally, bland turfed slopes of Lancelot Brown. For the Vale of Llangollen and the ladies within it, the picturesque won hands down.

On the shelves of the ever burgeoning library housed in the gothic summerhouse, prosaic works on botany, botanical illustration and practical gardening found themselves planted next to Gilpin's Lakeland 'Tours'. The works by Gilpin and Uvedale Price on the principles of taste in picturesque and sublime landscape gardening created a variety on the bookshelf only matched by the garden itself. In 1789 Eleanor's day book listed forty-four different kinds of rose, and a friend described the garden borders as containing 'every type of shrub and perennial'. In true picturesque style the gravel walk led through shade and light, passing shrubs and flowers with every variety of foliage; before reaching a deep hollow glen at whose tangled bottom a frothing brook leapt and clamoured over rough stones. Rustic bridges were built to span the Cufflymen Brook, and a font from the ruins of the Valle Crucis Abbey was placed beneath the runnel of a piped spring, surrounded with mosses and ferns.

As the romance and mystery of the ladies grew, so too did the romance of their gardens: the sounds of the Aeolian harp entertained visitors both within and without, views through painted glass inside were echoed by distant garden vistas to ancient mills. A semicircular seat under an old beech tree was enhanced by the inclusion of a garden motto to the woods and water. This use of inscriptions, tastefully disposed around the gardens to heighten emotional and intellectual response, was a favourite of Shenstone at his own gardens at The Leasowes, and Sarah and Eleanor rose to the occasion with their own selections, although tending to the less melancholy. After the death of Eleanor in 1830, Sarah only lived to enjoy their 'sylvan retreat', as the house of Plas Newydd was so often referred to, for a further two years. Gradually the Gothick Bird-Cote, Lady Eleanor's Bower and even the Model Dairy fell into decay, until only the Cufflymen tumbled on, bereft of its rustic bridges. Their final monument was their own, a stone tomb set in the churchyard, surprisingly restrained with only a hint of gothic arch. Seeking the solitude of perfect romantic retirement, Eleanor and Sarah had created not only a garden but a lifestyle that appealed to the picturesque tastes of the late eighteenth century.

Retirement into the country was not only the preserve of the scandalised. A world away from the snares and follies of society, sin and fashion in roughly equal measures, the country was seen by many as the ideal retreat of wives and daughters. Many fashionable and wealthy eighteenth-century families would spend at least half the year living on their country estates, but often the menfolk would return to the business of the city, leaving women to a retreat more enforced than sought. For the eighteenth-century 'bluestocking' this retreat took on an extra cultural meaning, with an increasing emphasis being placed on the connection between retirement and the idealised female companion. Joseph Addison, writing in *The Spectator* in 1711, envisaged the ideal wife as one who was a companion to her husband in good sense, consummate virtue, and mutual esteem. His description of 'Aurelia, a Woman of Great Quality, who delights in the Privacy of a Country Life and passes away a great part of her Time in her Walks and Gardens' discriminated between those women who enjoyed the company of the town, and those who went there merely to grow weary of it and have greater relish of their country retirement.[14] Woebetide the woman who did not find pleasure in the isolation of the country lane and the cares of the (model) dairy.

For women such as Elizabeth Montagu (1720–1800) who wished to identify with Addison's ideal of retirement, meditation and learning, gardening was thus as much an obligation as an option. With a marriage widely acknowledged to be a loveless match, the garden was both a refuge from disappointments and a symbol of unattainable perfection.

Perfection is a lot to ask of either a woman or a garden, but letters from Elizabeth while at Sandleford (her Berkshire estate) indicate a striving towards meditative appreciation of rural joys although she acknowledged also the loneliness of the isolated rural life. Before her marriage Elizabeth had identified herself with the pastoral 'farmeress'; during her marriage she became the image of the contemplative in Elysium, a somewhat more melancholic association. The death of her son, followed by that of her mother and brother in fact sent Elizabeth hurrying away from rurality towards the heady distractions of Tunbridge Wells and the soothing waters of the spas. Her London homes at Hill Street and Montagu House were famous for many years as salons for the intellectuals of the day.

It was not until the death of her husband that Elizabeth took on the fashionable improvement of the grounds of Sandleford as part of the contemplative package. Two weeks after his death she wrote to Elizabeth Carter, 'I may perhaps indulge myself with laying out two or three hundred a year in embellishing ye grounds, as ye money will keep the neighbourhood in better employment.'[15] Aware of her own ageing (she was 60 when she commenced the work) she wrote, 'As fast as time wrinkles my forehead, I smooth the grounds around Sandleford.' To smooth the Sandleford wrinkles she chose Lancelot Brown, the most fashionable of designers in the 1770s, while to actually labour on the works she employed the poor and out-of-work weavers of the local villages. With this combination of intellectual fashion, aesthetics and moral good Mrs Montagu reached as near perfection as one can. Of Brown's works at Sandleford she writes: 'He is forming it into a lovely pastoral – a sweet Arcadian scene. In not attempting more, he adapts his scheme to the character of the place and my purse. We shall not erect temples to the gods, build proud bridges over humble rivulets.'[16] Despite her protestations of being a 'poor widow with paltry plans' the greatly 'improved' grounds at Sandleford Priory attracted numerous visitations and admiration from society. For Elizabeth, as for the Ladies of Llangollen, creation of a pastoral retreat brought with it little actual retirement.

Unhappy marriage, scandal, divorce or elopement were fortunately not prerequisites for an interest in gardens. Jemima, Marchioness Grey (1722–97), was in need of no distractions from her mutually affectionate marriage to Philip Yorke, later 2nd Earl of Hardwicke. Her earlier life, it is true, had been less idyllic. With her mother dying when she was 5, her grandmother when she was 6, and her father overseas, she was brought up by her elderly grandfather the Duke of Kent in London and

Bedfordshire. The family seat of Wrest Park in Bedfordshire was Jemima's home for much of her life, and in 1733, with the death of her stepbrother, she became the sole heir to the Duke's estates. By special remainder she inherited the title of Marchioness Grey along with the estates, and on her uncle's death in 1741 Wrest became hers. That it came with some £12,500 of debts was admittedly an inconvenience, but perhaps a small price to pay. Working in close harmony with her new husband, Philip Yorke, Jemima was soon able not only to repay the debts but also to embark on a series of improvements to the grounds which were to reflect the couple's shared interests in landscaping, architecture and intellectual studies. After 1743 Wrest became their main residence and there Jemima was able to entertain her friends, including Catherine Talbot. Talbot's secret diary of her 1745 visit to Wrest gives an intimate picture of Jemima's life. Morning prayers were followed by a walk in the park; tea was taken in the garden buildings or, if wet, chess or billiards were played in the house. In the evening there was an hour's reading, which could include theology, political theory and the classics; she read French in the original but other languages, including Latin, Greek and Italian, in translation. Jemima asserted that women could profit from a life of scholarly retirement as well as men, and once commented sharply on Pliny's advocacy of a country life of study and exercise: 'I don't find how Mrs Pliny (for all his charming account of her and his letters to her) had any share in it.'[17]

Wrest Park gardens had been laid out in the fashionable Anglo-Dutch style at the end of the eighteenth century, with work ongoing during Jemima's childhood. The south face of the house looked out on to parterres with fountains and *allées*, while iron screens allowed views into the formal wilderness gardens beyond. A long central canal carried the eye towards the distant pavilion, created by the architect Thomas Archer in 1712, while a matching pavilion by the same architect sat astride the Cain Hill in the park to the east, a destination for longer walks. *Allées* of finely raked sand cut through the formal wilderness (the word wilderness itself comes from the verb 'to wilder' or to wander). Lined with tall hedges these were interspersed with formal glades, again high-hedged, containing brick or stone arbours and seats, statues, obelisks and columns. Statues also peopled the walks, joined the promenaders on the parterres and spectated at the bowling greens. So numerous in fact were the statues, that when they had fallen out of fashion and been melted down in the nineteenth century, Amabel de Grey noted that the garden felt lonely.

Such was the garden that Jemima would guide into the informality of the later eighteenth century. Jemima's love of the garden is evident from the frequency with which it is referred to in her many letters.[18] She was intensely proud of the grounds and intensely possessive of their beauty. Writing to a close friend about the arrival of Philip at Wrest (after a brief honeymoon in 1740) she expresses mock irritation that he 'stole a further walk – which I did not allow of, for I wanted to have been with him every time he was to see anything in the garden'.[19] A lesser man might have felt jealous, although his own family estates at Wimpole had absorbed his father's time and money. After settling into married bliss (and paying off debts), the years from 1744 onwards were full of 'works being done' in the gardens. The joy of walking in areas newly planted with flowering scented shrubs, including the roses, jasmines, lilacs and syringas, filled Jemima's letters to her childhood friend Catherine Talbot as much as the joys of marriage (if not more). As the romantic influence of the eighteenth century made itself felt, the straight canals were transformed to serpentine rivers, the springs became 'artless rivulets', the formal walks were perfumed with honeysuckles, and a rustic root house and 'ruined' bathhouse made their appearance.[20] A Persian or Mithraic-style altar was constructed as a reference to the couple's intellectual pretensions and Philip's contribution to the witty *Athenian Letters* (published in 1741). Antiquarians were fooled by its Persian inscriptions, and architects taken in by its claw-footed base although its knapped flint construction might surely have given a hint of its more local construction.

Payments to the workmen are recorded in the estate records, but letters from Jemima reveal her own very personal involvement in the additions and alterations. While touring other gardens and houses she sent back instructions for the workmen constructing the fashionable Chinese Seat at Wrest (possibly modelled on those seen at Kew), and to her widowed daughter Amabel[21] she keeps up an endless stream of queries on flowers and foundations. To Miss Talbot she writes: 'I am called upon to visit my workmen at the serpentine who are adding its meanders and improving it very much. It is at present the great object of my attention.' In addition to landscaping, and populating the menagerie and aviary, the choice of planting was also her concern. In 1775 she sent advice to the head gardener on beds to be planted along the ancient yew hedge and an opening up of a gap in the same hedge. She is also anxious for lists of plants sent by the nurseries for planting near the magnolias.

It was not just the lowly gardeners and workmen that formed Jemima's responsibilities at Wrest. Lancelot 'Capability' Brown was employed to 'improve' some of the waters and grounds in 1758–60 and again in the late 1770s. Jemima does not appear to have thought much of the great man. Dealing with affairs in her mother's absence, Amabel was due to entertain Brown when he visited the Park to check on progress. Jemima expresses sympathy for this enforced meeting in a letter to Amabel and suggests that to pass the dining hour she might 'set [Brown] to talk' on any subject, as he makes claim to being a politician, farmer, architect, lover of virtue and 'divine for ought I know'. Her instructions in 1779 include concurrence with some of Brown's schemes, but also the strict admonition that he is 'on no account to be allowed to shorten the terrace'.[22] She also expressed distaste for Stowe, where Brown had worked in the early part of his career, finding the sweeping landscapes too barren and lacking in scent and colour. A commemorative column (with suitably 'rustic' ornamentation) erected on completion of Brown's landscaping at Wrest carefully records that Jemima, Marchioness Grey, and Philip, Earl of Hardwicke, laid out the grounds with the 'professional assistance' of Lancelot Brown, a carefully worded tribute considerably less glowing than that given by most of his clients.

By the time of Jemima's death in 1797 Wrest had had over fifty years of female superintendence, taking it from the formality of the early seventeenth century into the more romantic closing years of the eighteenth. In the hands of her daughter Amabel (1751–1833) this superintendence continued for a further thirty-five years into the Victorian era. Amabel's main contribution was the glade of Graeco-Roman altars continuing the theme of memorials and antiquity, although she also nurtured the scents and sounds of the woodland gardens. A seated statue of Jemima as literate shepherdess, with book in hand, still survives in the gardens at Wrest, overseeing the restorations of the modern age.

Overseeing famous landscape designers appears to have been more often the responsibility of the woman of the house than has been previously suspected. In addition to Marchioness Grey, and Lady Montagu harrying the fashionable Brown, at Audley End (Essex) Lady Griffin had requested he include an ornamental garden within his usually rather more austere landscape design, a request that might have had something to do with his rather abrupt departure and subsequent financial dispute.[23] Lady Elizabeth Pope (1645–1719; Lady Lindsay by marriage) was recorded by the landscape designer Stephen Switzer as being continually 'Attendant and Supervisor of the works [at Grimsthorpe] without any regard to the rigid inclemency of the winter season . . . in the Measuring and Laying out the distances of her rows of Trees she was actually employed with Rule, Line etc.'[24] Shades of Lady Luxborough suggest to the reader that 'displanting' might also have been one of Lady Lindsay's specialities had anything been positioned wrongly. Switzer, probably on his first independent commission away from his employers London and Wise, cut avenues and rides through the plantations at Grimsthorpe 'resembling the nave of a baroque cathedral' under the ever-watchful eyes of Lady Elizabeth. John Vanbrugh was another landscape architect who came under watchful female eyes. Employed by the Duke, Vanbrugh never could come to an agreement with the Duchess of Marlborough and was eventually banned from entering Blenheim altogether as a result of disagreements over the demolition of Woodstock Manor.

Lady Catherine Parker also took charge of the layout of the grounds at her family's estates at Saltram. Described by contemporaries as a woman of judgement, taste and energy, Lady Catherine initially took on the improvements to the house and grounds during her husband's serious illness. That she continued to do so after his recovery might be down to others' somewhat less flattering appraisal of her as rather 'proud and wilful'.[25] Despite this rather overly practical approach to illness on the part of his wife, the couple appeared happy when moving into Saltram together in 1743. In addition to transforming the house from its old Tudor appearance and layout to the height of eighteenth-century fashion, Lady Catherine also oversaw the redesign of the gardens to include an amphitheatre and other contemporary features. A 'castle' with interiors by Robert Adams formed a pleasant summer retreat, and an orangery, greenhouse and lodges were added by Lady Parker's daughter-in-law, Theresa, in the second half of the century. Theresa's portrait by Reynolds (held at Saltram) shows her standing in a landscape of young trees, leaning against the type of classical urn that was so vital to any eighteenth-century garden design. A prospective plantation of some 38,000 trees ordered by the Parkers had arrived by ship at the nearby Devon ports only to be greeted by an unusually hard frost in this mildest part of England; some had obviously survived to form this romantic backdrop.

Fluttering on the edge of the eighteenth-century romantic garden was the burgeoning interest in natural history and, in particular, the study of insects. A remarkably high proportion of entomologists at this early period in the history of the study were women. As with plants, insects were even named after the women who studied them, such as Mrs Eleanor Glanville, of the Glanville Fritillary.[26] Famous though she was for her dedication to her plants and insects in the seventeenth century Mary, Duchess of Beaufort (see page 20), could not have competed with the collecting mania of Lady Margaret Cavendish Bentinck, 3rd Duchess of Portland (1715–85). From her marriage at the age of 20 until her death fifty years later, Lady Margaret spent most of her time and energy (not to mention the family fortunes) on her collections. Her interests encompassed natural history, entomology, porcelain and botany, each seen as appropriate areas for female study in the eighteenth century. Margaret had grown up at her father's house at Wimpole, Cambridgeshire, surrounded by books, paintings, sculpture, and in the company of writers such as Alexander Pope, Jonathan Swift and Matthew Prior as well as aristocrats and politicians. Unsurprisingly, she was known as a bluestocking and corresponded with Jean-Jacques Rousseau. Her gardens at Bulstrode, Buckinghamshire (known in court circles as 'the Hive' for the amount of work carried out there) boasted large botanic collections, worthy of visitation by those enthusiastic royals and collectors in their own right, King George III and Queen Charlotte. Her fellow collector Horace Walpole commented that few men rivalled Margaret Cavendish in the mania of collecting, and perhaps no woman. In an age of great collectors she rivalled the greatest.

Margaret employed Georg Ehret to illustrate her botanical collection from *c.* 1736 onwards. Ehret also worked on the collection of Hans Sloane, and illustrating Philip Miller's *Gardener's Dictionary*. Perhaps unsurprisingly, the omnipresent and energetic Mary Delany also recorded the collections at what she called 'the noble house'. It was here that she first had the idea for her famous flower collages or 'mosaicks'. Noticing the similarity of colour between a geranium and a piece of red paper that was on her bedside table Mrs Delany took up her scissors and imitated the petals. Upon entering the room, the Duchess mistook them for real: 'Her approbation was such a sanction to my undertaking . . . and gave me courage to go on with confidence.'[27]

The enormity of the Duchess of Portland's collections can be gauged by the thirty-eight days it took to sell them off after her death in 1785,[28] a sale that was made necessary by the running down of the family fortunes as a result of their acquisition in the first place. The story has strong echoes in the collecting mania and bankruptcy of Ellen Willmott, a century and a half later.[29] The Duchess may have been the introducer of the *Ginkgo biloba* (*c.* 1750) although other claimants are her

Portland Rose (*Rosa* 'Portlandica', syn. *Rosa* 'Paestana')

Named after the 3rd Duchess of Portland, avid collector of all forms of art and botany. While undertaking a Grand Tour of Italy in the 1770s the Duchess was supposedly handed a mysterious rose from the area of Paestum. Renowned as a rose-growing area under both the Greeks and the Romans, Paestum's rich volcanic soil produced some of the earliest-known repeat-flowering roses in Europe, possibly pre-dating (and bypassing) the later introduction of the Chinese roses. A rose that strongly resembles the mysterious *Rosa* 'Paestana' in fact appears on the wall frescoes of ancient Pompeii. In 1800, Georg Ehret renamed *Rosa* 'Paestana' the Portland rose, after his patroness, for whom he was carrying out a series of rose watercolours. It was later conjectured that rather than being an ancient rose, the Portland rose was an offspring of 'Autumn Damask', 'Slater's Crimson China', and possibly *Rosa gallica*. From 1800 to about 1850, *Rosa* 'Portlandica' was extensively hybridised in France. Crossed with Chinas, Autumn Damasks and Gallicas over 150 varieties were created, only to fall out of fashion with the arrival of the Hybrid Perpetuals. Only a handful of Portland roses still survive today; but this includes such gems as 'Compte de Chambord' and 'Marquise Bocella'. The original *Rosa* 'Portlandica' has the appearance of a repeating Apothecary rose with bright crimson, semi-double, highly fragrant flowers with bright golden stamens. The Portland rose was grown at Bulstrode House as part of the collections there and illustrated by Ehret from an original.

son, the Duke of Portland, and Lord William Cavendish, Governor of India. She is also rather bizarrely commemorated by a small genus of Central American shrubs and trees, *Portlandia*, all of which require stove conditions to grow in England and none of which appear to be popular today.

For every woman whose interests and responsibilities lay in management of estates or vast collections, there were many more who found domestic delight and diversion in managing the smaller flower garden. Among these were the ladies of the Fox Strangways family. Four generations of the Fox Strangways wives and daughters have been carefully brought back to life from their letters and diaries,[30] and with them their gardens have also flowered again. A love of plants threaded through all generations of the family at their houses at Melbury and Redlynch (Dorset) although, as with all family traits, it blossomed more in some than in others. Susanna Strangways Horner was a friend of Sarah, Duchess of Marlborough and, in common with the Duchess, a woman who knew her own mind. Widowed in 1741, on the death of a husband whom she had regarded as somewhat of a fool, she commenced considerable work on the gardens at Melbury. Keeping at least twenty people at work she removed the old-fashioned terraces and created 'one easy slope, that the water [of the enlarged canal] might be seen from the parlour floor'.[31] Cascades and serpentine rivers were built, ha-has dug, and the whole ground given a rather more romantic appearance with shrubberies and winding walks in the style of Stephen Switzer. A small gothic temple and a rustic cold bath might have made even the romantic Eleanor Butler and Sarah Ponsonby feel at home, while the enlarged canal complete with gilded dragon boat would have reminded Jemima of Wrest Park. However, alongside this larger-scale landscaping Susannah also paid particular attention to the planting of flowering shrubs, both in beds in the lawns and along the borders. Purchased from the Blandford nurseryman Francis Kingston, these included 'fifty-four roses, forty "lawrenistines", twenty laburnums, twenty jessamines, ten dwarf syringoes, and ten *Hypericum fruiticosum*'.[32]

At Redlynch, the family's other main seat, improvements were also in hand, under the direction of Elizabeth, Countess of Ilchester. The grounds here had not contained a flower garden prior to her arrival, being largely in the geometric style. Romantic elements had consisted almost exclusively of tree and shrub clumps, named rather bizarrely after friends and relatives of Stephen Fox (Elizabeth's husband-to-be). An erratically spelt series of accounts documents the development of the gardens following Elizabeth's arrival. A 'statue on the tarrice', 'garden wales', a new 'garding', an orangery and a menagerie were all installed, alongside a new motto on the temple. By 1750 a 'Ladies Garden' had been completed as part of a series of alterations to give the garden a rococo style. This predominantly female fashion for rococo combined the serpentine and romantic with an opportunity to display the latest flowering (and scented) shrubs, often set in clumps or kidney-shaped beds. When Lady Ilchester wrote to her husband in February 1750 she enthused that her garden 'looked so pretty and full of flowers', although given the season one suspects this must have been somewhat of an exaggeration. Horace Walpole (who appears to have been everywhere and known everyone!) also noted the 'new' flower garden when he visited in 1762, as undoubtedly did Charles Hamilton, of Painshill, another friend of the Foxes.[33]

As instructed by Charles Evelyn, Elizabeth took an active role in the management and direction of her garden. While away she writes giving instructions on matters as diverse as mowing the lawns, the placement of orange trees and myrtle cuttings (we hear of the myrtles again later in the year when they appear to have taken and are in good health, although the holly trees merely 'seem all alive'). By the 1760s more exotic plants were being acquired, still from Francis Kingston, and blue phlox, zinnias, and twelve 'best blowing carnations' gave rise to a need for twenty-four hand-glasses. A second Lady Ilchester created a second informal flower garden, and by the time that Mary Strangways was growing up in the 1790s, a love of flowers would have come naturally. Mary's father wrote to her when she was staying in London to tell her of the progress of spring among the auricula and hyacinth at Redlynch. Promoting the vision of ideal female retirement among the flowers his letter concludes, 'I rather think you would prefer . . . this poor country life to sunshine through a Claude in Burlington Street.'

Mary was destined to dedicate much of her life to her own gardens at Penrice, Glamorgan, where she moved on her marriage to Thomas Talbot in 1793. It was rumoured in Mary's family that she had only agreed to marry Thomas because she had fallen in love with his newly landscaped gardens. Perhaps she took to heart the advice of her aunt Susan who at the end of a long life (and ten years of widowhood) had written: 'Crocus border in its glory, and many other good symptoms of spring and very fine weather. Those, you will allow are pleasures, and the pleasures of Nature don't depend so much on others as most pleasures do.'[34] Susan need not have worried about the attractions of other pleasures, as Mary was to become dedicated to her garden. As her son was later to say, 'Gardening was her passion . . . and I do not believe the attraction of all the gaities in London would have induced her to forego seeing the snowdrops or the crocuses at Penrice in blow for one single day.' Her garden was admired by all her friends and visitors for its beauties and variety. Rockwork outcrops (artificial), a grotto and ponds provided a naturalistic habitat for some plants, while others bloomed in the beds, borders and hothouses. She ordered both traditional old florists' varieties (auricula, primula, ranuncula, carnations, pinks, etc.) as well as flowering shrubs and roses, and newly introduced plants and exotics. Mail-order suppliers meant that Glamorgan was not as isolated from seedsmen as some felt it was from society. Plants came by the Swansea boat from Bristol having made their journeys from the Sweet and Miller nurserymen, or from Loddidges of Hackney.

Mary was an observant gardener and kept a notebook of orders to be made, changes to the garden, dates of flowering, and cultivation techniques. In 1803 she wrote recommending sandy soils in a warm place for the Guernsey lily (hers had just come into bloom by the wall of the kitchen garden). She also advised her sisters on the layout of their gardens, and sent plants to supplement the advice. Their own ignorance must have pained her; although answering the query sent by Louisa as to what is the name of the 'beautiful, white, tallish thing'[35] would be a challenge that any gardener would relish. Louisa would later become mistress of Bowood where some of the finest formal gardens of the Victorian period were laid out by Robert Smirke. The inclusion of a new pinetum at Bowood in the 1840s would certainly have been a test of newly found naming abilities on Louisa's part.

By the end of the eighteenth century Mary's domestic bliss was further enhanced by watching her own children garden. Children's gardens were to become popular in the Victorian period, but an early start was made at Penrice, perhaps as a result of reading the works of Richard and Maria Edgeworth on education and the role of gardens in childhood. Letters from the children appear to reflect a certain preoccupation with the edibles of the garden (gooseberries, strawberries, cherries and melons are recorded by a young Jane in a letter to her mother), but roses, lilacs and pinks were also learnt early. As they grew older the children actually carried out the sowing and planting themselves, although Mary also spent time on the less attractive tasks of weeding, preparing and slug hunting. Dressed in a loose-fitting cloak and informal dress, Mary carried out much of the physical work in her own gardens, even during her (frequent) pregnancies. In 1798 she was gardening the day before her confinement with Christina, and in 1803 the garden was occupying her until a few days before her son was born.[36] Digging was her especial delight and recommended (no doubt with explicit instructions) to her many female friends and relatives. Little wonder that her network of descendants, relatives and friends reverberated through the next century at gardens such as Highclere, Killerton, Bowood and Mount Edgecumbe.

For Mary Talbot domestic bliss appears to have grown on a well-prepared soil, but for others it takes root in the most unsuitable of mediums. Charlotte Haynes (1763–1849) appears to have overcome a degree of disagreeableness in her husband that would have sent many a lady into the arms of another. On Charlotte's marriage in 1783 to John William Egerton, she was equally unaware of his future unexpected inheritance and his insufferable conceit. Charlotte's 'ability to appeal to her husband's conceit, to flatter and sympathise and to ultimately overrule with such grace and charm that he seems never to have realised'[37] was all that enabled them to continue in apparent harmony. It must have been an ability that many wives longed for in the days before divorce became commonplace. An army officer at the time of their marriage, John William Egerton inherited the title and estate at Ashridge on the death of his cousin Francis, 3rd Duke of Bridgewater (as well as estates in Shropshire, Hertfordshire and Buckinghamshire). Suddenly worth some two million pounds, the couple embarked on a programme of socialising, building and landscaping; aided in the last two by the architects James and Jeffry Wyatt and the landscape gardener Humphry Repton. Ashridge had originated as a monastery of the Bonhommes order but had been deserted during the religious upheavals of 1534, despite an enjoyable visit being recorded by Henry VIII just three years before. Elizabeth I spent part of her childhood there, and in 1550 she was briefly its possessor under the settlement of Henry VIII's will. A prayer book, embroidered with complex knot patterns as if from a garden, survives from Elizabeth's happier hours spent in the house and gardens. A New Year's gift to her stepmother Katherine Parr, it is bound in canvas and embroidered in blue, silver and gilt, with a wild pansy or heartsease at each corner. To complete the work Elizabeth stitched seven flowers along the spine before placing the initials 'KP' at the centre.

Many years passed between Elizabeth's garden-inspired stitch-work and the building of the new mansion, but gardens have a strange way of making connections across the centuries, so it comes as no surprise to discover that the new Countess, Charlotte, found Ashridge the ideal setting for her own creations. With its surrounding park and gardens, Ashridge was largely rebuilt by about 1814, only eleven years after Egerton's inheritance. Gone were the monastic buildings and in their place stood a magnificent gothic hall. Frequent visits by Humphry Repton, accompanied in these last years of his life by his son, were recorded by the steward of the house. Usually both 'Lord and Lady B' are carefully noted as being present when Repton walked the grounds, or presented his designs in his typical 'Red Book'. However, unlike Jemima's rather condescending relationship with Brown at Wrest Park, Charlotte appears to have enjoyed the company of Repton at Ashridge and Repton in turn appears to have been especially charmed by Charlotte. He expressed a genuine fondness for the site, staying as a guest several times and being present at the traditional beating of the bounds. A watercolour entitled *A Garland of Flowers from the Garden at Ashridge* was a proposed present from Repton for the Countess, although never actually given. It was Charlotte who chose to put into motion (or not) the suggestions made by Repton and it may have come as a disappointment to him that not all of his carefully illustrated plans were translated into reality. Indeed, at some period his Red Book of designs for Ashridge appears to have been temporarily lost or mislaid, but then Charlotte had ideas of her own for the gardens.

In 1824 Henry Todd, Chaplain to the Earl of Bridgewater, wrote a detailed description of the house and gardens, allowing an insight into the work that had been carried out and the role of the Countess. Writing of the Monk's Garden, for example, he notes that 'The profusion also of flowers which abound here, as well as in the walks and conservatories together with the elegance of their arrangement, sufficiently indicates the care and attention bestowed by the Countess of Bridgewater upon her delightful pursuits of the garden.'[38] It was the Monk's Garden in particular that Charlotte had much altered from the original Repton design. Although sympathising with the idea, she chose to relocate it, and wisely altered the proposed rather funereal layout of grave-shaped flower beds that Repton had illustrated. Other areas, such as the Rosarie, were laid out much as Repton suggested and survive into the present day. Dying in 1823, the Earl of Bridgewater left Charlotte as chatelaine of the house, gardens, park and extensive estate for the remaining twenty-six years of her life. His brother, an eccentric resident of Paris, left a legacy of £13,500 for the erection of an obelisk on the Ashridge Estate in memory of a cousin, the canal-building Duke of Bridgewater. Charlotte, confident as ever in her own taste and judgement, used the money to build not the design submitted by the Earl, but instead one of her own selection. Although childless, Charlotte brought life and laughter to Ashridge, as well as colour and taste to its gardens, until her own death at the age of 80, by which time the work had passed from the Regency to the new Victorian Age.

FOUR

Inspiration and Perspiration

ARTISTS AND NEEDLEWOMEN

In Spring when Flow'rs your garden grace,
With needle or pencil you can trace,
Each curious Form, and various Dye,
So represent unto the Eye,
Noble proportion ev'ry Part,
That Nature blushes at your Art

John Rea, *Flora* Dedication addressed to
Lady Hanmer (1665)[1]

To be able to draw flowers botanically and fruit horticulturally . . . is one of the most useful accomplishments of your ladies of leisure, living in the country.

J.C. Loudon, *Gardener's Magazine*[2]

The needle, the paintbrush, scissors and shell collection may seem a world away from the spade and the hoe, but for generations of middle- and upper-class women these were the only tools allowed. As any form of physical labour was usually seen as socially and sexually demeaning, their relationship with gardens and more specifically flowers was kept alive through the accepted female occupations of art and needlework, collage and flower arrangement. For a few the tools became those of a trade, but for most they were the marks of social standing, of polite accomplishment and years of enforced leisure. Needlework in all its forms – tapestry, embroidery and clothing decoration – had its professionals and its dilettantes; although long hours at the needle created a skilled workforce among those even of the highest social status. Some female botanical artists of the seventeenth and eighteenth centuries fought to take their place in the halls of artists' academies or earn an independent income from their art, but others were content with the hired drawing master and the amateur easel. Producers of 'flower paintings' far outnumbered botanical artists, and came from a broader spectrum of female society. Many paintings never left the homes in which they had been produced, although the burgeoning of societies for amateur artists encouraged exhibition to wider audiences than family and friends. The Royal Society of Watercolourists and the Society of British Artists both received contributions from female artists, and the Society of Female Artists was of course exclusively their preserve. To make a living from your skills was one thing, but at least one woman went further and founded a manufactory, combining financial acumen with membership of the Society of Artists. It is a rare country house garden that has no trace of the magical Coade stone ornament, usually better preserved than those of genuine stonework. Plants in stitches, flowers in frames, sculpture in the garden: no aspect of the arts was without its women and no woman complete without some form of botanical artistry.

William Morris, himself an exceptional creator of botanical motifs, once likened the art of embroidery to 'gardening with silk and gold thread'.[3] Speaking in the nineteenth century, he was putting into words a connection between embroidery and gardening that went back many centuries. Flowers, plants and gardens have appeared on textiles almost since their creation, and examples exist of Egyptian cloth with floral motifs. In England there was a very specific connection between women and the domestic production of tapestries and embroideries of all kinds. Samplers, embroidered pictures, cabinets decorated in raised work, cushions, hangings, fireguards, furniture covers, all portrayed the outside world come inside and acted as witness to the housewife's skills. In addition, waistcoats, dresses, shawls, purses and even shoes might be decorated with silks in a rich evocation of the flowers of the garden. Mary Delany's court dress alone contained some 200 flowers on the overskirt, while Queen Elizabeth I's gowns contained not only flowers but also meaning, as the embroiderer chose the virgin eglantine. Even the busy Duchess of Portland worked fire screens portraying her exotic plants. By examining just a few of the silk and gold threads it is possible to gain an insight into this predominantly feminised area of plant and garden history.

Display, decoration and delight in pattern and colour were hallmarks of the Tudor and Elizabethan ages. Knot gardens, foot mazes and topiary in the Tudor garden carried through into interior decoration and costume. Intertwining plants, bright flower heads and complete garden scenes covered the walls and furnishings of the home as well as the clothes of its inhabitants. Gardens and gardening were seen as having both practical and symbolic meaning in all walks of life, from the virgin queen reflected in the closed cup of the foxglove, to the earth itself, compared by John Gerard to a 'robe of embroidered works set with orient pearls and costly jewels'.[4] Elizabeth and Mary, queens and half-sisters, were both famed for their embroideries, albeit in very different circumstances. Mary and her waiting women embroidered 'fifty-two different flowers in *petit point* drawn from life' while residing at the home of Bess, Countess of Shrewsbury at Hardwick Hall. Some of the hangings that adorn Hardwick Hall were created by Bess and her ladies in waiting, although a tapestry of Elizabeth as Diana is the hand of a professional. A red velvet cushion, recorded in an inventory of 1601 and still at the Hall, portrays a garden with flowers in each bed and surrounded by scrollwork, reflecting the knot gardens that these industrious needleworkers would have looked out on.

At Loseley Park (Surrey) a chair cushion decorated with pinks and roses in a blue and white pot was stitched by Queen Elizabeth I herself, and used supposedly by one of her maids of honour. An embroidered book cover, again with knot pattern, was worked by the young Elizabeth while at Ashridge for her stepmother Katherine Parr. Reminding one of the grottos and statues of her courtiers' gardens, is another embroidery by Elizabeth, this portraying the encounter between the virgin Diana and the hunter Actaeon. Conserved at Parham Park, the central scene of the piece is ringed with animal and plant motifs, and giant violets overshadow the dogs of the hunter. Herbals, as well as pattern books, were frequent sources of inspiration for needlework and the single plants would be pricked out and transferred to material for stitching. The resultant embroideries are studded with flowers as singles or cut slips, often out of scale and free from any earthbound reality. Giant pinks tower over rose bushes and miniature oaks bow down to tulips as large as houses. Also loosed from reality are the seasons: spring and summer flowers dance together across cushions, and daffodils are visited by dragonflies, in a world where decay and death are unknown.

Celebrated in prose and poetry as the harbinger of eternal spring, this everlasting garden was welcomed by Elizabeth I into the court. In addition to the tapestry hangings and embroidered furnishings Elizabeth and her ladies-in-waiting wore highly embroidered gowns where flowers were contained within lines and knots. A portrait by Marcus Gheeraerts the Elder in 1585, known variously as the *Peace Portrait* or the *Wanstead Portrait* (private collection), depicts Elizabeth in a gown decorated with periwinkle and a cape embroidered with the bright red Tudor rose. Behind her we spy a small enclosed garden, quartered, and with a covered walkway – embroidery, gardens and painting combine. In the *Rainbow Portrait* by Isaac Oliver (*c.* 1600, Hatfield House) Elizabeth's gown is embroidered with English wildflowers, as the Queen poses in the guise of Astraea, the virginal heroine of classical literature.[5] Honeysuckle, heartsease, eglantine and strawberry are threaded onto a gown of pale cream. Her headdress is decorated lavishly with pearls symbolising her virginity, while a serpent clasps a ruby, representing wisdom overcoming passion. Aged 60 at the time of the portrait, the Queen appears scarcely out of her teens: eternal spring indeed. One of the most incredible dresses of the age, supposedly embroidered for the Queen by Bess of Hardwick, shows sea serpents and whales vying for space with daffodils and violets, woodcocks and iris. Nature run riot in threads. *Lady of the Hampden Family* (Robert Peake, *c.* 1610–15, Museum of Art, Rhode Island) portrays a gown that is a riot of embroidered flowers and fruit. Rather than the wildflowers of the traditional English spring, *Lady of the Hampden Family* has embroidered skirts of crown imperials set amid the honeysuckles.[6] Dressed for a masque and placed in a grassy bower, palms and laurels surround her symbolising chastity and faith in love. *The Persian Lady* by Marcus Gheeraerts the Younger (Hampton Court) also stands poised between the stage and marriage. Shown with the chaste laurel and hind, her hair falls loosely over a dress alive with the brightly coloured flowers of the newly exotic Elizabethan garden.

During the mid-seventeenth century the number of flowers available, and their colour range, increased considerably and these newcomers swiftly joined the native flowers embroidered on both clothes and samplers. Spot samplers, where a number of individual motifs are created as opposed to a picture, are common from the seventeenth century onwards and nearly always include flower and plant motifs. Typical examples include violas, strawberries, pinks, tulips and roses, while vines and acanthus adorn the more ambitious. *The Needle's Excellency*, a pattern book published in 1631, has as its frontispiece a young girl (symbolising industry)[7] working her embroidery while seated in a garden, but few will have taken living flowers as their model. Butterflies, bees and caterpillars also crawl across the 'band' samplers, which show a continuous or repeat picture. There was a considerable overlap between florilegiums, with their wealth of botanical illustration and exotic collections, and embroiderers' source books. Crispin van de Passe's *A Garden of Flowers* or *Hortus Floridus* (1614) contained engravings and descriptions of all types of garden flowers, and proved as invaluable to the embroiderer as to the gardener.[8] The Victorian garden writer Mrs Theresa Earle owned an original copy of *Hortus Floridus* and noted that 'some philistine lady in the last century has, with patient industry, pricked out some of the flowers and insects all round for the purpose of taking the outlines for needlework'.[9] In Henry IV's gardens at the Louvre his director of gardens, Jean Robin, supplied flowers for the king's embroiderer Pierre Vallet, who used them to create designs to be worked by Marie de Medici and the ladies of the court.

Many embroidered pieces of this period include a house and garden or just a garden. Most of these are stylised but some appear based on real gardens, perhaps those in which the embroiderer worked or looked out on to. Samplers in particular are a rich source of gardens, and as nearly all samplers are 'signed' by their creator we know that they were the preserve of girls or young women. Margaret Mason completed a band sampler in 1660 showing a squared knot garden with central fountain in front of a crenellated house. Such gardens would have been slightly old fashioned by this period but not out of place in a traditional family or country manor house. Certainly embroidery could reflect fashions in the garden. A stumpwork cabinet of the mid-seventeenth century, decorated with episodes from the Story of Abraham, opens to reveal a small orchard resembling Ralph Austen's 1653 work *A Treatise of Fruit Trees with The Spiritual Use of the Orchard*,[10] and the rise in popularity of orchards and fruit growing during the Commonwealth period generally may be reflected in an increase in the number of fruit trees in embroidery. Similarly, the fashion for topiary and clipped plants in the Dutch style was reflected in samplers of the early eighteenth century. In 1752 Elizabeth Cridland included clipped topiary and potted orange trees in her sampler, now held in the Victoria and Albert Museum. This geometric style of garden design suited the cross-work and tent stitch most often used in samplers, and the move to portray the naturalistic gardens of the late eighteenth century onwards must have presented a considerable technical challenge. An embroidery of *c.* 1785 by Elizabeth Brain (Victoria and Albert Museum) manages against all the odds to convey the atmosphere of the 'Capability' Brown parkland. A sinuous walk or drive leads through a grassland park where deer graze under a clump of naturally shaped trees. Honeysuckle and other twining plants decorate the edge of the picture, lending it a rococo touch which would have been unappreciated by Brown.

Garden buildings, so beloved of the eighteenth- and early nineteenth-century garden designer, are also carefully portrayed by these young needleworkers. Follies, ruins and idyllic rural scenes were shown on a mid-eighteenth-century settee worked by Anne Southey. The pastoral theme of music in the garden includes instruments to a backdrop of goats and sheep grazing among flowers. Aged only 13, Ann Curren completed a sampler depicting a pavilion set within an informally planted landscape instantly recognisable as typical of its 1830s date. One should, however, be wary of always equating decoration with garden reality. A mid-seventeenth-century tent-stitched picture (in a private collection) shows dwarf fruit trees with oversized fruit forming a landscape where camels, elephants and giant dragonfly roam. Perhaps not a reflection of the true state of the countryside during the Commonwealth period.

Embroidery remained an important female accomplishment into the nineteenth and early twentieth centuries, but it was increasingly joined by a range of 'polite' occupations including shellwork and grotto decoration. Grottos have long had a connection with women and women gardeners. One of the first created in England was the Grotto of Diana at Nonsuch, devised by Lord Lumley as a reference to the Virgin Queen. By the following century the most famous grotto creator, Isaac de Caus was creating a much-embellished room-grotto for Lucy Harington, Countess of Bedford (1581–1627) at Woburn.[11] Justly famous for its elaborate mosaics and mechanical sea monsters, its putti and its nymphs, the Woburn grotto survives five centuries on. De Caus may have been responsible for a grotto at Moor Park, also possibly for Lucy. In the eighteenth century the fashion for rustic and picturesque garden buildings resulted in a plethora of grottos, baths and summer-houses all in need of internal embellishment. One of the most famous was that at Goodwood House, the home of Sarah Lennox, Duchess of Richmond (1706–51), where in the late 1730s the grotto was elaborately decorated by the Duchess and her daughters Caroline and Emily. This ornate building with its stunning sea views required entire shiploads of shells for its completion, and in 1739 Captain Charles Knowles of HMS *Diamond* filled his holds with specimens to assist the Duchess in her work. Thousands of shells, flints and fossils were brought to them by relatives and friends, including the 'officers serving abroad',[12] and these were used to decorate the interior walls and ceiling, while polished horses' teeth lined the floor.

For those less fortunate in their choice of friends and acquaintances, specialist dealers charged exorbitant sums to feed the fashion. William Shenstone declared that the grotto of Susanna, Viscountess Fane (d. 1792) cost her £5,000, which was 'about three times what her house is worth'.[13] In the 1760s, Princess Amelia found salve for a frustrated engagement in her cold plunge pool in the grotto at Gunnersbury, blissfully unaware it would later be chosen as the scene of a brutal (fictional) crime by the writer Deryn Lake.[14] At Walton (Warwickshire) the daughters of Charles Mordaunt seized upon an octagonal bathhouse in the wooded grounds, transforming the interior with festoons of shells and other decorative items. Originally built by Sanderson Miller as a cold plunge over a spring, the 'pepperpot' was converted into the home of a 'nymph or triton' by their creative makeover. Fortunately for them (or perhaps for their father) the ladies did not have to resort to specialist dealers for their materials. Living next door to their Walton estate was Mrs Anne Dewes, sister of one of the most famous female grotto creators: Mary Granville Delany.

Mary Delany (1700–88) seems to have been dogged by ill luck in early life, or as she was later to put it, 'early inured to disappointments and vexations'.[15] Her father had been a staunch Tory and supporter of Queen Anne, and there had been hope that Mary would become a maid of honour to the Queen. Alas for herself and her family, Anne's death brought an about-turn in the politics of the country and their high hopes were dashed. Exiled into (relative) poverty in the country, rather than welcomed at court, it might have seemed to Mary that things could not get worse. Little was she to know that just two years later she would be married to a man over forty years her senior, whose very appearance she found repulsive and character distasteful. 'Never,' she said, 'was woe dressed out in gayer colours than when I was led to the altar, I wished from my soul I had been led, as Iphegenia was, to be sacrificed.'[16] She was to spend seven years in misery married to the 60-year-old Alexander Pendarve (Lord Lansdowne) of Cornwall before being released by his death. During that time her repugnance for him never ceased, although she gave him the care and nursing of a dutiful wife.

Having had to repel several other unsuitable and pressing suitors even when her husband was alive (including a suicidal maniac), Mary was not in a hurry to swap widowhood for matrimony. She spent nineteen years as a widow before making her own choice of Reverend Delany for her second husband. Despite having attained a scholarship and a deanery, Delany was the son of a servant; and in addition to upsetting her family, the marriage led to a change in Mary's social status. As the wife of an Irish clergyman of humble background she no longer had access to the court parties that her marriage to Lord Lansdowne had given her. Retirement to Ireland appealed to Mary, and her descriptions of her domain are reminiscent of Plas Newydd and the Ladies of Llangollen. Writing to her sister she describes the gardens as including 'a good kitchen garden, two fruit gardens, little wild walks, private seats, lovely prospects, a beggars hut and a brook with a purling rill'.[17] It was during these peaceful years of her second marriage that Mary developed further the skills and interest that she had already shown in abundance: shell collecting, grotto decoration and embroidery.

Mary had begun shell collecting on earlier tours of Ireland, and had sent back barrels of shells for her own and others' amusement. Now she was even better placed, with access to Irish shores and contacts in Irish ports. Soon the eating parlour at the Delany house at Delville was embellished with her 'finds' and an ornamental grotto overlooking the sea was constructed and similarly decorated. With the garden flowers and wild plants of the roadsides to inspire her Mary also returned to embroidery, a skill she had learnt as a girl. At first she made furnishings for her new home including winter and summer covers for dining chairs with seasonal flowers. A design of oak branches and roses in chenille on a black background was originally favoured for seats for her husband's chapel, later also decorated with shellwork, but this was thought to be 'too gay' and a crimson diamond pattern was eventually settled upon. Flowers were the dominant motif of her items of personal adornment and dress. Aprons, handkerchiefs, bodices and skirts were all alive with a profusion of brilliant silk flowers. She embroidered a white linen coverlet in a foliage and knot pattern for her godson. The coverlet still survives in Ulster Museum in Belfast, its patterns demonstrating a continuation of design when knot gardens themselves had long gone.

Her greatest achievement, created before the years of retirement in Ireland, had been her court dress. Court dresses of the early to mid-eighteenth century were commonly emblazoned with flower motifs, and the extraordinary widths of the skirts (being held sideways out from the body with padded supports) resulted in substantial panels for the display of this decoration. Combined with the stomachers, petticoats and jackets, court dresses would resemble nothing less than a series of garden borders on the move. Selina, Countess of Huntingdon, was one of the first to wear the fashions at a court ball attended by Mary Delany. The Countess's dress was covered with 'the pattern of a large stone vase filled with ramping flowers that spread almost over a breadth of the petticoat from the bottom to the top . . . no vases on the sleeves but two or three on the tail'. The Duchess of Queensbury favoured white satin with 'brown hills covered with all sorts of weeds, and every breadth had an old stump of a tree . . . round which twined nastersians, evy, [*sic*] honeysuckles, periwinkles, convolvuluses and all sorts of twining flowers which spread and covered the petticoat'.[18]

Mary had embroidered her own court dress with these examples in mind, although with less of the picturesque touches. The outfit comprised a stomacher of black velvet with a line of embroidered pinks down the centre with lily of the valley either side; a petticoat encrusted at the hemline with large flowers and leaves with scattered flowers above; and an overskirt with over 200 flowers and plants on a background of black silk. Although some of the species were the same, each had a different twist to the leaf or tendril making it unique, as in real life. The flowers on the ensemble included many of the natives that she later delighted in on her walks around the country lanes, supplemented with traditional garden plants including convolvulus, bluebell, roses, winter jasmine, hawthorn berries, love-in-the-mist, sweet pea, forget-me-not and lily of the valley. This last was Mary's favourite flower and it grew in profusion in her garden in Ireland. It is interesting to note that it was the native flowers that drew her attention in her earlier life, whereas her later paper flowers included the many exotics and novelties provided for her by hothouses and conservatories. Mrs Delany was not alone in her embroidery skills. Her close friend Mrs Forth Hamilton of Finglass also used plants and flowers in her own decoration, but added to this a riot of butterflies, moths, dragonflies, ladybirds and even the occasional small snail! The latter perhaps not something that the strictest of gardeners saw as essential to the garden, but recalling the early tapestries with their millefleurs backgrounds or the jewelled borders of early illuminations.

Widowed for the second time in 1768, Mary moved back to England and to court life. Living as a companion to Mary, Duchess of Portland at Bulstrode, she was surrounded by the botanical, shell and entomological collections of her host. At the age of 73 she wrote to her niece Mary Port, 'I have invented a new way of imitating flowers, I'll send you next time I write a sample.' This 'new way' comprised cutting coloured paper into the shapes of leaves, stalks and petals, and assembling them on backing paper as paper collages or mosaics. Initially Mary regarded this new pastime as merely a 'whim of my own fancy', but the encouragement of all around led to her eventually creating nearly 1,000 pieces. Threads between art and botany and embroidery run through the century but nowhere more strongly than in the work of Mrs Delany. Visitors to the Bulstrode collections included Queen Charlotte, Sir Joseph Banks, Philip Miller (of the Chelsea Physic Garden), as well as the prominent botanical artist Ehret. These contacts in the world of botany and gardening meant that Mary Delany had a wide range of source material for her collages and they in turn came to be regarded as a valuable method of recording botanical detail. Soon specimens for recording were being sent to her from the hothouses of the nobility and court. Made of coloured papers from China, she cut each leaf, stem and petal with scissors by hand at life size, recording the Latin name, and sometimes the location of the plant, on the back of the work. Backgrounds were plain black, giving a startling three-dimensional effect.[19] Mary referred to her collection as a *Hortus Siccus* (literally a dried garden), the term usually reserved for a dried herbal collection. Erasmus Darwin included Mrs Delany in his poem 'The Love of Plants':

> So now DELANY forms her mimic bowers,
> Her paper foliage, and her silken flowers;
> Her virgin train the tender scissors ply,
> Vein the green leaf, the purple petal dye;
> Round wiry stems the flaxen tendril bends,
> Moss creeps below, and waxen fruit impends.
> Cold Winter views amid his realm of snow,
> DELANY'S vegetable statues below.[20]

In 1781 Queen Charlotte presented Mrs Delany with an embroidered pocket book worked in gold and spangled ornaments, containing knife, scissors, pencil, rule, compass and bodkin. Probably embroidered by the Queen herself, the gift unfortunately arrived just as Mrs Delany's eyesight was failing and at the age of 83 she finally decided to lay down her scissors and paper. In the ten years since she had invented her paper collages she had produced nearly 1,000 pictures. Ten large volumes now contain these pictures, each volume indexed with botanical and common names written in her own clear hand. Many more pictures were given as gifts or in return for flowers and some of these are scattered in museums and private collections. After the death of the Duchess of Portland, Mary spent the remaining years of her life at court at the invitation of the Queen, who was anxious that such a talented lady should not spend her final years in poverty. The small pocket book given by Queen Charlotte survives today in the Royal Collections, being placed there after Mary Delany's death.

By the mid-nineteenth century a different form of embroidery had emerged, but one still reliant on the motifs and patterns provided by the garden. Making use of the new dye processes, the very bright colours of Berlin wool work imitated the colourful bedding schemes of the Victorian garden. In fact the patterns for this work shown in the contemporary publication *The Young Ladies Journal* may be directly compared with patterns appearing in contemporary gardening publications. Jane Loudon, in her *The Ladies' Companion to the Flower Garden* (1841), suggests that a garden pattern might be marked out on the ground exactly as one might copy 'the paper containing plans for Berlin worsted work'. Her husband John Loudon went further, suggesting that 'We venture to assert that there is not any lady who can design a pattern and embroider a gown, that might not, in a few hours, be taught to design flower gardens with as much taste and skill as a professional landscape gardener.'[21]

The Arts and Crafts movement in turn brought a renewed focus on the role of flower and plant patterns in embroidered textiles, including a revival of tapestry hangings and floor coverings. Gerard's *Herball* yet again proved a valuable source not only for plant and flower design but also for the natural plant dyes used to create the subtle blues and greens for which Arts and Crafts textiles are so famous. William Morris led a revival in male involvement in tapestry, but much of the work for his own home was carried out by his daughter May Morris and wife Jane. The gorgeous bed hangings designed and executed by May Morris for the four-poster bed at Kelmscott are a testimony to Morris's belief in gardening with silk and gold thread. Embroidered in glowing gold and subtle reds and greens, the hangings depict a medieval-style garden with wooden trellis entwined with roses and rich with bird life. For the less ambitious, patterns could be purchased through the company of Morris and Co. These included flower designs for cushions, fire screens and other household adornments, to allow the woman of the house to achieve the Arts and Crafts look.

Gertrude Jekyll,[22] perhaps the most famous female garden designer and plantswoman, was heavily influenced by the work of Morris and the

Arts and Crafts movement. Originally trained as a painter and competent in woodworking crafts, she also collected embroideries. Her collection was composed of both old and antique pieces from the many countries she visited, and supplemented by her own embroideries in coloured cottons, silks, wools and chenille. Some of her pieces were displayed as part of the London International Exhibition at New Bond Street in 1870, and attracted further commissions. The painter Hercules Brabazon commissioned a set of six flower and berry cushions, while a table cover was created in 'rich tones' for Lord Leighton. Her designs for periwinkle and iris from the Brabazon set were published by the Royal School of Art Needlework in 1880. Much of her embroidery (and her wallpaper designs) contains intertwining flowers, stems and stalks, tendrils and leaves. However, as with her gardening, she was insistent that the flowers should be placed with attention and care and not be an ill-assorted collection of colours.

While their sisters and friends plied their skills in threads, other women were occupied with the brush and easel. In the sixteenth and seventeenth centuries the art and tradition of the illuminated manuscript merged with the quest for accuracy in the scientific recording of plants. A series of watercolours produced for wealthy patrons, including the Medici in Florence and Rudolph II at Prague, resulted in the establishment of European botanical art. Although the majority of the painters were male, a surprising number of well-regarded professional artists were women. Unfortunately we know little about these women (or indeed some of their male counterparts). An 'Anastaise' is mentioned as a flower painter by Christine de Pizan in *c.* 1405[23] but nothing more is known of her. Clara Peeters (*c.* 1594–1657) was a phenomenally precocious painter whose first still life was painted when she was 14. Born in Antwerp she worked in Amsterdam and The Hague where she painted still lifes of flowers, fruit and other objects. Giovanna Garzoni (1600–70) worked in Rome for the Cassiano dal Pozzo in the late 1620s, before travelling to Naples, Turin and Paris. She found French ways difficult to adapt to, returning to Florence and eventually Rome. Known for her botanical knowledge and artistic sophistication, her flowers are often placed on a stippled background of iridescent colour.

Maria Sibylla Merian (1647–1717) was born in Frankfurt in the mid-seventeenth century and led the independent life we rarely associate with women at this time. Maria was part of a family of professional artists: her father was an engraver, her stepfather a flower painter, and her first husband a pupil of his. From an early age she pursued a career that combined painting with botanical and entomological studies, and after separating from her husband in 1685 she travelled with her daughter Dorothea to collect and draw insect and plant life. The botanical (and zoological) studies she created were to lay the foundations not only for her own work *Metamorphosis Insectorum Surinamensium* (1705), but also for the Linnaean system. She also published *A New Book of Flowers* made up of her own illustrations, and supplemented her income by teaching embroidery.[24] It is tempting when viewing the work and career of Maria Sibylla Merian to see her as a direct forerunner of Marianne North, whose later travels led to the identification of new species, and of Margaret Mee who also travelled to the South Americas.

Germany was an important centre for botanical art in the seventeenth and eighteenth centuries. The Deitzsch sisters, Barbara (1706–83) and Margereta (1726–95), with their unusual botanical illustrations against a dark, almost midnight, background, shared their physician patron with Georg Ehret while working in Nuremburg. Ehret was later to come to England and carried out a series of commissions for patrons including Margaret, Duchess of Portland and the Duchess of Norfolk and Leeds. It is possible that the black background of Mary Delany's botanical mosaics was influenced by the work of the Deitzsch sisters. In the previous century Elizabeth, Countess of Carnarvon (née Capel, 1633–96) had used her own talents to produce a series of exquisite botanical watercolours, some of which survive in the Royal Collection. A portrait of Elizabeth Capel and her sister Mary[25] by the court painter Lely, shows the two young women seated in front of a romantic landscape. Mary holds a small wreath of ivy, probably indicative of her enthusiasm for poetry, while Elizabeth holds in her lap one of her own early botanical paintings of a tulip. Lady Anne Capel (daughter of the 2nd Lord Capel) was also painted by Lely, with a magnificent and unusual backdrop of flowers and foliage, while Henry Capel grew oranges and myrtles in the grounds later to become Princess Augusta's Kew collection. The link between garden creation, plant collection and botanical and flower painting was never so familial as with the Capels.

Aristocratic and royal patronage extended to female artists in both England and France in the eighteenth century. The court of Louis XIV included the painter Anne Vallayer-Coster who was appointed official flower painter to Marie Antoinette. In England, Queen Charlotte employed the artist Mary Moser (1744–1819) to oversee the decoration of the painted pavilion room at Frogmore House. Perhaps the first 'professional' female flower painter in England, Mary Moser made an early entry into the world of successful artists, winning the silver medal from the Royal Society of Arts at the tender age of 15, and going on to become one of the most sought after, and expensive, flower painters of her day. Crossing the divide between flower paintings and botanical illustrations she was most famous for her Dutch style, and several of her paintings can be found in the collections of the Royal Academy. Working predominantly in watercolour and gouache (although her father was a skilled worker in enamels), many of her flower paintings have dark backgrounds reminiscent of the works of the Deitzsch sisters. She used flowers and plants taken from gardens and conservatories as her subjects, and at Frogmore House included specimens from Queen Charlotte's own collections. Her painting for the pavilion at Frogmore was rumoured to have cost the royal purse £900 and is at the more botanical end of her work. Despite being a founder of the Royal Academy in 1768 Mary did not appear in person in John Sander's 1772 study *The Academicians of the Royal Academy* (at a life drawing class). Instead she is included (alongside the artist Angelica Kauffman) as a head and shoulder portrait hanging on the wall.[26] Unlike Kauffman, whose portrait is shown looking directly at the life sitter, Mary Moser stares away into the distance, preoccupied perhaps with the variety and colour of the plant world above the fleshy tones of the life class.

For every professional female flower painter or botanical artist there were many more for whom art was only one of many social accomplishments.[27] Elizabeth Burgoyne, known as Mrs Montagu Burgoyne, was one such. Over forty of her botanical illustrations (in watercolour on vellum) survive in the collections of the Fitzwilliam Museum, Cambridge, as part of the Broughton collection. She was possibly a pupil of the botanical artist Ehret, as were many aristocratic women. Unlike Ehret, however, Burgoyne was esteemed not only for the accuracy of her paintings but also for her 'social and domestic virtues'. These virtues, alongside her work on botanical illustration, led William Curtis to dedicate the first volume of his *Botanical Magazine* to her in 1787. It is perhaps a relief to lesser mortals to note that even such an exemplary artist, wife and all-round domestic goddess could make errors – mistakenly labelling a Rock Rose as *Halimium lasianthum* rather than *Cistus lasianthum*. Less is known of the virtues or otherwise of Amelia Fancourt whose botanical watercolours are also held in the Broughton collection. Classed as a 'gifted lady amateur' she stands for so many vanished women of the late eighteenth and nineteenth centuries whose accomplishments included flower illustration. Some had professional tutoring by the best artists of the day, but many more must have worked under the guidance of a local drawing master, using the published works of the great artists as their exemplars. In *A New Treatise on Flower Painting or Every Lady Her Own Drawing Master* (1816), George Brookshaw noted that 'Many ladies I have had the honour of teaching sketched flowers so correctly after my manner that I mistook them for my own drawings.'[28]

Lucy Cust (active 1815), one of five daughters of Brownlow Cust, 1st Baron Brownlow, chose rather more exulted exemplars, and drew in the style of Ehret and Redouté. Her work is of professional quality and includes plants such as the *Paeonia suffruticosa*, newly introduced into England in 1802 and first flowering in 1806. The Brownlows owned the estate of Belton, known for its gardens and park, and it is possible that Lucy's specimens came from the hothouses there. Many artists chose to draw newly introduced flowers and plants, strengthening the link between plant collecting and illustration that had been forged in the seventeenth century. This continued into the twentieth century, with artists such as Margaret Stones (b. 1920) who worked on the flora of Tasmania for *Curtis's Botanical Magazine* (1967–78) and also recorded plants first introduced into Kew by the nineteenth-century plant hunters.

Employment as either original artists or copyists for the new botanical and horticultural magazines of the period could bring public admiration. More prosaically it could bring in much needed income. Augusta Innes Withers (active 1827–65) (known as Mrs, but this may be a formal title) produced plates for magazines such as the *Transactions of the Horticultural Society* and the *Pomological Magazine*, as well as advertising herself as a teacher of botanical illustration. Working from her home at Grove Terrace, Lisson Grove (London), Mrs Withers was a member of the Society of Lady Artists and met with considerable success illustrating new plant introductions. Her plates adorn James Bateman's *Orchidaceae of Mexico and Guatemala* (1837–43), a monumental work by the owner of Biddulph Grange, published as a limited edition of just over one hundred copies. Surviving paintings by Mrs Withers include the *Datura rosei* from South America in the Fitzwilliam Museum. Royal patronage resulted in the position of Royal Flower Painter in Ordinary to Queen Adelaide, wife of William IV. An interesting comparison may be made between

Mrs Withers's illustration of the Datura made in the quiet backwaters of Fulham, and that made 'on the spot' in Brazil by Marianne North just a few decades later. The illustration by Mrs Withers is technically superb, crisp and detailed, portraying a solitary immaculate flower with three leaves on which every vein is shown. That by Marianne North shows a flower at the instant of pollination by a humming bird, the leaves lush and thick-looking. Insect holes mark the fertile life cycle of birth, growth and death of the Brazilian forests. One portrays nature as cultured perfection, the other nature in reality.

Originally from Bungay in Suffolk, Margaret Meen (*fl.* 1775–1824) settled in London during the active period of her artistic life[29] and worked on the Kew collections just a few years before Mrs Withers; the same plants may even have been visited by both artists. Regarded by art historians as a highly gifted amateur she was nevertheless active in the art market, selling her paintings and publishing work based upon them. A number of her paintings were made for Lord Bute while he was garden adviser to Princess Augusta. These passed into the Tankerville Collection before being re-purchased by Kew in the 1930s. Her own work *Exotic Plants from the Royal Gardens at Kew* was published in 1790. This was intended originally to be a biannual work but unfortunately ceased publication after only two issues. Her classification as an amateur is interesting given the evidence of her fifty-year artistic career, her exhibition at the Royal Academy (1775–85) and financial gains from her work. 'Amateur' was a label that was to haunt women for many years. Gertrude Jekyll was famously described as an amateur gardener by herself and by her family and friends. Another amateur botanical artist for whom publication was an aim, and the market a lure, was Arabella Roupell (1817–1914). This long-lived lady was married to an official of the East India Company and took the opportunity of a posting in the Cape of Good Hope to illustrate lesser-known plants of the area. Her pictures caught the eye of Sir William Hooker and following his encouragement she published a book of ten plates on the *Flora of South Africa by a Lady* (1850). A rare copy of this, and a further eleven plates published posthumously as *More Cape Flowers by a Lady*, is held by the Royal Horticultural Society Lindley Library.[30]

Given the restrictions placed on women travellers it is no surprise that the majority of female illustrators and copyists worked from specimens provided by patrons or editors, from hothouses and conservatories in England. However, a few followed the early example of Maria Sibylla Merian and travelled to find new species and varieties to add to their illustrative collections. The best known of these is Marianne North (1830–90). One of very few women at the time to have a gallery of their own, Marianne North conforms to a definable pattern of spinster explorers who beat an independent path through the Victorian undergrowth.[31] Fellow spinster travellers include Isabella Bird, Gertrude Bell and Mary Kingsley, all of whom chose the more distant outposts of the world rather than the comfort of the domestic hearth. Marianne's diaries *Recollections of a Happy Life* (published posthumously in 1893) inspired Elizabeth von Arnim (see Chapter 6) to travel, albeit to the slightly less exotic regions of Rügen in Germany. For Marianne North travel and movement appear to have been a psychological need; a form of rheumatic fever accompanied by severe headaches overwhelmed her whenever she stayed in one place for any length of time. As her diaries frequently record, over-delayed departures would be hastened by severe pain and practical immobility.

Marianne's early travels were in the company of her father who, despite being the Liberal MP for Hastings, spent considerable periods of each year abroad. She regarded her father as the 'one idol and friend of my life' and after the death of her mother, in 1855, she accompanied him on journeys of increasing distance. Initial travels to the Alps and Greece were followed by a trip to Egypt, via Albania, Corfu and Syria. It was while on a later journey in Munich that her father fell ill and died on reaching home in 1869. During these early travels, and while at home in Hastings, Marianne had occupied her time by drawing plants and flowers 'from nature'. She had had lessons in painting from a young age, including some from the Dutch female artist Miss van Fowinkel in the 1850s, and had spent time painting at Chelsea Physic Garden and the Royal Botanic Gardens at Kew, where she was once presented with a hanging bunch of *Amherstia nobilis* by Sir William Hooker. It was to her painting, and her travel, that she turned on the death of her father.

Marianne commenced her travels as soon as the old household in Hastings could be broken up, taking with her a single servant and her painting materials. Italy was her first destination, but finding that independent travel suited her there was then little pause in her worldwide itinerary for the next twenty years. Beginning with Canada and the United States in 1871, the West Indies followed in 1872 and Brazil the following year. After overwintering back in England (during which time she learnt to etch on copper), she fled the cold on New Year's Day of 1875 to spend the next two years in the then remote areas of Madeira, California, Japan, Singapore, Borneo, Java and Ceylon. After a brief

Giant Poker Lily (*Kniphofia northiae*)

Stunningly architectural and wonderfully exotic-looking, this 'red hot poker' is from the temperate regions of South Africa. A giant among the kniphofias it reaches some 6–8ft in height, and can cover as much area again with its wide rosette of leaves. Its thick flower stalks with their red and yellow tubular flowers are strangely phallic in real life, but even more so in Marianne North's portrayal of the plant in its own habitat. Marianne travelled to South Africa in 1882, having noted that as 'All the continents of the world had some sort of representation in my gallery except Africa . . . I resolved to begin painting there without loss of time'. Travelling by railroad, horse-drawn carriage (driven by a drunken local) and on foot, she was drawn particularly to the giant *Proteas* of the Cape area. Spending weeks in the gardens of Dr Baines she painted amid bouganvillea, ipomea and *Mesembryanthemum*. *Strelitzia reginae* (named after Princess Augusta) were subjects of her paintings, as were the giant pokers which were to bear her own name. Her painting of the kniphofia in its rocky habitat near Grahamstown survives in the Marianne North Gallery at Kew, one of many hundreds of unlikely looking exotics frozen in the subdued London light.

sojourn back in the rather less tropical climes of Victorian London, she set off for India where she painted banyan trees and rhododendrons against a backdrop of temples and mountains. She was one of the first to paint the great lily of Naini Tal (*Lilium wallichianum*) in its natural habitat.

Painting directly what she observed, usually in the open air, had been a way of life for Marianne North since those early years with her father. It was this immediacy and vibrancy born of direct observation that not only set her paintings apart, but also made them of such importance to plant collectors and horticulturalists. Travelling with sturdy easel and folding chair, pictures record Marianne capturing plants within their actual habitats, however remote or difficult that habitat might be. Single specimens are rarely shown; instead a brilliant waxy bloom shares the canvas with an array of insects, birds and vegetation, as would be seen in real life. Bread fruit dwarf the wooden huts of Jamaican settlers, wild llamas graze beneath the monkey puzzles (*Araucaria araucana*) of Chile, while Mount Fujiyama forms a magnificent backdrop to the *Wisteria chinensis* in Japan. These are not botanical drawings clinically detailing each part of the plant at each stage of life, but rich luxuriant portrayals of a flower or pod almost at the point of senescence. The Ginger Lily (*Hedychium gardnerianum*) being visited by the firetailed sunbird of India is not merely fully open, but at that moment when a flower changes from bloom to decay. An Angel's Trumpet (*Brugmansia arborea*) visited by a humming bird in Brazil will swiftly lose its crisp edges and hang limp and tattered, echoing the insect-nibbled leaves which make up the backdrop. Often Marianne North's paintings recall the *Vanitas* paintings of the seventeenth century rather than the clinical botanical observations of the nineteenth.

In order to capture this brief moment in the flowering of tropical plants, her drawings were created swiftly, as her subjects so often bloomed and died within one day. Unlike most female painters of the period Marianne North used oils rather than watercolours, finding them more suitable for both her own temperament and the climate of the countries she visited. Paintings were created on prepared paper which was only fixed to canvas once the painting was back in England (the hazards of the journey back to England would also favour oils over delicate watercolours). Oils allowed her to portray the vividness of the colours and gorgeousness of the fruits and flowers; but both her style and her choice of materials led to criticisms. In 1882, at the opening of the Marianne North Gallery, the *Gardeners' Chronicle* for 6 June 1882 described her paintings as 'skilful, dashing works', and there is something in the use of the word 'dashing' that has the nature of a double-edged compliment. Writing in 1950, Wilfrid Blunt judged that the paintings were 'almost wholly lacking in sensibility' making 'a disagreeable impression'.[32] Sentiments that had also abounded among her contemporaries, more used to delicate watercolours and patient detail.

Marianne's works often created an air of sensual uneasiness as nectar glistened in droplets and stamens obtruded from crimson petals, but she was firm in her belief that her paintings formed a valuable contribution to botanical study. From an early age she had been an enthusiastic gardener, interested both in the outside garden and the hothouse. She had become acquainted with Sir William Hooker, then the Director of Kew, through early visits to the gardens with her father, and when his son Joseph Hooker took over the directorship she remained close to the work and collections of the Royal Botanic Gardens. Many of the plants she recorded were barely known either botanically or horticulturally at that period, and at least four were totally unknown to Western science. Four species and several varieties were subsequently named after her. One of these, *Crinum northianum*, from Borneo, was actually first described botanically using her drawings and paintings, and was noted in the catalogue as paying 'the highest compliment to the scientific accuracy' of the painting. However, other critics were not as kind.

Perhaps it was an awareness of this mixed reception that prompted Marianne to consider the fate of her works after her death. Eventually she decided that a gallery should be constructed at Kew dedicated to their display. The project was first mooted in the *Pall Mall Gazette* following an exhibition in 1879, but money was not forthcoming from the Royal Horticultural Society. Instead it was left to Marianne herself to organise and fund the gallery, with the agreement of Sir Joseph Hooker for its location in the gardens. Employing the architect James Fergusson to create a gallery that would maximise the weak London light, Marianne spent the winter of 1879/80 arranging the paintings. The sheer number of paintings, and their close positioning with no wall space showing between the narrow frames, created an overwhelming impression on the visitor. Paintings were arranged by country with little or no regard for composition, with landscapes jostling still lifes, and botanical details nestling with mountain temples. Two hundred and forty-six specimens of different woods also collected on her travels added to the rich selection of hues, with no space left undecorated. Her funding also included the production of a catalogue, the first edition of which sold out of its print run of 2,000 copies six months after the gallery finally opened in 1882. The gallery still exists, with the paintings placed exactly as Marianne dictated. The only concessions to the twenty-first century are the artificial light to assist the visitor and a modern seat. A gallery attendant has the unenviable task of selling the limited choice of twenty postcards to visitors who wish to purchase a copy of one of the 832 pictures housed there. Alas the facilities for refreshments, which Miss North envisaged, were never created, as Joseph Hooker felt that the British public would be too difficult to keep in order for such a facility to be a success. Perhaps Hooker was concerned about the effect her vibrant, colourful and sensual paintings might have on the normally respectable visitors to the gardens. Her final travels in the 1880s were to take in Australia, New Zealand and South Africa before she finally

Pitcher Plant *(Nepenthes northiana)*

Many a Victorian spinster might have shied away from the bulbous, red-lipped cavities of the hanging pitcher plant, but Marianne North was made of sterner stuff. During her travels in the limestone mountains of Sarawak (Borneo) in 1876 she noted that several varieties were of types previously unknown. Carnivorous plants were of great interest to Victorian collectors, who could nurture them in their newly affordable glasshouses. Marianne North recorded nepenthes both in Borneo and the Seychelles, which commemorated the centennial of her visit there by issuing nepenthes stamps using her artwork. It was from her original painting that Harry Veitch, of the renowned Veitch nurseries, was able to identify the Sarawak nepenthes as a new variety, and honour it with her name. The nepenthes craze lasted through the final decades of the nineteenth century, fuelled by nurseries and collectors such as Hooker and Burbidge. *Nepenthes burbidgeae* is named after Burbidge's wife (perhaps in an attempt to pacify her for his extended plant-hunting absences); although even an 'eggshell porcelain blotched with crimson red' pitcher plant such as *burbidgeae* still has an appearance unlikely to endear it to the more prudish Victorian female. By 1889 the *Nepenthes northiana* had been lost from cultivation, no longer being listed by Veitch's nurseries. However, by 1893 a specimen must have flowered as it was hybridised to create *Nepenthes* x *mixta*. The vision of a garden where the giant elongated heads of kniphofia mingle with the bulbous blotched bags and gaping openings of the nepenthes is, to be honest, not one to be recommended.

settled in a quiet country house in the Cotswolds for the last years of her life from 1886 until her death in 1890.

After studying at the St Martin's School of Art, Margaret Mee (1909–88) also specialised in painting exotic flowers and plants in their own habitats. Often working with the São Paulo Botanical Institute, she travelled throughout the Amazon recording the flora of its forests. Margaret's first expedition was in 1956 and it was then that she began to keep the diaries that give such a fascinating insight into the life of a twentieth-century botanical artist. From surviving raging rapids to fending off drunken prospectors with a revolver, Margaret documented the many hazards she experienced on her expeditions.[33] Although her partner also worked in Brazil, Margaret often travelled alone through the dense jungles or with locals to help guide canoes through the hostile rapids. Her initial objective, to search out and illustrate the tropical rainforest flora, was later combined with a growing concern at the commercial plunder of the great forests. One of the main ambitions of her later life was to paint the rare night-flowering *Selenicereus witterii*, the Amazonian moonflower. The plant does not flower every year, and when it does, the flowers open for a single night. Near Manaus she located a plant with buds, and with a companion waited through the night until it opened. She then sketched by the light of a fluorescent torch, taking the colours the following day from the by then closed flower. Margaret was killed in a car crash in 1988 after attending the opening of an exhibition of her paintings at the Royal Botanic Gardens in Kew, where many of her paintings are still held.

Women such as Margaret Meen, Marianne North and Margaret Mee were exceptional in the very public nature of their careers, and the continuing fascination that their lives and works hold.[34] Fame and success were not, however, the lot of the vast majority of female botanical and flower painters of the Victorian period or even the twentieth century. With the growth of the middle classes in the mid-nineteenth century came an increase in the number of 'leisured' women looking for an outlet for their creativity (and an occupation for their solitary hours). Often not sufficiently wealthy to afford private drawing masters, nor permitted by their husbands to attend public classes, these women turned to books for their instruction in the arts. As books on gardening for ladies were written by women, so it seemed natural that books on art for ladies should also be written by someone who would understand the special circumstances of these suburban females. When Mrs William Duffield[35] (1819–1914) set pen and brush to paper in 1856, it was this market that she had in mind. A medallist from the Society of Arts, and member of the Royal Institute of Painters in Watercolours, Mrs Duffield was well qualified to instruct and inspire. Going into several successful editions, her *Art of Flower Painting* reflects the sheer numbers of women who were active in this area.

An examination of Ray Desmond's splendid *Dictionary of British and Irish Botanists and Horticulturalists, including Plant Collectors,*

Flower Painters and Garden Designers reveals the names and scanty details of some representatives of these largely nameless and unremembered women. Usually little survives of the work these women produced other than a brief description in the Academy catalogues, or an occasional solitary painting in a local collection. From Mrs Frances Mathilde Adams (1784–1863), who painted flowers for Queen Adelaide and exhibited at the Royal Academy, to Annie Marie Youngman from Saffron Walden, who studied at the Royal Academy School and produced landscape and flower paintings, almost all are listed as exhibiting 'flower' rather than garden or landscape paintings, and almost all appear to have drawn not from life but from the seclusion and isolation of an indoor studio. We may picture them with their flowers obtained from their own gardens or the hothouses of wealthier friends, or less usually from botanical gardens. A sketchbook of South African flowers in the Merseyside Museum is all that is known of Miss Rebecca Mills (fl. 1810s), the daughter of a military man. Original works of even talented amateurs are often lost as generations lose touch with their ancestors and little value is placed on family heirlooms. Where now are the works of Miss Agnes Moore (fl. 1880s), Miss Mary Moody (fl. 1870s), Catherine Lucas (fl. 1870s) or Miss Florence White (fl. 1880s–1910)? All are listed in the carefully researched pages of Desmond's *Dictionary* but only survive courtesy of the registers and roll calls of their artists' schools. Marianne North is one of the best known female flower painters of her day, but who has heard of her less well travelled, married sister Catherine who also recorded the natural world with her brush?

Helen Allingham (1848–1926), that consummate painter of the idyllic cottage and garden, has most definitely not been forgotten. This genre of Victorian country cottage art has not only maintained its popularity but has actually served to colour our vision of history. For many people the history of Victorian rural life *is* the vision that Allingham portrayed, complete with rambling roses, honeysuckle round the door, ducks at the gate, and small kittens playing on the path. Helen Allingham (née Paterson) was born near Burton-upon-Trent and studied at the Government School of Design in Birmingham before going on to the Female School of Art (1866) and finally the Royal Academy Schools in 1867. Helen's aunt, Laura Herford, had been the first woman to gain admission to the Royal Academy Schools in 1860, and her grandmother Sarah Smith Herford had also gained limited recognition for her oil painting. While at the School she was heavily influenced by the work of fellow artists of rural life, including Frederick Walker and Myles Birket Foster. It was not, however, until her own move to the village of Witley, Surrey, that the cottage and garden became her principal theme. It was through the influence of such designers as William Morris and Gertrude Jekyll that she came to prioritise the garden and cottage over people in her landscapes. Her technique as an artist was unusual, and was described by a contemporary as 'entirely opposed to mechanical reproduction . . . obtaining effects by rubbing scratching and scrubbing . . . so that the blooms blend amongst themselves and grow naturally out of their foliage'.[36]

In the past there has been some debate about the degree of historical accuracy in Allingham's attractive pictures. The typical presence of a small kitten or ducklings suggests a degree of sentimentality which does not fit easily with modern interpretations of the hardships of Victorian rural life. Recent studies, looking, for example, at similar cottages recorded photographically by Gertrude Jekyll, suggest that both architectural details and typicality of garden planting are generally correct. Certainly the plants seen in Allingham's cottage gardens reflect those described in the literature of the period. Hers are predominantly traditional garden flowers including rosemary, lavender, roses, lily, hollyhock and jasmine – often plants that had medicinal uses in addition to their attractiveness and thus earned their place in the garden twice over.

Allingham was not alone as a female garden artist in this period. Her early forays into the countryside, while working for *Graphic* and *Cornhill* magazines were in the company of Catherine (Kate) Greenaway (1834–1900). Allingham recorded that they were always made welcome in the gardens or orchards they wished to paint due to the 'scrupulous thoughtfulness for the convenience and feelings of the owners' exhibited by Greenaway. Although much of Greenaway's work includes flowers she was not predominantly a recorder of gardens or plants. Her long-standing, and largely unrequited, relationship with Ruskin had a damaging effect on her personal life, and her time spent in country gardens with Helen Allingham must have come as a relief. She also gained the support of Lady Dorothy Nevill, and became a close friend of Violet Dickenson. Kate Greenaway's relationship with women and gardens was completed in one of her final works: the illustrations for Elizabeth von Arnim's *The April Baby's Book of Tunes* (1900).

Helen Allingham's sister, Caroline Paterson (later Caroline Sharpe), was also an accomplished painter of garden scenes. Often of an even more sentimental style than her sister these typically contained children in clean white smocks hugging small animals. However, beyond these are the plants and flowers of a carefully observed garden. Children are frequently included in garden watercolours by female artists. Mary Lucas's *Collecting Nosegays* (private collection) is a typical example. Two very small children, replete in spotless white dresses, aprons and white mob-caps, totter down a narrow path between flower borders overflowing with a profusion of pinks and mauves. Rather than gathering the flowers they appear almost engulfed in the riches they have to choose from. The identification of both the children and the garden has long since been lost (perhaps they were Mary Lucas's own?), but the idyllic summer moment has been captured for ever.

One of the liveliest of the cottage garden painters was Theresa Stannard (1898–1947). Daughter of the more famous Arthur Claude Stannard and niece of Lillian Stannard, Theresa's light, almost animated style was a contrast to the soft romantic quality of earlier female watercolourists or the botanical accuracy of Beatrice Parsons. A precocious artist from a painting background she exhibited at the Royal Academy in 1915 at the age of 16. She continued working throughout the inter-war years and was a popular artist with the royal family, who purchased several of her works. Her depictions of gardens are detailed and in many ways appear to us as perhaps more honest, with their mixed jumble of less carefully designed planting. Yellows and reds sit uneasily next to each other against clashing backgrounds of orange brick. In 1928 the *Birmingham Post* commented that although her pictures were fresh and clear they lacked 'the restfulness of the well arranged garden' and suggested that Miss Stannard 'still has something to learn about the value of elimination in picture painting'.[37] Little did they realise that future generations of garden historians would be grateful for her honest detailing of the country cottager's garden.

Theresa's aunt, Lillian Stannard (1877–1944), provided some of the careful detail of flowers and plants missing from her niece's work. An extremely talented garden artist, her fascination was with the flowers themselves rather than the context or setting. Born into a family of painters in Bedfordshire, she became one of the best known of the flower painters in England by the age of 30 and many of her pictures were reproduced in gardening books in the first part of the twentieth century. Among the most famous is perhaps *The Gardens of England* by Charles Holme, released in three volumes between 1907 and 1911 and showcasing many of the most talented garden artists of the period.

So accurate and detailed were her depictions of flower borders that the *Bedfordshire Times* commented in 1899 that her 'exact drawing and colouring should be of great value to publishers and men of science'.[38] Lady Ludlow commissioned her to paint the gardens at Luton Hoo, and she also painted a series of pictures in the Cambridge Colleges, although many of her paintings are unprovenanced and titled according to their general subject rather than place (*A Sunny Corner*; *An Old Water Garden*, etc.). Some of the cottage gardens are undoubtedly from around the family base of Bedfordshire and Hertfordshire, and recognition of specific houses will undoubtedly come with delight and surprise to their new owners.[39] In many of these it is difficult to judge which aspect held more interest for the artist, the cottage and garden setting or the plants within it. Thus the art of the cottage garden was to meet the long tradition of female botanical artists.

Some of the most detailed portrayal of flowers within garden art can be seen in the work of Beatrice Parsons (1870–1955). The peak of Beatrice's career coincided with the period of nostalgia for the 'small country manor house' so beloved of designers such as William Robinson and Gertrude Jekyll and artists such as George Samuel Elgood. Her work often captured the interplay between the traditional formal garden and the wilder gardens of Robinson's *The English Flower Garden* (1883). Beatrice Parsons had a thorough academic training, studying at the Royal Academy Schools, and her early works depict largely religious scenes, perhaps demonstrating the influence of her brother Karl Parsons, a religious painter and designer of stained glass. It was not until she reached her early thirties that garden scenes began to take preference. An art dealer named Dowdeswell, intuitively spotting both a subject and style of instant appeal to the Edwardian market, offered her a one-woman exhibition at his own gallery in 1904. Forty-four garden pictures were exhibited, of which forty sold instantly and Beatrice Parsons became the professional garden artist of the period. Working in Italy, France and Algeria as well as England, Beatrice portrayed the golden afternoon of the country house and garden, typified by the flower garden at Blickling, Norfolk, or the walled gardens in *Garden Scene*. Her works were commissioned by E.T. Cook, editor of the Arts and Crafts-style magazine *The Garden* and publisher of *Gardens of England* which was produced with her illustrations. She worked on subtle English gardens such as Gravetye, the manor house of William Robinson, as well as the bright colours of the Mediterranean at La Mortola and Villa Maryland. However, she also worked on generic pictures with titles such as *Spring*, *Lily Pond and Roses*, *Sweet Peas* and *Our Lady's Flowers*. Her work was used by Sutton's Nurseries to adorn the front covers of their seed catalogues for several years in the 1920s, a testament both to their attractiveness and their accuracy. She painted through the early decades of the twentieth century, portraying the Edwardian garden as a constant in those ever changing times. Whether through war or age, the 1940s saw the end of her career, and she died almost forgotten in 1955.

If such a renowned and talented artist as Beatrice Parsons could be forgotten what chance had the less celebrated female artists of this golden era of garden painting? Thankfully gardening books of the early twentieth century were often illustrated with high quality works by these artists, and survive where the originals are lost. Charlotte Georgina Trower (1855–1928) illustrated Skene's *Flower Book for the Pocket* in 1935, and the wonderfully named *British Brambles* (1928), but little else survives of her output. The paintings of Margaret Waterfield (1860–1950) can be seen in *Garden Colour*. Published by Dent in 1905, this book included written contributions by Ellen Willmott, Rose Kingsley and the Hon. Eleanor Vere Boyle. Eleanor Boyle (1825–1916) also wrote and illustrated *Days and Hours in a Garden* (1884), *A Garden of Pleasure* (1895) and *Gardens in Summer* (1905). Her earlier books had been for children and she had used the money from these to finance works on the estate of Marston, where her husband was rector (his father owning the estate). Following his death she devoted herself to gardening and illustration, portraying her own garden at Huntercombe Manor, Buckinghamshire, where she finally died at the age of 92.[40] Interestingly, there appears often to be a correlation between a female botanical author and the use of a female artist, perhaps networks of support were even then being built up. Mrs Sidgwick and Mrs Paynter commissioned the Pre-Raphaelite-style artist Mrs Cayley Robinson to illustrate their children's book of gardening in 1909, eschewing her rather better-known brother.

Of all the hundreds of creative women for whom the garden was a focus, few could claim their work survives in such numbers or in such good condition as that of Eleanor Coade.[41] Working not with paintbrush or embroiderer's needle, Eleanor chose an artificial stone in which to create her lasting memorials. Catering for the rise in popularity of statuary, urns and vases in eighteenth- and nineteenth-century England, Eleanor's manufactory produced literally thousands of highly fired ceramic imitations. Affordable, long-lasting and almost indistinguishable from real stone they were an immediate success. Even today over 650 historic gardens in England contain Coade stone pieces, while a further 500 are thought to have been lost, either through the destruction or sale of the garden or loss of the pieces. A rare example of a successful businesswoman of the late eighteenth century, Eleanor (1733–1821) had been born into a family not strong on financial success. Her father was a bankrupt (at least once) and undoubtedly an influence on Eleanor's own decision to remain unmarried, the only way in which she could retain vital control of her own finances. In 1769 she set up a business in artificial fired ceramics at the King's Stairs in Lambeth, a business that was to remain phenomenally successful until her death over fifty years later.

Dealing directly with architects and designers such as Humphry Repton, John Nash and Charles Barry, Eleanor Coade ruled over her male foreman and gave short shrift to any caught 'freelancing' with her secret Coade stone recipe. With an external appearance of fine-grained limestone, the 'ceramic' she created was made from a mix of ball clay, 'grog' (crushed stoneware), flint, fine sand and soda-lime silica. Fired to a very high temperature in one of the factory's enormous kilns it withstands weathering better than real stone. She exported her 'stone' pieces to North and South America, the Caribbean, Poland and Russia. In 1784 her catalogue contained 700 pieces, the largest of which was the River God designed by John Bacon. This 3-metre-long god cost one hundred guineas and was purchased for the gardens at Ham House (originally the seat of the Duchess of Lauderdale). Wrest Park (Bedfordshire) contains two Borghese Coade stone vases, Audley End (Essex) a lion couchant, while other examples are scattered in the royal gardens of Buckingham Palace and Windsor Castle. Smaller gardens often contain one or two vases or urns, for example at Sezincote, or in several gardens at Lyme Regis (her home for a few years). A recent exhibition at Lyme included pictures of a Coade stone gate pier with a coot in raised relief. A reminder that, at least in Dorset, her name should rhyme with the water bird rather than the toad. Crossing the line between creativity and manufactory Eleanor Coade represents one extreme of women in Georgian and Victorian England. For every one Eleanor Coade striving for independence through their own inspiration and perspiration there were a thousand others for whom creativity in the garden was a spiritual, and sometimes a financial, lifeline.

FIVE

An Antidote to Levity and Idleness?

THE VICTORIAN WOMAN PLANT COLLECTOR AND GARDENER

> May [botany] become a substitute for some of the trifling, not to say pernicious, objects, that too frequently employ the leisure of young ladies of fashionable manners, and, by employing their faculties rationally, act as an antidote to levity and idleness.
>
> Priscilla Wakefield, *An Introduction to Botany*, Preface (1796)

Just twenty years after Charles Evelyn dedicated his *Lady's Recreation* to the botanically gifted Duchess of Beaufort, something unpleasant was stirring in the glasshouses of England. In 1736 the Swedish botanist Carl Linnaeus startled the world with the publication of his classification of the plant world. Trained in botany and medicine, Linnaeus (1707–78) spent the early part of his career working on a revolutionary new system for classifying plant and animal life. Based first at Upsalla and then at the University and Botanic Gardens at Leiden, by 1736 he was ready to publish his *Systema Naturae* or System of Nature. Embedded in Linnaeus's studies was his belief that there was a natural order of living things, an order that once comprehended by man would reveal the Divine Order.[1] Unfortunately for Linnaeus, the system he came up with was condemned by some critics as not so much divine as loathsome harlotry. The reason for such critical outbursts, and the reason for Linnaeus's equally unfortunate impact on women botanists, was quite simply sex. Linnaeus's taxonomic classification was based almost solely on the number and arrangement of the reproductive organs. Working under Linnaeus's new system any prospective botanist would henceforth be forced to peer into the male and female organs of any plant they wished to identify. Worse was yet to come. The groupings that he proposed included not only those that had single male and female parts but others that contained multiple male organs[2] or both male and female organs. He himself expressed his classifications using parallels with human society which, although couched in florid terms, clearly spelt out the sexuality of their nature. In 1729, for example, he wrote: 'The flowers' leaves . . . serve as bridal beds which the Creator has so gloriously arranged, adorned with such noble bed curtains, and perfumed with so many soft scents that the bridegroom with his bride might there celebrate their nuptials with so much the greater solemnity.'

Although it got off to a shaky start, by the last quarter of the eighteenth century the Linnaean System had spread throughout Europe and was set to become the established method of classification. Queen Charlotte Sophia allowed the President of the Linnean Society to instruct herself and her daughters in the new system in their painted botanical rooms at Frogmore House. Not all mothers (or more especially fathers and husbands) were to be so broadminded. Even within Frogmore House there was concern that the learned President should avoid any unnecessary explanation of 'the generation of animals', and should not shock the delicacies of the Queen and the Princesses with his teachings.[3] How he managed to impart the Linnaean system without breaching this propriety is a mystery (as no doubt were his much censored teachings to the royal family). Under the onslaught of sex in the lecture room and stamens in the hothouse, botanical studies among women began to decline. What few botanical studies were still felt appropriate in the rather looser moral climate of the Regency period were finally ousted with the advent of the nineteenth century and Victorian morality. In a moral climate where the human ankle was felt shameful, the technicalities of vegetative reproduction were nothing less than pornographic.

As early as 1790 Richard Powheel had accused 'botanising girls' of 'exchanging the blush of modesty for the bronze of impudence'. In a vision on a par with Linnaeus's own descriptions of botanic studies Powheel sees these women as they 'point the prostitution of a plant; dissect its organ of unhallow'd lust, and fondly gaze at the titillating dust'.[4] Needless to say the orchid house was out of bounds for any woman of moral sense and decency.[5] Accompanying the horror of sexuality was the belief that the scent of the flowers in the hothouse could itself overwhelm the unwary. A writer, probably the great Joseph Paxton himself, suggested of orchid houses that:

> Not one in ten of the houses expressly devoted to their culture, can be entered by the most robust among the higher classes, much less by delicate persons or by ladies, without experiencing highly uncomfortable and overpowering sensations, and entailing unpleasant and even dangerous consequences. Everyone will acknowledge that this is a state of things which urgently demands some remedial measures, if such can be applied consistently with the safety and prosperity of the plants.[6]

One wonders what the eighteenth-century 'queen of the hothouses', Mary, Duchess of Portland, would have made of such a claim.

For frustrated female botanists, help was at hand in the shape of the frond. In his classifications of plants Linnaeus had been thwarted by the several species that had no obvious sexual organs or means of sexual reproduction. These he grouped together within the class *Cryptogamia*, a class that included algae, lichens, fungi, mosses and other bryophytes, and ferns. While algae, fungi and lichens only appealed to the most dedicated plant lover, ferns were to be the salvation of a generation of women determined upon botanising and collecting.[7] As Shirley Hibberd so sagaciously opined in his book *The Fern Garden: How to Make, Keep and Enjoy It* (1869): 'Ferns . . . belong to the sub-kingdom of vegetables called *Cryptogamia*, a sub-kingdom so called because it is the custom of the population to celebrate marriages in the dark, so that it can scarcely be averred to marry at all.' This delicacy in all things conjugal made the fern the ideal subject of study for the shy Victorian female. Surely no father or husband could have doubts about the suitability of studying a plant so admirably coy about its private life. Modest, neat, never adorned with gaudy colours, and obligingly at home in the shade of the suburban garden – it is difficult to tell whether the subject of description is the ideal fern or the ideal woman.

Shirley Hibberd's book, which ran into eight editions, reflected the popularity of his subject and as such was second only to his *Rustic Adornments for Homes of Taste* (1856). This work also contained a lengthy discussion on the role of the fern both indoors and out, and its title encapsulated all that the Victorian middle classes held dear. A man with his pulse on the Victorian suburban market (perhaps to an even greater extent than John and Jane Loudon), (James) Shirley Hibberd had first caught the public imagination at the age of 25 with his collection of articles: *Brambles and Bay Leaves: Essays on the Homely and Beautiful.* Reviewed by the *Gardeners' Chronicle* as being composed of 'rural subjects . . . treated from the sentimental view' these were ideal for family consumption. In a period of profound political and social unrest, the stress on an outward show of domestic morality and respectability had never been greater. With the opportunity for combining adornment with education, rusticity with suburban living, and neatly sidestepping any qualms over the sexuality of plants, the fern reigned supreme.

The Fern Garden also extolled the virtues of the Fern House or Indoor Fernery. Hibberd's own Fern House (or more correctly Mrs Hibberd's) had been created at his house in Stoke Newington when a greenhouse for tender plants had been carelessly cast into shade by a neighbour's building activities. Rather than sue his neighbour, Hibberd quickly adapted the now damp and dark glasshouse to a home for shade-loving ferns. Being attached to the house the lean-to was eminently suitable for being under the care of the female of the house, and as Hibberd proudly declared a few years later, he had 'scarcely met with a fernery to surpass Mrs Hibberd's, in beauty and interest, though it is on an extremely small scale'.[8] For himself, he maintained a massive construction of rockwork and gothic tracery in the main gardens distant from the house. Sexual division between responsibilities for the indoor and outdoor fern gardens also played a large part in the popularity of the ever-adaptable fern. Indoor window displays, Wardian glasses and cases, winter gardens, conservatories and 'attached' lean-tos all lay within the respectable remit of the lady of the house. The outdoor fern garden usually fell within the domain of the man of the house.

With such opportunities for display and decoration within her dominion all the housewife (or prospective housewife) needed was instruction on how to care for the ferns she placed in it. Here there was also an array of choice. When Shirley Hibberd published *The Fern Garden: How to Make, Keep and Enjoy It* in 1869, his book was merely joining a whole library of works already available to the eager nineteenth-century collector. As part of a much wider movement towards the study of natural history, entomology, and even geology, journals and magazines on the subject of all things 'natural' had been widely available from the 1830s onwards; the *Magazine of Natural History* for example was started in May 1828 by none other than John

Loudon. In 1837 George William Francis had officially launched the fern craze with his work *An Analysis of the British Ferns and their Allies.* Not perhaps the catchiest of titles, and one that his possible relation, George Heath Francis, was to improve upon later in the century. *A Handbook of British Ferns: Intended as a guide and companion in fern culture* was published by Thomas Moore in 1848, aimed at both the scientific and the popular community, and the following decades saw publications as numerous and varied as the ferns themselves. George Heath Francis was obviously better at marketing than William Francis, and 1877 saw the arrival of *The Fern World*, followed the next year by his *Fern Paradise: a Plea for the Culture of Ferns.*

As 'fernmania' grew it spread beyond the hallowed portals of the home, and collecting excursions to the Lake District and other suitable destinations became popular.[9] An engraving in the *Illustrated London News* of July 1871 portrayed a mixed outing to collect ferns, with the accompanying opportunities for social contact between the sexes. A far cry from the sexless fern residing under its protective glass dome, excursions to collect material for both botanical study and garden decoration undoubtedly also served other purposes, allowing young people to meet outside the strict confines of the domestic hearth. Entire areas of the Lake District were stripped of their natural beauties by the hordes that descended each weekend armed with their collecting baskets, rugs, and books on identification. For those who could not travel such distances, however, flora and fern guides to more suburban areas were also available; James Brewer's *A New Flora of the Neighbourhood of Reigate, Surrey* (1856), for example, specifically drew attention to the richness of the ferns in the area. Although many of the early books on ferns were written by men, they often contained references to the suitability of the study of the culture of ferns for women, although there were exceptions. Echoing the Victorian division between 'polite botany' for ladies and 'scientific botany' for men, these were often condescending or patronising and rarely advocated serious scientific study by women. Describing the typical 'fern hunter' in 1888 Charles Druery apologised for his terminology, stating: 'When we write him or his, we must beg our lady readers to transmute the pronouns to suit themselves, since we are indebted for many of the most remarkable finds to the sharp eyes of the ladies, and trust, therefore, to make fully as many disciples amongst the fair sex as amongst the (so called) sterner sex'.[10]

Despite the distaste with which publication by women was commonly held, books on botany had been available by women for women through even the leanest times of the late eighteenth and early nineteenth centuries. Priscilla Wakefield's *An Introduction to Botany: In a Series of Familiar Letters* (1796) had been enormously popular. Claiming in botany a relief and cure for depression of spirits, levity and idleness among the fairer sex, the book sought to instil good habits and healthy behaviour in its female readers, as well as a somewhat censored version of the Linnaean system. In addition to her works on botany Priscilla Wakefield published moral tales and other popular science books, but 'Wakefield's Botany', as it became known, was still popular into the middle of the nineteenth century despite increasing competition for her market.

In 1817 Sarah and Elizabeth Fitton addressed the 'rising generation and the fairer sex' in a further series of letters on botany, this time supposedly between mother and son. *Conversations on Botany* contained eighteen letters, by the end of which the mother had explained (in considerable detail) how one could identify a poppy as *Papaver rhoas*. Instruction through epistolary means was enormously popular with female writers (and readers) of the period. Used to exchanging confidences via letters, and preferring perhaps to take instruction from a 'friend', these books of 'dialogues', 'letters' and 'exchanges', were common throughout the nineteenth century. Other examples include Maria Jacson and her *Botanical Dialogues between Hortensia and Her Four Children* (1797); Harriet Beaufort's *Dialogues on Botany* (1819) and the rather gushing *Wonders of the Vegetable Kingdom Displayed: In a Series of Letters* (1822) by the religious children's author Mary Roberts. That the dialogues were meant to reflect real conversations is sometimes difficult to believe. Two women walking together in the early spring were supposed, for example, to have had the following exchange on encountering a snowdrop:

> *Ingeana*: What elegant simplicity and elegance is in this flower! It belongs I believe to the sixth class of the Linnaean system . . . but it seems to me to be two flowers . . .
> *Flora*: The whole is but one Flower: this part . . . is called by our ingenious translators of the immortal Linnaeus, the nectary.[11]

Even Jane Loudon chose the epistolary form when she wrote *The Lady's Country Companion* in 1845. Supposedly addressed to a recently married lady who has moved to the country and needs advice on gardening and other domestic matters, this gives a delicious insight into the domestic concerns of the period, covering everything from ordering furniture and arranging the housekeeper's room to keeping monkeys and macaws and purchasing 'shoes and other apparatus' for country walking. 'You complain my dear Annie, [Jane Loudon starts to her imagined correspondent] that when I wrote to congratulate you on your marriage, I did not send you any of the advice I promised.' Unwilling, she explains, to disturb the happiness of the honeymoon, she has put off her letters until the happy couple have actually arrived at their future dwelling. Now, however, she has been spurred to reply by a plea for advice on felling some lofty Scotch pines, 'the most gloomy of all the vegetable race'.[12] The letters continue for nineteen chapters, and supposedly over several months, during which we learn more about Annie's needs and worries as well as solutions to these domestic difficulties. The semblance of having received a reply is kept up throughout, as Annie is thanked for the sketches of the location of her flower garden, admonished for still expressing a preference for town over country, and patiently reminded to write again with a description of her soil type. Indeed, Jane Loudon had 'not intended saying anything about the kitchen garden, as it hardly comes within the ladies province', until her hand is forced by Annie's sending to 'tell me you are so much annoyed by your old gardener never having the things you want when you want them, that you think of farming a small-kitchen garden near the house'; advice of course follows. A hundred years later Gladys Rawson was to use a similar disguised 'question and answer' form in her book *Eve's Garden* (1940) 'to help the average woman who likes pottering in her garden'.

With the recognised market in introductory books on wider botanical subjects by women authors, and the rising popularity of the fern, it was inevitable that a book on fern collecting and culture would soon be tackled by a member of the 'fairer sex'. In 1855 Anne Pratt, an established writer on a range of flower and seaside-related topics, published *The Ferns of Great Britain and their Allies the Club Mosses, Pepperworts and Horsetails*. In her introduction Anne Pratt notes that ferns are popular with those who have little botanical knowledge or experience, but goes on to say that the study of the fern may offer more difficulties than many other flowering plants. Although addressing the prospective fern (and clubmoss) collector as 'he' the tone of the books, published by the Society for Promotion of Christian Knowledge, fits closely with other books aimed at women. Her discussion of the use of ferns in decorating the house and the indoor fernery also hints at a female readership. Five years later Mrs Phebe Lankester published

A Plain and Easy Account of the British Ferns; although for those hoping for a simple introductory work the subtitle *together with their classification, arrangement by genera, structure and functions, and a glossary of technical and other terms* might have been just a little off-putting. Long neglected in the annals of botany and garden history Mrs Lankester (1814–74) deserves much greater recognition.[13] Born Phebe Pope, she married the physician and naturalist Edwin Lankester but, unlike many women of the period, continued her own studies after her marriage. Her book was supposedly aimed at the 'lover of nature who might not be acquainted with botany' and her introduction and tone recall strongly the work of Jane Loudon (who twenty years earlier had addressed herself to women who wanted to garden but had not the acquaintance with horticulture to understand the publications put out by men such as her own husband[14]). *A Plain and Easy Account of Ferns* was later enlarged several times (one of the last being in 1884). These enlarged editions included an odd mix of folklore, physic or medicinal recipes and historical references, next to technical details on pollen, stamens and ovules. The Common Hart's Tongue, for example, is noted as an astringent and a remedy for burns, while the Eagle Fern is an excellent manure (a comment that would appear to conflict rather with its status as a 'collectable' fern).

Nona Bellairs was less scientifically rigorous in her approach to the cryptogamia family. Her *Hardy Ferns: How I Collected and Cultivated Them* (1865) has the sort of forthright title that addresses and encourages the novice, promising not just knowledge but also an opportunity for excursions. The fact that it was sandwiched between her other publications *Going Abroad* (1857) and *Wayside Flowers: or Gleanings from Rocks and Fields towards Rome* (1866) suggests a writer with rather broader interests than those of the specialist Mrs Lankester. Miss Bellairs was noted for going on lengthy tours to collect her specimens, and 'doing what [she] advised other fern-lovers to do: I packed up a large hamper full and sent it off by rail home'. Expressing regret for the stripping of the countryside she rather contrarily notes that 'if the present rage continues I see no hope of any known species being allowed to remain in its old haunts'.[15] The rage did continue if the rush of publications is anything to go by. In 1856 Charlotte Chanter had guided more hamper-packers to the ferns' remote dwelling places with *Ferny Combes: A Ramble after Ferns in the Glens of Devonshire*; while Margaret Plues was more wide ranging in her *Rambles in Search of Flowerless Plants* (1864). In other publications Margaret also 'rambled' in search of mosses (1861), ferns (1861) and wild flowers (1863). That she rambled rather than setting out on expeditions is typical of female terminology in a period when women collected as a polite accomplishment and men botanised as a scientific study.

As the journal *Phytologist* noted of the publication *A Handbook of British Ferns*, part of its immediate success was due to its being small enough to be carried in a lady's reticule. That women did use these books is evidenced by the bookplates and inscriptions on the flyleaves of the works produced by both men and women authors. The collection in the library of the University of Cambridge Botanic Garden[16] contains many examples with women's names written as owners, or inscriptions indicating that the work was a gift from or to a woman. In Charles Johnson's *The Ferns of Great Britain* (1855) is the handwritten dedication, 'Given to Anne Maria Walker from her affectionate Uncle William. Bath April 1859'. Marginalia in a different hand, almost undoubtedly contemporary and most likely the recipient's, notes plants identified in locations including Bath, Pembrokeshire, Devonshire, Lansdowne and Derbyshire. Anne Maria Walker obviously took her hobby to heart.

It was to the many less rigorous (but undoubtedly very popular) publications that Shirley Hibberd addressed himself in the introduction to his own work. Belligerent on the rash of books by authors with little scientific background he states, 'it has become the fashion to consider a knowledge of the subject rather a disqualification than otherwise'.[17] That he should follow this with a description of the botanical qualities of the fern that included the memorable line 'it can scarcely be averred of them to a certainty that they really marry at all' may suggest that he felt that ignorance was in fact in many cases bliss. The popularity of the fern house as recommended by Hibberd continued unabated through the 1860s and 1870s. One builder in the 1860s claimed to have constructed over seventy in one neighbourhood of London alone.[18] Of even greater popularity was the fern outing. Again Hibberd hints at this with his glorious description of 'picnicing, archaeologico-exploring and holiday perambulating'. George Francis Heath had been even more enthusiastic with his description of 'rambles . . . through winding mazes of green lanes; through ferny hollows, up ferny hills; over moorland and meadow; by the daisied margins of gurgling brooks and . . . into the deepest shade of spreading woods'.[19]

With her book on fern identification firmly placed in her reticule, the female fern-collector responded to the call of the daisied margins. Fortunately for her she was not being called on to stray too far from home, as independent women travellers were even more alarming to decent society than the Linnaean system. In the eighteenth and nineteenth centuries, travel abroad was difficult for women. Only those from very limited spheres of society would travel, and even fewer would be permitted to travel alone. Spinsters of a 'certain age' lacking family and of restricted independent means might look to Europe or (less often) the empire as an attractive option, combining higher social status with lower living costs. Those fleeing scandal, prosecution, or persecution might also take refuge in the relative anonymity of foreign climes while reluctant wives of government officials were soon to be found in every far-flung corner of the empire.

That any of these categories of women devoted time and energy to the recording and collection of plants might seem unlikely in the extreme, but the lure of the rare plant is not easily denied. While trailing their governor-generals through impenetrable thickets, or pausing in their scandalous flights to and from lovers, a flower would be noticed, a plant collected, and the inevitable baggage train further encumbered. Overcoming heat and exhaustion they sketched, pressed and dug their way across the plant world, pausing only to consider the unsuitability of their clothing for such horticultural endeavours. From the common border plant to the prized exotic, it would be a rare garden that did not owe a debt to these intrepid, and often troubled, women.

Lady Elizabeth Webster (1770–1845) was 23 when she ran away with the even younger Lord Holland, leaving behind an astounded husband and outraged family. The subsequent birth of their son Charles out of wedlock further fuelled Elizabeth's notoriety, and the Hollands were forced to reside abroad for several years. While living in Spain Lady Holland encountered the magnificent and flamboyant flowers of the dahlia. Determined to have the South American flower enlivening her autumn months back in London, she sent tubers[20] ahead of her. At Holland House they were carefully tended and eventually blossomed, taking the fashionable horticultural scene by storm. Twenty years later a still romantic Lord Holland was to commemorate both the dahlia and Elizabeth in verse: 'The Dahlia you brought to our isle, Your praises for ever shall speak: Mid gardens as sweet as your smile, And colour as bright as your cheek.' One suspects that the appealing qualities that had led Elizabeth to elope with him had lain elsewhere than poetry.[21]

Dahlia mania spread through the Continent in the first half of the nineteenth century and over 1,500 different varieties of dahlia were created. Admired by Joseph Paxton at Chatsworth and avidly collected by John Wedgewood (who was said to have over 200 named varieties), a whole garden was devoted to them by Maria and James Batemen at Biddulph Grange. John Claudius Loudon assured his readers that dahlias were 'the most fashionable flower in this country' in the mid-nineteenth century.[22] Lady Holland was almost beaten into second place for the honour of the praises of the brightly coloured dahlia by another woman traveller in Spain. Marchioness Bute (d. 1800), wife of the then British Ambassador to Spain, had attempted to introduce the 'Cocoxochitl', as it was then known, in the 1790s. For some reason the introduction failed (perhaps the burden of the name proved too much), leaving the way clear for Lady Holland in 1804. Its subsequent renaming after Dr Dahl, a Swedish pupil of Linnaeus, relieved us of the possible culture clash of *Cocoxochitl* 'Bishop of Llandaff'. To further complicate matters the dahlia is sometimes known as Georgina on the Continent. Charlotte-Jane, Marchioness of Bute, had to be content with the introduction of the *Zinnia elegans*, although its common name 'Youth and Age' might have been a worrying appellation for any Victorian woman.[23]

Travelling rather more conventionally than Lady Holland, was Lady Sarah Amherst (née Archer, Dowager Countess of Plymouth) Lady Amherst (1762–1838) was an avid plant collector and was greatly facilitated in her interest by her husband being appointed representative to China in 1816 and then governor-general to India in 1823. Whether it was the plant collecting or the husband that came first, she made the most of the opportunity to travel in distant and seldom visited regions, collecting among others, *Clematis montana*[24] and *Anemone vitifolia*, the white autumn-flowering anemone.[25] Her most famous acquisition, however, was the *Amherstia nobilis*, or 'Pride of Burma'. Described by Sarah in 1826 as being of 'unequalled . . . magnificence and elegance' the *Amherstia*'s importation was not to be an easy matter. Following the arrival of a picture of a specimen plant, the Duke of Devonshire at Chatsworth suffered a strong pang of plant lust. He immediately dispatched the plant collector John Gibson to India to obtain an *Amherstia* for Chatsworth, but alas on its arrival in England neither the combined efforts of his head gardener, Joseph Paxton, nor the tropical conditions of the Chatsworth hothouses could entice it to flower. Similar lack of success was met with at Syon House and Kew with further specimens. However in 1849, twenty-three years after it was first described, Mrs Louisa Lawrence of Ealing[26] was able to throw open her hothouse doors and proudly display the first ever English blossoms. There the *Amherstia* blossomed for six years until the death of Louisa, when it was transferred to Kew. It continued for three years in its new home before dying. During those three years it was painted coincidentally by the artist Marianne North and its flowering was also marked by the honour of a presentation of one of its blossoms to the young Queen Victoria. This elegant 'tree' thus had a female collector (after whom it is named), a female 'nursemaid', female painter, and admiring female monarch.

Lady Amherst almost managed to add the perhaps even more sought-after Tree or Mountain Peony to her list of introductions.[27] Delegations of English ambassadors had been dispatched to China to attempt to free this magnificent shrub from its native soils, including Lord Macartney who arrived replete with greetings from His Majesty King George III. Lord Amherst arrived in China to press the same suite in 1816–17 bringing not only royal greetings but also an entourage fit for royalty. One suspects Lady Amherst awaited the results of the deputation to 'free the peony' (and other restrictions on foreign travel and exportation) with bated breath. But it was not to be and the *Paeonia suffruticosa* made tortuously slow progress towards English shores, with only one or two smuggled plants making the long journey until the 1840s, when Robert Fortune was responsible for an influx of several species. The Amherst name is also commemorated in Lady Amherst's pheasant (*Chrysolophus amherstiae*). This much sought-after pheasant is native to the mountains of China, Tibet and Burma, and Lord Amherst was responsible for sending the first specimen to London in 1828. The bird did not survive the journey, but the ornithologist Leadbetter nevertheless used the specimen for his official description in 1829. The family connection with gardens continued via marriage with the Tyssen Amhersts, to blossom again with the Hon. Alicia Margaret Tyssen Amherst (1865–1941), who wrote a *History of Gardening in England* in 1895.

Wives of governors, representatives and consuls loom large in the history of plant collecting and recording; but it can sometimes be difficult to judge whether they are there due to an innate interest and enthusiasm for their subject matter, or as a cure for the stultifying boredom of diplomatic life in foreign climes. Lady Amherst was certainly a very active plant hunter and appears to have travelled at times independently of her husband in pursuit of rarities and exotics. Another woman who one feels seized the opportunities with outstretched hands was Christian[28] Ramsey, Countess of Dalhousie (1786–1839), wife of the 9th Earl of Dalhousie. Following her husband first to Canada (Nova Scotia) and then to India the Countess collected and botanised as she went. Her exquisite botanical watercolours (a considerable achievement in the conditions of the Himalayas) survive in the Kew collections and testify to her remarkable powers of observation. Her private letters are also full of descriptions of flora and fauna and bear witness to an interest surely beyond that of the bored diplomatic wife.[29] On their way out to India, Christian had collected plants on Madeira and St Helena and at the Cape of Good Hope, and had stayed in constant communication with Joseph Hooker, to whom she was to write again concerning her discoveries in Simla, Penang and Burma. Her donation of plants to both the Hooker Herbarium and the Botanical Society of Edinburgh (to which she gifted some 1,200 specimens) allowed Hooker to compile his *Flora Indica*. Robert Graham named a new genus of tropical shrubs (*Dalhousiae*) after her, although the rhododendron that is more commonly associated with her name (*Rhododendron* 'Lady Dalhousie') is in fact named after her daughter-in-law Lady Susan. Joseph Archibald, head gardener at the couple's gardens at Dalhousie Castle, described the Countess in the *Gardener's Magazine* of 1826, saying, 'few . . . attained such proficiency as her ladyship in the science of gardening'.[30] High praise indeed from a Victorian (male) head gardener. Lady Dalhousie's enthusiasms also appeared to rub off on her son James, 10th Earl of Dalhousie (1812–60), who became the youngest viceroy ever sent to India. Meeting with the famous collector Joseph Hooker on the journey out, James was to facilitate plant hunting both by enthusiastic support and, more practically, by the construction of the railways and canal systems. *Rhododendron* 'Lady Dalhousie' was his reward.

Not all plants given female names in this period were the result of happy discoveries by wives and daughters. It was the fragrance of the *Rosa banksiae* that resulted in it being named after the wife of Sir Joseph Banks rather than her actual involvement in its discovery. QueenVictoria did not battle with the Amazonian rainforest to recover the *Victoria amazonica*, and even the redoubtable Ellen Willmott sent Ernest Wilson to China to collect the *Rosa willmottae* rather than go herself. Roses appear to be one of the worst flowers for taking the names of females who have had little or nothing to do with their breeding. Lady Hillingdon, the famous society hostess who is said to have coined the phrase 'shut your eyes and think of England', gave her name to a pale yellow rose. A climber by habit, *Rosa* 'Lady Hillingdon' is said to be dreadful in the bed but great against the wall.

By the last decades of the nineteenth century plant hunting was being driven predominantly by the large commercial nurseries, such as Veitch's of London and Devon. In order to obtain rarities and maintain supplies from around the world, they employed professional plant collectors and hunters. By the very nature of their employment these were exclusively male, often combining swashbuckling characters with relatively limited horticultural background. This change in perception of the plant hunter had the effect of diminishing the role of the amateur and with it the female collector. Facing both social and cultural restrictions on independent travel (in addition to financial dependence), women of this period could not make a career of actively pursuing plants across the globe, even if they felt the urge. Instead they acted as the nurseries and nurturers of new introductions, creating havens where the tender seeds and plants could thrive and, hopefully, blossom. This role was encouraged by the publication of books such as Jane Loudon's *The Ladies' Flower-Garden of Ornamental Greenhouse Plants* (1848) and Louisa Johnson's *Every Ladies' Guide to Her Own Greenhouse* (1851). A new emphasis was placed on the role of 'ladies' in the conservatory and glasshouse, with perhaps unintended analogies between their own sheltered lives and those of the plants held within. Increasingly women were portrayed as being at home among the hothouse flowers, both in books and in art.

Lady in a Conservatory (*c.* 1870–80; location unknown), by Jane Maria Bowkett, was one of many popular Victorian paintings that portrayed women in their new setting.[31] Jane Bowkett was known as a painter of women and small domestic scenes, and it has been suggested that the detailed representation of a middle-class suburban conservatory may even have been modelled on her own greenhouse. A demure lady, all in white, tends a lily while around her, tender fuchias, pelargoniums and ferns await her ministrations. The scene is one of domestic peace and harmony, although the prominence of the lily stamens may hint at some sexual awakening. Often there appears to be an underlying tension in the portrayals. *Five O'Clock* (1874; private collection) by George Dunlop Leslie, has been variously interpreted. A middle-aged woman sits nervously by a tea table in a richly furnished conservatory or winter-garden. The room is large and elegant and the plants expensive. The outside world is blocked from view by their size and profusion. Two places are set for tea and questions focus on the identity of the expected guest. Is it a husband who is so anxiously awaited, or someone who will release her from her social passivity and domestic enclosure? In *Il Pensero* (1875; private collection), by John Atkinson Grimshaw, a young woman (again in white) exhibits a degree of frustration that is palpable even 100 years after the original painting. Trapped behind a shiny wooden table in a claustrophobic glasshouse, she is hemmed in on all sides by exotic and rare plants. She does not appear to be tending the plants, or even admiring them, but instead herself forms one of the exotic collection presented for the viewer.

This duality of women as nurterer and nurtured is most clearly presented in Walter Howell Deverell's 1853 painting, *The Pet* (Tate Gallery). Shown standing in the doorway between the domestic space of the conservatory and the external garden, is a young woman dressed in pink. A docile dog lies on the red tiles of the conservatory floor, while a bird within a small cage hangs just above the woman's face. She tilts her head to bestow a kiss on the confined creature. A further larger bird, perhaps a jay, sits on a cage by her feet. Unlike the lush planting in the previous paintings, clay pots contain out of season pelargoniums, stunted and leafless. Outside, however, we can glimpse a delightful garden with gravel path leading between herbaceous borders towards a distant shrubbery. A wild bird hops between light and shade across the wide path, the only free creature in the whole painting. In truth, the conservatory could be both a liberating and a constricting space, one which 'every lady' should approach with caution.

Specialising in exotics and hothouse plants, Louisa Lawrence, appears to have taken control of her conservatory, her garden and one suspects her husband. Louisa had 28 acres of grounds as her domain, surrounding Lawrencian Villa in Drayton Green and when these proved insufficient for her collections the couple moved to a larger garden in nearby Ealing Park. Introduced by John Claudius Loudon as 'Mrs Lawrence F.H.S., the lady of the celebrated surgeon of that name',[32] Louisa created 'the most remarkable' garden of its size in the neighbourhood of London. Its remarkableness, as noted by both John and Jane Loudon, was in its sheer variety. Even accounting for the acres laid aside for the small farm and decorative parkland, there was still plenty of room for the four different decorative gardens, the hothouses and the exotics, not to mention the array of statuary. Six gardeners were employed full-time as well of course as the ubiquitous lowly 'women for collecting insects and deadleaves'. No doubt at least some of the medals awarded to her extensive tender plant collections must have been owing to the care of the stove and glasshouses lavished by the gardeners; however the design of the gardens, the collecting and ordering of the plants, and the choice of planting was very much under the command of Mrs Lawrence herself.

John Loudon describes a staggering number of species as being present in the Lawrencian gardens in Drayton Green. This included 212

Amazon Water Lily *(Victoria amazonica)*

In retrospect it is nothing short of a miracle that the Amazonian water lily should have been named after an English queen. First 'discovered' in Peru by a Spanish botanist it was rediscovered twenty-five years later when a dried specimen was sent from Argentina to Paris by a French botanist. A German collector found it in the Amazon, but Guiana was the home of the first 'British' specimen, British only by virtue of having been collected by a plant hunter working for the Royal Geographic Society in an outpost of empire. Viable seeds finally arrived via Brazil, adding yet another nationality to this famous bloom. Its identification as a new genus by John Lindley gave the English the privilege of naming and Joseph Hooker argued for the name *Victoria regia* on the basis of the Queen's recent 'gracious' opening of Kew for 'public enjoyment'.[44] In November 1849 the first ever flower was presented to Queen Victoria courtesy of the Duke of Devonshire, the Kew specimens being reluctant to bloom. A later name change allowed both the Queen and the homelands of the lily to be honoured. Despite having numerous plants named after her, horticulture was one sphere of life that does not seem to have greatly interested Victoria. Albert, on the other hand, was fascinated by the work of the Horticultural Society. Queen Victoria had complained in 1859 that Prince Albert was so busy with the organisation that he had not time enough to take her for a walk. One of Prince Albert's last public engagements was on 5 June 1861, when he visited the Society gardens, conferring at the same time the title 'Royal' on the organisation.

species and varieties of hardy and half-hardy ornamental trees and shrubs; 130 species and varieties of hardy fruit trees; 600 species and varieties of hardy herbaceous plants; 30 species of British and American ferns (planted in rockwork); 140 species of alpines (also in rockwork); 34 species of hardy aquatics; 200 varieties of heartsease; 500 varieties of garden roses, creepers and standards; 12 varieties of ivy; 40 species of American plants; 992 (!) species and varieties of Botany Bay, China and Cape shrubs; 134 genera and 340 species of hothouse plants and

57 genera and 227 species of *Orchidacea*. It was particularly the orchids and other stove plants that caught the attention of the RHS, and for which she gained at least fifty-three medals, including the Knightian medal. A female orchid collector was unusual, a medal-winning one almost unheard of. But it was for the decoration and layout of the gardens that she has courted attention through subsequent years.

Poised on the cusp between the early nineteenth-century gardenesque and the Victorian eclectic, Mrs Lawrence had a rather overwhelming choice of styles and genres to choose from; and appears to have used them to the full. A detailed description of a 'tour' of the gardens was included in John Loudon's *The Suburban Gardener and Villa Companion* (1838). From here we learn that, after descending from the drawing room onto the lawn, passing on our way the foliated vase, ivy vase, pyramid of roses and 'rustic basket of pelargoniums',[33] we will look out on to 'an intricate maze of agreeable and beautiful objects'. A sufficient surface of naked lawn prevented these objects from appearing crowded, insists Loudon, although it must be said that the engravings that accompany the description testify otherwise. Indeed, later in the same description he admits that the view to the paddock 'affords an agreeable relief from the excess of beauty and variety on the lawn'. The sole adornment of the paddock being the carefully grouped Alderney cows.[34]

Areas of grouped plantations at Lawrencian Villa contained hybrid rhododendrons, azaleas and other shrubs treated in a mixed picturesque style. An Italian walk contained a rustic arch and vase at one end, with an elegant fountain at the other, while the main walk was lined with various statues on square plinths. Borders along the walk were filled with standard and climbing roses, with views to a rockwork arch and across to a garden bathhouse and the span-roofed greenhouse. No ordinary greenhouse this, as lofty finials and side arches, combined with a reclining statue over the entrance, gave the whole a grand air. The French parterre similarly contained a statue and several pedestal vases, while an area of more rustic rockwork was topped by a statue of Fame trumpeting, no doubt, the magnificence of the garden. Rockwork was a motif of the garden with further areas containing concealed springs to allow for the growth of aquatics. This combination of rustic adornments with classical statuary, including garden nymphs, Cupid and Mercury, strikes an odd note now, but would have been much more acceptable in the mid-nineteenth century. However, one does suspect a hidden meaning in Loudon's summing up that 'this villa may be considered a model of its particular kind'. Loudon does accept that 'there are many people of a simple and severe taste who will think that the Lawrencian Villa is too highly ornamented' but he goes on to argue that 'allowance must be made for individual taste'. Allowances were also made for Mrs Lawrence's 'devotion to the subject' and the limited area that she had available to display that devotion.

It is for her devotion to her plants, and in particular her hothouses, that we should indeed remember Mrs Lawrence. With Mr Lawrence usually away (we are told he kept his books and wine at a London house) there was plenty of time for Mrs Lawrence to indulge her gardening passions. In a period when so many women were nervously restricting themselves to the joys of the sexless fern Louisa was bravely and brazenly cultivating the sensual orchid and the hothouse exotic. Near-naked statuary of marble and bronze confronted the modestly-clad visitor, and one suspects many a fainter-hearted Victorian female encountered some confusing emotions among the shrubberies. Mr Lawrence's comments on the surroundings of his villa in Drayton Green are unknown, but if any Victorian could look with equanimity on a classical portrayal of the partly clothed human body it should have been a surgeon. The opinions of the lowly women who swept the dead leaves from the tidy lawns under the watchful eyes of Cupid also remain, unsurprisingly, unrecorded. Drayton Green was succeeded in time by a garden in Ealing, providing even more space for the glasshouses and rockwork that had become the passion of Louisa's life. It was at the villa in Ealing that Mrs Lawrence gained her greatest success and everlasting famc by bcing the first person in England to flower the *Amherstia*. One can only hope that Mr Lawrence appreciated it.

Rockwork was not exclusive to the gardens of Mrs Lawrence. Thanks to the artificial rocks of James Pulham and sons, and the cheapness of labour to haul real rocks, alpine plants had never had it so good. Uprooted from their tenuous hold on the Alpine slopes they were transported to miniature mountain ranges in the suburbs of England. Larger in scale than most was the alpine garden at Hoole House (Cheshire), created by Lady Broughton. Modelled on the mountains of Savoy, with the valley of Chamonix, snow and strata were mimicked by careful use of grey limestones and white marble. All the planting on the slopes was Alpine, although the entire edifice loomed over a pancake-flat lawn with rows of brightly coloured circular flower beds. Pictures of the garden show astounded visitors wandering through miniature fir trees on the lower slopes and peering over snow-capped peaks. Jane Loudon described Lady Broughton's masterpiece as 'stand[ing] quite alone, the only one of its kind'.[35] One can perhaps see why. Dropmore, the garden of Lady Grenville, was arguably the origin of shaped beds containing grouped plants cut into lawns. Claimed to be an imaginative gardener, she was at her best when constructing rustic flower baskets out of garden and household detritus. Lady Grenville also championed the use of roses to such an extent that borders and walls were smothered in rose blooms, especially the newly fashionable French varieties.

Combining a love of exotics, a large garden and an even larger personal income, Lady Dorothy Nevill (née Walpole) (1826–1913) might seem a women to be envied, even by Mrs Lawrence. However, few gardening women would wish to share in the disappointments and distress of Dorothy Walpole's early life. A portrait of her as a young woman of 18 shows a slightly shy-looking, eager girl, hands clasped tenderly to her bosom, eyes demure. Only hindsight allows us to know that this was a woman on the edge of disaster. Daughter of the 3rd Earl of Orford, Dorothy's homelife included political and social parties attended by the great and the good; but beautiful and vivacious Dorothy was unfortunate enough to attract the attention of one of the not so good. George Augustus Smythe, Tory politician and rake, was variously described by contemporaries as 'unprincipled' and 'radical'. His list of conquests is so long as to make one wonder he had time to fit in Dorothy in 1847.[36] Alas that he did. At the tender age of 21, Dorothy was publicly compromised by this accomplished seducer, supposedly in a Hampshire summerhouse. With a reputation in ruins Dorothy was hurriedly forced into marriage with an elderly cousin, while her erstwhile seducer was sent packing to Europe. Her family may appear to have acted rather harshly given that her father was an addicted gambler and her brother had eloped with Lady Lincoln (herself notorious for flouting society's conventions), but the Nevill family were still trying to gain a better foothold in society and this must have seemed the last straw.

Reginald Henry Nevill was a serious religious man over twenty years Dorothy's senior and although the family's choice, he cannot have been her ideal husband. He was, however, wealthy, with £8,000 a year and he was prepared to let Dorothy spend it. Wealth was a consolation for the hastily arranged wedding and, as many scandalised women have done before and since, she turned first to shopping and then to horticulture. In 1851 the Nevills acquired (in addition to their London house) the country estate of Dangstein, along with its 23 acres of gardens. Near Petersfield in Hampshire, the gardens were to become famous for their collections of exotics, their fine herbaceous borders and their numerous aviaries and menagerie. With its collections of porcelain and pictures, Dangstein was also to become the centre for house parties allowing Lady Dorothy to 'collect' society around her, despite the fact that she was not accepted back at court until 1901. Although she collected many plant rarities, Dorothy's particular obsession was the hothouse exotics. She had seventeen hothouses built at Dangstein to contain her collections, and corresponded with William Hooker at Kew and then his son Joseph on the subject of her new specimens. The Dangstein Palm House was the most splendid of the glasshouses and the first of Lady Dorothy's constructions. Semi-domed, it measured 80ft by 50ft and was heated by both air and water. A filmy-fern house was constructed in 1872 for the growing of Hymenophyllum, Todea and Trichomanes.[37] Facing north-west and slightly sunken, it provided the cool moist conditions essential for these plants. Lady Dorothy's orchid collection rivalled that of Mrs Lawrence, with over 320 plants being housed by 1861, including almost all the species then known. A list was available for those houseguests and visitors who were interested, as indeed there was for all the plantings.[38] Aquatics and insectivorous plants were not neglected, and the Madagascan lattice plant (*Ouviranda fenestralis*) was one of Dangstein's showpieces alongside various species of Nepenthes, although not it seems *Nepenthes northiana*. She was not a woman to shy away from the sexuality of the orchid (perhaps it would have been better if she had been) and sent some from her own collections to Charles Darwin, corresponding with him about his studies. In addition to the exotics there was a pinetum containing newly introduced Wellingtonias and monkey puzzles. An engraving in the *Journal of Horticulture* of 1872 shows a group of small gangly monkey puzzles being rapidly overshadowed by firs.[39] All of these gardens were kept in the most immaculate condition by a team of thirty-four gardeners overseen by Mr Vair, the Scottish head gardener.

Reginald Nevill died in 1878 after a long and painful illness. He left his 62-year-old wife with an income variously reported as £2,000 or £800 a year, neither of which would be sufficient to maintain the magnificence of the Dangstein gardens. A sale was declared. Part way through the negotiations to transfer the plant collections to Kew, the Zulu War broke out, diverting all the Treasury's thoughts and funds away from ferns and palms. Over five days in the summer of 1879 1,000 orchids, 1,000 stove ferns, 200 carnivorous plants and masses of palms and other rarities were sold. The Prince of Monaco chartered a steamer to transport those he bought in a separate private sale, while other tropical trees went to the King of Belgium. A mere three vanloads of plants were transferred to Dorothy Nevill's new gardens at Stillyans, East Sussex, along with the faithful head gardener Mr Vains. A small start in what was to be a new interest in hardy and Alpine planting.

A fascination with lilies and fuchsias, as well as with hardy ferns, was a hallmark of James and Maria Bateman, owners of Biddulph Grange. James Batemen had collected orchids from his student days, but it was Maria who was later to be known as 'that distinguished liliophile'. Together they created an extraordinary garden filled with many of the imported American plants of the day. Specimen trees including the monkey puzzle and Wellingtonia towered over hybrid rhododendron and Japanese maples, while brightly coloured dahlias occupied the specially designed terraced gardens of a sunken garden walk. The famous 'Chinese' and 'Egyptian' gardens were jointly designed by Maria and her husband and the artist and designer Edward Cooke. Cooke was the son-in-law of George Loddidges, of Loddidges Nursery, and so had little problem in obtaining specimens of the latest imports. Although it is often difficult to entangle the complexity of responsibility in a gardening relationship, it is certain that Maria was active in the design and layout of the gardens. As Maria Sibylla Egerton-Warburton (an interesting coincidence of names with the seventeenth-century plant illustrator) she came from a creative gardening family. Her brother created the gardens at Arley Hall and her family had been responsible for gardens in their home county of Cheshire. As well as their joint names over the entrance to the garden cottage, the complex gardens on the top terrace at Biddulph were named 'Mrs Bateman's Gardens', although recent research indicates a chequered history. Biddulph House was destroyed by fire in 1896 (a year after Maria's death[40]), but much of the gardens survived and are being actively restored. 'Miss Bateman' still survives as a clematis (*C.* 'Miss Bateman') growing alongside *Clematis flammula* on the posts and chains leading to the Wellingtonia avenue.

Husband and wife or brother and sister partnerships often make for difficult gardening but the wealthy Rothschild family turned it into an art, with gardens across Europe belonging to uncles, daughters, sisters and granddaughters. Miriam Rothschild of the twentieth-century wild and butterfly gardens was related to the Baron Ferdinand de Rothschild of Waddesdon Manor (Buckinghamshire) being granddaughter of the 2nd Lord Rothschild. Ferdinand's sister, Alice, as well as advising him on the creation of Waddesdon (in particular the rose beds and aviary), established her own gardens next door at Eythrope. A mere 60 acres, the gardens were described enthusiastically by the *Journal of Horticulture* in the 1890s. Called the Pavilion, the Eythorpe house itself was only used in the daytime as the proximity of the estate to water resulted in Alice's doctor forbidding her to sleep there. Regardless of this hydrophobia, Alice had the rivers widened and artificial islands placed in them. A wilderness and wild garden complemented the naturalised planting of the rivers. Twenty acres of lawn lay in front of the house, studded with flower beds, shrubberies and specimen trees in a definitely 'unnatural' style. Frameworks of iron, filled with soil and moss, allowed 'three dimensional' bedding in the form of giant birds and other shapes. Views of the arrangements survive showing alarmingly green birds rising from starbursts of pelargoniums.

At Sedgwick Park, Sussex, Emma Henderson and her husband Robert employed the architects Ernest George and Harold Peto at their house and gardens. Director of the Bank of England, Robert Henderson was anxious to build a house to impress, but the garden and its planting were the domain of his wife. Articles in *Country Life* from 1901 onwards record the fine formal gardens stretching away from the house in a series of hedged walks. A rectangular lily pool is redolent of the Italianate style of some of Peto's later commissions (for example at Easton Lodge for 'Daisy' of Warwick), and the planting was said in *Country Life* to have given 'the result exactly the same as that given by a garden in an olive grove on the Riviera'. Emma Henderson developed a Japanese theme for the gardens, and alongside Japanese lanterns and long-legged cranes she planted white-flowered yuccas, giving an exoticism to the Sussex flagstone terraces. A yucca is forefront in a *Country Life* photograph of 1901, showing the rectangular pool and rock gardens in their initial design. It was Emma Henderson herself who was said to have overseen her eight gardeners and the developing gardens.[41] At Bicton Lady Louisa Rolles and her husband also enjoyed joint management of the gardens, constructing a hermitage where they could take tea in peace together. A poem of 1839 placed over this hideaway commemorates the divine retreat, 'choice of the prudent and envy of the great', that they found there. Despite their disparate ages (in 1839 Lady Louisa was 45, her husband 83), the final lines of the poem summed up their future as 'this life I relish, and secure the next'.

Another lady who undoubtedly oversaw her own domains was Diana Beaumont (d. 1831). Popularly known as Madame Beaumont she was said to be proud, untrusting and unpopular. She dismissed workers, agents and labourers at will, and ruled the estate at Bretton (in the West Riding of Yorkshire) with a rod of iron. Her one-time gardener, Robert Marnock (later to be famous for his work at Kew), appears to have been the only employee who admired her. Diana was a keen horticulturalist, spending both her energies and the Beaumont funds on hothouses and plants to fill them. She commissioned John Claudius Loudon to build a conservatory that became known as 'The Far Famed Dome', to join an already complete ornamental conservatory by Wyatt. The domed conservatory was 60ft in diameter with a huge copper crown. In 1832 this conservatory and its famed collection also went under the hammer as Diana's son, Thomas Wentworth Beaumont, had little interest in horticulture and more in money.

Organising and ordering of designers, head gardeners and workforce was something at which women garden-owners were accomplished, along with the responsibility of spending (although not actually earning) money on the garden. But how many women actually worked in their own gardens? The women of the Fox Strangways family in the early nineteenth century certainly recorded many days spent working in the garden either on their own or with children, and Diana Beaumont also conducted her own plant 'experiments', but few can have approached the garden with as much gusto as Caroline Hamilton (1780–1861). *The Garden Notebook* of Caroline Hamilton allows us an almost unique insight into the day-to-day activities of a Victorian middle-class woman who had a very physical relationship with her garden. A small, handwritten, leather-bound volume details the year-round pattern of sowing, planting, trimming, pruning, digging and seed ordering for the years 1827 to 1846. Caroline (née Tighe) had married Charles Hamilton in 1801 and the two had moved into Charles's late eighteenth-century family house, Hamwood, in County Meath. Here Caroline created an 'old world'-style garden of herbs, roses, box hedges, vegetable and fruit plots and tall beech hedges. Despite some early mentions of 'Charlie', and a more or less constant background of unsatisfactory male helpers, it is obvious from the notebooks that Caroline herself carried out much of the hands-on gardening. 'Trim the gravel walk in the wood. Dig border on right hand going towards the flower garden, border opposite Morello Cherry . . . Clean back alleys near the Beech hedge. Dig the square where the red Cabbage is' – a formidable list with which to commence the New Year, but one that did not seem to cow the formidable Caroline.[42] *The Garden Notebook*

Euphorbia 'Mrs Robb's Bonnet' *(Euphorbia amygdaloides robbiae)*

Mrs Mary Anne Robb was travelling through Turkey and Greece in 1898 when she spotted the tall and striking cousin of the English spurge. A plant lover who had already corresponded with the Royal Botanic Gardens at Kew, she ordered her accompanying official dragoman to excavate it from its soil (using a handy potsherd). Determined to have it in her garden at Liphook, Hampshire, but with no suitable receptacle in which to transport it, she placed the newly displaced plant in a hatbox for its journey back to England. None the worse for its unusual receptacle, the Euphorbia thrived and became known popularly as 'Mrs Robb's Bonnet'. What happened to the bonnet it displaced is not recorded. Visited by plant lovers including E.A. Bowles and William Robinson, her 150-acre garden at Liphook was full of unusual shrubs and flowers, including a rare cowslip in a shade of orange which appears since to have been 'lost'. Mrs Robb had an unusual approach to keeping possible plant hunters away from her own garden. A sign was erected asking people to 'Beware of the *Lycopodium*', which only the most dedicated of gardeners would be able to interpret as a rather unusual warning of a usually peaceful club-moss.[45] Mary Anne Robb was also a collector of trees, being recorded in Henry John Elwes's work on the most remarkable trees in Britain as growing one of the few examples of a Sassafras in the country. Her house, Goldenfield (or Goldfield), in Liphook, was designed by the Arts and Crafts architect Phillip Webb, and has her name as the 'builder'. Inherited by her son it was unfortunately sold and split up in the late 1920s.

records details of work done, work to be done, and work sadly undone. It covers details such as the pruning regime for particular rose varieties, tips on how to get rid of caterpillars, and the rather unusual claim that 'Ducks and cats are very useful in the garden'.

The only drawing that survives of the garden layout is also in Caroline's own hand. It shows neat rectangles of fruits and vegetables, but does not venture out into the main flower gardens so the exact form of these flower and shrub borders is unknown, although *The Garden Notebook* indicates shelter was created by 'rooms' of beech hedges in what must have been a windy and wet area. Lists of the plants that Caroline grew indicate that the 'old world' style of the garden was combined with the acquisition of newly introduced varieties. A large and rich herb garden and old-fashioned 'clove' carnations, pollinated by her own bees, contrasted with the latest varieties of roses – including the 'Macartney Rose' (*Rosa bracteata*) introduced from Peking in 1793 and named after the same Lord Macartney who had failed to 'liberate' the Tree Peony. Flower borders overflowed with favourites still with us today: Soapwort, Astrantia, Yellow Flax, Teucriums, Thalictrums, Hollyhocks, Lady's Mantle, Hawkweeds and Agapanthus (which she kept well watered to encourage profuse blooms). Shrubs and trees included the 'new' double-flowering cherry, broad-leaved *Euonymus*, *Jasminum wallichianum*, *Eccremocarpus scaber* and *Cotoneaster affinis*. Protection from insect pests and aphids was provided by chemical washes and companion planting; onions being planted between carrot rows and potatoes used to attract celery worms. Caroline records early summer and late autumn fruits being protected from weather and pilferers by the tall hedges.

This very practical approach to the garden is combined with a spiritual and philosophic element, as one would expect from a correspondent of John Wesley and Edmund Burke. Slightly more unexpected is Caroline's friendship with Eleanor Butler and Sarah Ponsonby at Llangollen.[43] Caroline's cousin, Mary Tighe, was a well-known romantic writer publishing poetry including *Psyche or the Legend of Love* (1805) and recollections of her life. Mary corresponded with the equally romantic Ladies of Llangollen, and Caroline also formed part of the correspondence circle. Caroline compiled biographical notes on Mary's life and must have been influenced by her poetry and romantic philosophy; however, with the exception of very occasional lines of religious verse *The Garden Notebook* remains extremely practical. Caroline's attitude to gardening was one of enjoyment certainly, but an enjoyment built on observation, personal experience and physical discovery rather than on romantic verse or picturesque ideals. As the century progressed it was to be an enjoyment that more and more women would discover.

SIX

By the Ignorant for the Ignorant

WOMEN WRITE ON THE GARDEN

It is so very difficult for a person who has been acquainted with a subject all his life to imagine the state of ignorance in which those are who know nothing of it, that adepts often find it quite impossible to communicate the knowledge they possess. Thus though it may at first sight appear presumptuous in me to teach an art of which for the greater part of my life I was totally ignorant, it is in fact that very circumstance which is one of my chief qualifications for the task.

Jane Loudon, *Instructions in Gardening for Ladies*, Foreword (1840)

Ignorance may in some circumstances be bliss, but in a garden it usually spells disaster. As Victorian women fought their way out of the fern house and into the shrubbery they were suddenly assailed with doubts and questions. Women who had never used gardening tools before needed to know how they should be used and, indeed, what tools were available, and even 'what was a spade anyway'? Those that did not know one garden shrub from another sought information on identification, and once identified the relative merits of one over another. From the suburban housewife installed in her new suburban villa came the question, where should the various gardens be situated? What style should they be in? The newly independent widow wished to know how to keep up a garden at least cost and the unmarried spinster how to garden without bending down. And they all, without exception, wanted to know what to wear while doing it.

Available books on garden planting, or 'gardener's dictionaries' as they were frequently known, gave the impression that to venture into the garden at all one needed first to gain an education in chemistry, botany, soil science and even astronomy. Thompson's *The Gardener's Assistant*, published in 1859, spends several pages discussing the importance of establishing the angle of the hour line according to the degree of latitude, while the table on the chemical composition of different ashes could put even the most determined horticultural student off gardening for life. John Abercrombie's *Every Man His Own Gardener* (1767) was similarly demanding, despite its all-inclusive title. 'By the educated for the educated' might have been more honest. Books on botany and plant identification rarely dealt with the niceties of garden design, even when they included technical details on propagation and stove houses. Gardening magazines were aimed at either plant collectors or head gardeners, often seeking to impress as much as educate. As Jane Loudon sadly explained, a person who has been acquainted with a subject all their life 'often finds it quite impossible to communicate the knowledge that they possess'.[1] Fortunately for the frustrated female would-be gardener, this situation was about to change.

Writing in *The Story of the Garden* in 1932, Eleanour Sinclair Rohde examined the history of books for the female gardener who, she argued, had for centuries been responsible for the domestic garden. She was only able to name two: William Lawson's *The Country Housewifes Garden* (1617/18) and Charles Evelyn's *The Lady's Recreation*, which came out almost 100 years later. Not exactly a crowded genre. Lawson's book had been addressed to the newly literate 'gentle' housewife (or one with a husband that was willing to read to her). Discussing the herb, kitchen and flower gardens he combines practical advice with a slightly condescending tone. Having listed a range of plants he goes on to say that 'garden herbs are innumerable, yet these [following] are common and sufficient for our Country Housewife'. Charles Evelyn's *The Lady's Recreation* was published as part of his larger work on *The Art of Gardening*, rather more of an afterthought than a blow for female liberation. After stating that the 'curious part' of gardening in general has always been an amusement for men, Evelyn admits the management of the flower garden to be a 'diversion of the ladies', and in particular ladies of leisure. This then was a book aimed at the upper end of the social classes, rather than the more prosaic gardening audience who looked in vain for advice on growing cabbages, turnips and skirrets. Although aimed at the supposedly flower-fixated female, both books also discussed the properties of soils and layout of the garden, rather than dwelling on the plants alone.

For those women who were able to read books in French there was another option available. *Le Jardinier François* (1651) by an anonymous author was addressed to the 'women, but particularly to the household managers'. Claiming the priority of the garden over other occupations and interests the author lists the garden's charms, its role in production for the house and kitchen, and its possible economic benefits, before going on to acquaint readers with actual gardening tasks. Described by June Taboroff as a highly professional work intended for serious gardeners,[2] any woman able to acquire (and read) this book would have been well trained in horticulture. Over 200 years later Viscountess Frances Wolseley noted the superior garden knowledge of French housewives over English, and one wonders if the *Jardinier* was the ancient root of this superiority? In seventeenth- and eighteenth-century England, the outlook was rather bleaker.

Books by women on household matters occasionally touched on flowers and herbs, although more often on their uses for physic or decoration. In the early seventeenth century Elizabeth Grey released *A Choice Manuel of Rare and Select Secrets in Physic and Chyrurgy*, which included herb-based recipes for treating illnesses. These had been collected by Elizabeth, Countess of Kent, who as a noblewoman could defy the usual embargo on publications by women herbalists. She went on to publish a second work on recipes for food of all kinds, again using herbs to complement the dishes. Hannah Wolley (also spelt Woolley or Wooley) wrote on the use of plants and flowers for 'dressing the house' in her rather racy-sounding *The Queen-like Closet or Rich Cabinet* (1675). A prolific writer, Hannah also gave advice on *The Accomplish'd Ladies Delight* and *The Gentlewoman's Companion* in the 1670s. Born in 1622 Hannah worked as a servant in a noble household but after marrying decided to make her living from writing books of advice aimed at women of all classes. In a series of publications she covered cookery, deportment, manners, decoration of the house, and some medicinal matters; as well as 'pleasant discourse and witty dialogues' between the sexes. Floral decoration was, however, as near as she got to gardening.

The eighteenth century saw the arrival of the first illustrated herbal by a woman, with Elizabeth Blackwell's two-volume work *A Curious Herball* (1737–9). Elizabeth drew the illustrations as well as writing the text (and identifying the plants), and combined medicinal usage with hints for cookery. This was no specialist apothecary text but written in English and aimed at a more general audience. Intended to appeal to 'such as are not furnished with other Herbals',[3] it was issued in weekly parts and was thus more affordable for those on lower incomes. It was the issue of low income that had prompted Elizabeth to write in the first place. In common with many women who chose to expose themselves to the public by becoming authoresses, Elizabeth wrote for money. Her husband had been imprisoned as part of a lawsuit and Elizabeth needed not only to pay his debts but also provide herself with a living. Her *Curious Herball* was a tremendous success, and not just among the English-speaking herb users at which it was originally aimed. The book found favour with the Worshipfull Society of Apothecaries, grateful no doubt for an insight into the traditional herb-lore that it contained, as well as admiring of the high quality of her illustrations. Elizabeth came from a predominantly merchant background, but her uncle was a professor of medicine at the University of Glasgow, undoubtedly aiding her initial introduction into the world of the professional apothecaries and physicians. Elizabeth's *Curious Herball* was eventually taken up by Christoph Jakob Trew in Nuremberg and an enlarged edition, translated into Latin, was published as *Herbarium Blackwellianum* (1750–60).

Although not publishing in her own name, Lady Anne Monson (*c.* 1714–76) also contributed to the spread of plant knowledge beyond the bounds of the Latin-speaking professional. A plant (and insect) collector Lady Anne encouraged and later assisted the nurseryman James Lee in undertaking a popularised version of the work of Linnaeus which was eventually published under Lee's name as *Introduction to Botany: Extracted from the Works of Dr Linnaeus*. Still a respectable married member of titled society at this period (she was later to divorce), Lady Anne refused to be named publically in the published work. The Linnaean System was also at the heart of Charlotte Murray's *The British Garden, A Descriptive Catalogue of Hardy Plants, Indigenous or Cultivated*, published in 1799, in two volumes. Charlotte attempted to give its readers both a descriptive catalogue and instruction on how to discover the name of any plant by examining it along Linnaean principles. Daughter of the 3rd Duke of Atholl (himself famous for his forestry schemes), Charlotte (1754–1808) was writing for wealthy young beginners in botany. Using tones so familiar in women's books she enthuses, cajoles and encourages people to cultivate an interest in plants and flowers. To us it may seem strange that the Linnaean system was seen as so essential to the beginner, but in the eighteenth century its relative newness made it of paramount importance even to those who could not tell one flower from another.

Monsonia speciosa

Great-granddaughter of Charles II, Lady Anne Monson (*c.* 1714–76) was a celebrated botanist and plant collector. Determined to spread botanical knowledge beyond its restricted academic circles she popularised the work of Linnaeus, working with the nurseryman James Lee on a popular *Introduction to Botany* (1760). Whether it was the botanical researching or the impending publication that was to blame, she divorced her first husband in her late forties and remarried a colonial army officer stationed in India. New opportunities for travel brought with them opportunities for plant collecting and recording, and Lady Anne made several forays in the areas around Calcutta, hiring native artists to record the Indian flora and insects. Breaking one long sea journey she met pupils of Linnaeus at the Cape of Good Hope, and took the opportunity to botanise with them. Linnaeus himself dedicated the *Monsonia speciosa* to her. He accompanied it with a dedication to set the botanical heart racing: 'I have long been trying to smother a passion which has proved unquenchable and which now has burst into flame. This is not the first time that I have been fired with love for one of the fair sex . . . Who can look on so fair a flower without falling in love with its innocence . . . But should I be so happy as to find my love for you reciprocated, then I ask but one favour of you: that I may be permitted to join with you in the procreation of just one little daughter to bear witness of our love – a little Monsonia, through which your flame would live forever in the Kingdom of Flora.'[55]

Books on plant identification, whether for use in physic or botanical study, are of course an essential part of the gardener's tool kit, however the rest of the tool kit remained severely lacking. Subsequent to Charles Evelyn's *Lady's Recreation* no other book came out in the eighteenth century specifically aimed at women actually contemplating work in the garden, and still no book at all written by women themselves. Women could of course refer to some of the publications aimed at the general gardener, works such as Thomas Hale's *Eden: or, a Compleat Body of*

Gardening published in 1757, or John Hill's *The Gardener's New Kalendar* (1758), but these were really aimed at large estates and kitchen gardens, with sections on management of fruit grounds supplemented by explanations of the Linnaean system. They were unlikely to appeal to 'polite' women of the period. What was needed was a book aimed specifically at the woman teetering on the edge of the flower border and wondering whether (and indeed how) to take the plunge. A book written by a woman and appealing to those interests that were promoted as being especially feminine.

Maria Elizabetha Jacson's[4] *Florist's Manual*, published in 1816, aimed to do just that. In her fervour for all things to do with 'this lovely order of creation', and her equally fervent need to supplement her finances, Maria wrote several books relating to plants and flowers, all of which sought to place the flower garden firmly within the feminine realm. Maria had already successfully assisted her (female) readers in the botanical education of their children with her *Botanical Dialogues between Hortensia and Her Four Children* (*c.* 1797). Now her aim was to assist them in 'the humble path of exhibiting to best advantage the moderately-sized flower garden' which, she enthused, should be 'replete with colour of every variety'. That Maria's own gardens (technically her father's, then her brother's, and finally those of a friend) were moderately-sized, and her preferred style mixed, or 'mingled' coloured beds, gave the book its very personal style. Rarities such as those cultivated by Mrs Louisa Lawrence held no thrill for Maria, who preferred a 'well-blended quantity' above rarity and variety, although she did insist that a conservatory was a necessity for winter gardening pleasures.

Maria was not afraid of putting forward her own opinions, particularly in the matter of taste and layout of the garden, and she offers the book as a manual of advice for friends, relatives and strangers who wish to procure a 'gay flower garden'. She may also have carried out several informal consultancies on design of gardens near her various homes, and in particular at Somersal Hall (Staffordshire), where she finally settled. She was a close friend of Lady Broughton who was to become famous for her rock garden (later described by John Loudon), and the circular and S-shaped flower beds at Lady Broughton's gardens at Hoole appear to have been designed and planted according to Maria's suggestion. Maria's *Manual* included diagrams for possible bed layouts, and although it does not give the prescriptive plantings that were to become common in the following decades, she lists suitable herbaceous plants and annuals in catalogues. Decrying 'the unnatural appearance of artificial crags of rocks and other stones interspersed with delicate plants', Maria gives short shrift to rock gardens, although perhaps bearing in mind her friendship with Lady Broughton she adds that these are admissible in more extensive establishments.

The *Florist's Manual* was a very influential book of the period, but has suffered historically by being immediately overshadowed by the numerous encyclopaedic works of John Loudon, and later of his wife Jane. Although not specifically addressed to women, its tone and style plus the very fact of female authorship, made them the obvious audience. The *Manual* was, in fact, extensively quoted by John Loudon in his 1834 edition of the *Encyclopaedia of Gardening*, where he notes Maria's 'correct ideas' on design. He also included articles and reviews by her in his *Gardener's Magazine*. Whether he agreed on her proposal for humanitarian ways of disposing of slugs (treating them to turnip slices and then 'instant' drowning) is unrecorded. From caterpillars to beds, and bulbs to rockwork, Maria Jacson covered nearly everything that a woman who managed a garden might need to know. What she didn't tell you was how to actually do the work yourself, although her own financial circumstances suggest that Maria, who never married, must have done her fair share.

Slugs did not make an appearance, however humanitarian, in Elizabeth Kent's *Flora Domestica: or the Portable Flower Garden* (1823). A member of an artistic circle that included her brother-in-law Leigh Hunt, Elizabeth put the seal of respectability on the flower garden by combining poetry, painting and the garden in her book. She had created a celebrated roof garden at her home near St Paul's churchyard, utilising pots to create a floriferous and scented world within the heart of the city. In the preface to *Flora Domestica* Elizabeth declared that 'I am as fond of books as of flowers; but in all that regards authorship, I fear I am as little able to produce the one, as to create the others'. Her claim to ignorance was the convention of the time and both books and garden gained her a place not only in artistic circles but also among the gardening works of the period. Her *Sylvan Sketches: or a companion to the park and shrubbery* came out in 1825 and again contained 'illustrations from the poets' to overcome any doubts women might have of the cultural role of the flower garden and both books found a ready market with several editions being published. Given the lack of any actual horticultural instruction one might see them as asides in the annals of women writers on the garden, but Elizabeth went on to write essays and reviews for John Loudon's *Magazine of Natural*

History, taking with her one suspects many of her female readership and introducing them to a more scientific basis for horticultural study. Nine of those essays were dedicated to an explanation of the Linnaean system, a subject that does not easily lend itself to poetical illustration or romantic tones. Her combined fame as poet, botanist and garden creator was an inspiration for many to follow.

Rosa, the anonymous contributor who wrote for the periodical *Cottage Gardener* in the years 1849–50, combined the practical approach of Maria Jacson with some of the poetic phraseology of Elizabeth Kent. Waxing lyrical on the joys to be had from a garden furnished with 'jessamines' and honeysuckle, she mixes morality with garden design. Well-kept hedges and gardens brimful of cabbages are used as sure indicators of thrifty and industrious characters dwelling within; an unkempt garden and untrimmed hedge being the mark of people rather more acquainted with the Beer-House (a word which is printed with the moral force of capitals in the magazine). 'Innocent' flowers are the continual subject of Rosa (the series of articles was called *My Flowers*), such as the single traditional roses, winding clematis, the herb garden and the simple posy. Apple and pear trees are seen as the property and responsibility of the husband, while the creeping and winding plants (needing strong supports) are those of the wife. *My Flowers* was dropped after some forty-six instalments, but Rosa was able to continue in the same moralistic vein in *Our Village Walls, Hints for Humble Households*, and finally *Home Suggestions*. Her own final suggestions were on how to cope in reduced circumstances, an intimation of her own cessation of employment.[5]

Unemployment, sickness and death stalked the lives of Victorian women. Combine this with their absolute dependence on the financial success and probity of the male members of the family and it is little wonder that 'disappointment' was a frequent if not constant companion in their lives. Gardening, fortunately, could be recommended as an antidote to those disappointments. Miss Louisa Johnson had, one suspects, a very particular disappointment in mind when she recommended gardening. Speaking from the heart she declared in *Every Lady Her Own Flower Gardener*: 'A flower garden, to the young and single of my sex, acts upon the heart and affections as a nursery acts upon matronly feelings. It attaches them to their home; it throws a powerful charm over the spot . . . and it lures them from dwelling too deeply upon the unavoidable disappointments and trials of life, which sooner or later disturb and disquiet the heart.'[6] Spinsters such as Louisa

Johnson inhabited a very particular and often difficult niche in Victorian society. Too often dependent on uninterested male relatives, women who should have been able to lead active lives freed from the domestic rounds, were limited by straitened finances where every expense had to be justified. It is no wonder that *Every Lady Her Own Flower Gardener*, aimed specifically at the 'economical and industrious', and those who 'have gardens but cannot afford a gardener', should find a ready market among those in similar circumstances to its author.

Published in *c.* 1839[7], Johnson's was the first book to cross the dividing line between the romantic, the academic and the practical. Advertised as being written for the lady with 'a passion for flowers' but with no education in 'the deluge of Latin terms', it catered for those who required to 'know the hardiest flowers, and to comprehend the general business of the garden, undisturbed by fear of failure, at the most economical scale of expense'. That the lady concerned would be doing a considerable amount of the gardening work herself is also indicated in the subtitle of the book: 'for the industrious and economic only'. Equipped with the necessary protection of a stout Holland apron with ample pockets, and a pair of India rubber boots, the single female was recommended to venture forth to indulge her passion for flowers at all seasons; stopping only for rain or snow. Louisa does, however, appear to baulk at some of the physical tasks even within the 'small compass' that she envisages for her lady gardener. Some may be regarded as too menial (weeding the gravel path), or too arduous (planting of ornamental shrubs), or too heavy (rolling the lawns). For such tasks she suggests that even the economically challenged might procure the temporary services of 'an old man, a woman, or a stout boy' for little expense. The labourer or 'stout active girl' appear again when pruning of the larger ornamental shrubs is discussed, while even a child will do to weed the gravel paths. A clear division is made between the 'lady' who may be unequal to the physical fatigue of planting, or even in some instances bending, and the 'old woman' or 'stout girl' who can be cheerfully (and cheaply) employed to do those same tasks. Although some allowance might be being made for age, the insidious effect of the corset may also be blamed for the difficulties that the female gardener encountered. Restrictive clothing worn especially by middle- and upper-class women made even the lightest physical task exhausting by constricting the breathing. Bending down might also be hampered by corsetry, although Miss Johnson recommends the raised flower bed for those who find themselves and their visitors unequal to bending.

While Miss Johnson may have been aware of the possible physical limitations of her readers, she nevertheless expected them to aspire to a certain amount of labour. She may not, it is true, describe the use of the spade in the detail that Jane Loudon was to do, but Louisa Johnson still recommends that a spade is purchased. Her list of essential garden tools differs little from that of Jane Loudon's, except perhaps in being limited by economy. A light spade, two rakes, a light garden fork, a watering pot, hoe, trowels, shears, a pruning knife and a 'stout deep basket' for weeds, are listed as the only essentials. An 'avroncater',[8] apparently then very fashionable for heavy branches of larger shrubbery plants, is admired but dismissed as too expensive. As Louisa wisely points out, a great deal more tools may be seen decorating the walls of some amateur's tool sheds, but they appear to have been purchased more for display than use. To add to the tools in the shed one might contemplate the purchase of a jobbing gardener to assist with the heavier tasks on a more regular basis if economy allowed. If this was to be the case Miss Johnson added the recommendation: 'if she has any regard to her own comfort [a lady should] obtain a man who does not know too much . . . for it is unpleasant to be subject to the invisible sneers of a man who considers you wrong'.[9] The sneers of the opposite sex were something that female authors commented on with frequency. Elizabeth von Arnim recorded that her instructions on planting were either ignored or derided by increasingly recalcitrant gardeners, until the memorable day when one 'dejected gardener' went mad. Armed with a spade in one hand and a revolver in the other he proceeded to berate Elizabeth when she mildly requested him to tie up a fallen creeper, 'after which there was nothing for it but to get him into an asylum as expeditiously as possible'.[10] In 1940 Gladys Rawson was still catering for 'the woman who is at the mercy of the jobbing gardener' and who needs to have sufficient knowledge 'to arm her in verbal battles with the gardener'.[11]

The success that greeted *Every Lady Her Own Flower Gardener* encouraged Louisa Johnson (and her publishers) to bring out *Every Lady's Guide to Her Own Greenhouse* a few years later, having already appended a small section on glasshouses and window boxes to the 1851 edition of her earlier work. Repeal of the brick and glass taxes had put ownership of a small glasshouse within many people's reach, and with it came a further opportunity for the woman of the house to practise her skills in nurturing. A small step for some from the children's nursery to the plant nursery, but one that Miss Johnson had not had the opportunity to take. Whether it was her very slightly melancholic outlook or her overt stress on economy and industry (who after all wished to be counted among the 'disappointed' or poor in life?), Louisa Johnson's book was unfortunately to be ousted from the bestsellers in just a few years. Despite several editions, the small pocket-sized work was to be replaced on everyone's bookshelves by the comprehensive and enthusiastic *Instructions in Gardening for Ladies*.

The indefatigable, if occasionally overshadowed, Jane Loudon (1807–58) burst into ladies' gardening in 1840 and continued to dominate until her death almost twenty years later. Turning away from the theme of disappointments and trials, her upbeat go-for-it attitude is apparent from the first page. Although she modestly demures to the academic training of so many male authors, she argues firmly for the necessity for a book such as hers, a book that will quite literally make understandable the processes of gardening to those who wish to garden. Her advice was practical, her approach persuasive. Not only did she tell you that you would need a spade, but where you might buy it, and how to use it (in detail!). Her market was the new middle-class woman faced with more garden and free time than money and gardeners. Unlike Louisa Johnson who had predicted that 'in large towns, under the coal, smoke, shade and gloom' a gardener's lot would be disappointment, Loudon embraced the suburban gardener. She was, after all, one herself.

The success of her approach may be judged by the astonishing sales of her work. On the first day alone, 1,350 copies of *Instructions in Gardening for Ladies* were sold and within the first year it went into three editions (some editions adding the word *Practical* to the title). An American edition was printed in 1843 sparking a movement for 'gardenesque'-style gardens there. New books of instruction followed aimed variously at ladies with flower gardens, ladies with greenhouses, ladies with children, ladies recently moved to the country, newly married ladies, ladies interested in botany – in short every type of lady with even a passing interest in plants. Jane Loudon's output was to be almost as prolific as that of her husband. However, whereas his was based on a combination of a lifetime's horticultural training and a natural propensity towards prolixity, hers was based on an ability to write clear, appealing text and a level of knowledge suited to her readers. Her approach was neither too romantic nor too scientific. Whether she was explaining the 'Chinese layering system', the creation of a moss house, or the recurvature of the calyx in a *Fuchsia globosa*, Jane Loudon could keep you reading. It comes as no surprise to discover that before meeting her horticultural husband, she had been a novelist.

Born into a middle-class family in 1807, Jane Loudon (née Webb) was an only child, whose mother died when she was 12. Her father, an engineer from Birmingham, turned to his daughter for consolation and companionship, accompanying her on a year's travel on the Continent. Rather unusually, he indulged his daughter's creative nature to the extent of encouraging (and presumably funding) her in her desire to publish a volume of verse and prose. Unfortunately Mr Webb himself died when Jane was 17, and an examination of his affairs at death revealed that Jane would have to find some method of supporting herself. At the beginning of the nineteenth century there was little that a lone, single female could decently do as a career. Eschewing the more usual options of governess, lady's companion, milliner, or an early marriage, Jane Webb decided she would continue to pursue her writing career. Her first work was a continuation of her prose and verse pieces under the rather uninspiring, although accurate, title of *Prose and Verse*. There is nothing unusual about the work, except perhaps for the fact of its publication, and little to indicate that the author was to follow it with something quite different.[12]

In 1827 Jane published her second work, *The Mummy! A Tale of the Twenty-Second Century*.[13] A complete break from her previous publication, and serving as a testament to a rather unusual and vivid imagination, *The Mummy* was a cross between a science fiction novel and a Victorian melodrama. Set in the year 2126 it contained (in common with many of the futuristic novels of H.G. Wells) many surprisingly prophetic features of a practical nature. Jane's futuristic world, detailed in three volumes, included such features as air conditioning in houses, coffee machines, mass-produced clothing, milking machines and, perhaps more importantly for one of her readers, steam mowers and well planned public parks and cemeteries. Against this backdrop of a utopian society lies a moralistic tale of the search for the secret of the afterlife, and the conclusion that despite cheap travel and universal education, enquiring into matters beyond our own sphere only makes us wretched. Contentment, it concludes, is to be had by making ourselves useful to our fellow creatures. Whether it was the rather gothic romantic interludes, the strong moralistic tone, or the imaginative scientific utopia of the tale, the book became a minor success and drew attention from reviewers in a range of publications. One of these was John Claudius Loudon, editor and founder of the *Gardener's Magazine*. A glowing review in the magazine (rather surprisingly under the heading 'Hints for Improvements') was followed by a request to meet the author, a meeting that must have been rather a surprise for John Loudon, who had no idea the author w... meeting, in February 1830, went well and as with all good ... century romances they were married within the year.

Before their marriage Jane had just had time to write two m... books. *Stories of a Bride* in 1829, and *Conversations on Chronology* in 1830. After this premarital flurry, production stopped until 1839 when she took up her pen again to write *Agnes, or the Little Girl who could keep a Promise*. For most middle-class women in this period, marriage would have meant the end of any opportunity (or necessity) for work beyond the domestic confines. However, the Loudon household was not a normal household. John Loudon was a workaholic, a man driven with the desire to educate and improve in all forms of horticulture. John Loudon's writings were not only prolific but also founded on extensive personal experience, experimentation and knowledge. Just a short dip into one of his many publications can leave one reeling with facts, figures, opinions and instruction as breathtaking in its detail as it is dense in its prose. For the rest of their married life Jane was to combine the duties of wife, secretary, amenuensis, travelling companion, nurse and author. Perhaps fortunately the duties of motherhood were confined to their one child, Agnes.

Difficult though it must have been not to feel overwhelmed and overshadowed by such a husband,[14] Jane commenced to find a contributive rather than merely supporting role in the constant output of works from their family home and offices. Until her meeting with John, her experience of botany and gardening had been confined to the usual lessons that might be expected to be taken by a female of her class, combined with walks within the gardens of her father's home at Kitwell. Writing as an adult, Jane remarked that 'As I child I could never learn Botany. There was something in the Linnaean system that was excessively repugnant to me; I never could remember the different classes and orders, and after several attempts the study was given up as one too difficult for me to master.'[15] The opportunity for personal study under her new husband must, however, have added some new appeal or understanding with regard to Linnaeus, for Jane records that soon she was involved both in the study and the practical joys of gardening. An opportunity to attend a series of lectures at the Horticultural Society, specifically targeted at 'ladies', was taken up with enthusiasm, and the lessons of Mr Lindley added to those of Mr Loudon.

For someone surrounded by the written word Jane might have turned to a manual of instruction to supplement her new learning. However, as

...e was to note in her own work, none was then available for someone who started from a basis of ignorance. *Instructions in Gardening for Ladies*, published in 1840 (ten years after her marriage), was a breakthrough in gardening for women. Jane instructed her lady readers on the actual physical accomplishment of gardening. Digging, weeding, planting, budding, pruning, manuring, potting and basketwork were all considered as activities within the reach of the suburban woman at whom Jane's book was aimed. Each month in her gardening calender was filled with intense physical activity. Even December, which starts with the restful statement that 'This month is a perfect blank both for the flower and fruit garden', goes on, 'except for collecting soils, making composts, preparing labels . . . and for pruning the larger and more hardy deciduous trees and shrubs'.[16] Not quite the perfect blank the exhausted housewife might have looked forward to.

In one of the most quoted passages of her considerable output Jane establishes unequivocally the active role that her lady readers should play in their garden. Commencing with an acknowledgement of the 'small and delicately formed hands and feet of a woman' which she admits may at first sight seem 'peculiarly unfitted' for the laborious employment of digging, she goes on to explain in careful detail how the operation and labour of digging may be simplified and rendered sufficiently easy for a woman to accomplish. To the modern reader the detail may seem almost farcical, including as it does guidelines as to which end of the spade to insert into the earth, the angle of insertion and the 'throwing forward of the body' as an aid to lifting the soil. However anyone who has ever watched a novice spade-wielder at work can empathise with Jane in her desire to leave no detail out.[17] That she concludes the section with an admonition and instruction on cleaning and storing the spade is further indication that little other assistance is envisaged in the gardens of her readers. There is a very interesting contrast between Jane Loudon, brought up surrounded by the written word, and Gertrude Jekyll who was physically creative from an early age. When considering the importance of digging Jekyll informed her readers that 'It is no use asking me or anyone else how to dig . . . better to go and watch a man digging and then take a spade and try to do it.'[18]

Instructions in Gardening for Ladies did not exist merely to instruct those for whom financial considerations had led them into the garden. Within its 400 pages were to be found in turn, exhortations, enticements and cajolery to turn away from the life of indolence to one of physical activities. Gardening was not to be a necessity but an enjoyment. Thus instructions for digging included not only the realisation that the novice digger may have 'comparatively feeble power', but held out the promise that by doing 'all the digging that can be required in a small garden, [the reader] will not only have the satisfaction of seeing the garden created . . . but she will find her health and spirits wonderfully improved by the exercise, and by the reviving smell of the fresh earth'.[19] Nervous debilities, migraines, melancholy and hysteria were almost endemic among middle- and upper-class women in the eighteenth and nineteenth centuries. Jane Loudon's assurance of revived spirits and renewed strength must have held out a lifeline to many women literally wilting under the tedium of a restricted domestic role.

As a status accoutrement to her husband, many a newly married woman found her situation little changed from her life under parental control. Domestic servants brought a certain status and relief from domestic chores, perhaps analogous to the acquisition of the dishwasher and washing machine of the later twentieth century. However, the leisure options for the Victorian middle-class woman were considerably more restricted than her modern counterparts. Relief from domestic drudgery all too often brought with it an enforced idleness injurious to physical and mental health. As Elizabeth von Arnim exclaimed after a secretive session of digging and raking, 'It is not graceful, and it makes one hot; but it is a blessed sort of work.'[20] Louisa Johnson had hinted obliquely that one of the main practical difficulties that beset the female gardener was her undergarments. From the stays of the seventeenth century, to the corset, crinolines and suspenders of the nineteenth, women had been squeezed, pulled and tied into undergarments that restricted and rearranged the reality of their physical shapes. Although some of these garments made allowances for the necessities of life, for example corsets for pregnancy or easy loosening fasteners to facilitate eating, few allowed the wearer the ease of movement or breathing essential for physical activity.[21] The 'ideal' figure could only be maintained by a woman of sedentary lifestyle. A woman wearing full skirts and a tight waist would thus be seen as an outward indication of a household with a sufficiency of staff; a sufficiency that reflected on the status of the male householder. Status was in the eye of the beholder and the waist of the wife.

With her usual practical approach to overcoming such difficulties, Jane Loudon opened her seminal work with a frontispiece illustrating the appropriate clothing for the lady gardener and her young child.[22] Risibly impractical to the modern eye it is difficult to conceive of the relaxed informality of this dress for the period. An ankle-length dress, with two small rows of frills, forms the basis of this outfit, with no visible sign of padding, petticoat hooping or extreme tightening. Over this is an apron with two very practical pockets (one of which has a pair of scissors poking out) while the sleeves are gathered up to the elbows. In her text Jane also recommends a pair of gauntlets to protect one's hands and to cover the lower arms (presumably also protecting the sleeves of any garment). A pair of clogs or overshoes suitable for walking on uneven and dirty ground complete the outfit, although notably both Louisa Johnson and Jane Loudon recommend that one should not work in wet or muddy weather as this would be injurious to health. Unsurprisingly, the last two rather unattractive items (gauntlets and clogs) are not shown on the frontispiece model. It is after all best to break one's readers in gently.

The tools that litter the background of this happy mother and daughter illustration might have come as somewhat more of a shock for the casual browser. A hoe, rake and watering can indicate a preparedness for the usual range of tasks that might be recommended as suitable for the female gardener. The spade, however, hints at an unusual level of physical activity for a woman above the lowest classes, while the wheelbarrow would normally be seen as beyond the ken of any lady. In the 1890s in reply to her rival Cecily Cardew's admission that she called a spade a spade, Gwendolen Fairfax was still able to state convincingly, 'I am glad to say that I have never seen a spade. It is obvious that our social spheres have been widely different'.[23] Perhaps she might have benefited from an edition of Jane Loudon. A comment in the foreword to a later book by Jane Loudon (*The Lady's Country Companion*) replies to what Jane describes as 'numerous' applications for information as to where to purchase these tools, suggesting that women such as Gwendolen were to become a minority.

The initial impetus for Jane's own horticultural career had been the financial disaster of John Loudon's massive *Arboretum et Fruticetum Britannicum*. This extremely thorough and heavily illustrated work had left the family over £10,000 in debt. It was no coincidence that *Instructions in Gardening for Ladies* came out within eighteen months of the expensive, if acclaimed, tome. Once into her stride, however, there was no stopping Jane, and books and magazines appeared under her name as regularly as those of her husband. Unfortunately, however hard she worked and however successful her publications, she was never to be free of the accumulated debts. In the three years between her first publication and John's death (from overwork) in 1843, she published at least five further books as well as editing *The Ladies' Magazine of Gardening*, an unfortunately short-lived venture. These books largely addressed areas of special interest, such as *The Ladies Flower-Garden of Ornamental Bulbous Plants* (1841), or *The Ladies Flower-Garden of Ornamental Annuals* (1840), but she also found time to tackle the rather more general topic of *Botany for Ladies* (1842). Up until the publication of her own *Botany for Ladies* she had been recommending John Lindley's *Ladies' Botany*, but one presumes that she had decided to branch out on her own behalf. *Instructions* was also edited for the American market and Jane 'went global' in 1843. Children's books were also her domain and two works for young people were written at this time.

The years between her husband's death in 1843 and her own in 1858 were not easy for Jane, as she struggled to support herself and her daughter in scenes considerably less idyllic than that shown on the frontispiece of *Gardening for Ladies*. John Loudon's creditors seem to have made an appearance even at his death scene, and despite a continual outpouring on all things horticultural and female, Jane was doomed to hardship and debt. Agnes appears to have been rather spoilt and was not the support her mother might have wished, although she too was later to launch into print. *The Lady's Country Companion*, written by Jane in 1845, was addressed to a (largely) imaginary lady who had recently moved to the country and needed instruction on just about everything. It drew on Jane's extensive experience of keeping house firstly for her father, then her husband, and then by herself. Covering everything from setting a fire to keeping a pet squirrel, brewing beer to making clothes for the poor, it adds rather surprisingly that 'the management of sheep . . . certainly do not come within a lady's province'.[24] It may be just as well that Jane did not proffer much advice on the subject of sheep, as the one piece of information she does impart, that they are 'subject to nearly the same diseases as rabbits', appears alarmingly erroneous. Advice is even given on going for country walks and admiring clouds, subjects which, one imagines, even the most hardened of urban refugees could have managed unaided had she had the time after accomplishing all the other various duties.

Life was not kind enough to Jane to allow her much time to admire clouds, and despite the continued good sales of many of her publications the gloom started to gather. Publishers became less interested, her own magazine ceased production, and her editorship of *The Ladies Companion at Home and Abroad* (a weekly magazine) was ignominiously given to a man by the publishers.[25] Her indomitable spirit and belief in self and womanhood are encompassed in the last words she wrote as editor of that same publication. In a piece composed under the most difficult of personal circumstances – widowed, single parent, poor and newly unemployed – Jane wrote: 'Real and vital happiness depends only on ourselves. If once the mind can grasp this truth, and with firmness and courage resolve to draw happiness from sources whence alone it springs, no storms from without will permanently shake us, no fears depress, no trials overcome us.'[26] If any woman had triumphed over the disappointments and trials of life, it was Jane Loudon.

Following Jane Loudon's tidal wave of books there was, not surprisingly, a pause in the publication of works by women. Some on related subjects came out, such as Miss Maling's *The Indoor Gardener* (1860) and Annie Hassard's book on *Floral Decorations for the Dwelling House* (1875), but nothing approaching the comprehensiveness, or indeed enthusiasm, of Jane. Other (male) authors began to include reference to the fairer sex or the lady of the house in their introductions; although more often than not condemning them to the fernery or the superintendence of the flower beds. Gardens controlled by women were still being featured in gardening magazines, proving them to be active and successful gardeners, but these women appeared to be too busy in the garden to put pen to paper. Frances Hope was one exception to this rule. Up early and at work late in her garden at Wardie Lodge, near Edinburgh, she was remembered by a close friend as 'working as hard as men and doing everything much better than they'.[27] Her hard work may explain why her rather coyly named *Notes and Thoughts on Gardens and Woodlands* (1881) was not published until the year after her death, although still beating by eighteen years the similarly named *Wood and Garden* by Gertrude Jekyll. Hers is a conversational book of advice on plants and planting styles from a practical gardener. Jane Loudon would have appreciated the description of Mrs Hope as gardening with 'lilac sun bonnet . . . short skirts, soiled gauntlets and heavy shoes'.

'I am not going to write a gardening book, or a cookery book, or a book on furnishing or education'; so commenced Mrs Theresa Earle's

Pot-Pourri from a Surrey Garden (1897). An appropriately named mixture of advice, admonition, instruction and encouragement, the book in fact covered all of the areas denied by the above statement, as well as several more. Having much in common with Jane Loudon's *The Lady's Country Companion*, Mrs Earle's tone was personal, direct, resolutely cheerful, and destined to be very very popular. This first mix of advice was followed rapidly by *More Pot-Pourri from a Surrey Garden* (1899), *A Third Pot-Pourri* (1903), *Pot-Pourri Mixed by Two* (1914), and in a startling and inexplicable departure from the established pattern, *Gardening for the Ignorant* (1912). Largely neglected in the present day,[28] Theresa Earle (1836–1925) became a household name in the 1890s, with the first *Pot-Pourri* going into twenty-eight editions and translated into several languages. The success was as much a surprise to Mrs Earle as to her publishers, and it was initially rumoured by critics that it was due almost entirely to the social standing of the authoress. Mrs Earle did indeed have a wide circle of friends and acquaintances ranging from Oscar Wilde and George Eliot, to her niece Lady Constance Lytton (who wrote an appendix to the first *Pot-Pourri*). However, even the widest circle could not account for the overwhelming sales and the sacks full of complimentary letters.

As Mrs Earle was the first to admit, there were detractors of her rather individual style. Suggestions were apparently made by some of her most earnest 'fans' that she 'rest on her laurels and write no more', and in a subsequent *Pot-Pourri* she cheerfully noted that some of her earlier recipes had caused 'panic in some minds and indignation in others'. It was this irreverent style of writing that undoubtedly helped to make the books such a success. Indeed, it would otherwise be difficult to see quite why a book written as 'desultory notes . . . on paper'[29] should have been quite so popular. At the commencement of her writing career Theresa Earle stated that 'I am merely, like so many other women of the past and present, a patient gleaner in the fields of knowledge, and absolutely dependent on human sympathy in order to do anything at all.' Sentiments which, although in keeping with the traditional attitudes of many Victorian women, underestimate Mrs Earle's own experience. Born into an aristocratic family (her mother was the ninth child of Baron Ravensworth, her father great-grandson of the 2nd Earl of Jersey) she spent much of her childhood living on the country estates of wealthy relatives. Despite the early death of her father, funds were sufficiently ample to allow the family to travel on the Continent and play an active social role. Theresa was presented at court and even offered the position of Maid of Honour to

Queen Victoria. She had an active social life and finally, at the relatively advanced age of 27, married Captain Charles William Earle.

Theresa's first steps into authorship had come a year before her marriage in 1863, when she was pressurised by an adoring curate (as she claimed) to write two articles on the occasion of the marriage of the Prince of Wales. The articles appeared in the parish magazine for Watford. Not perhaps a publication with a large circulation and probably even less actual readership, but a forerunner of what was to come. Reading excerpts from these articles one is struck by the confidence of style with which they were written. They abound in references to taste, appropriate decoration and reflections on the fashions of the day.[30] She signed neither of these articles and it is probable that Charles was unaware of them, or of her subsequent ideas on publishing a book on art for amateurs. Thirty-four years later when the first *Pot-Pourri* was ready to hit the bookseller lists, a horrified Charles is said to have offered her 100 pounds if she would agree not to publish. Somewhat ironically when the publication did go ahead, it was under the initials of her husband as 'Mrs C.W. Earle'.

With such little experience of authorship it might seem surprising that a well-provided-for woman should decide to embark on writing. However, both the book's appearance and its content become easier to understand if one remembers again the importance of letter writing among female friends and relatives of the period. By the age of 61, Theresa Earle had a lifetime's experience of letter writing to build on, and in publishing her book was drawing together those thoughts and advice which she had been dispensing so freely over the previous decades. She appears to have been known within her social and family circle as a provider of continual advice and wisdom covering the very subjects she was to draw on for *Pot-Pourri*. It was in fact while giving advice on the subjects of gardening and furnishings to a 'foreign friend' (one Madame de Grunelius) that the idea of writing a book first came to Theresa. With the encouragement of her niece Lady Constance Lytton, whom she was nursing at the period, she set about recording her predominantly practical and sensible advice. As a relatively well-travelled, well-read and progressive woman (by Victorian standards), her counsel and opinions were to be greeted as manna from heaven by those with less experience and confidence. One of her main topics was to be gardening, a topic abundantly suited to the arrangement of the chapters by months of the year; but exactly what was that experience with reference to gardens and gardening?

Despite the best efforts of the immensely practical Jane Loudon or the more ladylike Louisa Johnson, the genteel or aristocratic lady was not usually to be found with spade in hand and it is doubtful that Jane Loudon's detailed advice on how to wield a spade had ever formed essential reading in Mrs Earle's youth. Indeed, it is fascinating to note that the books on gardening recommended on the very first page of *Pot-Pourri* are all by male writers on the subject. They include William Robinson's *The English Flower Garden* and his translated version of the French *The Vegetable Garden*, with Johnson's *Gardener's Dictionary* supplying the deficiencies of the first two (as she said) and providing information on cultivation under glass.[31] The reader is also encouraged to refer to the weekly gardening magazines and to always look up plants in a suitable garden dictionary, widely available at the time. However, the information to be gleaned from these works is not always (or indeed primarily) expected to be physically carried out by the lady reader, but instead passed on to their gardeners. As *Pot-Pourri* reasonably points out, 'Nothing is more unjust than the way a great many people find fault with their gardeners' as 'How can a man who has little education and no experience be expected to know about plants that come from all parts of the world.' It is therefore the role of the well-read woman to come to the aid of her gardener by providing him with information and instruction. Notably Theresa's tone changes during the long period of authorship, and by 1912 (by which time she was 76) she appears, perversely, to be undertaking considerably more physical work herself.

The gardens that Theresa was in charge of she describes as comprising 'a small piece of flat ground surrounding an ordinary suburban house'. However, any visions that one may have on reading this of a small narrow garden of, say, 100ft long by 30ft wide are instantly banished by the information that 'Kitchen garden, flower-garden, house and drive can scarcely cover more than two acres'. This 'ordinary suburban house' is also located some 16 miles from London, which in the 1890s must have been stretching the concept of suburban to beyond its limits. This garden was only seen in the warmer seasons as for much of Theresa's writing career the Earles lived for five or six months of the year in London, where Theresa maintained indoor planting with pots and flowers often sent up from the suburbs. A detailed description of these indoor pot plants takes up some six pages of the 1897 edition of *Pot-Pourri* and gives the impression of a room filled to overflowing with a collection of exotics and evergreens, necessitating a machete to negotiate one's way to the piano. However limited her hands-on role might have been, Theresa Earle's joy in the garden is obviously genuine and heartfelt. Taking a few days out from the London season to visit the suburban home she writes: 'I came from London to pass two or three days in the country and look after my garden as usual. How delightful it is to be out of London again! There is always plenty to do and enjoy. How the birds sing as if it were spring!.'[32] Most, if not all, of the doing is in the nature of 'overseeing' and 'giving instructions' to the gardener, although a discussion of raising seed and bulbs betrays some experience of the practical. March sees a recommendation to plant asparagus by digging three spits deep and adding such delights as the 'emptying of cesspools, butchers offal and dead animals'; an entry not for the squeamish and a topic not usually thought suitable for the average upper-class woman. But although she might have been typical in circumstance, Theresa Earle was definitely not average in character.

In terms of gardening style, Mrs Earle recommended the new 'natural' or 'wild' gardening as advocated by William Robinson. She describes the early Victorian tastes for baskets, vases, rustic summer-houses and laurel beds as 'execrable' while the 'planting and laying out of grounds are equally bad'. This bias probably explains the lack of recommendation of Jane Loudon or Louisa Johnson, as both writers pre-dated this wilder style. Both Loudon and Johnson were present on Mrs Earle's bookshelves, however, alongside almost every famous writer from the seventeenth century onwards. These bookshelves contained a collection of garden books that might easily form the basis for a modern day distinguished gardening society or antiquarian library. Arranged chronologically, they commenced with the 1614 *Hortus Floridus*, continued through 'both the Parkinson's' (1629 and 1640), and included an original copy of Gerard's *Herball* (1633 Johnson edition). They carried on (chronologically) with most of the major works on gardening and botany published in the eighteenth century, including a staggering sixty-seven volumes of *Curtis's Botanical Magazine*. Her collection of nineteenth-century books continued in the same vein, including the entire seventeen volumes of Mr Loudon's *Gardener's Magazine*. That Theresa Earle herself knowledgeably burst into print becomes less of a surprise with such material at her fingertips.

To the modern mind the most extraordinary aspect of Theresa Earle's books is not that they were written in the first place, or that despite their repetitive titles they were a success, but the sheer range of topics covered. 'Gardening as employment for women' is gaily followed by 'A list of flowering creepers'; 'tips on cleaning hands and fingers after weeding' snuggles up close to 'the decline of vegetable culture in the Middle Ages'. 'The abuse of athletics' (!?) was considered to come within the same scope of interest as 'uses for rainwater', 'what young girls should read' and 'other people's gardening difficulties' (the last a perennial favourite with gardeners). Hidden within the pages are hints on the use of 'tomatoes as an aperient for the liver', a discussion on whether sundials may be regarded as 'affected' in a suburban garden, and the rather disarming declaration (in regard to poultry keeping) that 'nothing one does at home ever pays and so there is no point in keeping [financial] accounts of it'.[33] Nothing and no one remained unconsidered. Section headings read like a journey through the matters and concerns of Victorian family life, as in many ways they were. The reader is securely taken both by the hand and in hand, and led by an experienced friend through the difficulties and pleasures of family life. By the time of her death, in 1925, Theresa Earle had come to be regarded as a recognised expert on horticultural matters by no less an authority than the Director of Wisley Gardens. But for her numerous friends, family and readers she was so much more.

The year 1899 saw the arrival in print of that greatest of experts on gardens and horticulture, Gertrude Jekyll (1869–1944). Illustrated with her own photographs and written in her accessible and friendly, yet authoritative manner, *Wood and Garden* was to be the first of many publications bringing the distinctive Jekyll style to gardens and bookshelves across the English-speaking world. Concentrating almost exclusively on the garden (with the exception of *Flower Decoration in the House*, and two books on local architecture and customs), Jekyll communicated to her audience both the sheer exhilaration of the act of garden creation and the technical knowledge required for success. No one reading the sentence 'Weeding is a delightful occupation, especially after summer rain'[34] can feel in doubt of the fact, but if they did the explanation of the effect of a light rain on the soil and an account of the varieties of different root forms to be encountered would persuade them of the technical reasons for that delight. Her genius lay not just in her writing but also in her designing and planting, and it was her 'professional' career in garden design that set her apart from all of the other women writers of this period. Although Maria Jacson had possibly carried out a few design commissions ninety years earlier, hers had not been a career founded on design, and none of the other women who had chosen to write of horticulture had ventured to practise beyond their own garden walls. No wonder then that Jekyll was to dominate the first part of the twentieth century with a dedicated following that still survives today.[35]

Elizabeth von Arnim (1866–1941) was another woman who gathered a dedicated following, although in her case perhaps out of all proportion to her actual gardening worth. Married rather unexpectedly to a German Count she found social life in upper-class Berlin (and her husband) stultifyingly dull. An outing to one of the Count's many country estates fixed the idea in her mind of living in this derelict Pomeranian *schloss* surrounded by the joys of its rambling gardens. Elizabeth appears to have had almost no experience of gardening before her arrival here in the idyllic month of April 1896 and, indeed, no training or real experience afterwards. Despite this, her book *Elizabeth and Her German Garden* (1898), in which she recorded her delight in the gardens and their gradual transformation, was a runaway success. Redolent more of Frances Hodgson Burnett's *The Secret Garden*[36] than any horticultural work, *Elizabeth and Her German Garden* was described by wildlife gardener Dame Miriam Rothschild as being about 'love and affection, spring and picnics on frosty afternoons, and the leisure we have forgotten ever existed'.[37] It is the garden that shines forth as the leitmotif of the book. 'I love my garden' is the first sentence that greets the reader, and 'the happy flowers I so much love', the last. Between these two exclamations, Elizabeth chronicles the frustrations of the novice gardener, the social constrictions that prevented any type of physical work, the plants that finally managed to flower, and the (male) gardener who went insane. Unsurprisingly, reviewers were mixed in their appreciation, with one suggesting that 'even the amateur gardener will be disappointed'. *The Times* appreciated it for what it was, a book whose charm lay 'not in its horticultural record, but in its personal atmosphere, its individuality of sentiment, and its healthy sympathy with nature and outdoor life'.[38] Her garden itself also had a mixed reception. E.M. Forster, who stayed there in 1904 to tutor Elizabeth von Arnim's children, complained that he 'could not find it', but could only see paddocks and shrubberies, lilacs, roses and meadows.[39] Hugh Walpole, a tutor in 1907, found its beauty in its wild uncouth nature, 'a garden of trees rather than flowers'.

Elizabeth von Arnim was eventually to become a popular author of all kinds of light-hearted family and travel-related books. Her marriage to the 'man of wrath', as she called him, unsurprisingly failed and she fled Germany to England, Europe and America, writing for her income.

This fifteenth-century illustration for Pietro de Crescenzi's manuscript on garden and estate management shows a woman tending a carefully shaped plant, while others gossip in the background. De Crescenzi himself is seen, right, pointing out tasks to the landowner. *(British Library, London, UK/The Bridgeman Art Library)*

Noblewomen used gardens both for privacy and for assignations with their courtly lovers. The turf seat shown in this fifteenth-century illustration for De Crescenzi's manuscript is typical of the period. *(Musée Condé, Chantilly, France/Lauros/Giraudon/The Bridgeman Art Library)*

Above left: This chair cushion, which survives at Loseley Park, Surrey, was embroidered by Elizabeth I and shows her skills with floral work. *(Loseley Park, Guildford, Surrey, UK/Mark Fiennes/The Bridgeman Art Library).* ***Above right:*** *An Unknown Lady in Fancy Dress*, by Marcus Gheeraerts the Younger (*c.* 1561–1635), depicts a woman wearing a heavily embroidered costume containing many flower motifs. She is dressed as the 'Persian Virgin' of myth. *(Hampton Court Palace, Middlesex, UK/The Bridgeman Art Library)*

Below left: Portrait of a lady thought to be Elizabeth, Duchess of Beaufort, *c.* 1715, one of the most famous female collectors of 'exotics' which she nurtured in her hothouses at Badminton. *(Private Collection/© Philip Mould, Historical Portraits Ltd, London, UK/The Bridgeman Art Library).* ***Below right:*** Lady Eleanor Butler and Miss Sarah Ponsonby (the Ladies of Llangollen) walking their dog. In the background is their Gothic arch and font. *(Mary Evans Picture Library)*

Above left: *Nepenthes northiana* (pitcher plant), painted by Marianne North in Sarawak, Borneo, and named after her. *(Reproduced with the kind permission of the Director and the Board of Trustees, Royal Botanic Gardens, Kew)*

Above right: *Amherstia nobilis*, painted by Marianne North and named after Lady Amherst. *(Reproduced with the kind permission of the Director and the Board of Trustees, Royal Botanic Gardens, Kew)*

Right: Mary Delany invented the art of flower 'mosaic' using coloured paper. This example is a cotton-headed thistle (*Carduus eriophorus*), *c.* 1772–82. *(British Museum, London, UK/The Bridgeman Art Library)*

The Goodwood Shell Grotto was decorated by Sarah Lennox, Duchess of Richmond, and her daughters with shells sent by Naval officers serving abroad. *(Tim Imrie/Country Life Picture Library, 1997)*

Lady in a Conservatory, by Jane Maria Bowkett (1839–91), is one of many Victorian paintings which depict women within the confines of the glasshouse. *(Roy Miles Fine Paintings/The Bridgeman Art Library)*

Above: *A London Garden in August*, depicting Mrs Spooner tending her plants, appeared in *Gardens of England* (1908) by E.T. Cook with paintings by Beatrice Parsons. Mrs Spooner herself was also an accomplished artist. *(Reproduced with the kind permission of the Geffrye Museum, London).* ***Below left:*** Frontispiece from *Every Lady Her Own Flower Gardener*, by Louisa Johnson. Aimed at the industrious and economical lady gardener and originally published in 1839/40, this popular book went through many editions. ***Below right:*** The *Children's Book of Gardening*, by Mrs Sidgwick and Mrs Paynter, contains illustrations by Mrs Cayley-Robinson showing girls carrying out various garden tasks.

Pruning Class, c. 1910, Studley Castle Horticultural College. The college was founded by Daisy, Countess of Warwick, who was concerned at the plight of the 'one million women' who were prevented from obtaining careers. *(Reproduced with kind permission of the Museum of Garden History)*

The Right Kind of Women Gardeners at the Glynde School for Lady Gardeners. *(From* In a College Garden, *by Viscountess Frances Wolseley, John Murray, 1916)*

Beatrix Havergal, principal of Waterperry, tending grape vines. This portrait was taken by Cecil Beaton in 1943 when he visited the school on behalf of the government to document the war effort. *(Reproduced with kind permission of the Imperial War Museum. Crown Copyright)*

With a pressing need for food and a shortage of labour, organised groups of women and girls created allotments on bomb sites, such as this one in London (1942). *(Reproduced with kind permission of the Imperial War Museum. Crown Copyright)*

LADY GARDENERS AND THEIR FUTURE.

By the Hon. Frances Wolseley.

Ernest Smith

THE HON. FRANCES WOLSELEY, DAUGHTER OF LORD WOLSELEY, MOWING THE LAWN OF HER GARDEN

By the early twentieth century women were being specifically targeted in advertisements for lawnmowers. This picture of Viscountess Frances Wolseley, founder of the Glynde School for Lady Gardeners, shows the push/pull method of mowing. *(Mary Evans Picture Library)*

Narcissus 'Great Warley', originally bred by Ellen Willmott and still flowering at Warley Place in Essex in 2006. *(©Ailsa Wildig)*

Some of the titles strike us as unbelievably fey, and one wonders who bought such works as *The April Baby's Book of Tunes* (all her children were called by her after the months of their birth). *The Solitary Summer* was, however, also popular with female readers of gardening books, and her travel book *The Adventures of Elizabeth in Rügen* was in the collection of Viscountess Frances Wolseley. The travels in question were inspired by Marianne North's publication of her own travels in 1898. Elizabeth was also a visitor at Munstead Wood, and a photograph taken by Ellen Willmott of her (as an adult) reading in the summer-house appears in Jekyll's *Children and Gardens*. Drawn together as if in a novel, Marianne North, Gertrude Jekyll, Ellen Willmott and Frances Wolseley are all part of Elizabeth's garden story.

Elizabeth and her German Garden was influential as one of the first books in a totally new genre of garden writing. A book that chronicled both the physical and the emotional making of a garden, it shared with the reader the highs and the lows of garden-making, and allowed an insight into other women's struggles both in the garden and in their lives more generally. As more women turned to the garden for their enjoyment and satisfaction so they began to write about their experiences, their successes, their struggles and their failures. Moved to fill moments away from toil with the spade to toil with the pen, some included instruction within their remit, but many just sought to share the joys and the triumphs of a garden they could, at last, often call their own. By the middle of the twentieth century this initial trickle had turned into a torrent as the sharing of 'breaking of nails, back and heart'[40] in the pursuit of the garden became an obsession. Increasingly, women gardeners based in other parts of the English-speaking world also sought to share their gardening experiences, creating a heady mix of styles.

One of the first into print with garden angst was Mrs Leslie Williams, *A Garden in the Suburbs* coming out in 1901. Hardly an inspiring title but certainly less self-effacing than Mabel Osgood Wright's *The Garden of a Commuter's Wife* (1911).[41] Living in Fairfield, Connecticut, Mabel wrote several books based on her garden and her life with her (English) husband, and one can only hope that the title was ironic. Rather more upper class was Lady Ottoline Morrell (1873–1938) who shared her Italianate garden with readers in *Ottoline at Garsington* in 1918. This is one of the rare titles that actually refer to the authors themselves, most preferring to hide behind a garden location or style. *My Garden in the Wilderness* by Kathleen Murray

(1915) and *Gardening in Sunny Lands* by Lady Martineau[42] were two of the many that recorded gardening life for those ex-patriots living in Europe or the far-flung parts of the empire. Kathleen Murray spent much of her life in India and Simla, creating two gardens at Behar. Louise Beebe Wilder lived and gardened in Baltimore at the turn of the century, but inspired women (and men) with the possibilities of rock gardening, publishing eight books including *Adventures in my Garden and Rock Garden* (1924). Whether you lived in the town (*My Town Garden* (1927), Lady Frances Seton) or the country (*Eve's Garden* (1940), Gladys Rawson), were ignorant (*Gardening for the Ignorant* (1912), Theresa Earle), or plain foolish (*Fool's Garden* (1936), Muriel Stuart) there was a book by a woman gardener for you, the woman gardener.

One of the most famous, and certainly one of the most entertaining, of this genre was also one of the last.[43] *We Made a Garden* charts the relationship between Margery Fish (1892–1969), her husband Walter, and their garden East Lambrook, in Somerset. Written in 1956, after the death of Walter, the work sheds a wry humour on the labours of the diametrically opposed gardening couple: Margery, a lover of the informal, the small and the neglected, and Walter who is described at the outset as embodying the precise and obsessive attributes of the male gardener. Two acres of wilderness, divided originally into two tiny gardens and orchard, had faced Margery when they had decided to move away from London in 1939. Filled with 'old beds, rusty oil stoves, ancient corsets, pots, pans, tins and china, bottles, glass jars', the state of the garden would have intimidated most people but not apparently Walter. Most of these stray items would in fact eventually make their way into the rock garden which Walter suggested would make an attractive feature and which Margery enthusiastically agreed to. That is until she discovered his interests lay not in the alpines that might one day adorn such a garden, but instead in finding a rapid and easy way of disposing of the larger items of rubbish. Once this had been accomplished the rock garden was handed over to Marjory, who spent the next twenty years trying to extract the rubbish that he had hidden.

Much of the joy of the book comes from the disarming charm with which Marjory contrasts her own self-doubt with the strongly held opinions and habits of her husband. 'When it came to the job of making paths . . . this was a subject on which Walter had very strong views', as he did over the level of flower beds in relation to the lawn, the placement of dahlias, the way to water, and the use of dwarf plants in rock gardens

Geranium cinereum 'Lambrook Helen'

Few garden writers have plants named after them, and even fewer have plants named after their gardens. The gardens at East Lambrook, created by Margery Fish with the 'assistance' of her husband Walter, have become famous as a result of her popular books and writings. Now owned by a new family, the gardens have been restored and opened to the public, including a new plant nursery and the National Collection of hardy geraniums. Although the plants in the restored gardens are those that would be familiar to Margery Fish, a newly discovered hardy geranium was discovered in a nearby village in 2005 and named in honour of the gardens. Extremely hardy, the geranium brings its vivid pink flowers to any type of garden. Maintenance free, colourful and adaptable, it would have thrilled Marjory Fish, who undoubtedly would have let it set seed in the remains of Walter's gravel driveway. The geranium is named after a combination of the gardens of Margery Fish and the name of the finder's wife, two women in one plant.

and crevices ('poking belly-crawlers into rat-holes'). His own gardening was militaristic in style. All-day, seven-day-long watering episodes were planned in campaigning detail; while the brilliantly coloured clematis with which Walter covered the walls responded with complete obedience to his 'indicating to each leaf over which wire it should go'. Walter, we are told, would 'no more have left his grass uncut or the edges untrimmed than he would have neglected to shave'. In contrast Marjory documents her own early mistakes, and indeed her later ones, with humour: the rock garden with rocks placed at angles such that the rain washed the new soil and plants away in the first downpour; the ill-fated water garden in the boundary ditch; and the daffodils laboriously planted and then rather more rapidly trampled by the cows let in to graze in the orchard. The death of Walter, heralding the slow disintegration of the gravel drive, left Margery alone in charge of a garden that gradually changed in style. The borders became wilder and the edges softer in 'traditional' cottage style. East Lambrook Manor became famous under her management, attracting visitors to its overflowing borders and orchard. But it is the chronicle of the early days, the struggles and the failures, alongside the successes, which is so fondly remembered. Self-effacement among female garden writers was still alive and well, and being used to humorous effect in the mid-twentieth century.

Having covered the subject of 'how to do the garden' and moved successfully on to 'how I did my garden', the way was free for a history of 'how the garden used to be done'. A gap in the market was spotted, a woman filled it, and in 1896 garden history was born with Alicia Amherst's *A History of Gardening in England*. In 1892 architect and garden designer Reginald Blomfield had produced an overview entitled *The Formal Garden in England*, but his was a specific agenda to promote the modern role of the architect in contemporary garden design and to incite argument against the promoters of the wild garden.[44] Rather than contemporary design it was the history of gardens that intrigued the Hon. Alicia Amherst (1865–1941).[45] Initially commissioned as a series of articles on garden history to be written by a young botanist called Percy Newberry, the work had been abandoned by Newberry for unknown reasons and passed on. Only 24 years of age, Alicia was a well-qualified candidate to take up the baton from the botanist. Intelligent, hard-working, and skilled in reading early botanical and herbal manuscripts, it was almost as if she had been in training. She had the further advantage of access to an exceptionally rich library full of rare herbals and gardening books collected by her father. Not satisfied even with these sources she also undertook research on original manuscripts in Norwich Priory and the archives of Trinity College, Cambridge. *A History of Gardening in England* (1896) includes a wealth of quotes taken direct from authors including John Gerard, Parkinson, Francis Bacon and John Evelyn as well as the then comparatively 'recent' Humphry Repton, Shirley Hibberd and William Robinson.

As an early history of garden design and designers it is exhaustive. Importantly for the future study of the subject it was also garden- rather than architecture- focused. The book presented a surprisingly modern approach to the social and cultural history of garden design that would presage the garden historians of the early twenty-first century. As she clearly reasons in her later book, *Historic Gardens of England* (1938), 'There is much more than meets the eye in English Gardens. Even the most insignificant have their story to tell, for every stage of English history is reflected in them.'[46] Disappointingly, however, Alicia Amherst did not include the stories of medieval herb-wives, Tudor weeding women and eighteenth-century female garden creators in her work; social history had not yet become emancipated. Jane Loudon was the only woman whom Alicia refers to in any detail, and Gertrude Jekyll, whose own first book would not be published for another three years, merited only a footnote to a photographic caption. To Alicia, however, these women were almost contemporaries and as such had no role in a book on the history of the garden.[47] Despite this lack of emphasis on women's role in garden history, Alicia was a staunch supporter of females in practical gardening. In 1900, writing under her married name of Hon. Mrs Evelyn Cecil, she enquired of the Revd William Wilkes, then Secretary of the RHS, as to whether he could recommend to her a lady gardener to take charge of a garden. His reply was that he knew none, as women did not suit the work, nor the work women, an attitude that cannot have endeared him to a woman who knew the likes of Jekyll and Willmott.

Soon Alicia was not alone in the neglected garden of history. In America Rose Standish Nichols produced the excellent *English Pleasure Gardens* in 1902; described by a reviewer at the time as 'like a solid and substantial dowager among the lighter and more frivolous garden-sisterhood'.[48] While in Germany Marie-Luise Gothein (1863–1931) published the comprehensive two-volume *A History of Garden Art* (1913). Lavishly illustrated, this provided an overview not just of English garden history, but also Near Eastern, Classical and European. Art historical, rather than social in its approach, it was thorough and academic. Marie-Luise was born in Prussia and had attended the University of Breslau (now Wroclaw). Having studied art and history of art her interest in garden history was triggered by a move to Karlsruhe, where an eighteenth-century garden and landscape had been created around the palace. She travelled around the libraries, gardens and palaces of Europe while researching her work, and combined her scholastic approach with a personal appreciation of vistas and views. Her two-volume work was published first in German and then translated into English. After the death of her two sons in 1913 and her husband in 1923 she abandoned European gardens for the more exotic plantings of China, Japan and Bali. Learning Sanskrit, she published *Indian Gardens* (1926, in German) and was awarded an honorary Doctorate by the University of Heidelberg shortly before her death.

Back in England Eleanour Sinclair Rohde (1881–1950) produced a series of books on herbs and 'old English gardening books', and edited works by early horticulturalists including William Lawson and Sir Thomas Hanmer. Titles such as *Rose Recipes from Olden Times* reflected her fascination with the gardens and kitchens of the Elizabethan period, and she acknowledged that her own garden favourites were 'Flowers that were commonly grown in Cottage Gardens and have remained almost unchanged through the centuries'.[49] When it came out in 1935 her *Shakespeare's Wild Flowers* was one of the earliest books to use his plays and sonnets as a source of garden lore, although it has been imitated frequently since. A student of medieval and Tudor history and a hands-on gardener, she was equally at home in the British Museum and her parents' garden in Reigate, Surrey. Friends with Gertrude Jekyll, Vita Sackville-West and Maud Messel, she was able to draw on both historical manuscripts and the best of contemporary garden designers.

Despite her Oxford academic background, her most famous books, *Old English Gardens* (1924) and *The Story of the Garden* (1932), achieve a wonderful balance between intellectualism and interest. Poems and anecdotes (of the appropriate periods) are interspersed with description and detail. Reading them over seventy years later one is struck by the freshness that Eleanour breathed into twelfth-century wage accounts or seventeenth-century descriptions of the potato (newly arrived on English shores). When Eleanour enthuses that 'The outstandingly interesting features of [Hughes' *The American Physitian* [*sic*]] are the notes on plants used medicinally by the Indians and the list of English weeds introduced by the settlers',[50] she manages to make the reader feel genuinely interested. Long excerpts from other works, which liberally intersperse her own writing, were obviously chosen by her from an enormously wide range of original garden works, accounts and diaries. They add a variety and interest that is often missing from modern works quoting increasingly selective quotes from earlier ones. Her bibliography in *The Story of the Garden*, arranged chronologically and commencing in 1495, runs to over thirty pages and lists herbals and manuals now rarely heard of.[51] It is good to see that despite Eleanour's disclaimer that she has only included the most important Victorian works, Jane Loudon appears with several of her books.

Eleanour had obviously become interested in the history of women in the garden by 1932, as she makes especial note of instructions to lady gardeners. Advice and references come from authors such as William Lawson (*Country Housewife*), Charles Butler (*Feminnene Monarchie,* 1623), on bees, and Charles Evelyn, and she also notes the advice of the seventeenth-century writer William Coles that 'Gentlewomen if the ground be not too wet may doe themselves much good by kneeling upon a cushion and weeding'. Remarking on the paucity of books aimed at women before the nineteenth century she comments, 'This paucity is all the more remarkable because at least since the medieval days the garden had been regarded as the special province of the housewife.'[52] From the mid-nineteenth century she records a 'spate of books' aimed at women flower lovers, commencing of course with those of Mrs Loudon. The Honourable Alicia Amherst is only given two mentions, although the two women were obviously in contact as Eleanour thanks Lady Cecil personally for allowing her to reprint a complete list of plants given by Master Jon Gardener in his fifteenth-century treatise on gardening, *The Feate of Gardening*. This had been transcribed and published by Alicia Amherst with comments based on her own historical knowledge.[53]

In this small world of women gardens, Eleanour Rohde was a close friend of Maud Messel, who lived and gardened at Nymans, Sussex. In 1931 she dedicated *The Scented Garden* to Maud Messel, with thanks to Colonel Messel, and their friendship appears to have become close. The library at Nymans was full of antiquarian and specialist books, on such subjects as roses, herbs and scented plants (a particular interest of Maud Messel's), and must have been of intense interest to Eleanour. In 1933 she published an article on the Nymans library collection in the RHS *Journal*, including comments on the most notable items, their authors and their influence on contemporary thought. Written in Latin, German, French, Flemish and Italian, the books must have been an exciting challenge to Eleanour's undoubted capabilities. One can only imagine her heartbreak (and that of the Messels) when in 1947 the entire collection was lost in a devastating fire that destroyed most of the house.[54] Eleanour worked with Eric Parker, brother-in-law of Leonard Messel, on her publication *The Gardener's Weekend Book* in 1939 and she made reference to Nymans in almost all her works.

While the 1950s brought both Nan Fairbrother's *Men and Gardens: England and its Gardens from the Anglo-Saxons to the Modern Age* (1956) and Dorothea Eastwood's rather neglected *The Story of Our Gardens* (1958), Eleanour Rohde's work was the most authoritative and influential on the subject until the last decades of the twentieth century. By then a new generation of garden writers, many of them women, were making their own contributions to the history of the garden.

SEVEN

Virgins in the Beds

SCHOOLS FOR WOMEN GARDENERS

It must be borne in mind that horticulture is still a comparatively new profession for women, and that unless those who enter it strive to give full time and application to learning its details they cannot hope to be successful . . . they should spare no pains to gain a complete education, for only then, when they are themselves worth something, can they expect remuneration.

Hon. Frances Wolseley, *Gardening for Women* (1908)

Emerging from a period when middle- and upper-class ladies were shielded from the realities of sex and soil, horticultural careers for women might seem an unlikely prospect. However, for an increasing number of the female population the matter of employment, and in particular paid employment, was a pressing issue. Gardening with its 'considerable amount of freedom, refining influences . . . and health and happiness to body and mind'[1] held out a possible solution for these 'surplus women'.[2] But this was not a solution without difficulties. Victorian estate gardens, with their armies of under-gardeners and battalions of garden boys, had a rigidly structured hierarchy, with little place for women in the traditional career structure from journeyman to head gardener. Boys taken on at 12 or 13 years of age would gain instruction from the men above them, often accompanied by hardships and punishment. Living in an all male bothy or hostel, career gardeners on their way up would move from one estate to the next, gaining experience and on-the-job training, before achieving the dizzying heights of head gardener and the opportunity of a house and marriage. Women simply did not fit in to this structure. Working-class women of course had always had a toe-hold in the country-house garden. Uniformly underpaid and unnoticed, they worked for a low day rate, often casually or seasonally, coming in from the nearby village. Occasionally one comes across a woman weeder on the wages lists of larger estates, or more often a woman who 'cooked and cleaned' in the bothy. John Loudon noted a weeding woman at Aubrey Hall when he visited in 1823. Or more correctly, rather than noticing the woman herself, it was the metal-tipped weeding gloves that she wore that drew his attention.[3] She remained anonymous. In the 1890s the garden staff at Englefield House (Berkshire) included two women weeders, from a staff of over twenty gardeners.[4] Clearly, however, weeding and cleaning were not jobs for the daughters of the professional classes, nor jobs that their parents would be likely to allow them to do. The solution of garden careers for women was to come not in the grounds of the established country houses, but instead in the gardens of newly formed women's horticultural schools.

Opportunities for women to train in gardening and horticulture became available from the 1890s, when a small number of general horticultural colleges opened their doors to women. The Horticultural College at Swanley, Kent let in its first female students in 1891 although in 1899 Mr Propert of that same college argued that such work was undesirable in every way, resulting in the women gaining masculine muscles and the loss of the proper womanly shape. Essex County Council had permitted women to study at its Chelmsford College from *c.* 1895 and at that same 1899 meeting declared that they made resourceful and intelligent gardeners of the highest standard (they made no mention of their shape).[5] The University of Reading, Berkshire, had also initially offered facilities for women students at its Lady Warwick Hostel in the autumn of 1898, although these were later reduced when the students were moved. These relatively large horticultural and agricultural colleges continued to offer horticultural courses into the twentieth century, but they did so alongside increasing provision by smaller women-only private schools and colleges.

Although there was often little clear distinction between the two kinds of provision in terms of qualification, the private gardening schools often provided a smaller 'family' atmosphere, albeit a female-only family. Typically, the proprietors were single females, sisters or, in the case of Waterperry Horticultural School, a female partnership. Often the schools only lasted as long as their proprietors, being closed at their death or retirement, although three provided instruction into the 1930s. Only one school, Waterperry, near Oxford, survived the Second World War and continued into the 1970s. For many women these, generally smaller, establishments with their emphasis on practical as well as examination-led training provided a less intimidating and more encouraging environment in which to develop their careers. Their families were also encouraged by the thought that their offspring would be mixing only with similar daughters of professional men; men who could afford the not inconsiderable fees. These women of talent and industry, well read and well educated, even before entering the garden schools, were envisaged as graduating not to the bothy but to the role of head gardener, or perhaps sole gardener.

Between the years of 1899 and 1922 at least nineteen of these private schools were set up.[6] The vast majority were established in the pre-war period, with a further handful during the interwar years. The impact of these private schools, and even that of the three larger public colleges, might seem small to us; but for the aspiring female gardener and horticultural worker the prospects were indeed blooming. Practical experience was not all that could be gained from these schools. Although only four private schools were RHS recognised, many of the others offered their students the opportunity to take the RHS General Examination, a recognised qualification to show future prospective employers. The little-known Elmwood Nurseries, Cosham (later moving to Aldersey Hall, Chester) under its three sister proprietors the Misses Cornelius Wheelers, presented ninety-seven successful lady students for the RHS General between 1907 and 1939; while the Thatcham Fruit and Flower Farm, run in partnership between Miss Hughes Jones and Miss Sowerby managed 118 between 1909 and 1925.[7]

It is interesting to note that during more or less the same period the Glynde School, Sussex, under the charge of Frances Wolseley, only presented thirteen students. It is the high profile and penmanship of its proprietor that has, however, made this school famous. Viscountess Frances Garnet Wolseley[8] (1872–1936) was a champion of the rights of lady gardeners, and wrote extensively on the subject in articles and books. Her works include *Gardening for Women* (1908), *In a College Garden* (1916) and *Women and the Land* (1916), the last written very firmly with the war effort in mind. It seems rather odd that she presented so few students for examination, and one can only presume that the gaining of the RHS qualification was considered by her to be not as essential as the practical experience that the school offered in all areas of horticulture.

A brief biography of Frances Wolseley's early years does little to explain her later commitment to the vital role that gardening and horticulture could play in women's lives. Born in 1872, daughter of the 1st Viscount Wolseley, she spent a restless childhood following her father's postings. Presented at court on her 21st birthday, she took part in the usual social round of balls and parties, presumably with the expectation that a happy married life was to follow. Despite a neat figure and attractive and vivacious demeanour, marriage did not follow and Frances seems to have been drawn to the active country life, rather than the glitter of the ballroom. In 1899 the family settled in Glynde, Sussex, and Frances (now at the dangerously advanced age of 27) confirmed her interests in horses and dogs rather than suitors. During her leisure she found time to become involved in the garden at her parents' house, known as the Farm House. She planted borders in the walled garden and created decorative rose swags and wreaths; what the reaction to this was from Viscount Wolseley's own gardening staff we will never know. Perhaps it was such as gave rise to the advice she was later to give her students on immediately establishing authority over any male staff when taking up a new position. There is no indication as to where Lady Frances gained her own gardening skills; maybe she was content to learn from the gardener's experience, supplemented by the many books on gardening available.

During this period of her life Frances Wolseley was to develop the conviction that was to change the rest of her life; that women who are bound to work for their livelihood might find in gardening a career that satisfied both their economic and their intellectual needs. The possibility of finding acceptable careers for women had already been mooted by several notable women, including Mrs Creighton (a campaigner for women's rights) and of course Daisy, Countess of Warwick (a philanthropist, gardener and later social reformer). There appears to have been an understandable connection between women's emancipation and the gardening schools, and Adela Pankhurst (daughter of Emily) attended Studley Horticultural College. The vision of the gardening profession that Frances Wolseley put forward was one calculated to appeal both to the women themselves and their families. Gardening, she argued, 'offers a considerable amount of freedom, the refining influence of poetry and beauty, contact with intelligent, interesting people, and health and happiness to body and mind'.[9] It is interesting to speculate how many professional gardeners, either in the nineteenth century or the modern day, would be able to agree wholeheartedly with this assessment of the delights of a gardening career. Perhaps the gardeners on her father's estate at Glynde were exceptional.

On her thirtieth birthday (more usually an occasion for sorrow among Victorian spinsters), Frances founded the Glynde School for Lady Gardeners. Initially created on land in the Wolseley's own garden with her father's necessary permission, it was the first step towards her own career. Her objects in establishing the school were recorded as: 'to give a more thorough foundation in the management of all the more hardy garden plants; to improve taste in the laying out and arrangement of gardens; to teach the daily routine work of a private garden, so essential to those who wish to become private head gardeners; and to give students responsibility and thus enable them more easily to undertake posts when their course of training is completed'.[10] The aim was to produce a lady gardener who 'does not wish to supplant able, clever men head-gardeners . . . [but] desire however to assist by lending intelligence, good taste and refinement to our great gardens'.[11] Such qualities were apparently all too often found lacking in male head gardeners, known instead for drunkenness, ignorance and belligerence, as outlined by earlier writers such as the moralistic Rosa. Applicants, whom Frances herself interviewed, were committed to a two-year programme of studies for which they were to pay £20 per year for practical instruction plus extra for additional lectures. Lodgings and meals were also additional. These comparatively high fees (certainly higher than the public horticultural colleges) served to define the class of women who would attend the school. In common with all the Lady Gardening Schools[12] the students were boarders and formed what Frances herself described as a 'community'. The atmosphere at the schools must have had much in common with some of the superior class of girls' boarding schools: hard work and observance of the rules (enforced by fines), balanced by outings and extra-curricular activities. Again in common with most of the other schools and colleges all the girls wore a uniform. This varied between the colleges, and indeed during the lifetime of any one college, but that at Glynde was typical in attempting to balance practicality with female modesty and social approval.

After a brief time at the Farm House the school expanded sufficiently to make it necessary to purchase extra land and Frances acquired the south-facing 'Ragged Lands'. Before the move she had been able to take only ten or so pupils, now this increased considerably, although the prospectus still referred to numbers as being 'limited'. In her book *In a College Garden* written fifteen years[13] after the setting up of the college,

Frances Wolseley described the development of the garden as it was built up 'from a cornfield, devoid of house, tree or shrub, to a garden complete enough to afford ample preparation to those women who wish to make a livelihood by gardening'. Containing 5 acres, the garden at Ragged Lands was laid out as a series of enclosed gardens, allowing students to work on fruit, flowers and vegetables within a small space without losing the attractiveness of the overall design. There were wide cross paths of grass, known as 'The Cross Roads', and flower borders were planted along these, as well as geraniums in large pots at the centre. A pleasure ground area with birches, horse chestnut and poplar was created, giving the students further skills in tree management in addition to orchard areas for training in fruit production (apple storage was also excavated in part-sunken cool sheds). Terrace gardens were created due to the steep slope of the grounds, and a terrace placed in front of the main house. This house was erected especially for Frances herself to live in, in addition to providing administration offices and student accommodation.

Students carried out a full range of tasks under the tutelage of Elsa More and Mary Campion, both early graduates from Glynde. The syllabus for the school included both manual and more skilled duties, although Lady Wolseley admitted that in the vast majority of gardens, male under-gardeners or labourers would still be essential for the 'mechanical work' necessitating physical labour. Vegetables, flowers and fruit were all grown and sold, assisting both with advertising the skills of the students and with the funding of the college. Saleable produce was a high priority in the first years of the school, supplementing funding and thus keeping down the fees. With the coming of the war this emphasis on production took on an added importance and a handbarrow loaded with fresh vegetables was taken to the nearby village once a week as vegetables became scarcer in the market towns. Further areas of the gardens were planted with annuals, including sweet peas; and an alpine area gave experience in that most popular of garden features of the period. Wild areas were also encouraged, and the planting of bulbs in meadow areas, well away from the flower borders (which new intakes of students would dig afresh each year) was both practical and fashionable in the era of William Robinson's *The Wild Garden*.[14] Robinson was himself a supporter of the school, although unlike Alicia Amherst he did not seek to employ any female gardeners at his own property of Gravetye Manor, Sussex.

Photographs of the Glynde students at work (and rest) adorn Frances Wolseley's books and allow us to gain an insight into the day-to-day activities of the school. They also provide precious glimpses of some of the very first women who chose gardening as a career.[15] Attired variously in their winter uniform of khaki skirts, leggings and jackets, or summer long skirts and straw bonnets, the students pause for the camera, with tools in hand. A solitary but indomitable young woman, in oversized flat cap, solid boots and leather gloves, shoulders a fork with tines the length of her forearms. Looking determinedly into the distance, her shoulders are set square and her jaw firm. She makes an ideal frontispiece to *Gardening for Women*; and a marked contrast with Jane Loudon's befrilled and smocked figure of sixty years earlier. In other photographs young girls and women wield spades, push wheelbarrows and pull the handcart. They stand among the borders, like gnomes in a suburban garden, or pause in the act of tying in sweet peas. The planting out of the King Edward VII Sanatorium Garden in Midhurst (1907) was a further opportunity for recording the world of Glynde pupils. In their summer attire among the roses, the students could pass for a ladies' garden party who have become overenthusiastic in the admiration of the rose beds. But the presence of three wheelbarrows firmly grasped in the hands of fellow students indicates a more professional involvement with the garden. The King Edward VII Sanatorium Garden was a triumph for the promotion of awareness of the female gardeners. Designed by Gertrude Jekyll, laid out by the pupils of Glynde, much of the planting was produced by Jekyll's own nursery at Munstead Wood. Jekyll was a patron of the Glynde School, as was the eccentric genius of female plant breeding and collecting, Ellen Willmott, and the eclectic writer Theresa Earle. Sadly neither Jekyll nor Willmott appears to have thought of employing gardening women in their own gardens. Ellen Willmott once famously wrote to Beatrix Havergal, principal of Waterperry, that women would be 'utterly hopeless and unsafe in the borders'.[16]

In 1915 Frances Wolseley (now 43) retired from the day-to-day teaching and administration of the school. This enabled her to devote more time to her writing. She had also become increasingly involved in the education of women to work on farms during the war. By 1915 the demand for women gardeners had become 'imperative and general' as male gardeners left for the trenches of war. One senses a note of triumph as Frances records letters asking for female gardeners from 'owners of large private gardens, who had maintained, until then, that men-gardeners alone could do the work and that women were all right as companion gardeners or to do jobbing gardening in seaside towns, but altogether impossible to consider for the supervision of large places'. 'The reaction', she notes, 'had come at last and was almost laughable in its suddenness and haste.'[17] Whether the training they had at the gardening schools stood these newly-in-demand women in good stead for all the tasks now required of them was debatable. More than gardeners had been lost to the war effort and requests came to the Glynde School for women who would be able not only to garden but also take on the duties of chauffeurs, work the electric light engine, feed the pigs and mind the children's pony. This at the same time as nurturing the orchid collections, raising fruit under glass and tending the stovehouses.

Training at the Glynde School, even before the war, had anticipated that women would often take on a range of roles, but perhaps not this wide-ranging. Schooling in all aspects of garden management and horticulture was a thorough one and it was expected that at the end of it the trainees would be sufficiently skilled to be taken on as head gardeners in the smaller establishments. This might lead after a few years to a post in a larger garden for those who wished, although the tone of many women's writing over this period indicates that the distrust and even hostility they encountered in these positions gave all but the most determined a disinclination for the large estates.

Writing in 1896, having visited the newly opened women's branch of Swanley Horticultural College, Theresa Earle had been immediately struck with the idea that 'a new employment might be created for women of small means out of the modern increased taste for gardening'.

Gardens around so many of the houses in the newly created suburbs might be transformed by the hand of the female gardener. 'The dullness of the small plots of ground', Earle went on to argue, 'was entirely owing to the want of education in the neighbouring nurserymen, whose first idea was always to plant laurels or other coarse shrubs.'[18] A comment that can hardly have endeared her to her own nursery suppliers. A lady gardener, Earle went on enthusiastically, might easily undertake to lay out these plots in endless variety, supplying them through the year with flowers and plants suited to the aspect of each garden. The increased cost involved in this seasonal supply of plants was not a matter that Theresa Earle dwelt on, but at least might have consoled the few nurserymen whose reading matter included *Pot-Pourri*.

Other career options, or in the terminology of the period 'openings', might be found in the larger villas. Blithely unaware (one presumes) of the possible misinterpretation of her suggestion, Mrs Earle went on to say that single ladies living in larger villas might 'prefer a woman head gardener with a man under her to do the rough work'.[19]

Recording her visit to Swanley Horticultural School in the March entry of *Pot-Pourri*, Theresa Earle was very supportive of the general aims of the school. She was, though, concerned that many of the women there were too young to have fully committed themselves to a career in gardening. Some of the girls she saw were only 16 or 17, whereas she felt that 18 or even 20 was a better age at which to be able to decide on a profession in gardening.[20]

Although some pupils may have fallen by the wayside, Swanley Horticultural School produced some high-profile women gardeners. Sylvia Crowe (1901–97) and Brenda Colvin (1897–1981), famous for their work on urban landscapes in the postwar period, were both graduates. Brenda Colvin was one of the founder members of the Institute of Landscape Architects and helped to establish the position of women in what had been a predominantly male field. Frances Perry (1907–93) also studied at Swanley before going on to become horticultural adviser to Middlesex County Council, author of *Water Gardening* (1938) and columnist for *The Observer* (following on from Vita Sackville-West). She had married into the famous horticulturalist family of the Perrys, but it was her own work that resulted in her being honoured with the RHS Victoria Medal in 1971.

Glynde School produced its own roll-call of names who went on to influence later generations of gardeners, either as designers, plants-women or head gardeners. Perhaps the most famous of these was Chrystabel Prudence Goldsmith Proctor who studied at Glynde before going on to complete her training in France, Germany and Tuscany between the wars. After ten years as Gardening Mistress at St Paul's Girls School, and a spell at Bingley Training College, she came to Girton College, Cambridge in 1933 and stayed until 1945. Here she was in charge of 46 acres of garden and grounds as well as playing a vital role in the production of vegetables and fruits during the war years. She moved on to become Estate Steward at Bryanston School in Blandford, Dorset before retiring in 1950 to travel to East Africa and Australia and settling for a while in Kenya. Chrystabel wrote poetry throughout her life, in addition to diaries, journals, and a privately printed biography of her close friend Helen Neatby, whom she lived with in Kenya and back in England. Among other correspondents in horticulture she communicated with Gertrude Jekyll and her old 'principal' Frances Wolseley, until the latter's death in 1936. As if this output was not enough, Chrystabel Proctor also wrote on gardening and education, preparing for publication works on the layout of school grounds and speaking on the importance of gardening at schools.[21] Frances Wolseley must have been proud of such a student.

From the earliest days the future careers of the pupils at Glynde were envisaged on a global as well as suburban scale. Alongside careers as head gardener, or in market gardening, landscape gardening, jobbing gardening, nature study teaching and floral decoration, Frances Wolseley also advocated the emigration of newly trained female gardeners to the colonies. South Africa in particular was 'unhesitatingly recommended' for a range of female workers including nurses, teachers and home helps. Similarly, excellent prospects were presumed to lay in store for female gardeners. By 1908 there had already been examples of women's success, predominantly in the fruit farms on the Cape Colonies; while more 'earnest and adaptable English Women' were wanted to similarly boost production and techniques of dairying, bee-keeping and flower growing. Although the climate of the Cape prevented any actual physical exertion on the part of white women their services were needed, according to Frances Wolseley, to organise work for the natives. 'Intelligence and enlightenment'[22] were needed to superintend the mere mechanical work of the kaffirs and thus bring about a revolution in the productivity of the area. A specialist course in colonial horticulture (for women) had been instigated at Swanley College, where they were trained in dairy and fruit production as well as fitted for work in private gardens in the Cape. It was recognised, however, that the climate and soils of Kent did not necessarily prepare one for the rigours of the colonies, and the South African Colonisation Society was urged to consider assisting with the creation of a college for lady gardeners actually within South Africa.

That some prospective female colonists might have had little idea of what awaited them in the African colonies is indicated by the preparatory hints given to them in *Gardening for Women*. Under the discussion of clothing, for example, it is advised that furs are best left at home, while light and unwashable materials are 'unwise . . . as the red dust is terrible all over the country'. Warm underwear was recommended for the bitterly cold nights, and a chiffon veil would be a 'great comfort' in the dust storms. For the few prospective horticultural colonists undeterred by this sartorial advice, the unequivocal statement that a 'woollen cholera belt' was essential, even in the hottest of weathers, might have been the final straw. For the adventurous few who gave little heed to physical comfort and none at all to fashionable appearance, there were other considerations and dangers. A considerable source of anxiety was the question of leaving white women 'unprotected' among kaffirs. In a small garden where only one woman and a boy were needed the danger was apparently less, but in larger gardens two women would be needed not just to control the flower borders but also for the necessity of 'protecting each other'. Surely few who read this summary of prospects for the lady gardener in the colonies can have agreed with Frances Wolseley's conclusion that the career held out 'decidedly good prospects' to ladies who could 'face some degree of adventure'. On a final note it must have been a comfort to know that travelling to the colonies by boat one could at least take one's own English bicycle (it was in fact recommended), although cycling in a veil might present hazards of a different kind.

Nearer to home, for those of a less adventurous nature, the direction of even a large garden might be open to qualified lady gardeners. It is not difficult to imagine the battles that some of these women might have to overcome to gain the respect of the male gardeners who would be in their charge. Again the advice given by Frances Wolseley treads a fine line between practical and optimistic. When confronting the question of the authority that a head lady gardener must exert she not only places complete confidence in 'the right sort of woman' but also indicates the appropriate method of attaining that authority: 'Let her, without hesitation, dismiss the first drunken under-gardener she meets with, and the others will respect her.'[23] What one should do in the absence of a convenient alcoholic on the staff is not revealed and one can only presume that it was such a common problem among the poorly paid gardeners that one would always be to hand.

It is presumed in the few books of the period that comment on this subject, that a women in sole ownership of a garden will welcome the idea of the female gardener, both as someone who will maintain the garden and as a companion in their own horticultural endeavours. Theresa Earle noted that many women felt happier talking to other women on the subject of what they wanted done, and under the strict social conventions of the period a live-in female gardener would be seen as eminently appropriate in a household maintained by a woman. The 'companion gardener' was also a category much promoted by Frances Wolseley, someone who would share her knowledge and taste with her female employer as they pottered among the flower beds and borders. Male employers were, however, cautious about this relatively novel idea. There was even a lingering belief that faced with a woman employee the man of the house would feel forced to go and dig himself, to spare the physical infirmities of his newly hired gardener. Firmly held ideas of gender differences could, however, work both ways. Although the female gardener might be seen as weak physically, she had talents aplenty widely associated with her sex which would make up for this small lack. True artistic taste combined with superior aesthetic judgement were hers by nature, and for the college graduate this combined with a scientific education to raise her above the male gardener. Taste in colour, apparently singularly absent in the average male gardener, also came naturally to the female, along with lightness of touch for indoor flower displays and a background in the arts. To these qualities highlighted by Frances Wolseley, Theresa Earle added the suitability of a woman for work in the greenhouse producing year-round colour with knowledge and care. Honesty and trustworthiness completed this exemplary model gardener, as 'the lady gardener is a gentlewoman, and therefore possesses these qualities' in Frances Wolseley's eyes. The absence of drunkenness and ability to resist other 'temptations' (unspecified!) deemed less open to a lady must also have set her apart from many male gardeners.[24] With all these in her favour it is not difficult to see why demands were made not just for equal careers but also equal pay and rather above average conditions.

There was, however, still the reluctance of the male employer (and fellow employees) to be overcome. No lady gardener would wish to take up her post without the full confidence and backing of her employer, and many male householders apparently still wavered. If they could not be convinced of the superiority of the female gardener an appeal could instead be made to their own sense of proprietorship of the garden. It was well known that traditional male head gardeners had a reputation for feeling they owned the garden, often being more interested in exhibiting the fruits, flowers and vegetables than passing them on to the owners. For some householders winning the local and even national exhibitions engendered a real sense of pride, but for others it appears to have been more of an inconvenience. Head gardeners who grew carnations for exhibiting rather than for the house, and marrows for prizes rather than the family table, were a byword at the aristocratic dinner table. Whether myth or reality, the obstinacy of the male gardener was not to be met with in the lady gardener. The 'friend whose judgement and taste can be relied upon'[25] would not only grow sweet peas for the house but would actually arrange them exquisitely and bring them to you with polite, sober courtesy. A testament both to her excellent training and her natural inclination.

With so many presumed natural advantages to the lady gardener, not to mention the social and financial disadvantages that women were desperate to overcome, colleges for lady gardeners sprung up like mushrooms in those early decades of the twentieth century. The Glynde School under Frances Wolseley is now one of the best known, but many of the others had notable successes, gaining a place in history through their students rather than their owners.[26] Thatcham Fruit and Flower Farm School of Gardening, near Newbury, Berkshire, was one of several schools that combined a market gardening business with instruction and training. It opened in 1906 under the principal Miss Hughes Jones and continued to provide training until *c.* 1925. In 1908 a description of the school and its prospectus emphasised the balance between theoretical and practical work, preparing students to either gain a livelihood or merely superintend their own garden. Courses at Thatcham included horticulture, bee-keeping, carpentering [*sic*] and jam making. In addition, a newly created French garden, on the 'Maraîche' system was run by a French tutor, with fruits and vegetables being forced out of season under frames and cloches. Soils, manures, botany and floral work completed the theoretical courses. Students were expected to attend the school for two to three years before being regarded as ready to qualify.

One of the most famous of the Thatcham students was Beatrix Havergal (1901–80) who went on to found the longest-running school for women gardeners, Waterperry Horticultural School, Oxfordshire. After completing her training at Thatcham, Beatrix Havergal found a post as head gardener at Downe House, a boarding school for girls. Here she met Miss Avice Sanders (1896–1970), who was working as the cook at the school and with whom she was to strike up a lifelong partnership. Together the two women founded the Pusey School for Lady Gardeners in 1929, with Beatrix Havergal in charge of the horticultural training while Avice Sanders ran the administration and domestic sphere. The school was an instant success and within a few years the couple moved on to larger premises at Waterperry, near Oxford. Taking over an old manor house owned by Magdalen College,

Oxford allowed them to expand, with additional full-time teaching staff and students. College life at Waterperry had much in common with a religious boarding school or nunnery. The day began with weak tea and chores at 7 a.m., followed by communal prayers before breakfast; the working day commenced at 9.15 a.m.

In *Waterperry: A Dream Fulfilled*, Ursula Maddy recalled the tepid tea, the strict rules and the long confessional meetings following any incident of plant neglect or death. Confessionals of any other kind were unlikely to be needed as contacts with men were strongly discouraged if not actually forbidden. Ordinands from the nearby Cuddesdon Theological College came once a year for several years; but the theatricals and ghost walks that were the highlights of these visits were eventually judged by their Principal (later the Archbishop of Canterbury) as likely to lead the young men astray and the visits were discontinued. A woman student who married not only had to leave the school but was considered lost to the profession. In the context of the period this was not as draconian as it now sounds; even in the mid-twentieth century male gardeners would be expected to be unmarried at least until they reached head gardener status, while female teachers were expected to leave their posts once they married. A married student could not therefore be expected to ever gain employment at the end of her course. In 1954, when Bridget Ross-Lowe told Beatrix Havergal that she was engaged to be married on the completion of her course, she was met with the horrified reaction 'But what about the garden?' From that moment on Bridget was regarded as having wasted her education and her life.[27]

Some of the strictness may have been due to Beatrix's own family background. The Reverend Clement Havergal was uncompromisingly Calvinistic, and her mother, although more romantic in her leanings, was also deeply religious. A high level of discipline was, however, common to almost all the schools, with fines being imposed for neglect or damage to plants. An ex-student at Waterperry still recalled the day she accidentally knocked the top off a cucumber seedling as the most traumatic day of her life, some forty years after it had happened.[28] On the fate of any students who committed other social transgressions the record is silent, but as it is also silent on the close partnership between Avice Sanders and Beatrix Havergal this is perhaps not surprising. In the words of Sue Bennett, 'Such was the force of Beatrix's personality that no-one commented on the fact that she and Avice habitually shared a bedroom.'[29]

Assessment for the prized Waterperry Diploma was unusual even among the private schools, in that it covered not only the horticultural but also the social skills of the candidate. Punctuality, friendliness and reliability were assessed alongside abilities in actual gardening, and although this may seem somewhat eccentric, these social skills in fact play a vital role in the running of a staffed garden. The original aims of the school had been to instil both the theoretical and practical horticultural knowledge that would result in a 'first class gardener' and reliability would certainly be one of those attributes. Only fifteen RHS passes were gained at the school during the time that the students were entered for the RHS examination (1930–9) but the Waterperry Diploma itself was of sufficiently high standing to secure posts for many of its graduates. In fact the Diploma was particularly prized, as Beatrix Havergal's dislike of bureaucracy and administration made assessment and the issuing of Diploma credits an irregular event.[30] If marking was irregular, teaching was of the highest standard, as might be expected from a woman who had herself won the Royal Horticultural Society Victoria Medal of Honour. The school was regularly approached with offers of positions for final year students, and many years after its closing ex-Waterperry students were still being sought.

Women who graduated from Waterperry to become famous gardeners in their own right included Pamela Schwerdt, Sibylle Kreutzberger and Valerie Finnis (later Lady Scott) among others. After completing their training Schwerdt and Kreutzberger advertised in the national press looking for either a plot of land on which to start a joint nursery garden or a position in an established garden for the two of them together. Replies included offers of land in disused kitchen gardens up and down the country.[31] They were finally lured to Sissinghurst, to work in the gardens created by Vita Sackville-West and Harold Nicolson, where they stayed for over thirty years carrying on the life of the garden after the death of Vita in 1962 and overseeing the transfer into the hands of The National Trust. A colour photograph taken in the 1960s records a visit by Beatrix Havergal to Sissinghurst, Pamela Schwerdt and Sibylle Kreutzberger dressed in corduroy three-quarters and long woollen socks, Beatrix in a solid brown double-breasted overcoat.[32] In 1981 they were awarded the Associateship of Honour by the Royal Horticultural Society, and in 2005 they were both still lecturing on horticulture.

Valerie Finnis, the photographer of the Sissinghurst visit and other women gardeners, was also a product of Waterperry. Born in 1925 she spent the war years maintaining a 25-acre field of vegetables and driving trucks of fruit to Covent Garden. After the war she joined Waterperry as a member of staff and built up a nursery of alpines, swapping plants with other famous women gardeners including Margery Fish. She left Waterperry after twenty-eight years to marry Sir David Scott, a famous plant collector, and moved her alpine collection to their home at the Dower House, Boughton, Northamptonshire, also home to Sir David's collection of rare shrubs and trees.

Founded by Daisy, Countess of Warwick,[33] the Studley Castle Horticultural and Agricultural College for Women was another of the foremost women's training establishments of the early twentieth century. Education, and in particular education of women, was one of Daisy's principal aims. 'I have often thrown discretion, money and self-interest to the winds when I have been caught by the glamour of an idea,' claimed the social hostess and long-time mistress of the Prince of Wales; although the fact that it was to education that she alluded might have surprised some. Sounding vaguely like a beauty competition contestant, Evelyn 'Daisy' Maynard, Countess of Warwick (1861–1938), listed 'the encouragement of gardening as a hobby for women' in her entry in *Who's Who*. As if to convince any sceptics, the entry contained the supporting note that she had 'already written an interesting account of the subject'.[34] The Lady Warwick Hostel (at first within the auspices of Reading University) was set up by Daisy in 1898 with the aim of providing women with an education in rural and agricultural work and moved to Studley to enable greater numbers to attend.

With her usual combination of idealism and practicality, Daisy had originally outlined a much grander scheme for the support and education of women. Rather than training merely to work for other people, she had envisaged the creation of communities of 'unmarrying women'. These women would be placed in settlements of six to twenty holdings, each worked by two women sharing a cottage and acting as partners. Each settlement would contain one or more women who had trained at Studley and were thus able to guide the others in their work. The scheme (perhaps unsurprisingly) met with ridicule from agricultural commentators such as Lord Willoughby de Broke (Master of Foxhounds and owner of 18,200 acres). Lord Willoughby regarded the proposed settlements as being formed by 'soft-handed delicate women from towns' with not 'the remotest bearing for good or evil on the future of agriculture'.[35] One wonders whether Lord Willoughby looked back on those words sixteen years later as the Women's National Land Service Corps swung into action for the future of agriculture and the country.

A course of instruction at the Lady Warwick Hostel was of two years' duration and included flower and fruit growing, tomato and mushroom production, bee- and poultry-keeping and dairy work. An initial sum of £2,000 was raised as capital for the venture, with contributors including Suttons (seed merchants) and Huntley and Palmers (biscuits) as well as Daisy herself. By 1901 demand for places (and the newly qualified students) was exceeding supply, and the college moved to new premises at Studley Castle in Warwickshire where it was renamed The Horticultural and Agricultural College.[36] In 1938, on the eve of war, Studley College opened a new wing to accommodate its expanding numbers, a ceremony at which Lady Warwick was to have an honoured place but was prevented by her fatal illness. Eventually recognised as a Technical Institute by the Board of Education, the College remained successful until 1969.

Whether the school ever achieved the founder's aims of finding hope and employment for the 'million surplus women' whose plight Daisy had written about in 1899, is unlikely, but certainly it provided hope and independence for hundreds. In addition to taking vocational horticultural students Studley was unusual in that it would take students with some emotional problems. Dr Lilias Hamilton, the first warden at Studley, had qualified as a doctor in 1890 and (finding a female practice difficult to establish in England) travelled to India where she set up a successful private practice in Calcutta. In 1894, in a rare moment of peace between Britain and Afghanistan, she was appointed court physician to the Amir of Afghanistan but later rebellion led to her returning to a private consultancy in London, and then to the Transvaal and eventually to Studley.[37] Its last Principal had a somewhat less exotic background. Elizabeth Hess had trained at the private Practical Gardening School for Ladies at Regent's Park (run by the Royal Botanic Society of London from 1899 until 1931) before joining Studley in 1956 and staying until its closure. An Elizabeth Hess Scholarship is still awarded annually by the Studley College Trust in memory of Miss Hess (who died in 1996) to those at the beginning of their careers.

While few partnerships are as well known as that of Beatrix Havergal and Avice Sanders, or perhaps as close as theirs was, joint women proprietors were not uncommon in the female gardening schools. Like-minded women, whether friends, business partners or sisters, were often to be found running horticultural schools and market gardens. Almost always unmarried, one at least would have training in horticulture while the other might provide essential administrative or domestic skills. The

Elmwood Nurseries and Horticultural School, Cosham, was run by the sisters Misses Cornelius Wheeler, for the almost forty years of its existence from *c.* 1902 to 1940.[38] Set up by Ruth Cornelius Wheeler using £1,000 given to her by her father, she was subsequently joined by three of her sisters (Sylvia, Amy and Laura) before she herself left to get married. Laura became Principal of the school in 1915, while Amy ran the household and Sylvia went on to qualify and eventually teach. Laura Wheeler was later to be involved in the Women's Farm and Garden Association, chairing the Committee on Education and Employment from 1934 to 1937, taking over the chair from a Studley graduate. Another female partnership was that of Miss Turner and Miss Kitson who set up the County and Colonial Training School at Arlesey, Hitchin. The School taught gardening as part of its wider training of women heading for adventure in the colonies.

Several former students of the early women's schools went on to set up their own colleges on graduating. While Beatrix Havergal was perhaps the most illustrious student to set up her own school, Stella Frost, who had originally studied at Thatcham, advertised independently for pupils from 1911 before then setting up her own school at Terenure in Ireland in 1919. Miss Baker and Miss Morrison, both graduates from Swanley, ran the School of Gardening at Corstorphine, Edinburgh, and the Breedons Norton School was founded by Miss May Crooke, originally of Studley. Teaching, was yet another career opening for the successful student, and indeed many stayed on at their own schools to teach for a short while after completing their studies. Staff positions at Waterperry were particularly prized, while at Glynde two of the first pupils stayed on to teach for many years. Teaching was ideally suited to the more academically minded pupil, and a profession where she would not be exposed to those invisible and visible sneers of a male workforce.

Setting up a school of one's own needed financial backing, even if it were to be an adjunct to a market gardening enterprise. Frances Wolseley was well aware of the costs of setting up in market gardening and recommended it only for those students who had 'both brains and capital', unlike jobbing gardening or companion gardening. Not all of the students who passed through the growing number of schools and colleges in the first decades of the twentieth century would have been able to afford a capital investment of this kind. Although the schools were primarily aimed at the 'daughters of the professional classes', and much emphasis was laid by Frances Wolseley on the merits of employing the trained gentlewoman, financial wealth was not easy to come by for the single female. Those who did set up schools and businesses usually did so as a result of gifts from their fathers, perhaps many despairing of ever having to provide a dowry and thus anxious to provide for some long-term security for their spinster daughters. The initial decision to attend the training courses, particularly those that involved two or more years of residential study, was itself a considerable financial commitment. Unconcerned about competition to her own school, Frances Wolseley listed the prospectuses and costs of other gardening schools in England and Europe in her own *Gardening for Women*. In 1908 fees for courses typically ranged from £55 per annum (for a full course at Thatcham) to £96 a year at Swanley (including a study bedroom) and £120 at Studley (again with bedroom). Shorter courses for only two weeks on particular topics might be as little as £5. Extra lectures and boarding might be an additional cost where not specifically included, or lodgings might have to be found within the vicinity when boarding places were not available. Set against these were the evening classes which gave theoretical instruction as part of the much broader course options. At the newly formed Science and Art Evening Centres across south London, such as Plumstead (Greenwich), Forest Hill (Lewisham) or West Norwood (Lambeth), individual sessions might be purchased for 5*s*. The training must, however, have lacked the practical input of the residential schools.

To give an idea of how fees related to income it may be noted that the Swanley College recommended the following wages for its students after graduating: for head gardeners in larger establishments up to £100 a year with rooms, light and vegetables, but grading down to as low as £20 a year for very small establishments; under-gardeners up to £80 a year, companion gardeners £100 down to £30; while landscape gardeners might expect to charge a fee of between 2 guineas a week to 2 guineas a day. Although the fees varied depending on both the scale of the garden and staff and the experience of the employee, it is apparent that in most cases it would have taken several years for the women to recoup the monetary investment spent on their training. It is also apparent that these were not fees that could be afforded by working-class girls and women. For a few of these the public colleges may have offered a way in to their chosen career, but for many more the only way into the garden was via the same dead-end route that women had taken for the previous centuries, as low-paid weeding women.

When, in 1896, Kew outwardly set an example of the liberal employer by taking on three women as journeymen-gardeners, Kew's own director, Sir William Turner Thiselton-Dyer designed a uniform that would be 'unlikely to provoke their male colleagues'. Brown bloomers, woollen stockings, waistcoat, jacket and peaked cap combined to prevent the new intake from arousing any passions from their work-fellows, or indeed any suspicions of their actually being women. Women they might have been, but in the rather less liberal words of Sir Joseph Hooker, then in his eighties, they were 'not ladies in any sense of the word'.[39] The bloomers, however, were to be a siren call to male Londoners. 'They gardened in bloomers, the newspapers said; so to Kew without warning all Londoners sped; From the roofs of the buses they had a fine view of the ladies in bloomers who gardened at Kew.' Published in *Fun Magazine* in 1900, this ditty highlights one of the major difficulties facing females entering the gardening profession. Photographs of the young women referred to in the ditty show what to us seems a more than decorous covering of the Kew uniform. Tweed or woollen jackets cover woollen waistcoats, shirts and ties, while the

Dianthus 'Mrs Sinkins'

Raised from the workhouse to the country house garden, Dianthus 'Mrs Sinkins' is a story of success that many a gardening-school pupil might wish to emulate. Catherine Rowe was born in Maidstone, Kent, in 1837, the seventh of thirteen children. Marrying John Sinkins sometime in the middle of the century she was established as matron of the Eton Union Workhouse in Slough by 1881, the workhouse where he was master. Both were keen gardeners and included pinks in the workhouse gardens, where they seem to have experimented with their stock to achieve new colours. Extra stock was sold to the nurseryman Charles Turner, who was able to purchase the new dianthus on the stipulation that it was named after Mrs Sinkins. First exhibited in 1880 and advertised for general sale in 1883, it became extremely popular. With a white flower and fully scented, it loves sunny well-drained spots and can happily be planted next to its daughter 'Miss Sinkins', also raised in the Slough workhouse.

offending bloomers are tweedy plus-fours tucked into thick woollen socks; only the hands and faces are bare. Decorous though they may look to us, in the late Victorian period any reminder that the female of the species had two legs, rather than being supported from the ground merely by a voluminous skirt, was enough to set pulses racing. In general, horticultural school gardens were less open to public view than that at Kew, but still the issue of clothing was an important one. Any uniform had to combine female modesty with practicality, and suitability to the weather with neatness.

Photographs of pupils at the various schools indicate a considerable variation in uniform at least in the pre-war years. In the innocent first years of the twentieth century, summer uniforms included long, quite voluminous skirts with full-sleeved blouses and full-length aprons. Ties were an essential part of the uniform, as they would have been for the male gardener, and so were hats. In summer, straw hats replaced the inevitable male flat cap and interestingly the women appear never to have used the bowler hat, the accepted status headwear of a (male) head gardener or foreman. Other photographs of women students[40] suggest an initial period of experimentation with smocks, all-encompassing full-sleeved overalls and boaters. This latter, at the Espanas School in Sweden, must have proved extremely difficult to balance while shovelling. Soon, however, uniforms settled down along the Glynde School model. At Waterperry regulation green breeches were tucked into thick socks and a green overall tied at the waist, with shirt and jacket.

In a discussion of 'Dress for Lady Gardeners' Frances Wolseley recommended a skirt with cotton or khaki drill knickerbockers during summer, and woollen underclothing both in summer and winter, eschewing the normal petticoats of the period. A turn-down collar with tie gave 'freedom of movement' while a starched stand-up linen collar gave a neat appearance for the head gardener. Writing in 1908 she stated that 'skirts should always clear the ankle to give freedom of movement' and added that a waterproof lining assisted in washing off any mud accumulated on the skirt at all times of year. The ubiquitous straw hat was essential for keeping off the sun, but alas for the followers of fashion, it should be kept plain and not decorated with flowers or chiffon. Cabbage leaves could be added on the inside to help keep the wearer cool, although obtaining cabbage leaves in the height of summer might have been tricky. Winter wear included a tweed jacket, mid-calf-length heavy skirt over breeches, spats and boots.

For those schools that survived into the 1914–18 period, and the few that made it to 1944–8, the allowances for female dress were to change dramatically. As women became out of necessity the predominant workforce both on the land and in other physically demanding roles, dress styles reflected this. Photographs of women hay-making, ploughing and sheep-sheering during the First World War show skirts hitched up to just below the knee, although doubtless dropped to a more modest length out of work hours. By the 1940s, both students and Land Girls were seen in dungarees and short-sleeved shirts, having cast aside their straw hats, ties and knickerbockers. For those early 'blooming' students at Kew, however, there had been a quick response to the leering London hoards. The new recruits had been promptly issued with long mackintoshes to wear when within the public gaze.

England was not alone in its movement to train women gardeners. Throughout Europe, America, Canada, and even Australia, horticultural schools were being set up by enterprising women who felt that the role of women should extend beyond the domestic sphere.[41] Dr Elvira Castner had set up a school of pomology and horticulture at Marienfelde, Germany after experiencing an epiphany in the sea port of Baltimore. Seeing crates of apples being loaded for export to Germany she realised that by setting up a school of pomology for women she could not only assist German women seeking gainful and respectable employment, but also reduce Germany's dependence on imports. Born in Prussia in 1844, Elvira had studied at a boys' school before becoming a teacher in Berlin and then training as a dentist in Baltimore. Botany, however, had always been an interest and she established the first ever German School of Horticulture for women in 1894. Intake in the first year was a slim seven students, but by 1904, seventy-seven students had completed the course at Marienfelde, of whom thirty-eight had obtained gardening situations, nine were self-supporting in some way, and eighteen were 'occupied at home'. It is interesting to note that only four had gone on to marry.

Another pomological school existed at Wolfenbüttel in Germany, where training in pomology was complemented with chemistry, botany, garden design and zoology. This last had a very unusual slant for a zoology course, covering only those aspects relevant to 'the foes of plants' and the destruction of those foes. At a school at Schleswig-Holstein the main concentration was again on fruits, although vegetables were grown in the two hothouses and eighty forcing frames. Pot plants were produced for sale, as one suspects were most of the vegetables, to assist in the funding of the school. The German schools recorded great demand for well-trained ladies, with demand over-reaching supply and salaries being on a par with men. In Holland the only horticultural school (in 1908) was not intended to provide women with a career, but merely to enable them to decorate and lay out their own garden. A more liberal attitude prevailed in Sweden and women 'of all classes' could attend the Gardening School at Agdatorp. This stress on 'all classes' contrasts with the attitude in many of the English schools where only intelligent, 'educated ladies' of the professional classes were encouraged. As Frances Wolseley suggested, for the 'secondary school girl it would seem that farm and not garden life holds out more suitable prospects . . . in the company of the farmer's wife'. Success in English private gardens was dependent on 'higher educations and qualities of directorship which do not come easily to maidservants'.[42]

In the liberal, and supposedly classless, United States of America, schools and colleges of horticulture had been founded on a very different basis to that in England. Each of the forty-five states had a college of agriculture supported by public funds, and the colleges were open equally to men and women in the expectation that they would study and then go on to work together. Women who wanted to train in horticulture, fruit farming, etc., thus did so within those colleges. There were occasional supplementary Schools for Lady Gardeners, such as the one at Lowthorpe, Groton, Massachusetts, run by Mrs Low. For $100 a year (in 1908) tuition was given in trees and shrubs, botany, garden design, drawing, surveying and engineering (as related to landscape work), and care of the greenhouse. Boarding was an extra $30 a month. The course lasted for two years, at the end of which you would be suited for design and planting of flower gardens, supervising greenhouses, planning and laying out small estates and also, interestingly, planting small parks for village improvement societies.[43]

Such improvement societies were a less common source of employment in England, but one career opportunity that did exist both sides of the Atlantic was the teaching of botany and nature study to children. With some reservations as to the inclusion of the sexual aspects of botany, nature study had become fashionable subject to teach children both at home and in school from the middle of the nineteenth century. The royal seal of approval had been given to gardening for children by Queen Victoria, who had had gardens created for each of her children at Osborne House. The royal children were expected to keep these up with minimum assistance from the gardeners, and tools were made for each of them. Long absences from the Isle of Wight must have made any care bestowed by the prince and princesses rather intermittent, but it was the thought that counted. Queen Victoria had also been pictured as a young princess watering the flowers. With such an example before them governesses and teachers throughout the land were busy introducing their pupils to plants, fruits, flies and ferns. Nature studies could be included in school syllabuses at all levels, although they were particularly popular in junior schools, the subject transforming itself to chemistry and botany at senior school.

Gardening for children had been increasingly popular in the last part of the eighteenth century, and a steady stream of books recommended that children at school and at home be given a small patch of ground to sow, tend and crop. Maria Edgeworth (1768–1841) had been one of the first children's garden authors, basing much of her writing on her own gardening experience. Books such as *The Parent's Assistant* (1796) and *Early Lessons* (1801) instructed children in keeping their own garden plots and filling them with plants for consumption and decoration. Her own family's seat at County Longford still had its feet firmly set in the early eighteenth century when Maria arrived there in 1782. On a humble scale, it had been laid out in the original Dutch taste almost in imitation of the frontispiece of Miller's *Gardener's Dictionary* of 1731. At first it was to be Richard Lovell Edgeworth, Maria's father, who developed the gardens into a more fashionable English landscape style. However, by the turn of the century Maria herself had taken a strong interest in them and the role of gardens in education.

Preferences in bedding plants may seem an odd starting point for instructions on moral rectitude, but for writers such as Maria, or Mrs Horatia Ewing, these were natural companions. In her *Letters from a Little Garden* (1886), Mrs Ewing addressed the children of the middle and upper classes on the acceptable fashions in planting and the natural superiority of hardy plants over annual bedding. Anxious that they should not insult their elders she also cautioned them not to be rude about other people's carpet-bedding, even if it did display a deplorable lack of taste. Mrs Ewing published for the Society for Promotion of Christian Knowledge and her books depict serious hard-working children eager to learn. In *Mary's Meadow* (1886), Mary decides she will read a copy of John Parkinson's seventeenth-century *Paradisi in sole Paradisus Terrestris* in order better to be able to make her garden. That a girl of about 10 years of age should choose to read this text at all would be extraordinary to modern parents, that she chooses to do so while simultaneously making a bonnet for herself is frankly beyond belief.

Charlotte Yonge's *The Instructive Picture Book: or Letters from the Vegetable World* (1858) was less discriminating, dealing with fruit and flowers rather than class-ridden garden design, but less practical in its approach. Charlotte was also a novelist and included superbly detailed descriptions of Victorian-style gardens in novels such as *Heartsease* (*c.* 1854). For children who wanted to garden rather than botanise or merely pester their parents with plant-related questions, the breakthrough came with Mrs Sidgwick and Mrs Paynter's *Children's Book of Gardening* in 1909. Illustrated by Mrs Cayley-Robinson, this gave instruction and encouragement in a book specifically aimed at children, rather than at adults who wanted their children to garden.[44] The first edition of this book had an illustrated cover with a picture of a well-dressed girl carrying a potted lily between rich flower borders.

Quick-growing and relatively 'foe-free' crops were preferred for school gardens, and radishes and carrots rather than lilies were favourites. Writing in 1906, Lucy Latter, a practising teacher, claimed that the introduction of nature studies had resulted in wide-ranging improvements in one school. 'Each year has shown an increased gain to the children intellectually as well as physically and morally,' she claimed. 'The children pass on to the senior schools with a quickened power of observation, a far greater amount of intelligence, a keener desire to learn, and a greater refinement of the heart.'[45] In her Garden Diary for June, Lucy Latter records: 'A grand feast of radishes, shared by many of the children's parents and some friends, formed a happy climax to this month's work.' A record of crops growing in the school grounds was still something kept by schools into the 1950s and in some it is coming back into fashion, often with the support of local Garden Trusts.[46]

An increasingly important component of school nature studies was a school garden and, to accompany the garden, a teacher in charge of nature studies and gardening. Frances Wolseley, never one for missing an employment opportunity for the students under her care, also included a chapter on 'The Teaching of Nature Study' in *Gardening for Women*. On the subject of including nature studies on the school curriculum she claimed: 'The right application of nature study and all that it embraces, to the education of children, is one of the most important developments of our day. All those who are ambitious for the prosperity of our future England should give very careful consideration to these matters.' In an unusual extension of her own concerns to the children of the working classes, she noted that 'Love of nature . . . is not only wholesome for children of the upper classes. It is good for them, but more especially do we need an increase of such knowledge amongst the poor little waifs and strays of our great cities and towns, who have so few bright moments in their grey lives.'[47] Noting that England was far behind Germany in the promotion of nature study for children (interestingly, Lucy Latter also appears to have taken inspiration from European practice), Frances Wolseley then went on to promote the employment of trained lady gardeners and horticulturalists to teach these studies across England. She had been informed, she states, by 'one of the greatest authorities', that science mistresses did not exist in sufficient numbers to supply the demands for them and thus it would be no trouble for well-trained ladies to obtain work of that kind. Combining training for gardening in the colonies with training for teaching nature studies Viscountess Wolseley even ventured to hope that 'it is within the realms of possibility that there may be women teachers of nature-study wanted in South Africa and in India'.[48]

Regardless of the needs of South Africa and India, the future of the female gardening schools was not as rosy as Frances Wolseley had hoped. Writing in 1916 she had noted with satisfaction the increasing demand for women gardeners as more men were sent to the front, but with the return of peacetime, jobs again went 'to the boys'. Changes in society gave increasing opportunities to women from the very classes that schools like Glynde had appealed to, and soon the typing pool was competing with the flower bed. For those who did decide on a career in horticulture the agricultural colleges were able to accommodate female students alongside their male counterparts, and fewer felt the need for the all-female boarding school experience. More women were becoming gardeners, but few were choosing to start their careers in a private gardening school. Of nineteen private garden schools that opened in the first years of the twentieth century only one was still taking students after the Second World War and that was Waterperry. Its lesser-known rival, Aldersey Hall, closed in the 1930s when the Principal Miss Laura Wheeler went on to work with the Women's Farm and Garden Association. Perhaps the very closure of the schools suggested that the battle had been won, and that there was no longer a need for the separate Ladies Gardening School. Perhaps women were no longer banished (with a sneer) to the conservatory or the flower bed. Perhaps the 'intelligent, educated and well read' lady gardener had everywhere replaced the slow-thinking, rule-of-thumb, inartistic man gardener. Perhaps.

EIGHT

Geniuses, Spinsters and Eccentrics

INTO THE TWENTIETH CENTURY

> There must have come a time when, almost without knowing it, she reached the point where she could no longer be bothered to conceal the fact that she was more knowledgeable, quick-witted, and intelligent than most of the men she knew.
>
> Audrey le Lièvre, *Miss Willmott of Warley Place: Her Life and Her Gardens* (1980)

Female gardeners of the late nineteenth and early twentieth centuries experienced a rapidly changing society in which their own roles were constantly redefined and eventually transformed. Small wonder then that women such as Ellen Willmott, born in the years before Queen Victoria's widowhood and living almost to the eve of the Second World War, were regarded as eccentrics in their later years, albeit eccentrics of genius. Born to fulfil the role of society hostess, dutiful wife and doting mother, these women shared instead a desire to create and a genius for design. Many cheated the destinies that their birth and circumstances had planned for them, turning away from the commitments of the children's nursery and the parental sickbed to forge instead a life among the nursery beds of the garden. Ellen Willmott once famously claimed that 'my plants and my gardens come before anything in life for me'.[1] Unsurprisingly, Ellen Willmott never married or committed to any long-term intimate relationships, devoting her time to her gardens and plants, in common with Gertrude Jekyll. Others, such as Vita Sackville-West, led lives that combined unconventional relationships with unconventional approaches to gardens. Both Norah Lindsay and Daisy, Countess of Warwick had unstable relationships outside of the garden, with marriages that did not outstay the changing of life's seasons. In the case of Daisy it is difficult to see quite when she fitted in any gardening around a frantic social whirlwind of affairs, country house parties, socialist causes and women's gardening schools. For Gertrude Jekyll and Vita Sackville-West, writing was interwoven with planting, adding to that air of genius in seclusion that so often surrounds those who work with the pen. Penury also served to enhance the sheen of eccentricity in too many cases. Whatever their backgrounds or circumstances, all of these women turned to the garden, for inspiration, consolation, or as an escape from the restrictions of their lives. It was in the garden that their creative geniuses blossomed, and their personalities outgrew the confines of their age.

As Louisa Johnson said, the garden cures one from dwelling too deeply upon the unavoidable disappointments and trials of life,[2] and so it was perhaps especially fortunate that Harry Lindsay handed over the garden at the Manor House, Sutton Courtenay, Oxfordshire, to his new bride Norah Lindsay (1873–1948[3]) as a wedding gift.[4] Norah (née Bourke) had not quite reached the age of 22 before marrying, and the marriage was not to be an everlasting one. After two decades, and despite the appearance of two children, Colonel Lindsay departed from Norah's life, leaving her with the garden as both consolation and career inspiration. Norah Lindsay's planting style was, perhaps surprisingly in the circumstances, gloriously romantic. The flower borders at Sutton Courtenay overflowed with a profusion of blossoms that spilled over the edgings onto the lawns and paths. Taking inspiration partly from Italy and partly from the plants themselves, her style was 'shabby chic' meets Italian villa. Not blessed with the level of wealth of many of her friends Norah's gardens are largely lacking in the architectural features that were to become a hallmark of this period and style. A single sundial acted as a focal point for a low pavement, with thyme and santolina nestling in the cracks and sending scents into the summer air. The pool with its lead cherub fountain and a backdrop of dark yews and junipers echoed rather than imitated the cypresses and stonework of villa gardens. Gravel paths led to the different areas of the gardens, while an old brick wall divided the Long Garden from the jewel-like Persian Garden. As Christopher Hussey commented, it was 'something exquisite, in which colour, atmosphere and romance blur the lines of objective truth'.[5]

A love of Italy and in particular 'the crumbling shrines of the ancient gods of Florence and Rome'[6] inspired not only Norah but also many of her contemporaries. In 1904 Edith Wharton had published *Italian Villas*

Eryngium giganteum 'Miss Willmott's Ghost'

It would be possible to create an entire garden with plants that Ellen Willmott claimed as her own, from the first snowdrops of the year (*Galanthus plicatus* 'Warley Belles', 'Warley Duo', and 'Warley Long-bow') to the late summer and autumn flowering *Ceratostigma willmottianum*, with its intense blue flowers that even Jekyll must have admitted onto her list of 'pure blues'. Collected by 'Chinese' Wilson the latter was raised by Miss Willmott herself. Prostrate veronica ('Warley Blue'), tough epimediums (x *warleyense*) and delicate campanula (x *haylodgensis* 'Warley White') would vie for space with roses (Ellen Willmott) and corylopsis (*warleyensis* (now *willmottiae*)) – from the western Szechuan. Many were named by her, some named after her, and others were found by plant hunters funded by her. The best known, however, perhaps better even than its namesake, is the giant eryngium 'Miss Willmott's Ghost' (*Eryngium giganteum* 'Miss Willmott's Ghost'). This superb metre-high silvery grey thistle gets its name not from its breeding but from Miss Willmott's own habit of carrying a few of its seeds wherever she went. Gardens that she had visited were honoured with a few pinches of seed of this tough and virtually ineradicable plant. Next spring the owners would recognise the serrated grey leaves as they pushed upwards from their tough thistle-like root. With sinking hearts they would recall the sharp-eyed eccentric woman who had knowingly appraised their garden planting and whose presence would be felt for many a year.

and Their Gardens, reflecting the favoured style. Additional influences came from the gardens of Le Nôtre and Norah's friends would call her 'Le Nôtre Lindsay'. But it was the flower schemes seemingly artless in their grading of blues, purples, pinks, lemon yellows and greys that attracted most attention. Although Norah demurred that the 'thoughtless abundance' was as much accident as design, the careful colour mixes of blues, purples and yellows with mixed rose hedging of lemons and creams betray a firm guiding hand. Red and scarlet, again with their accompanying roses, were placed carefully in other areas of the garden, and although the candy pink of the valerian might mingle with the violet of the *Iris laevigata*, it did not overreach hospitality by trespassing into the golds and reds of the hotter borders. A jewelled mix of herbaceous and perennials, threaded through with self-seeded annuals and invaders from other garden areas, still maintained its original design. The winsome 'faerie fishing rods' of *Dierama pulcherrimum* cheek by jowl with the less fey architectural yucca, gave a nurtured impression of recent abandonment as vegetation thrust its heads and roots through warm stone slabs and peeped through balustrades.

A series of pools led eventually to the River Thames and its meadow banks, introducing the sight and sound of water into the garden and attracting dragonflies and other shimmering insects on hazy summer days. Describing her approach to the garden, Norah made the style seem effortless and ancient as if 'the flowers and trees had chosen their own positions, and like the house had been overlooked by the rushing tide of men'.[7] All manner of seedlings were left to form clumps in places of their own choosing claiming, as she said, 'squatters rights' that in 'nine out of ten' cases succeeded. As all gardeners will know, an artless appearance is in reality the result of a lot of hard work. A photograph of Norah taken for *Country Life* in 1904 shows her leaning on the sundial in her Manor House garden, wearing a tight-waisted skirt, large bonnet and a georgette blouse. To many she appears rather wistful and pensive, the pale face and long aquiline nose creating an air of romance. Jane Brown describes Norah as looking 'like a candidate for the Coterie of Souls'[8] (her sister-in-law Violet Lindsay was a member of this intellectual and cultural circle). However, it is also possible to see in the photograph a woman coolly appraising the impression she wanted to give to others, while also critically assessing the state of a distant flower bed.

Witty and vivacious, Norah Lindsay numbered among her friends some of the most influential country house hosts of the period: Nancy Astor at Cliveden (Buckinghamshire); Nancy Tree (later Lancaster) at Kelmarsh (Northamptonshire), and Lady Emerald Cunard.[9] Contacts were made through the influence of her mother Emma Bourke, who had been a very close friend of Edward VII; one of many women who the Prince of Wales had been 'close' to. As Norah's need for money and genius of style grew together, her hostesses were to become her customers. And as admiration turned into requests for advice, advice would result in invoices. Although she moved among the wealthiest members of society Norah herself experienced periods of penury, particularly following the end of her marriage, and gardening became her mainstay. As she noted in a letter to her daughter, the mid-1920s found her with no money, no house and no husband. Submission of an invoice at the end of a weekend garden party might be seen as eccentric, if practical, behaviour; however, with hostesses as wealthy as the Astors and the Trittons (of Godmersham Park, Kent) the small matter of payment did not place too much of a strain on hospitality.

Eccentricity had been an essential part of Norah Lindsay's charm from her earliest days. Her niece, Lady Diana Manners, recalls her as dressed mostly in tinsel and leopard skins, with baroque pearls and emeralds, serving chicken kedgeree and raspberries and cream for lunch. Tinsel and leopard skin were abandoned when more practical gardening matters were being addressed, although one suspects that the baroque pearls might well have been seen in at least the more aristocratic flower beds. By the late 1920s and 1930s, when Norah's gardening career was at its height, she was a slightly more substantial woman in her fifties and early sixties. Her appearance by this period had less tinsel and more tweed, less bonnet and a touch more waist. Hats such as the one in the 1904 photograph were, as she herself said, impossible to wear let alone garden in. Underneath the cultivated air of romanticism and ethereal wafts of silk was a woman who was no stranger to the soil; her letters record 'arduous hours' spent in the borders where she favoured the 'diehards' over the fleeting flowers, and the 'lolloping bush'[10] over the tender annual.

Describing her own garden Norah attributed the lack of formal bedding to a combination of 'distaste and economy',[11] a typical combination of the aesthetic and practical expressed in much of her writing, although on occasions the romantic does appear to triumph. Penury entered Norah's life two decades after gardening but from then the two rapidly became partners. Norah did employ a head gardener, himself helped by a variety of garden boys from the village, but as she noted, a laissez-faire attitude to gardening meant fewer garden staff to patrol the borders. It was this easy and relaxed style that was to form the ideal backdrop for the house parties of the country house set of Edwardian England and its creator was soon in demand both as guest and garden adviser. It was the sheer lavishness of the flowers, the overwhelming richness of the beds, and the all-pervasive summer evening scents at Sutton Courtenay, that led to commissions from her friends and demands that similar gardens be created as backdrops for their own summer garden parties.

Nancy Astor commissioned Norah to decorate the interior of Cliveden in the same lavish style and was not disappointed as guests gasped both from astonishment and a need for fresh air as the June flowers filled the rooms with scent. Outside Norah used the pure blue of forget-me-nots to carpet the parterre beds in waves that echoed the skies of a still summer's evening. At Port Lympne (Kent) she created designs for the Great Stairs and the terraces below, as well as the herbaceous border and the two small enclosed gardens viewed from the house. Filling Port Lympne with flowers was made easier by the fact that the owner, Philip Sassoon, was only resident in August. The purples and mauves of the Aster Terrace, or the dahlias of the Striped Garden, did not display their emptiness in the bleakness of March or dreary days of December. Other clients and friends included Philip Kerr (Lord Lothian) at Blickling (Norfolk) where she slept in the golden Chinese guest bedroom while designing golden, yellow and silver beds of crocosmia, *Stachys olympica*, golden roses and achilleas.

The gardens at Kelmarsh Hall (Northamptonshire), home of Nancy Tree (later Nancy Lancaster), niece of Nancy Astor, were also strongly influenced by Norah in the years 1928–33; although Nancy Lancaster is remembered as a gardener in her own right, as well as a partner in Colefax and Fowler, arbiters of the 'English country taste'. The Long Border at Kelmarsh still has the power to arrest, with its richness and profusion following from the perfect colour combinations in the double borders. Mrs Gilbert Russell, yet another female client, employed Norah to design a small parterre for her at Mottisfont Abbey (Hampshire), recognising the closeness between the responsibility for interior and exterior house decoration at this period. As dinner parties drifted into garden parties and the garden came into the dining room, the borders and parterres became as much a backdrop for socialising as the flower arrangement and flower paintings of earlier centuries, and the responsibility for their decoration fell to the hostess and housewife. Certainly Vita Sackville-West encountered Norah's designs while attending a house party at Godmersham, recording on her return to Sissinghurst yet *another* wonderful Norah Lindsay flower border at the 'too beastly-rich Trittons'.[12] Many of the gardens Norah designed were featured in *Country Life*, often without any attribution to the designer. This must have been galling to Norah who was always ready to credit her own influences. Whether it was the gardens of Italy, Le Nôtre, the books of Gertrude Jekyll, or Norah's frequent house guest Ellen Willmott, she confessed to learning from them all. The subtle blend of

Italianate formalism with sheer wild abundance was, however, Norah's own. All this was not achieved without hard work. Norah worked on designs every morning from 5.30 a.m. until 8.30 a.m. in bed, no doubt waiting for the other house guests to get up. When she was being paid a daily rate, such as at Rotherfield Park, she would charge about £5 a day. At Cliveden, where she could be called in at any time, she earned a retainer of £100 a year, for which she worked hard. Norah was summed up memorably by a contemporary in the comment 'if you had money she was there to spend it'.[13] With more than 200 commissions over the twenty-odd years of her gardening career, Norah spent a lot of people's money.

Ironically, perhaps, the garden with which she was most closely associated, other than her own, is now remembered almost solely for its male owner, Lawrence Johnston. Hidcote Manor, Gloucestershire, still typifies the overflowing approach to planting championed by Norah. A myriad of seemingly endless garden 'rooms' display their riches of scent and colour throughout the seasons, although especially the spring and summer months. Hidcote was purchased by Johnston's mother, Gertrude Winthrop, an American who came to England in 1907 when Johnston was already 36 years of age. At first it was she who had the greatest influence on the garden, then considerably smaller, using the money she had inherited from two husbands. With the end of Johnston's army career in 1914 his focus turned to Hidcote and he devoted himself to the garden (and his garden at Serre de la Madone on the French Riviera) until his retirement to the Continent in 1948, shortly before his death. Identifying influences on the design and planting of these well loved and much visited gardens has become almost a national pastime; and it is fascinating to note how many of these were actually women.

Anna Pavord, in her guide to the gardens, notes the presence in Johnston's library of works by Gertrude Jekyll including *Colour in the Flower Garden* (published 1908), and the probable influence of the Munstead Wood borders on the Red Borders at Hidcote. The Italianate Pillar Garden with its clipped yews and Long Walk betrays an Italianate influence that could have been inspired at least in part by the pages of Edith Wharton's 1904 work on *Italian Villas and Their Gardens*.[14] Other commentators have noted similarities of design between Hidcote and Sissinghurst, Vita Sackville-West's own garden that was also being created at this period. Vita herself, describing the gardens for the *Journal of the Royal Horticultural Society* in 1949,[15] summed up

Rosa de Rescht

Recognised as a plantswoman rather than a designer, Nancy Lindsay's name occurs as many plant varieties, forming a rather intriguing selection. *Arum italicum* 'Nancy Lindsay' is a rich green foliage plant of the late winter/early spring whose silvery patterns herald the coming of the spring bulbs and lighten the dark soil; *Colchicum autumnale* 'Nancy Lindsay' appears at the opposite time of the year, bringing a splash of colour to shade as the darker nights draw in, and is suitable for gardens in colder climates. Nestling in among these rather specialist plants the *Dianthus* 'Nancy Lindsay' comes as somewhat of a light-hearted surprise in the borders. The plant that Nancy herself claimed as her own was the Rosa de Rescht. This deep rich velvet damask rose was 'discovered' in Persia by Nancy on her plant-hunting trip in 1945. Blooming in distinct cycles, the flowers are 4–5cm across and exude an exceptionally sweet and intense damask scent. Its mystique is heightened by the mystery of its discovery and loss. A possible description of it appeared as early as 1843 in a catalogue from the firm of Rivers of London, but its identity is unsure and the name given ('Pompone perpetual') of no help. Ellen Willmott referred to the lost Persian rose, the Gul e Reschti, in her work *The Genus Rosa*. By 1922 an unnamed rose of the same description was claimed to have been growing on a ranch in Idaho, but not until many years later was the claim substantiated. And so Nancy Lindsay is credited with the 'rediscovery' of this exquisite (but well-behaved) rose during her equally mysterious, undocumented plant-hunting expedition to Persia in 1945. Coincidentally it is classified in England as a Portland Rose, a class of roses named after Margaret, Duchess of Portland.

the planting style as 'spilling abundance' with plants 'seeding themselves where they did not rightly belong', a description that could have applied equally to Sutton Courtenay.

Of all these influences, however, it is that of Norah Lindsay which is best documented and recorded. Norah may have met Johnston at the house and gardens of Bobbie James, another American garden maker, at

St Nicholas, Barrow-in-Furness. Certainly by the late twenties, the last important phase in the creation of the Hidcote gardens, Norah had become an important influence on Johnston. Her hallmark style of massed flowers, mixing cottage and rare plants, self-seeds with rarities, can clearly be seen in many areas of the garden. Norah also persuaded Johnston to plant the Rose Borders at Hidcote; she herself adored roses and had a whole hedge of *Rosa damascena* at Sutton Courtenay. Her daughter Nancy had admired the wild roses of Persia during her plant collecting expedition there in the 1930s, expeditions perhaps partly financed by Johnston as he became too old to travel himself. During the thirties and forties Norah worked directly with Johnston at Hidcote, adding contrast and luxuriance to his design and colour principles.

Alas insufficient information is available on the developments in those years to be able to fully compare this working relationship with other gardening partnerships such as Jekyll and Lutyens or Sackville-West and Nicolson. As Jane Brown has suggested, it was perhaps the distaste of fellow woman gardener, Vita Sackville-West, that resulted in Norah being 'written out' of the Hidcote story. Although her planting style was emphatically written in, her name was conspicuously missing from Sackville-West's 1949 article on Hidcote.[16] So close was their working relationship, and so involved was Norah at Hidcote, that Lawrence Johnston had planned that she would come to live in the house, on his retirement to Menton, while the gardens themselves would go to The National Trust. The costs of the Manor House at Sutton Courtenay had long ago proved too much for Norah and the house had been let out for much of her later life.[17] Hidcote, to which she had devoted so much of her latter years, was however never to be her home; Norah died suddenly in 1948.

With Norah's death the green mantle of Hidcote fell to her daughter Nancy. Nancy Lindsay (she never married) had also been close to Johnston in those final years and was perhaps a better plantswoman than her mother. Here one might have thought was the ideal candidate to keep alive the spirit of Hidcote as it passed into National Trust hands. However, in addition to her emotional attachment to Hidcote, Nancy shared with her mother a lack of adherence to the norms of society, perhaps enhanced by her travels in Persia. An air of eccentricity and emotional involvement, even when combined with specialist knowledge of planting, does not lend itself well to a committee structure and Nancy Lindsay was to be absent from The National Trust advisory body for Hidcote after only a few short years.

James Lees-Milne, then working for The National Trust and responsible for the negotiations, described Nancy Lindsay as 'like an old witch, very predatory and interfering'. He continued, 'She maintains that she has been deputed by L.J. [Lawrence Johnston] to supervise these gardens in his absence abroad. We were not overcome with gratitude.'[18] As Lees-Milne went on to note, although Nancy Lindsay was at the actual signing ceremony with Lawrence Johnston, there was no formal condition made of this involvement and so her position was a difficult one. Over the following months letters passed between Nancy Lindsay and The National Trust about the garden which Nancy felt she was committed to supervise; a position for which she felt uniquely suited on account of both her long involvement with the site and her friendship with Johnston. The National Trust felt otherwise, stating bluntly after the receipt of one particularly long letter, 'The Gardens Committee must try and get rid of her'.[19] It was perhaps this rather acrimonious ending of the relationship between the Lindsays and the new carers of Hidcote that resulted until recently in a continued under-emphasis of the role that they played in the heyday of the gardens.[20]

Nancy Lindsay remained at the Manor House Cottage, Sutton Courteney until her death, despite the sale of the Manor itself. Here she kept some of her beloved roses, including those she had collected on her travels in Persia and some no doubt that she had brought first to Hidcote, before reaching their eventual resting place at the Manor Cottage. Some she offered to Vita Sackville-West including the rare mauve *Rosa centifolia* 'Tour de Malakoff' and the double golden briar rose from Persia. She is recorded as becoming increasingly eccentric in her later years, although still sharp enough to impress Graham Stuart Thomas on his visit to the Manor House Cottage for his book *Old Shrub Roses* (1955). A book incidentally with a foreword by Vita Sackville-West herself. As a plantswoman she would be pleased to be remembered in the Hosta 'Nancy Lindsay' (a sport of *Fortunei Hyacinthina*). Described as a mottled gold and green fading later to a dull mid-green, it seems appropriate for someone who had such a brilliant start but faded to obscurity.[21]

The seemingly endless round of country house parties that formed part of high society in the late nineteenth and early twentieth centuries may appear to be an unlikely breeding ground for a gardener, but Norah and Nancy Lindsay were not lone blooms. Several of the circle in which Norah moved are now recalled as much for their gardens as their social skills. Lady Ottoline Morrell created gardens at Garsington Manor (perhaps inspired or even part designed by Norah, but under the firm hand of Lady Ottoline). Her involvement in flowers was to be expected as Lady Ottoline was descended from the Cavendish-Bentinck line and her half-brother succeeded to the dukedom of Portland in 1879. Lady Sibyl Colefax was largely responsible for ensuring the safety of Hidcote in the hands of The National Trust, causing a rupture with Nancy Lindsay by doing so; and Mary de Navarro (née Anderson) retired from acting to make an Arts and Crafts garden at Court Farm, Broadway, with the help of the painter Alfred Parsons. Few, however, had quite the social profile of Daisy, Countess of Warwick.

Beautiful, reckless, and wealthy beyond most men's wildest dreams, Frances Evelyn Maynard (1861–1938) was one of the most desirable women at court in the 1880s. Her father's death had been rapidly followed by that of her grandfather's, leaving her as sole heiress to the considerable family estates at the tender age of 4. Queen Victoria, with sound financial accumen, felt that the wealthy heiress would make an ideal wife for her own son, Leopold. 'Daisy' however had a different view, and refusing the Prince turned instead to the arms of his Equerry, Lord Brooke, heir to the Earl of Warwick. Lord Brooke was a member of the close-knit and influential Marlborough House set and on their marriage Daisy became readily accepted at Marlborough House and gardens. Gardens which she later described as 'the finest surroundings for flirtation to be found in the Metropolis'.[22]

Flirtation rather than planting was certainly uppermost in her mind at this time and after marriage came the affairs. Her first ended in a scandal, as she publicly berated Lord Beresford for unfaithfulness when his wife's pregnancy was announced. Turning for comfort, with rare predictability, to the person who had acted as go-between, Daisy commenced an affair with the Prince of Wales that was to last for nine years. A photograph dated 1885 shows members of the Marlborough House set, including the Prince of Wales, posed languorously on the steps of Daisy's house, Easton Lodge in Essex. A decade later they were to be replaced with leading lights of the socialist and trade union movements as Daisy's interests swung from sex to socialism, and from the Prince to the Salvation Army.

With the Lodge itself full of numerous guests and their entourages, Daisy created a quiet hideaway on the edge of the estate where she and select friends could retire. It was around this cottage of Stone Hall that Daisy created her first gardens. Typically Victorian in their sentimentality they included The Garden of Friendship, The Border of

Sentiment, The Rosarie and The Shakespeare Border. Each garden was themed, as reflected in their names, and each plant was labelled, with handmade labels in the shape of butterflies and other creatures. Those in the Shakespeare Border included quotes from the bard's plays and sonnets; while the Friendship Garden was composed of gifts from friends with a heart-shaped label identifying the giver and the date. The Shakespeare Border was a comfortable mix of traditional and native plants, if primarily known for their symbolism rather than their inherent beauty. By the mid-1890s although the gardens of Friendship and Sentiment appear to have lived on, Daisy's own sympathies and loyalties had undergone a transformation, with her dramatic and public conversion to the cause of socialism. In a campaign to bring gardening, and more specifically horticultural and agricultural careers, to the mass of women, Daisy set up an agricultural school for women in 1898 and founded *The Woman's Agricultural Times* in the same year. Cheekily using the patronage of her ex-lover, now King Edward VII, she also raised funding for the Studley Horticultural College for Women in 1903.

A newly found enthusiasm for socialism did not lead to any diminution in her collection of gardens, or indeed her ability to spend money on them. In 1902 Harold Peto, landscape architect and designer of the Italianate School, was commissioned by Daisy to undertake a transformation of the main gardens surrounding Easton Lodge. Under the direction of Daisy, Peto created a sunken, stone-flagged garden, set around a 100ft balustraded Italianate Pool, planted with lilies from the exclusive French breeder Latour-Marliac. Around the old croquet lawns a series of vast arched pergolas dripped with roses and scented plants, forming shady galleries of scents and colours, while woodland walks led to a tree house and maze. Utilising labour from the Salvation Army home for inebriates, a Japanese Garden was created stretching from the pergolas down to the lower lake, where a tea-house, temples and Japanese figure 'greeted' visitors. This vast effort of landscaping and earth shifting was achieved over a long wet winter and must have been a rather sobering experience for the sixty-seven souls employed to transform vision to reality.

In 1918 her house at Easton Lodge was burnt down for the third time in its history, the fire being caused by a sick pet monkey who had been wrapped in a blanket and set near a stove for extra warmth. The west wing and servants quarters were gutted and the architect Philip Tilden was called in, contributing also a new series of stone walks and flower beds to one side of the house. The Peto Pavilion, popularly if wrongly ascribed to Harold Peto's alterations, was also constructed at that time, and a pavilion brought from Maresfield Park in Sussex to sit at the head of the Japanese Garden valley. This latest phase of garden creation was to be the beginning of the end. The seemingly endless supply of wealth was finally running dry and by the mid-1920s Daisy was already beginning a period of retrenchment, selling off the outlying estates at Dunmow to her tenants. Between this time and her eventual death in 1938, Daisy became increasingly concerned with issues of animal and social welfare and less attracted to the formal or sentimental aspects of gardening. At Stone Hall, once the centre for her Sentiment and Friendship gardens, she fenced off an area of 4 acres to create a bird sanctuary; noting in her autobiography *Life's Ebb and Flow* (1929) that the overgrown gardens were now alive with birdsong. In 1937 she decided to create a nature reserve in the park itself, with Shetland ponies, St Kilda sheep, and deer. Aviaries were built to hold her collection of 330 bird species, and a retired keeper from London Zoo was employed to care for them. So successful was she in her new guise of wildlife gardener and bird protector that she was asked to write a foreword to *The Observer's Book of British Birds*. Daisy finally died in 1938 surrounded by wildlife and wilder gardens.

Wild flowers and plants had been a vital inspiration in Gertrude Jekyll's childhood years and were to remain so throughout her life. In later years Jekyll (1843–1932) recalled wearing out her first copy of that all-time favourite, Revd C.A. Johns' *Flowers of the Field* (first published in 1853 but republished throughout the nineteenth century). Using this delightful but learned work to identify plants she brought home from her rambles among the fields and lanes gave her, as she later recalled, 'the first firm steps in the path of plant knowledge'.[23] Although Jekyll is often thought of as a late developer in gardening, having spent much of her early adult years involved in arts and crafts, she saw a direct link between those early childhood rambles and her later flowering as one of the greatest 'amateur' garden designers. The rambles inspired her to her own efforts at cultivation and the creation of a small child's garden at the house in Guildford. It was this childhood love of practical work with the soil that she remembered all her life. 'It is', she said, 'because I have been more or less a gardener all my life that I still feel like a child in many ways.'[24] With her endearing nickname of 'Bumps', her deep and genuine love of the natural world, and her positive and infectious enthusiasm, it is easy to see the child within the plump, bespectacled, elderly lady who regards us sagely from her portrait. Her energy and appetite for physical activity almost denied us any portrait, as she found no time to sit for the artist William Nicholson. To while away the time while waiting for the sprightly 77-year-old to return from the nursery and potting sheds he painted a pair of her gardening boots, creating a 'portrait' almost as famous as that of the lady herself.

Despite her own long memories of the importance of the garden in her life there was little outward sign of a future career in garden design in the early years. Born in London in 1843 to a respectable and safe upper-middle-class family, her grandfather Joseph was an intellectual and scholar, while her father Edward was an army man. More remote ancestors were later to be described by her younger brother as 'respectable . . . but not particularly interesting'.[25] Edward retired from the Grenadier Guards on marrying Julia, Gertrude's mother, in 1836 and both parents were at home for much of Gertrude's childhood years. Julia's quiet, practical efficiency appears to have combined happily with Edward's high-spirited volatility and enthusiasms to produce the pragmatic yet enthusiastic character of Gertrude. She also carried on their aesthetic passions, although trading their love of music for the visual arts. The Jekyll family, parents and six children, moved to Bramley House, Surrey when Gertrude was 5, and this was to be her home for the next twenty years. Typical of their period the gardens consisted of parterres housing perlargoniums (Tom Thumb), lobelia, calceolaria and other bedding plants. A central vase contained an aloe. A shrubbery, small pine collection, Verbena Garden and walled kitchen garden completed the pleasure ground, all set within a wider estate of some 60 acres. A move to the larger estate of Wargrave Hill, where her father died in 1876, was followed by the return to the Bramley area and the beloved Munstead Heath. It was here at Munstead House that Gertrude was to create her first garden.

By the time of the move to Munstead House Gertrude was 35 years of age. Unlike some of her siblings she was still unmarried, a somewhat unusual state of affairs for a cultured, intelligent, relatively affluent daughter of respectable parents; but perfectly normal for a budding female gardener. Instead of undertaking the normal pursuit of marriage Gertrude had instead spent her time pursuing her own interests and in particular developing her skills in a range of arts and crafts. In 1861 she had enrolled in the Central School for Art and Design, then at South Kensington. Travelling to the school from her home she took lessons in segregated women-only classes from 1.00–3.30 p.m., including drawing, perspective, design, oil and watercolours, and also anatomy and botany. She was only the fourth female to enrol in the school and her presence there demonstrates not only her own determination but the supportive character of her family life. Sketches and paintings of Jekyll's survive from this period and indicate an accomplished, but not outstanding, student. Between 1865 and 1870 she exhibited nine pictures, one piece gaining the rather double-edged comment from Ruskin of 'very wonderful and interesting'. All nine were of animal subjects and one wonders if she deliberately turned away from the traditional female role of flower painter towards the animal world.[26] Two of these sketches, 'Froggy would a wooing go' and 'Portrait of Thomas in the Character of Puss in Boots', remind one strongly of Beatrix Potter in their clearly observed animal bodies.

Deteriorating eyesight brought an early close to her painting ambitions and she turned instead to a range of other crafts, including embroidery, wood carving, wood inlay, and even repoussé work. Just as her painting career ended so her reputation for other crafts was to take off and throughout the next decade she was in demand for room decoration and furnishings of all kinds. Her embroidery included flowers and plants taken as tracings or pricked out from garden books and botanical watercolours, continuing a tradition of many centuries. A commission for the redecoration of the rooms of the Blumenthals, at 43 Hyde Park Gate, brought Gertrude into contact with many famous artists and social notables of the period including William Morris, Burne-Jones, and others of the Pre-Raphaelite brotherhood. Their philosophy of close observation was to come through in her garden design. Travel also took up many months of her time, with trips to Algiers complementing earlier travels in the Levant and providing an Islamic influence that marks so much of the Arts and Crafts period. One wonders how much the rills of Hestercombe or the courtyard plantings at Munstead owe to these travels.

A few years after her mother's own return, Gertrude Jekyll heeded the call of her Surrey homeland. By 1882 she had purchased 15 acres of her own opposite the family's Munstead House. This was the plot on which she was eventually to create her own home and gardens, assisted by Edwin Lutyens. The description of Munstead Wood as recorded by Jekyll in *Gardens for Small Country Houses*, is not one to excite most gardeners. Triangular in shape, the site on 'the poorest possible soil' slopes down on the north and west sides. Made up of old sandy heath and pine plantation, only a small portion to the north had ever been used as arable land. Topsoil was in short supply. It was on this poor, acidic soil that Jekyll was to create one of the most famous gardens in

England, and from here she was to send out plants and designs to enhance many a small country house. While in the house that rose from this landscape she began to write the books that have guided generations of gardeners that have come after her.[27] Despite the strong emphasis on planning and design in her own books, the garden at Munstead did not have a definite plan at the beginning. Instead each area was treated on its merits with a piecemeal approach, which Jekyll later said resulted in some 'awkward angles' that needed to be reconciled.[28] A confession and regret that many gardeners may share in when looking back on their own gardens. Woodland areas were exploited to create maturity in the gardens, with areas of birch, sweet chestnut and an old Scots Pine being retained to create wooded walks on the southern and eastern parts. For the first few years of ownership Gertrude Jekyll still lived across the road at Munstead House, there being no house on the site of Munstead Wood. However, a chance encounter at a tea party in 1889 was to create not only a new home but also a new partnership in her life.

When Edwin Lutyens met Gertrude Jekyll at that tea party table she was already a mature woman of 46, busy establishing a reputation in gardens to rival her first in arts and crafts. Lutyens on the other hand was a young 20-year-old, just starting out on a career in architecture. It seems an unlikely friendship from a chance encounter, but something magic happened that day and the partnership of Lutyens and Jekyll (Ned and Bumps as they affectionately called each other) was born. In the following years Lutyens not only completed the house at Munstead Wood for its very particular owner, but also established a style that was to appeal successfully to owners across the country. A style complemented perfectly by the designs and plantings of Gertrude Jekyll. Jekyll emphasised the role of colour harmonies in garden design, while Lutyens championed the harmonies of vernacular architecture; Jekyll treasured the traditional old cottage garden plants, Lutyens the traditional old building materials; both valued craftsmanship and locality. The partnership could hardly fail. Their commissions together produced such outstanding works as The Deanery Garden (1899), Folly Farm (1906), Hestercombe (1908) and Lindisfarne (1910), as well as Munstead Wood. Separately they were to carry out hundreds of works both in England and abroad (Jekyll's commissions numbering over 400), but it was the partnership works that stand out across time.[29]

Munstead Wood remains the best-known collaboration between Jekyll and Lutyens, and one which has survived the ravages of time.

The Long Border with its careful modulations of cool greys, blues and contrasting yellows still builds to a hot crescendo of oranges and reds before cooling again into the distance. The Primrose Garden, set in a clearing of oaks and hazels, still survives and although her own strains of white and yellow bunch-flowered primroses (*Primula* 'Munstead Bunch', 'Munstead White' and 'Bunch Primrose Sultan') have departed, others have replaced them. Fifteen acres allowed areas to be set apart for specialist or seasonal planting; the iris and lupin borders, the Michaelmas daisy borders and the Pansy Garden were all recorded both in Jekyll's own photographs and by visiting artists. The Grey Garden, devoted to plants with grey and silver foliage with flowers of purple, pink and white, was in existence long before the more famous White Garden at Sissinghurst and may have partly been its inspiration.

Munstead Wood house was surrounded by planting. A terrace on the south side and carefully selected climbers over the walls gave the impression of house and land meeting, but neither overwhelming the other. Jekyll held the opinion that the happiest result was one where 'the architect and the gardener must have some knowledge of each other's business, and each must regard with feelings of kindly reverence the unknown domains of the other's higher knowledge'.[30] At Munstead Wood of course the architect and gardener had more than some knowledge, although still there were weekends of frustration and feuding as Jekyll imposed her own particular needs and style on Lutyens' ideals. Fanning out from the more formal gardens around the house were the wilder woodland and fern gardens, with walks leading through fields of daffodils or rhododendrons depending on the seasons. Ferns, Solomon's Seal and trilliums were used in shady areas, with stately foxgloves and silver birch giving points of colour in the green shade. Each area of the garden had its own character, carefully thought out and planted to make the best use of the conditions and the space. Even if the original divisions had been created in haste, they were planted with reference to the needs of the space and the needs of the plants. It was this, in addition to her understanding of the influence of colour, that made Jekyll's designs so successful.

In the first decades of the twentieth century Munstead was a honeypot for garden designers, garden writers and garden artists. Vita Sackville-West visited Munstead Wood in 1917, being taken there by Lutyens who wanted Lady Sackville (Vita's mother) to meet his Aunt Bumps. Vita recorded: 'Miss Jekyll rather fat, and rather grumbly; garden not at its best, but can see it must be lovely'.[31] Other visitors included the novelist and gardener Edith Wharton from America, who had the misfortune to arrive with a group of fashionable and ignorant sightseers, Mrs Francis King (an American garden writer) and Beatrix Farrand, who was later to save Jekyll's papers from destruction by taking them to her school of landscape studies at Reef Point Gardens, Maine. William Robinson, Dean Samuel Reynolds Hole, Harry Mangles and Ellen Willmott were all close gardening friends and were frequent guests until their own or Jekyll's infirmities made visits difficult. Although she corresponded with Frances Wolseley and became a patron of the Glynde School for Lady Gardeners there is no record that she ever employed any female gardeners trained at Glynde. Jekyll was a supporter of women's suffrage, making and embroidering a banner for the Godalming branch of the Association of Women's Suffrage. Unsurprisingly, Munstead Wood was beloved of garden artists. Created by an artist, with an artist's training and use of palette, the Long Border in particular drew Helen Allingham,[32] while Thomas Hunn recorded the Pansy Garden.

As her fame grew and design commissions came from all over England and Europe, she also began to write. At first she penned articles in magazines such as *The Garden* (edited by William Robinson) and *Country Life*, but at 56 years of age her first gardening book appeared. She quickly made up for her late start, penning inspirational but eminently practical books on an almost annual basis: *Wood and Garden* (1899) was followed by *Home and Garden* (1900) and *Wall and Water Gardens* (1901). *Lilies for English Gardens* (1901) and *Roses for English Gardens* (1902) were followed by a few plantless years (devoted instead to recording local vernacular architecture) but *Colour in the Flower Garden* arrived in 1908.

Gertrude Jekyll's eye for colour was unerring and the publication of her *Colour in the Flower Garden* must have been the despair of many a nurseryman or seed dealer. Perhaps due to her artist's training, or perhaps due to her extreme short sightedness, she both saw and recalled colour with an astounding accuracy and particularity. On her favourite colour, blue, for example, she was able to define it exactly by using examples from the plant world:

> When blue is named . . . what is meant is a perfectly pure blue, a colour that is perfect and complete in itself – that has no inclinations whatever to a reddish or purplish tone. It means the blue of *commelina*, of *salvia patens*, of *lithospermum*, and some of the gentians; of *Ipomoea* 'Heavenly Blue', of *Anagallis phillipsii*, of

> *anchusa* and the best delphiniums, with the lighter blues of forget-me-not, *Omphalodes verna* and *nemophila*. These and a few others may be described as perfectly pure blues.[33]

It must have been almost physically painful to her to see flowers described as 'brilliant amethystine blue' which she regarded as being 'a stone of washy purple colour' not even faintly approaching a real blue colour.[34] Typically, it was the blue of the delphinium flower that held her enraptured, rather than 'the duller colour of the third rate gem'. The use of the terms 'bright golden yellow', or 'gorgeous flame coloured' also left her incredulous. In her exasperated analysis of what was commonly meant by these colours one can just catch the sense of someone whose appreciation of colour has a finer tuning than common humanity, and who cannot quite understand how it is the rest of us get it so wrong. Again it is the plant catalogues that are guilty: 'Nothing is more frequent in plant catalogues than "bright golden yellow", when bright yellow is meant. Gold is not bright yellow. I find that a gold piece laid on a gravel path, or against a sandy bank, nearly matches it in colour; and I cannot think of any flower that matches or even approaches the true colour of gold.'[35] Woe betide the garden owner who expressed a preference for such colours as 'apple green' or 'pea green' or even the seemingly innocent 'snow white', to all of which she held up her hands in dismay. Her critical facilities were, however, balanced with a lively playfulness of observation. In *Children and Gardens*, for example, she shares the discovery that 'It is amusing to dress up a snapdragon seedpod, when it is brown and dry as an old woman. If you look at it you will see how curiously like a face it is, with large eyes and open mouth . . . If you shake her she weeps little black tears.'[36]

Although perhaps not as well disposed towards rabbits as Beatrix Potter, it was Jekyll's ability to empathise with children and animals (her numerous cats and a donkey named Jack who ate one side of her favourite rambling rose) that made her book *Children and Gardens* (1908) so natural. Many gardeners would have difficulty even embarking on such a title, and the worthy Victorian ladies who had gone before her had produced books that veered between staggering sentimentality and mind-numbing botanical correctness. To Jekyll, the topic appeared a natural one and no advice could be more welcome to children than 'There can be no doubt that the proper place for our shoes and stockings is on or near a garden bench.' Writing in her mid-sixties, she drew on a well of memories taking her back to her own childhood:

'more than half a century has passed [since first seeing a primrose copse], and yet each spring, when I wander into the primrose wood, and see the pale yellow blooms and smell their sweetest of scents . . . for a moment I am seven years old again and wandering in the fragrant wood.' She continues: 'Well do I remember the time when I thought there were two kinds of people in the world – children and grown ups – and that the world really belonged to children. And I think it is because I have more or less been a gardener all my life that I still feel like a child in many ways, although from the number of years I have lived I ought to know that I am quite an old woman.'[37]

Her old age was haunted by a degree of penury and hardship that it is difficult to understand given the popularity of her books and the sheer number of her designs. By the time of Jekyll's death in 1932 she had, rather predictably, come to be regarded as something of an eccentric. Her naturally large and healthy appetite and accompanying tendency to plumpness had produced a figure that was rather too round to be stern, but her thick round glasses and life-long adherence in public to black clothing and large hats, resulted in an old-fashioned slightly formidable appearance. With the death or departure of many of her old friends and plantsman colleagues she became isolated. Although Ellen Willmott was not to die until two years after her friend,[38] Jekyll must have been pained to observe the slow inexorable break-up of Ellen's magnificent plant collection in those final years of financial disaster, struggling as she was with her own retrenchments. She disliked 'modern contrivances', although she habitually listened to the radio her brother had installed for her against her wishes. Visitors became fewer after the early 1920s, and she became less likely to take casual visitors on tours, blaming her painful eyesight. In 1925 Mrs Francis King found the garden and Gertrude Jekyll 'little changed' since she had visited twenty years earlier. In those twenty years, however, much had changed in the world beyond the wood and perhaps it was no wonder that this remarkable woman, born in a different age, was regarded as eccentric.

Eccentricity did not just impress upon Ellen Willmott's later years, it was a trademark of her entire life. But it was through her gardens, and in particular her plant collecting, plant hybridisation, and her published work on roses,[39] that she was to earn lasting fame. So highly regarded was her work that she was elected a Fellow of the Linnean Society, the first ever woman to be thus honoured and, alongside Gertrude Jekyll, one of the first to receive the Victoria Medal of Honour from the Royal Horticultural Society. Ellen did not just specialise in roses but also bred new strains of snowdrops, daffodils and iris, as well as financing plant-hunting expeditions by E.H. Wilson, resulting in the introduction of many new plants from China. Warley Place (Essex), one of her three gardens, was estimated to contain over 100,000 varieties and species just prior to the First World War. Even during the war years the garden was described in *Country Life* as being 'a crowded gallery of masterpieces' that once seen in springtime was never to be forgotten.[40] Over 600 varieties and species of narcissus were planted along the daffodil banks including her own varieties *Narcissus* 'Warleyensis', *Narcissus* 'Great Warley' and *Narcissus* 'Warley Magna', while *Epimedium x warleyense* provided a rich foil for the bright spring yellows.

Born into similar upper-middle-class comfort as Gertrude Jekyll, Ellen (1858–1934)[41] and her sister Rose were fortunate in having a wealthy godmother who showered them with gifts. A cheque for £1,000 left on her breakfast plate on each birthday made Ellen a wealthy young lady by the age of 21. Her father came into his own inheritance in 1866, adding further to the family's social standing and wealth. In 1875 a new house was acquired to match this new status. Warley Place, Essex presented a face of the highest respectability to the world, with its carriageways and double entrance lodges, and with an estate of over 30 acres. More importantly for Ellen, then in her eighteenth year, and her sister Rose, 15, it allowed them to expand their already active interests in gardening. Although less well known than Ellen, Rose was also a gardener. Described by Ellen as having, even at the age of 15, 'a rare taste in effective grouping', she designed many of the beds and borders at Warley Place using herbaceous planting that was to remain there until its final sale. Her style was that of William Robinson and the *English Garden*, a world away from the Victorian bedding and ribbon borders that both mother and daughters disliked intensely. Mrs Willmott was also involved in the planting and Ellen later recorded that many a traditional Essex plant was hunted across the county by mother or daughters, ensuring it was present in the borders of Warley. The thrill of the plant chase, albeit in the somewhat unexotic territories of rural Essex, was to haunt Ellen for the rest of her life.

In addition to plant chasing, the two girls and their mother devoted themselves to the usual round of enjoyments, balls, visits, lawn tennis (at which Ellen was rather good), rides and walks. In the background, however, was always the garden. In the pleasure grounds Ellen constructed a Gipsy Hut near the pond with her own hands, and in 1879, for her twenty-first birthday, she claimed an area of ground to commence construction and planting of an Alpine Garden. Perhaps indicative of the scale of things to come, this was no small rockery to indulge a young girl's passing whim. Excavation of the Rock Garden was carried out not by the family's gardening staff but by the specialist firm Backhouse & Son of York. A deep gorge was planned by Ellen, sheltering the plants within and cutting wide sweeps and falls through the huge boulders. Deep curving steps passed through the planting and the path traversed a bridge, below which a fernery grotto was created.

In 1888 Ellen's godmother Helen Tasker[42] died, leaving the enormous sum of £140,000 to each of the sisters. Their fortunes were changed forever. By then almost 30 and beginning to suffer with inherited rheumatism, Ellen was no longer the gay and energetic girl devoted to dances and tennis. In their place was the self-determination and slight wilfulness that were to mark her adult years. No marriage had ever been in the offing, no broken engagement, or sighed-over absent lover ever recorded in her firm hand; instead that hand recorded the daily round at Warley and the trips abroad. Again the same question arises as with Gertrude Jekyll, Frances Wolseley and Nancy Lindsay. What circumstance of character or fate led to the derailment of that standard Victorian journey from childhood to coming out to marriage to childbearing? Was it strength of will, the obvious abilities and intelligence, or the independent character of these women that served to scare off possible admirers? Or did their interests lay elsewhere in the garden? Certainly in her later years Ellen was considered as being too independently minded to hide her disdain of men less intelligent or knowledgeable than she was. Disdain is not early learnt, however, and surely unlikely to have been present in a girl of 20. In each case gardening appears to have come before 'disappointment' and was not the 'heaven sent blessing' for those with unfulfilled lives envisaged by Theresa Earle.[43]

An early indication of impulsive extravagance was the purchase by Ellen of the Château at Tresserve near Aix. Accompanied only by Rose she bought the property while on holiday, using her own capital. The gardens at Tresserve and Warley were planned to be the joint responsibility of Rose and Ellen, but with Rose's marriage in 1890 Ellen was free to take on the responsibility that one suspects she had always longed for. Dividing her energies between the two gardens now, Tresserve and Warley Place, Ellen began to purchase enormous quantities of plants. Purchasing only from select sources, she gave the nurseryman Henri Correvon carte blanche to send her any new and interesting plants from his gardens in Geneva, also purchasing from him plants that could be obtained easily and more cheaply in England.[44] By the mid-1890s gardening and plant breeding had begun to take on the obsessive quality that was to eventually bankrupt her. Joining the Royal Horticultural Society in 1894, she was elected to the Narcissus Committee only three years later, having accomplished in that short time the work on the hybridisation and growing of daffodils for which she is still famous.[45] Ellen earned numerous Awards of Merit for her daffodils and in particular the *Triandrus* hybrids, including *Triandrus* 'Ada' named after the youngest sister who had died young, and *Narcissus* 'Warleyensis', an Ajax daffodil. Daffodils were only one of many bulb species planted in incredible quantities at Warley, with 10,000 *Camassia esculenta* bought in one order alone and planted to naturalise. Her dedication led to close connections within the nursery trade and soon she was both purchasing and supplying bulbs in the trade, becoming well respected for her skills and knowledge although also rather feared for her forthright appraisals of poor service or inferior bulb supplies.

In 1894, Ellen acquired the promising young Swiss gardener Jacob Maurer from the nursery of Henri Correvon. He was added to a staff that already comprised James Preece, the head gardener, Mr Candler, the foreman for herbaceous plants, and a small army of under-gardeners. At one time Ellen employed 104 gardeners, divided between her gardens in England and those in Europe, the impression of an army being emphasised by their uniforms, made to her own design. Maurer's arrival set the scene for the final transformation of both Warley and Tresserve into world-class collector's gardens. A rose collection was established including *Rosa fedtschenkoana*, collected in the regions Turkestan and Koram in the 1870s by Madame Olga Fedtschenko, who later worked at Kew.[46] A water plant collection was established in a series of gardens created from old ponds and the alpine garden was overhauled, and an alpine hut, thought to have been slept in by Ellen's hero Napoleon, was brought over in its entirety from Bourg St Pierre complete with herdsman gear and alpine furniture. Plants were daily packed and sent away to Kew or to shows, seed lists were created and sent worldwide, exchanges were made with some of the top professional breeders of the day. The year 1897 saw the award of the RHS Victoria Medal of Honour to Ellen. Seven years later Ellen was awarded the Fellowship of the Linnean Society, along with nine other distinguished lady botanists, the first women ever to be awarded fellowships. Things were looking good for women and for Ellen.

Ellen's interest in photography, an interest held in common with Gertrude Jekyll, resulted in her publishing a record of the gardens at Warley in 1909 as *Warley Garden in Spring and Summer*. Dedicated to her sister Rose, the book was a showcase both for the planting and its author's photographic skills, although it contained little text. A copy of the second edition (1924) was given by Ellen to Daisy, Countess of Warwick, with an inscription in Ellen's hand drawing attention to the connection between John Evelyn and Warley. Ellen was a great admirer of the seventeenth-century diarist and gardener, but her claims that the gardens were 'much as Evelyn left them' were far fetched in the extreme. Ellen Willmott had also used her photographs to help Gertrude Jekyll illustrate her book *Children and Gardens* in 1908. Although many of the photographs are by Jekyll herself, one of Elizabeth von Arnim (of *Elizabeth's German Garden* fame) seated in front of a playhouse is by Ellen. Writing about the photograph Jekyll describes Ellen Willmott as 'the greatest of living women-gardeners'.[47]

Not satisfied with the collections obtained through nurserymen, Ellen started to personally fund plant expeditions, employing Gerald Davidson to search out rare pelargoniums in the Cape to be sent back to her own hothouses. Other expeditions resulted in the introduction of *Iris willmottiana* and the dwarf *Iris willmottiana alba*. *Tulipa willmottiae* came from the eastern Armenian mountains, while Ernest 'Chinese' Wilson was pressed into further oriental plant forays despite the implorings of his young wife. Ellen's attitude towards the claims of the marital bed can perhaps be judged from her attitude towards Wilson's wife, who she described as a 'tiresome, ignorant woman unable to see the possibilities' of this dangerous expedition which was to be undertaken on behalf of the Arnold Arboretum and Ellen. Ellen was rewarded for her determination, and her personal 'bribe' of £200 to Wilson's wife, by his packages of rhododendrons, rose seeds and *Paeonia delavayi*. The roses in particular added to the stature of the rose collection at Warley, flowering earlier and in more profusion than those that Kew had received. In 1910 Ellen published the first part of her monumental work on *The Genus Rosa*, dedicated to Queen Alexandra. Illustrated by Alfred Parsons, the second volume was to come out in the inauspicious year of 1914 and only 260 copies were sold. Still regarded as one of the authoritative works on roses, it was given a genuine and authoritative tribute by Gertrude Jekyll in the *Quarterly Review*, describing it as an important and beautiful book,[48] although the National Rose Society did not review it until 1916;

perhaps because Ellen had accomplished it without their assistance or perhaps because it contained so many wild and species rose.

Not content with Tresserve and Warley, Ellen had purchased a further garden in the summer of 1906. Following her frequent visits to the Hanburys at their famous Riviera gardens at La Mortola, she purchased the villa and land of Boccanegra, barely 3 kilometres away from them in the Ventimiglia region of the Italian Riviera. Employing yet more gardeners and providing profits for yet more nurseries, Ellen planted Mediterranean plants that would thrive in such conditions. Figs, opuntia, acacia, orange trees, bay trees, pittosporum, cedars, eleagnus and yuccas – many plants that she could not hope to grow outside at Warley Place or even Tresserve. Creating a garden from almost nothing was expensive. Over £2,000 was spent at local suppliers, let alone the rare and specialist planting which she obtained from international and European dealers.[49] With three gardens in three different climatic zones she now spent her year chasing flowering times across Europe. Boccanegra in January for the Italian early spring, Warley for the late spring and summer months, then on to Tresserve often for the grape harvest, and Boccanegra again. Ellen kept up a constant correspondence with the head gardeners at each of the properties, and a series of pre-printed addressed postcards were left with the gardeners so that they might instantly communicate with her. Each visit would only last about a month and then it would be on again to the next garden, taking with her an entourage of servants, leaving behind an exhausted garden staff. She also kept up a constant flow of communication with Kew, and the Botanic Gardens of Oxford and Cambridge, claiming new introductions, checking identifications, querying growth regimes. Production of *The Genus Rosa* also took up much time, as disputes with Alfred Parsons and the publishers veered towards litigation.

Whether the cause was the strain of keeping up three astounding gardens, or the high costs of production of *The Genus Rosa*, the first decade of the twentieth century saw dangerous signs of impending financial instability. In 1907 Ellen was forced to borrow a sum of £15,000 secured upon her Warley Estate and farms, and a further £3,000 soon followed. Then in 1911 Preece, the head gardener, was asked to leave as an economy. This seems almost inexplicable as there were so many other economies that could have been made and Preece had proved himself a skilled and loyal man, but it was to become typical of her ill-management of financial stress. Perhaps Ellen felt that she herself could take over thus saving on wages, but she eventually employed a man called Fielder, a competent gardener who grasped the ways in which the garden was run and continued with the string of show successes. In 1912 the RHS awarded *Corylopsis warleyensis* the Award of Merit, one of the seeds of which had been collected by 'Chinese' Wilson, and there were many other awards. Awards of Merit, however, do not pay the bills, and both friends and solicitors tried to warn her of the impending doom. Incredible as it may seem she could not bring herself to sell one of her properties in order to free capital for the maintenance of the remaining two. She dreamt of renting one or more of the properties, or selling her more expensive musical instruments (she had two Amati violins as well as a Stradivarius) but somehow nothing came of the unattractive visions of financial retrenchment and storm clouds continued to gather.

In that most uncertain of years, 1914, a further blow came with the bankruptcy of her father's old firm, which had lent her considerable sums against the house. Fortunately for her the mortgage had been repurchased by a close friend (Sir Frank Crisp) who now took over the debt. She was bailed out, but only on the promise of selling Tresserve. Lavish rebuilding had taken place at Tresserve following a fire, and that added to ongoing plant buying had resulted in further debts in France, where a lawsuit was now pending. Selling would release her from those debts and help refloat Warley. In 1915, despite loans from Sir Frank Crisp of Friar Park, she was forced to ask for contributions from friends to provide for day-to-day outgoings. She toyed with the idea of starting a school of gardening, along the lines of the Glynde School, but again nothing came of it. Indecision and inability to cope with debt transfixed her. In addition to monetary problems the war had by now had an impact on the workforce at Warley, although ironically the call to military service must have at least relieved her of some of the enormous wage bill. When the time finally came, at Rose's insistence, to rent out Tresserve and Boccanegra and sell up much of the contents of these and Warley, Ellen was to take comfort in the fact that she could 'put it down to the war' and not lose too much face. Rose herself was meanwhile battling with the cancer that was to lead to her early death, another severe blow to Ellen. The Christmas of 1916 was spent alone, with few staff and only an oil heater in a house that, at the best of times, was icy. As war ended she was still struggling, and then just when it looked as though Warley would have to be sold she finally managed to sell both Tresserve and Boccanegra.

Financial and one suspects some mental relief came from these sales, and the next eighteen years were to see her finances reach an exhausted truce. Intermittent panics left Warley Place with fewer and fewer staff, and Ellen with slightly fewer of her rich possessions. A piece of jewellery, some rich inlaid furnishings, musical instruments from the past; all disappeared in ones and twos. Miraculously the awards for plants still kept coming in, the trips to the RHS Committee Rooms continued, and plant lists were still issued and distributed worldwide. This world of contrasts is nowhere better illustrated than in her famous shoplifting trial in 1918. One feels almost sorry for the store detective at the Galeries Lafayette who chose to apprehend the eccentrically dressed middle-aged lady. At the last minute an additional scarf was purchased direct rather than charged to her account as the rest had been. Alas, any receipt was absent-mindedly not retained and as Ellen and the scarf left the store, the detectives were following. Detained in the manager's office while the store arranged for charges to be brought against her, Ellen's phone call to Queen Mary and the subsequent hasty arrival of the King's Private Secretary must have horrified detective and manager alike. Typically she would not go quietly, but insisted on being publicly exonerated. After spending the night at the Marlborough Street Police Station, Ellen was cleared by magistrates the next morning; it was a public scandal for the Galeries Lafayette in an age when social deference was an essential attribute of such a store. On release from the court she declared it a victory for women's rights, claiming, probably correctly, that a less well-connected or less vociferous woman in the same position would have been convicted wrongly and unjustly by the testimony of men. When she died in 1934 Ellen was remembered by half her world as an eccentric, slightly cantankerous old lady dressed for a bygone age, but by the other half as a dedicated plantsperson, breeder and collector, and the greatest of women gardeners. A flurry of obituaries on both her personal and, more especially, her professional horticultural life followed. Then the silence of obscurity settled; a silence that many women gardeners share.

One can hardly accuse posterity of silence where Vita Sackville-West (1892–1962) is concerned.[50] Whether as poet, novelist, plantsperson, lover, traveller, gardener, or any one of the many personas that she gathered to herself, larger than life she strides across garden design of the twentieth century. Born nine years before the end of Queen Victoria's empire, Vita lived through two world wars and into the 1960s of sex, love and peace. In many ways she seems almost timeless, whether through her Tudor tower at Sissinghurst, or the ancestral home of Knole. Virginia Woolf's Orlando, modelled on Vita, weaves through the eternal centuries, changing sexual identity in much the same way that Vita weaved between past and present, male and female lovers. Her mother, Victoria Josefa Dolores Catalina Sackville-West (1862–1936), had been the result of an affair between the 2nd Baron Sackville and the Spanish dancer Pepita (Josefa de la Oliva). It was to be the fact that she was female rather than this romantic liaison that prevented her inheriting her beloved Knole. Cultured, romantic and solitary, she had the endless walks and courtyards as her childhood playground.

An early marriage at the age of 18 must have surprised those who knew of her intense relationships with women, and her contradictory solitary and independent nature. It was with her husband Harold Nicolson that she travelled, at first to Constantinople and later to Tehran, both countries with strong traditions of courtyard gardening and the mix of architecture and planting. They had already made a garden together at their house at Long Barn, Kent, but in 1930, approaching middle age, they bought the ruined and neglected Sissinghurst. This was to be a joint project, mirroring both their relationship together and their characters apart. The layout of the garden would echo the Tudor walls of Vita's Knole, thanks to the design schemes of Harold. His hard landscaping would be softened by Vita's romantic planting.

The White Garden, the Rose Garden, the Herb Garden, the Cottage Garden, the Lime Walk – the gardens at Sissinghurst are now so well known that they trip off the tongue. Each a garden in its own right, gardens within a garden. Each one small enough to be private but in all covering 7 acres. Vita Sackville-West did not invent the concept of the garden room but she did use it to superb effect. Setting the gardens within the brick boundaries of Sissinghurst, Vita and Harold created more walls of tall evergreens, giving structure and contrast to the overflowing planting within each room. The walls themselves were gardens, covered in roses, jasmines, clematis and ceanothus. Although the planting of each was different they all reflected Vita's love of 'cottage' or old-fashioned plants. The gillyflowers of the medieval noblewoman, the auriculas of Mistress Tuggy, and the herbs of Lawson's country housewife, all found a home in Sissinghurst's borders, nestling up to the springtime primroses from Munstead Wood. Not that Vita did not also include new planting; both she and Harold would visit plant fairs, buying, as Vita insisted, 'only the best'. Vita was a collector, listing those plants that she wanted and those she had seen. In Constantinople and

Persia she had literally collected in the style of Ernest 'Chinese' Wilson, now she collected in Chelsea or swapped plants with fellow gardeners. Her library contained books by contemporaries, as well as past masters, and Gertrude Jekyll and Eleanour Sinclair Rohde stood proudly next to Margery Fish and Parkinson.

As the war passed by overhead, Sissinghurst grew into its glory, and Vita into her role as plantswoman-gardener. Dividing her time between writing and gardening she produced the long poem *The Garden* in 1946, winning the Heinemann award for literature and a place on many a gardener's bookshelves. Opening the garden to the public (or as she called them 'the shillingses') came as no hardship and was a regular event from 1938. As well as the general open days, horticulturalists with a particular interest were welcomed at other times, often with more enthusiasm than offered to society friends. She made no effort for the visitors beyond carefully answering their questions, whereas friends would necessitate food and comforts, both sometimes a rarity at Sissinghurst as Harold so plaintively noted. In 1955 she was awarded the gold Veitch Medal of the RHS and, despite continuing with her novels, became better known to the world as a garden writer.

Writing for *The Observer* between 1946 and 1961 her columns were a wonderful mix of the practical and the romantic. On snails, for example, she admired the 'beautiful delicate shells' and decried the 'agony, during the dark hours, [of] these miserable members of God's creation' before going on to admit that to her the seedlings were more precious than the 'frail brother with its tender horns' and that the slaughter would go on (albeit with a slightly more humane anti-slug product than the traditional 'Meta-and-sawdust').[51] Sissinghurst to her was both a refuge and an inspiration, a lover and a companion. As she wrote about the tasks of the garden year, some of this intensity of feeling shone through, enlivening the most detailed list of plantings or seasonal chores. In the tradition of Jane Loudon, she was after all a novelist as well as a gardener. The arrival of Pamela Schwerdt and Sibylle Kreutzberger in 1959 (trained at Beatrix Havergal's school at Waterperry) gave Vita much needed support during the final years, and she in turn passed on her deep love and knowledge of the gardens until her death in the summer of 1962. Today Sissinghurst is known for its successful blend of the formal and informal, the structure and the planting. During Vita's life however visitors would as often remark on its oddity or 'curiousness': the result no doubt of a combination of genius and eccentricity.

NINE

At War and Peace

WOMEN TURN THE EARTH

> Years ago women – always defined as ladies – plied outdoor tools in semi-shame, afraid of being considered vulgar or unfeminine; now the spade is recognised as an honourable implement in female hands.
>
> Mary Hampden, *Every Woman's Flower Garden* (1915)[1]

In 1916 Viscountess Frances Wolseley joyfully recorded that all around her people were calling out for female gardeners. In private gardens, public parks, nurseries and market gardens women poured down the garden path responding to the clarion call of war, and the heartfelt cries of potential employers. As male gardeners were called up in their thousands they left behind them cooling hothouses and empty bothies. From the large country house with its army of garden staff to the suburban villa with its solitary jobbing gardener women were suddenly in demand. Glynde graduates trenched potatoes, housewives stripped sprouts, and the Girls Training Corps turned bombsites into allotments. No longer the confine of eccentrics or geniuses, spinsters or romantics, the war garden beckoned all who wished to come – and many that did not. Women's dress and women's roles would be revised and revised again in the drive for an efficient and effective female workforce on the land.

As the demand for women gardeners rose, so the prejudice against them declined. No longer was it social death to be able to identify a spade, or even to know how to use one. No longer was the vegetable garden a mystery to all but the lowest weeding woman, or the flower bed a refuge for the unfulfilled and disappointed. Eves of all ages, classes and backgrounds were firmly back in the garden. But would it last? Or would peacetime herald the return of the 'weaker' sex to the nurseries and kitchens from whence they had come? Certainly the period between the two wars saw a retreat as heroes returned from the battlefields of France to the battlefield of the sexes. Partial success in the campaign for female suffrage came in 1918 as a reward for their role on the home front, but for women with no property (the majority of the female workforce in peace and in war), emancipation did not arrive until 1928. As change gathered pace it began to affect every aspect of society, from education to clothing, income to outlook; equality of opportunity gradually spread like periwinkle into the shadiest recesses. For those women who lived and gardened in war and in peace it must have seemed a long slow struggle.

One cold night, in the February of 1913, three of the orchid houses at Kew were attacked by suffragettes. Whether the choice of the orchid houses was accidental, or inspired by the sexual connotations of the orchid and the orchid-lust of the predominantly male collectors, will never be known. Suffice it to say that glass panes were smashed, pots broken and plants destroyed. The *Gardeners' Magazine* described the protest as being 'as cowardly and cruel as one upon domestic animals or those in captivity',[2] a description containing perhaps unintended irony, as so many suffragettes were imprisoned at that time. Despite the almost farcical evidence of a handkerchief, a handbag, feminine fingerprints and an envelope bearing a paper with the words 'Votes for Women' (in an uneducated hand according to the *Gardeners' Magazine*) the particular culprits were never identified. Twelve days later the Refreshment Pavilion was burnt down. Perhaps dissatisfied with the limited impact of the orchid destruction and aiming for something of more direct relevance to the general public, suffragettes had struck again. Olive Wharry and Ida Inkle were arrested for the destruction of the public refreshment rooms.[3] Alas for the public, although plans for a new refreshment pavilion were put in hand, the intervention of the war meant the construction of a permanent replacement was delayed until 1920. When it did come it was a stark and purely functional building of no architectural merit.

Despite this somewhat inauspicious relationship between twentieth-century women and Kew, by 1915 the Royal Horticultural Society's gardens at Kew were employing an increasing number of women. Having initially taken on trainees at the beginning of the century they were in a better position than some to attract trained women staff. By

1916 the 'decorative department' was staffed almost entirely by women. Known as the Coutts' harem, from the name of one of the few men retained in the department, the women continued to care for the decorative pits throughout the war. Recalling the Victorian craze for the sexless cryptogamia, women were also used to staff the ferneries and some may even have made it back into the (re-glazed) orchid houses. By 1917 twenty-seven female gardeners and four sub-forewomen were employed in contrast to the mere handful at the outbreak of war.

Despite the often optimistic claims of their proprietors, the burgeoning numbers of women's gardening schools at the start of the twentieth century had had limited success in introducing women into the mainstream of the gardening profession. Female gardeners were still regarded as a novelty, most likely to gain careers in the rather more specialised employment markets than in the still misogynistic world of the country house garden. Writing in *Women and the Land* in 1916, a year which incidentally she described as being 'after the full tide of [the war's] force' and 'within measurable distance of peace', Viscountess Frances Wolseley was able to quote the following passage from the Agricultural Education Conference report:

> Since the outbreak of war, the demand for women gardeners has greatly exceeded the supply. In our opinion this demand will continue after the war to a much greater extent than formerly. Not only is the prejudice against women undertaking such work breaking down, but many employers who had not previously known that there were efficient women gardeners are now aware of the fact and will continue to employ them.[4]

At the Glynde School Frances Wolseley was inundated with requests from garden owners who, as they freely admitted, would never previously have dreamt of enquiring at the school. Frances Wolseley was confident in her students' abilities both to replace the men that had been called up and to maintain the gardens of the future when 'fewer men will be there'.[5] Demand was so high that she had to turn away some prospective employers. The gardening schools alone could not fulfil the demand for women workers, that was to be the role of the Women's Farm and Garden Union.

The year 1899 had seen the formation of the Women's Agricultural and Horticultural International Union (WAHIU) to assist both women wanting jobs on the land and employers needing trained workers. With

Dorothy Perkins Rose (*Rosa* 'Dorothy Perkins')

Abundant clusters of fluffy pink 'Dorothy Perkins' rose defined the English suburban garden in the first decades of the twentieth century. Originating in 1901, the delicately fragranced rambler survived the Dig for Victory campaigns of two world wars to adorn the archways and trellising of many a suburban semi. Few nowadays realise that it was the pretty-as-a-picture rose that came first and not the women's clothing chain which shares its name. American rose grower Mr Perkins, ambitious to create and supply better varieties, hired the hybridist E. Alvin Miller to develop a new fragranced rambling rose. The pink rose he created was named after the grower's granddaughter, Dorothy, and thus Dorothy Perkins was born. Success in America was followed by exports worldwide, and the rose arrived in England just in time to find a home in the gardens of the new suburbia. It was also chosen by Viscountess Wolseley to clothe some of the walls at Glynde. The National Rose Society of Great Britain awarded the Nickerson Cup to the Jackson and Perkins company for the best pink climbing rose. So popular was it, and so feminine in its appeal, that when a new women's clothing company was founded in 1916 it was named after the rose. The name was a wise choice, the clothing company grew, and almost 100 years later there are over 500 Dorothy Perkins' stores in England – though the number of 'Dorothy Perkins' roses in the country far outnumber the shops.

the outbreak of war the WAHIU (later renamed the Women's Farm and Garden Union)[6] was responsible for the setting up of the Women's National Land Service Corps (WNLSC), overseeing the placement of women throughout the country; although many a prospective employer still wrote direct to the schools, anxious to obtain well-trained career women rather than those who had experienced a more hasty response to the nation's call. Under the leadership of Louisa Jebb, one of the first women to read agriculture at Cambridge, the aim of the Land Service Corps was to give adequate training to enable all classes of women, not just daughters of professionals, to be generally accepted on the land.

'Create [ing] a favourable impression as to the value of women's work in agriculture by supplying a body of workers capable of making good impressions and thereby breaking down the prejudice of those of the farming community who are opposed to the employment of women.'[7] It was primarily farm work, both arable and dairy, although some women worked in market gardens and smallholdings carrying out a variety of tasks, most of which would have appeared on the syllabuses of the horticultural schools.

It was not until 1917 that the value of the Corps was fully realised by the government, who then integrated the scheme into the Women's Land Army (WLA). Revived at the outbreak of the Second World War (and in fact active between the wars) the Women's Land Army placed over 6,000 women in agricultural and market gardening. The horizons of the WNLSC and the Women's Land Army were of course broader than the confines of the garden. Farmwork included ploughing, sewing, planting, harvesting, riddling, milking, dung spreading, muck clearing, and of course crop weeding in the days before chemical herbicides. In many instances women joined the Women's Land Army with little knowledge of the tasks before them, and sometimes with no idea even of the existence of those jobs. For many enrolment meant not only a radical alteration in their work but the first ever contact with life outside the cities. The conditions in which they lived were a world away from the romanticised images presented by propaganda machines. Booklets handed out to prospective volunteers outlined some of the trials and tribulations they might encounter, but a warning about the lack of cinema and unavailability of fashions in the depths of the countryside cannot have been sufficient preparation for pig swill at dawn. For some the journey from city lady to country woman must have been a particularly tough one. For men and women alike it was a small step on the journey to equality on the land. By July 1918 over 113,000 women were employed on the land, without whom the harvests would have been impossible.

The Second World War again saw the mass mobilisation of the Women's Land Army, and tens of thousands of women responded to the call. As the propaganda machine swung into action women were asked to 'Lend a Hand on the Land', if they were not already active in some form of military work. In 1941 all women between the ages of 20 and 40 were obliged to register for war work, and although many went to the munitions factories, nursing or civil defence, over 80,000 registered with the WLA. Under the leadership of Lady Denham uniformed women again invaded the fields of England, this time with more experience at least of the working world, if not of the countryside. Supporting them in training was the Women's Farm and Gardening Association (WFGA), and the few remaining gardening schools and colleges. Connections between the WFGA and the schools had always been strong and remained for as long as such schools existed. Laura Cornelius Wheeler, principal of the Aldersey Hall School of Gardening for Women, had chaired the WFGA Committee on Education and Employment from 1934–7, taking over from an earlier Studley graduate.[8] Elizabeth Hess, lecturer at Swanley and later principal at Studley, was also keenly interested in the work of the WFGA, as was Kate Barrett, principal of Swanley for twenty-three years.

Waterperry was the only private gardening school for women to survive into the 1940s. Despite threats of closure from Magdalen College, who wanted to give the lease to the John Innes Institute, Waterperry entered the war in high spirits. An influx of Land Army Girls for training added diversity to student social life, and the arrival of heavy horses to assist in putting more land under the plough added variety to lectures. An intensification of vegetable cropping led to the opening of the Waterperry shop in the local covered market at Oxford. An enormous success it sold produce of all kinds, including soft fruit, flowers and pot plants as well as the inevitable wartime staples of potatoes and beet. The potato crop of 1941 formed the unlikely subject of one Land Girl's memoirs as she looked back on her time at Waterperry: a bumper crop covering 30 acres was beyond even the Waterperry students and eventually the army was called in. Soldiers were paid 3*s* an hour to help build an enormous potato clamp to store the potatoes in earth, while the women were paid the half-rate of 1*s* 6*d* for the same work.[9] Daphne Byrne looked back on her Waterperry months as 'immensely happy, immensely hard-working, and extremely uncomfortable', undoubtedly a combination experienced by many women working the land for the first time.

For most housewives the war on want began not in the farmer's fields or the venerable walled kitchen garden, but in the gardens of their own homes. In 1939 flower borders, lawns and even ponds were given one of the most rapid makeovers in garden history. Caught on the hop in the First World War, not anticipating either the length of the fighting or the possible blockade of food imports, the government was much quicker to react at the outbreak of war in 1939. Householders all over England were exhorted to stop growing flowers and devote their gardens to vegetables, while owners of larger gardens were urged to keep chickens or even pigs alongside the garden produce. Coal for boilers was severely restricted and hothouses were emptied of their exotic and tender fruits and flowers, to be replaced with the necessities of war. Many a walled garden saw its rose arches and long-established vines ripped up and replaced with cabbages and potatoes, although herbaceous plants in domestic gardens were often merely moved to one small area to make way for the compulsory vegetable plot. As Richard Suddell optimistically noted in his *Practical Gardening and Food Production in Pictures*, the 'present emergency' would not last long and one should expect to reinstate the flower beds as soon as the war was over.[10] Optimism was obviously Suddell's hallmark, as he also provides instructions on placing an Anderson Shelter so that it is inconspicuous. A tall order for the average suburban garden. With the 'Dig for Victory' campaign alongside 'Lend a Hand on the Land', women now became the targets of propaganda on several fronts. Urged to plant and provide, garden and cook, many juggled housework and children with unlooked-for jobs away from home or in office or factory.

Garden writers hastily added chapters on 'How to Adapt the Wartime Garden' to the 1940s editions of their gardening books; books that had sprung up to cater for the needs of the new suburban 1930s gardener.[11] Many a garden of well-trimmed lawns and primrose beds was transformed into a living dinner; often complementing smaller established vegetable plots at the bottom of the garden. Closer to the house, and usually needing less preparatory work than the newly laid out allotments, these vegetable gardens were more suitable for the busy housewife. Vegetables could be, and were, introduced into all corners of the garden. Rose trellising sprouted peas and runner beans, lily pools became sheltered marrow pits, and potatoes were squeezed in between the greenhouse and the coalbunker. Anderson shelter roofs proclaimed patriotism to the world, with lettuce and other shallow-rooted crops rejoicing in the freshly dug soil. Not that flowers were altogether neglected. In her book on famous American women gardeners written in 1962,[12] Buckner Hollingsworth recalls her sister, Mary Kirk-Simpson, 'planting tulips in a London garden during the Autumn of 1940 when bombs were raining down onto the city'.

Mr Middleton, 'the nation's favourite gardener', continued to write and broadcast through the war years, using the cartoon character 'Adam the Gardener' to illustrate his instructions. Adam was drawn as a weather-beaten, wiry, old man obviously beyond the age for conscription; thus there was no need to replace him with the rather more troublesome 'Eve'. Eve, or her 1940s equivalent, did however make a rather elegant appearance on the cover of Edward Brown's *Make Your Garden Feed You.*[13] Brown was the gardening expert for the *Daily Mirror* (Middleton being ensconced at the *Daily Express*) and was one of many writers who launched themselves onto the sea of novice gardeners at the outbreak of the war. There is no indication in the text of the book that it is aimed particularly at women, but striding across the front cover, is a determined woman in sensible shoes, trousers, shirt and headscarf. Confidently carrying a spade,[14] landscape rake and watering can this is not a woman on her way to assist with a 'little light weeding'.

It was not only suburban gardeners who were facing challenges in the wartime borders. Lady Eleanor Marjorie Williams also confronted privations and hardships in the seemingly idyllic village of Gorran Haven. At the outbreak of war she recorded her genuine sympathies with the local men, conscripted to guard the coast all night after their labours of the day. In the rural outpost of Cornwall, the men of Gorran Haven were mainly employed in the hard physical work of farming and fishing; exhausting enough without the all-night vigil, thought Marjorie. Little did she realise the labours that also awaited her. Already an active gardener before the war, Marjorie gradually began to increase the productive part of the gardens around her home at Lamledra. With the population of the village swollen by evacuees and supplies depleted by rationing, the substantial grounds around the house were to be invaluable. In the long bitter winter of 1940 she worked alongside Ray (the gardener) on a freshly ploughed strip between the kitchen gardens and the farm, preparing the ground for increased vegetable production. The strip was three-quarters of an acre, and the breaking down and preparation was done by hand. Marjorie recorded 'trenching day after day, often in fog and wind so cold that my hands can hardly hold the fork tight enough'. Indomitable in spirit, she added: 'The ground is breaking up well and it's good exercise. Every day in every way I get stronger and stronger etc. We have only been held up for three days by ground frozen too hard to work.'

Spirits were harder to uphold when Ray's long-awaited conscription finally arrived, his application for exemption as an agricultural gardener being insufficient. For nearly a year and a half Marjorie had worked under his instruction, learning sowing, pruning, spraying and crop routine, as well as dealing with the pump house engine; filling in as best she could for the lack of any garden boys and men. Now she was to be left alone with 2 acres of productive garden. On the evening he left she confessed, 'I did then feel desolate, and as if, broad as my shoulders are, they were not broad enough for what they would have to bear. I went into the empty garage, sat down with my head on the trestle table and wept.'[15] The hard and solitary work that she accomplished in the following months is a testament both to Marjorie and to the many other nameless women who carried on similarly throughout the country. Working on the land from 10 a.m. to 1 p.m. and 4 p.m. until dusk or dark every day, she somehow balanced her many other household duties with the trenching, planting, cropping and manure spreading. Forty-two barrow-loads of pig manure were carted over four memorable evenings; the task undertaken by dusk and moonlight in order 'not to shock' the coastguards or anyone else coming to visit the house by the sight of her struggles. Marjorie was eventually joined by a local man, too old for conscription, who assisted her for the duration of the rest of the war. Together they produced vegetables and fruit that were taken to a greengrocer at St Austell and sold at grower's prices. By the end of the war Marjorie Williams had earned £120 in National War Bonds and had supplied much needed produce to the people of Cornwall and London.

For those with commitments that kept them from the Land Army, and gardens too small to farm, the Allotment Army[16] beckoned during their few spare moments. The humble allotment, soon to be promoted as the parade ground of the Allotment Army had had somewhat of a shaky start in life. Born in the wake of the rural enclosures of the late eighteenth and early nineteenth centuries, allotment provision had been a contentious social issue, dividing tenants and landowners, factory owners and hands. Their ills had been denounced in the *The Penny Magazine* where it was claimed they gave rise to a superabundance of agricultural labour, unemployment, early marriage, the decline of the dependent wage labourer, non-attendance at church and an excess of children.[17] Not bad going for a small plot of vegetables. Some rural employers had attempted to introduce regulations that made the taking on of an allotment punishable by sacking. Urban allotments had fared little better, with strong opposition from employers only being ameliorated by a recognition of the appalling conditions of workers in the urban slums, and a somewhat optimistic view that allotments might tide men over periods of sickness or downturn of trade. There was strangely no suggestion that women might make use of them to tide them over widowhood, desertion or penury, although Louisa Wilkins (née Jebb), one of the early members of the Women's Farm and Garden Union, was a passionate proponent of smallholdings and allotments. After studying agriculture at Newnham she toured the country giving lectures on the benefits of allotments and in 1905 published a pamphlet entitled *The Small Holdings of England: An Enquiry into the Conditions of Success*.

By 1908, with the passing of the Small Holdings and Allotment Act, the provision of allotments fell within the authority of the local districts and some progress was made towards their increased availability, but it was to be the two world wars that finally saw their widespread establishment. From an estimated half a million allotments in 1913 provision grew to approximately 1½ million in the early years of the First World War, and by 1918 it was stated that one allotment existed for every five houses.[18] A variety of social and economic factors resulted in a slow decline to well under a million plots just prior to the outbreak of the Second World War.

On 4 October 1939 the Minister of Agriculture proclaimed the need for an increase of a further half a million allotments, which would feed another million adults and 1½ million children.[19] The 'Dig for Victory' campaign was born. By 1942, 10 million leaflets on how to cultivate and crop a typical 10-pole allotment[20] were being distributed, while further leaflets were available on hen- and pig-keeping. By the middle of the war over half the households of manual workers (defined by the male head of household even if absent or 'missing' or gone away) were raising vegetables in allotments or gardens. The Allotment Army was marching confidently across suburban wastes and urban parks alike; erecting towers for beans and digging trenches for potatoes, they paused only to establish outposts of brassicas in the gardens of the respectable 'semi'. Hard to come by equipment such as wheelbarrows was shared between four or five plots, while plot holders were expected to be catering for average families of five or six.

But who were the soldiers in this home-grown infantry? In 1914 over 1 million men had enlisted in the first few months of the war, and as both the scale of the conflict and the number of casualties rose, so did the depletion of men on the home front. By 1916 men between the ages of 18 and 50 were conscripted, unless in exempted occupations. The Second World War again saw immediate male conscription under the National Service Act and again, by the latter part of the war, men up to the age of 51 were conscripted unless ill, disabled or injured, or in reserved occupations. The garden army available to cultivate the home and allotment plot was thus increasingly one made up of women. Housewives and mothers who, due to their age or family commitments, were not suitable for the Land Army turned instead to the plot on their doorstep.

Although many of these women would have been a familiar sight pottering among the flower beds of their own back gardens, their appearance in the vegetable plot marked the final breakdown in the long-standing division between these two spheres of interest. Even Jane Loudon had only dared to suggest a woman might cultivate her own vegetable plot in the extremis of a recalcitrant male gardener. While in 1897 Mrs Earle had been satisfied in merely instructing the male gardener on the vegetables to be planted.[21] Even among the working classes, the productive garden had been regarded as the man's domain. Recalling her rural childhood before the wars, Flora Thompson stated that 'women never worked in the vegetable gardens or on the allotments, even when they had their children off hand and had plenty of spare time, for there was a strict division of labour and that was "men's work". . . and any work outside the home was considered unwomanly'.[22] Allotments in particular were considered the male preserve, being in the public rather than the private arena. To work with vegetables in the privacy of your own back garden might be a necessary evil for some women, but to brave public view and enter the male world of the allotment was almost unheard of. In many urban areas the absence of private gardens and the enforced link between vegetables and the public space of the allotment had served to actually intensify earlier sexual divisions before the war.

With millions fewer men and millions more allotments this was an attitude that had to change. In some instances the plot would be cultivated by younger sons or older male relatives, while the housewife confined herself to collection of the produce. Others took on the lighter tasks of planting out seedlings, hoeing, picking caterpillars from brassicas, or weeding and children were also conscripted to these monotonous tasks. For many allotment women the responsibility included the harder tasks of trenching, digging over and erecting crop protection, echoing, however distantly, the actions of the men at the front. What progress there was towards equality on the allotment took a distinct step backwards when peace finally arrived. Writing in the uncomfortable 1950s, caught between returning heroes and the forthcoming battle of the sexes, Martyn Hall ventured that 'There are some women who manage an allotment of their own, and most of them make quite a good job of it' but 'Many more give valuable help to their husbands in the lighter tasks of hoeing and weeding, and in gathering the crops'.[23]

Back at Kew, the Second World War had again seen women invade in more than usual numbers. Following a drop in the number of women gardeners employed in the interwar periods the conscription of male students and employees had hit hard. Again it was the decorative departments, as well as the propagating pits, flowers and rock gardens that saw most women gardeners. Membership of the Kew Women Gardener's Guild rose to twenty-seven just months after the first arrivals, echoing the numbers at the end of the First World War.[24] With a uniform of trousers and shirts they looked in many ways identical to those first early trainees in bloomers, although the flat cap had gone for good. During their free time the women donned overalls and clogs to tend the staff allotments on the Sundial Lawns. Official show allotments for the Ministry of Food and Farming were also maintained at Kew. Located close to the entrance kiosk these attracted visitors anxious to compare their own efforts with those of the professionals. As well as leading the way in allotments, Kew played an important role in providing herbs for the nation during both wars. Dangerous, unusual or slow-growing pharmaceutical products such as *Atropa belladonna*, and *Colchium* were a speciality of the gardens. Rather more unusually, seeds were collected by women from the chamomile lawns at Kew for sowing on airfields to camouflage them from above.

Other more common herbs were collected and grown throughout the country with traditional medicines replacing foreign and industrial pharmaceuticals. Medicinal herbs whose traditional collection had fallen into abeyance by 1940 became vital to the war effort and appeals were made for their collection by the Ministry of Supply (Directorate of Medical Supplies). Formed in the early years of the First World War as a county and often rural-based organisation the Women's Institutes were ideally placed to respond to this appeal, and alongside the Womens' Voluntary Service they organised county herb committees for the collection and drying of medicinal herbs from the wild. The National Federation of Women's Institutes acted as a central collector for *Unital digitalis* seed, while pennyroyal and *Atropa belladonna* came from gardens up and down the country. The Women's Institutes were also responsible for the coordination of jam and bottled fruit production, setting up 2,600 centres where surplus harvests from garden, allotment and hedgerow were preserved for the coming year. With sugar rationing from 1940 onwards, and jam rationing by early 1941, the tea tables of England would have been considerably poorer without their efforts. Supplies were not only marketed from the ever popular WI stalls around the country (as indeed they still are), but were also used for troop supplies, and the preservation kitchens became an annual event.

In peacetime it was to be the traditional herbs and wild flowers, rather than jam, that inspired so many women gardeners. Perhaps the tradition of the medieval herbwoman had been revived, or perhaps the mechanistic killing fields of the two world wars had reawakened an appreciation of nature. Whatever the inspiration the result was a love of the natural world and while the shelves of many a male garden shed groaned under the weight of herbicides and insecticides, women headed the return to nature. This was to be no poetical or fey relationship, however, but one often founded on influences from the medicinal, scientific and ecological worlds. Following on the heels of the First World War, and anticipating the needs of the Second, was Mrs C.F. (Hilda) Leyel (1880–1957). With a varied background including appearing on the stage and charity fund-raising for servicemen, Hilda Leyel became interested in the use of herbs during the First World War and went on to become a trained medicinal herbalist.

In 1927 Leyel founded The Herb Society to promote the use and understanding of herbal medicines, and a range of amateurs and professionals who attended society meetings were drawn to her knowledge as well as her eccentricities. In the same year she established the first of her shops presenting 'the elixirs, distillations, lotions and creams of our ancestors in an agreeable and attractive setting'. Naming the shops after the seventeenth-century apothecary Nicholas Culpeper, she set out to create a wholesome and clean store full of sweet-smelling herbs, superior lotions and soaps, tisanes and teas. A sharp contrast to the vision most Edwardians associated with herbal medicine, of 'small shabby rooms, dirty windows, dirty walls and dusty shelves, all suggestive of mysterious and probably evil practices'.[25] Leyel insisted on pure ingredients and simple, natural products. The Baker Street shop (London) was an immediate success, described in one enthusiastic review in *The Sunday Times* as 'radiant and alluring' with the charm of traditional English names on the spotless jars. Borage and basil, silverweed and marjoram, betony and lovage – all conjured up the image of traditional England.

By the mid-1930s Culpeper's had expanded to eight shops and Hilda Leyel had inspired a new generation of herb growers and users.

Mrs Leyel was also a prolific writer, reaching new converts with books on herb-related gardening and cookery as well as on actual herbs. *A Modern Herbal*, edited by Hilda Leyel in 1931, was based on monographs of English herbs written by Maud Grieve, fellow of the RHS. Mrs Grieve also had an outstanding herb garden at her home in Chalfont St Peter (Buckinghamshire) and had been active during the First World War training women in the harvesting, drying and preparation of medicinal herbs. She founded The Winns Medicinal and Commercial Herb School and Farm at Chalfort St Peter. Publications on herbs and herb gardening were popular in the 1920s and 1930s. Victorian patented medicines, and easy supplies from abroad, had had a devastating impact on traditional and home-grown preparations in the years before the First World War. The collapse in availability of those medicines had had a salutary effect, and many now turned back to the traditional treatments, fuelling a thirst for knowledge and sources. In addition to Grieve and Leyel's *A Modern Herbal*, Hilda Leyel also published *Compassionate Herbs* (1946), the history of herbs in her *Elixirs of Life* (1948) and other specialist uses of herbs. She also promoted her interests in a 'green diet', salads, and appropriate diets for children. Earlier books were rather more varied and sweet-toothed, as she collected together recipes for traditional English cakes, jams and preserves, and picnic fare for motorists.

Eleanour Sinclair Rohde (1881–1950) was on the committee that advised Leyel on the setting up and running of Culpeper's and shared Leyel's interest in herbs and their historic use, although for her the garden and the research library held more appeal than the medicine chest. A solitary and shy woman she was an ardent vegetarian and promoted the use of unusual or 'uncommon' vegetables. Her contribution to the war on the home front included the eminently practical *The War-time Vegetable Garden* (1940) and *Vegetable Cultivation and Cookery* (1944), and with the assistance of the Land Army girls she also ploughed up extra land at her own home. Her introduction to herbs came in 1916 when she attended a training school held by Maud Grieve at her Chalfont St Peter garden, and strong links were maintained between the three women.[26] By 1918 Eleanour had become a member of the British Guild of Herb Growers and was embarking on a lifetime of research into their history.

By the 1960s, the reawakened interest in traditional English herbs and wild flowers was accompanied by a growing appreciation of the role of the garden in conservation. Publications such as Rachel Carson's *Silent Spring* (1962) had ecologically minded gardeners everywhere turning chemically controlled weed-free gardens into ecological paradises. One of the founders of the modern environmental movement, Rachel Carson's critical examination of the impact of the agricultural industry reflected many women's concerns over the relationship between man and the environment. An empathy with nature and conservation can be seen running as a theme through the history of women in the garden. The Ladies of Llangollen constructed a gothic bird table in their picturesque garden sanctuary; Daisy, Countess of Warwick turned Italianate terraces into wildlife sanctuaries, while Jane Loudon recommended country wildlife walks alongside informal planting schemes.

A rare combination of gardener and rabbit lover Beatrix Potter (1866–1943) was also an early conservationist. Outwardly urban and confined, the London house of her childhood was filled with a range of pets and wildlife. Real-life models for Mrs Tiggywinkle, Tom Kitten, and Mrs Tittlemouse rubbed shoulders with the original Benjamin Bunny (actually called Benjamin Bouncer), who was taken out for walks on a harness in the family gardens when not posing for posterity. Following the success of *The Tale of Peter Rabbit*, Beatrix was able to leave London and buy Hill Top Farm in Sawrey, near Coniston. Here she created her own old-fashioned cottage garden worthy of any children's book. *The Tale of Tom Kitten* shows the front porch of the cottage with its pink rambling roses, white Japanese anemone, and outrageously plump snapdragons.[27] A description in 1924 records onions and sage among decorative phlox and Michaelmas daises, roses with peas, and strawberries with pansies. A delightful mix of traditional planting, kept under control with low box hedges to assist with deterring any passing Peter Rabbits.[28]

Beatrix Potter took her beliefs on conservation beyond the garden porch. Seeing the decline in the traditional hill sheep, she took on the mantle of Lake District farmer building up a herd of Hardwick sheep. During the First World War she produced wool and meat for the home market as well as vegetables and flowers from the garden, mirroring the efforts of Lady Eleanor Marjorie Williams during the next war, and many more women inbetween. Her commitment to wildlife and nature conservation resulted in her friendship with Canon Hardwicke Rawnsley and Octavia Hill, both involved in The National Trust from its earliest days. Octavia Hill (1838–1912) had herself founded a series of community homes with communal gardens for the poor of London, believing open spaces to be vital to physical and mental health. Dying just before the end of the Second World War, Beatrix Potter gifted her estate to The National Trust, preserving the garden, meadows and wildlife for future generations.

Despite their sympathies towards the wilder garden,[29] few women would consider going as far as Miriam Rothschild (1908–2005), who abandoned her entire garden to the wild. The extended Rothschild family created over one hundred gardens throughout Europe in the Victorian and Edwardian period, gaining 374 RHS awards between the years of 1899 and 1913. Alfred Rothschild, for example, had one of every British tree species in his garden collection and regularly sponsored plant-hunting expeditions, while Alice Rothschild, created a superb garden at Eythrope (Buckinghamshire). Following in the footsteps of her illustrious horticultural ancestry, Miriam (later Dame) Rothschild started to collect plants as a young child. At first she collected cacti and then progressed to orchids, with which she won prizes at the Chelsea shows. Balancing horticultural efforts with a scientific career she looked set to follow in the family tradition. War intervened, and work at Bletchley took her away from the gardens of Ashton Wold leaving them to fall into decay. Returning to restore and replant, 'one day the penny dropped and I realised with dismay that wild flowers had been drained and bulldozed, weedkillered and fertilised out of the fields, and that now we had a countryside reminiscent of a snooker table'.[30] Whether it was through love of insects, love of flowers, or more prosaically lack of gardeners, she was inspired to create a wildlife garden with a mix of native and cultivated species. In 1970 the first Meadow Garden was created on an old tennis court. Wild flowers also invaded the once immaculate Edwardian gardens, creeping in between the paths and colonising the old hothouses. Within twenty years over 115 different species flourished in a meadow that was eventually to measure 150 acres. Poppies, cornflowers, corn cockle and daisies flowered where debutantes had once bloomed.

Miriam's father, Charles Rothschild (died 1923), had also been instrumental in setting up a series of nature reserves across the country. A survey by Dame Miriam discovered that of the 280 potential sites he had nominated almost all had failed due to inappropriate management by farmers and planners. Farmers, gardeners and government must act as one to save our countryside was the conclusion reached by the survey. Bypasses and motorway verges should be sites for primroses, cowslips and buttercups, school gardens should flourish and butterflies and ladies smock should again be part of our childhood memories. Miriam Rothschild's 'Farmers Nightmare' mix of wild flowers soon found itself being sent to other sympathetic landowners as she repeated the actions of the many medieval women who had brought the world of wild plants into gardens. The Wild Flower Garden at Highgrove (for HRH Prince Charles) is one of many that now owe their diversity to a neglected tennis court and a remarkable woman.[31] In the introduction to *The Butterfly Gardener* (1983) she wrote: 'I garden purely for pleasure. I love plants and flowers and green leaves and I am incurably romantic – hankering after small stars spangling the grass.' Coming from a woman with eight honorary science doctorates in the fields of botany, zoology and entomology this stands as a testament to the power of the garden over the soul.

Working in harmony with the natural environment is also the key to Beth Chatto's designs, although her garden contains both unusual and native plantings. Situated in one of the driest parts of England with very varied soil conditions (from waterlogged spring-fed hollows to sun-baked gravel) the garden site was not one that would have inspired many people to garden design. However, rather than struggle against the odds, Beth Chatto (1923–) worked with them, creating a series of different gardens using plants adapted to each of the conditions. Her gardens at Elmstead Market, Colchester, have inspired people to throw away the water sprinkler and the hose, or the pump and the field drain, and instead garden with the climate and conditions they are given. For Beth Chatto, as with Miriam Rothschild, the garden, and the act of gardening, is seen as a form of therapy, an act of harmony with themselves, the earth and the environment. Her books on *The Dry Garden* (1978) and *The Damp Garden* (1982) (one feels they should stand on either end of the bookshelf), alongside her published gardening correspondence with the late Christopher Lloyd of Great Dixter,[32] display an empathy and harmony with nature alongside her undoubted horticultural skills.

These skills have been recognised by the RHS as Beth Chatto is one of the eleven females who currently hold the Victoria Medal of Honour (VMH), of which only sixty-three are awarded at any one time (one for each year of Queen Victoria's reign). Other holders include Valerie Finnis (Lady Scott), graduate of Waterperry and creator of the gardens at Dower House and Boughton House (Northamptonshire); Lady Anne Berry, who developed the famous RHS gardens at Rosemoor (Devon); and Mrs Helen Robinson, who developed the gardens at Hyde Hall (also RHS). Not only botanists and gardeners are honoured with the

VMH. The RHS recognises its close relationship with botanical art and flower arranging and the botanical artist Mary Grierson was honoured in 1997, while Mary Shirvill (Newnes) is a current holder as is her fellow flower arranger Julia Clements. Mary Pope (1899–1990), the founder of the National Association of Flower Arrangement Societies, was also awarded the VMH in 1979.

Since it was first awarded in 1897 to Gertrude Jekyll and Ellen Willmott, thirty-one women have been honoured with the RHS Victoria Medal. Their achievements range across the history of women's involvement in the garden and they include garden designers, botanical artists, horticulturalists, plant breeders and growers, flower arrangers, landscape architects, promoters of wildlife gardening, authors and garden historians. HM Queen Elizabeth the Queen Mother was honoured in 1961; over 800 years after Queen Eleanor created the Queen's Garden at Winchester the connection between royalty and gardens is still strong.

Geranium maculatum 'Beth Chatto'

It seems appropriate that a plantswoman dedicated to using plants in harmony with their environment should have an ever adaptable geranium named after her. Traditionally found in the borders of country cottages, the cranesbill or wood geranium is happy in partial sun or shade and all but the driest soils. *Geranium maculatum* 'Beth Chatto' has a pale lilac to pink flower with white centres, making it ideal to brighten shady corners or nod its heads over gravel paths. A long-flowering season and an ability to be rejuvenated seems to mimic its namesake, still working in the plant nurseries and garden in her seventies. One nursery even describes the flowers as elegant and sensual, perhaps anxious to please their rival. Who named the variety is unknown, at least by Beth Chatto. Should you want something a little more showy in the borders than the cranesbill, *Agapanthus campanulatus* 'Chatto's Blue' has a fine cobalt blue head of trumpet flowers. At home in the driest gravels of Essex, it was selected by Beth Chatto for its colour. Both plants are of course available from the Beth Chatto nursery.

At Highgrove, HRH the Prince of Wales chose the garden designer and historian Rosemary Verey (1918–2001) to advise on the gardens. Her own gardens at Barnsley House (Gloucestershire) were inspired by features of sixteenth- and seventeenth-century gardens, including knot gardens, lime walk and potager, but also open out to views and vistas of all scales. Reminiscent of Gertrude Jekyll's admission that there was at first no overall design plan for Munstead Wood, Rosemary Verey developed the 4-acre site gradually, starting as she said at her drawing room door (rather than her drawing board) and working outwards.[33] The potager combines the formality of box-lined beds with the modern colours of rainbow chards and pink and yellow cabbages to create an edible garden which has been inspirational. Whether it was her use of colour, or her mix of formal and informal that appealed, Rosemary was also asked to design the garden at Woodside (Windsor) for Sir Elton John. Scents and herbs also feature here, while at Otley Hall (Suffolk) she turned to medieval design and planting for inspiration.

In the tradition of many women gardeners, Rosemary Verey came later in life to gardening having originally graduated in social history. Although study and opportunities are now open equally to both sexes, and horticultural courses attract as many women as men, it is still the case that many women come to gardening as a second career or after a career break. The Women's Farm and Garden Association (WFGA), first set up in 1899, now runs a practical training scheme for these women, supplementing the theoretical instruction available through the Royal Horticultural Society. Women Returners To Amenity Gardening Scheme (WRAG) trainees work fifteen hours a week in a placement garden, receiving a small training allowance and structured practical instruction under a head gardener or direct from the garden owner.

The prejudice against women digging in public lasted much longer on the allotment than in the garden or on the farm. In 1969 a government report found that only 3.2 per cent of registered allotment holders were women and a mere 1.8 per cent were housewives, suggesting that the diehards of the vegetable plot were predominantly men. However, the figure was recognised even by the inquiry as underestimating the number of women who worked on allotments, as formal agreements of any kind were still usually placed in the name of a husband or male relative.[34] Even accounting for this bias, the committee did conclude that the allotment was still predominantly the man's sphere in the 1960s, despite gardening itself being an equally popular activity among both sexes. Vegetable gardening and digging were, they concluded, not attractive to the female sex. Perhaps more interestingly, they also remarked that many women were less able to leave the house for extended periods of time, having family commitments that kept them close to hearth and home. Thus if women were involved in vegetable growing it was more likely to be within the home garden than on an allotment site. Within the overall figures there was, however, variation between individual sites. Allotment sites with good community spirit and other amenities (in particular, toilets) tended to have higher numbers of female allotment holders, although which came first, toilets, good spirits or women, remained somewhat of an enigma. Thirty-six years later women are a common sight on allotments, both on their own and with partners and families. The battle for healthy food has resulted in a higher turnout that even the world wars managed, and some sites even have more women registered than men.

In 2002 the first book on practical allotment gardening by a woman was finally published, after 100 years of male instruction and advice.[35] Books by women on other aspects of gardening and garden history line the bookshelves, with notable contributions by authors such as Penelope Hobhouse, Rosemary Verey and Jane Fearnley-Whittingstall. Anna Pavord has combined garden historian, detective and plant specialist in her book on *The Tulip* (1999), and with *The Naming of Names* (2005) has followed in the footsteps of so many women who tackled the complexities of plant nomenclature, although for her Linnaeus is the beginning of the end. In other media, radio presenters such as Pippa Greenwood broke the mould of the male-only panels on *Gardeners Question Time* (BBC Radio), while Charlie Dimmock combined expertise on water gardens with a sexual frisson that had thousands turning on their televisions. Carol Klein combines presenting *Gardener's World* (BBC) with running a plant nursery, designing (her show gardens have won many gold medals at Chelsea Flower Show), and working in her own garden in North Devon. Drawn to gardens by a fascination with the natural world and a love of soil, she recalls bringing soil into the kitchen at the age of 6 to create an indoor flower bed. Removing rampant bindweed from heavy clay in her newly acquired Devon garden did nothing to quench this early enthusiasm and she still works the soil in between dispensing advice to men and women gardeners alike.

One of the newest most visited gardens in England owes its existence to a woman. Jane, Duchess of Northumberland was determined to create an exciting contemporary garden in the derelict gardens at Alnwick Castle (Northumberland). The site of earlier designs by

'Capability' Brown and the hothouses of the plant-hunting 3rd Duke, the gardens had been used in the Dig for Victory campaign, seeing the Italianate terraces of the nineteenth century transformed to vegetable beds. Neglected since the 1950s, it needed someone with the drive of the Duchess to build an exciting new series of gardens within the framework of the old. The Duchess's vision was of a garden to appeal to young and old, to bring laughter and surprise. Created by renowned Belgian designers Jaques and Peter Wirtz, using colour and scent, woodland and water, sound and silence, the gardens range from the treetop walks to the Grand Cascade. An unusual Poison Garden contains the same belladonna (Deadly Nightshade) that medieval women used to dilate their pupils and attract their lovers, and the digitalis once known as Our Lady's Gloves. Commissioned by the Duchess and designed by garden historian Caroline Holmes, the garden harks back to the ancient lore of the wisewoman but looks forward to the twenty-first century with its modern design features. A garden experience for everyone, the Alnwick Garden project is the result of one woman's very personal vision.

And so it seems we have come full circle. From a woman created in a garden to gardens created by women; from the women who weeded to the women who champion weeds. In the twenty-first century women are no longer a breed apart, a gardening oddity consigned to the flower bed or the fernery. No longer subject to the invisible sneers of our male counterparts, we play an active and equal part in the work of the garden as designers, gardeners, artists and plantswomen. In the immortal words of Vita Sackville-West, we are free to break our backs, our fingernails, and sometimes our hearts in the practical pursuit of our favourite occupation.[36] But we owe our place in Eden to those who went before us. The countless generations of women who dug and planted, stitched and sewed, collected and nurtured; owners and workers, the dreamers and the demonised. Virgins, queens and housewives, all have met and many have loved, in the garden.

APPENDIX

Gardens to Visit Created by Women

The following gardens were either created by, or have strong connections with, women who appear in this book. Only gardens that are open to the public on a regular basis have been included. To avoid frustration caused by changes to opening arrangements these have not been included here. Instead, those proposing to visit are recommended to check opening arrangements using the Internet or one of the many garden guides available.

The gardens are listed chronologically, although some such as Kew are associated with several women over a long time span.

Weald and Downland Open Air Museum,
Singleton, Chichester, Sussex PO18 0EU
Re-created medieval gardens on this museum site give visitors an opportunity to experience the world of the medieval and Tudor housewife and examine changes in gardens and plant availability through time. Herbs and cooking plants play an important role in these gardens.

Queen Eleanor's Garden, Winchester Castle,
Winchester, Hampshire SO23 8PJ
Eleanor of Provence and Eleanor of Castile are both commemorated in the re-creation of Queen Eleanor's Garden. Little is known of the original Winchester Castle gardens, and so this garden reflects fragmentary descriptions of several royal residences in the last part of the thirteenth century.

Hampton Court Palace,
Surrey KT8 9AU (Historic Royal Palaces)
Ales Brewer and Margaret Rogers were just two of the women employed by Henry VIII to keep his gardens immaculate. They also supplied him with wild strawberry plants. Queen Mary II was involved in the design and layout of the Privy Garden, while her collection of exotic plants was once housed in the Orangery.

Hardwick Hall, Doe Lea, Chesterfield,
Derbyshire S44 5QJ
The house contains embroideries and tapestries created by Bess of Hardwick and her ladies-in-waiting, including plant and flower embroideries. Walled

courtyards and a herb garden also contain plants that Bess would have recognised.

Royal Botanic Gardens, Kew, Richmond,
Surrey TW9 3AB
Now a World Heritage Site, the Royal Botanic Gardens incorporating the old estates of Kew and Richmond are associated with a number of important women including Queen Caroline, Princess Augusta, Queen Charlotte, Marianne North, Margaret Meen, Margaret Mee, and, of course, those unforgettable 'women in bloomers' who gardened at Kew.

Ham House, Richmond,
Surrey TW10 7RS
The Duchess of Lauderdale created the gardens in the last years of the seventeenth century, alongside her husband the Duke. Ham also contains some of the most impressive works of Eleanor Coade, including the Coade stone River God and a series of urns along the river front.

Wrest Park, Silsoe, Luton,
Bedfordshire MK45 4HS
Jemima, Marchioness Grey worked alongside her husband, Philip, to develop the eighteenth-century gardens. Her contributions include the Mithraic Pagan Altar, the Bath House, and the Root House (the latter now missing). She kept up a constant correspondence with her close friends, which includes many references to her gardening and landscaping. A statue of Jemima survives in the gardens. Her daughter Amabel continued her work.

Gardens of Easton Lodge, Warwick House,
Easton Lodge, Little Easton, Gt Dunmow, Essex CM6 2BB
Restored and re-created gardens associated with Daisy, Countess of Warwick and the Marlborough House set. A small museum contains an excellent selection of archives relating to Daisy and the gardens.

Waterperry Gardens, Waterperry,
Nr Wheatley, Oxfordshire OX33 1JZ
Within the area of the Waterperry Horticultural School run by Beatrix Havergal and Avice Sanders. The gardens contain herbaceous borders, rose garden and formal garden areas, now maintained by the School of Economic Science.

Kelmarsh Hall, Kelmarsh,
Northamptonshire NN6 9LT
Norah Lindsay laid out the long herbaceous borders in her typical overflowing style. These have been restored and form an important part of this attractive garden. Blickling Hall (Norfolk) also contains her planting.

Hestercombe Gardens, Cheddon Fitzpaine,
Taunton, Somerset TA2 8LG
One of the finest examples of collaboration between Gertrude Jekyll and Sir Edwin Lutyens. Planting faithfully restored to the Jekyll original layout. The garden contains water features, rills, and a long pergola, in addition to a small courtyard garden of greys, silvers and mauves.

Warley Place, Warley Rd,
Great Warley, Essex
Now functioning as a Nature Reserve, but one can still enjoy the displays of daffodils and spring bulbs planted here in their thousands by Ellen Willmott. The alpine garden and fernery are also being gradually restored. Limited opening.

Sissinghurst Castle Garden, Sissinghurst,
Cranbrook, Kent TN17 2AB
One of the most celebrated gardens in the world, created by Vita Sackville-West and her husband Harold Nicolson. Visitors can wander the garden 'rooms', admire the famous White Garden and also see the tower-room study where Vita worked.

East Lambrook Manor Gardens,
South Petherton, Somerset TA13 5HH
The 'Home of English Cottage Gardening', East Lambrook Manor Gardens were created by Margery Fish (with some hindrance from her husband Walter) from the 1940s until her death in 1969. They are recently open under new owners and are being restored to reflect Margery's plantsmanship.

Beth Chatto Gardens, Elmstead Market,
Colchester, Essex CO7 7DB
Created from 1960 onwards by Beth Chatto these include the famous Gravel Garden and Mediterranean Garden, as well as the Water Gardens, Long Shady Walk and Woodland Garden. There is also a nursery.

Alnwick Garden, Alnwick Castle, Alnwick,
Northumberland NE66 1NQ
Created under the inspiration of the Duchess of Northumberland, the garden is one of the most exciting contemporary gardens to be developed in the last century, a magical landscape which includes a Grand Cascade, Poison Garden, Labyrinth, Woodland Wood and many more features to entertain and excite garden visitors of all ages.

Many more gardens associated with women are open either by private arrangement or intermittently such as through The National Gardens Scheme; see *The Yellow Book* for details, www.ngs.org.uk

Notes

Preface

1. Viscountess Frances Wolseley, *Gardening for Women* (Cassell & Co, 1908), p. 5.
2. Eleanour Sinclair Rohde, *The Story of the Garden* (Medici Society, 1932), p. 184.
3. In the last thirty years only three books have looked at the special contribution made by women to the history of the garden: Sue Bennett, *Five Centuries of Women and Gardens*, published in 2000 to accompany an exhibition of that title at the National Portrait Gallery; Dawn MacLeod, *Down to Earth Women, Those Who Care for the Soil* (1982), which concentrated on the nineteenth and twentieth centuries; and Yvonne Cuthbertson, *Women Gardeners: A History* (1998), which focused on the contribution of female gardeners in America, although the wider context of Europe and the Near East is explored in its early chapters. Academic texts have also examined division in gender roles, including Mark Laird, 'The Culture of Horticulture; Class, Consumption and Gender in the English Landscape Garden' in Conan (ed.), *Bourgeois and Aristocratic Cultural Encounters in Garden Art, 1550–1850* (Dumbarton Oaks Colloquium), vol. 23.
4. Elizabeth, Countess von Arnim, *Elizabeth and Her German Garden*, (1898) p. 26.

Chapter One

1. Were she to come in contact with a swarm or hive of bees the whole swarm would instantly drop dead. Pliny wrote his *Natural History* in AD 77 and had an imagination almost as far reaching as his knowledge.
2. Ralph Austen, *A Treatise of Fruit Trees Together with The Spiritual Use of the Orchard* (London, 1653). This despite the fact that Beale was a correspondent with John Milton.
3. A notable exception to this was Jane Loudon's *Instructions in Gardening for Ladies* (John Murray, 1840), which tackled such tasks as grafting, pruning, budding and the maintenance of the fruit garden before its section on the flower gardens and lawns.

4. Few illuminations are actually English in origin, but the overlap of cultural life across northern Europe, and the close connection of courts in France and Spain, allow us to suppose a resemblance.
5. Written in poem form, the work of Jon (or Ion) dates to sometime in the fourteenth century. A copy is preserved in the Library of Trinity College, Cambridge, and was transcribed by Alicia Amherst. His list of plants was reproduced from Alicia Amherst's transcription in Eleanour Sinclair Rohde, *The Story of the Garden* (Medici Society, 1932), pp. 47 and 270–2.
6. Liberate Roll, 34 Hen. III. m.6, quoted in Rohde, *The Story of the Garden*, p. 39.
7. My thanks are due to Edward Martin of the Suffolk County Council Archaeological Service for this information, taken from the accounts of Lady Clare in the Public Record Office.
8. The author was fortunate enough to be a member of Clare College while researching for her Ph.D. and spent happy times in the gardens there.
9. John Milton, *Paradise Lost* (London, printed by Peter Parker, Robert Boulter and Mathias Walker, 1667).
10. Sir Anthony Fitzherbert, *Book of Husbandry* (1523), section 146, quoted in Christopher Thacker, *The Genius of Gardening: The History of Gardens in Britain and Ireland* (Weidenfeld and Nicolson, 1994), p. 51.
11. Rohde, *The Story of the Garden*, p. 185.
12. Teresa McLean, *Medieval English Gardens* (Collins, 1981), p. 116.
13. John Harvey, *Early Nurserymen: with Reprints of Documents and Lists* (Phillimore, 1974), p. 26.
14. Celia Fiennes, *Through England on a Side Saddle in the Time of William and Mary* (originally written 1697–8, Leadenhall Press, 1888), quoted in Laurence Fleming and Alan Gore, *The English Garden* (Mermaid Press, 1982) p. 69. Celia Fiennes is also rumoured to have been the inspiration behind the nursery rhyme 'Ride a Cock Horse', being the 'fine lady, upon a white horse'.
15. All figures taken from Harvey, *Early Nurserymen*, and referring to the early decades of the sixteenth century.
16. McLean, *Medieval English Gardens*, p. 219.
17. The Walters Art Gallery, Baltimore, USA, *Book of Hours*, W. 425, f.4, Flemish, early sixteenth century.
18. British Library BL Add Ms 38126, f.110, *Book of Hours*, *c.* 1500.
19. Rohde, *The Story of the Garden*, p. 185.
20. All quotes taken from Tusser, *Five Hundred Points*.
21. Jane Brown, *The Pursuit of Paradise: A Social History of Gardens and Gardening* (London, Harper Collins, 1999), p. 106.
22. All quotes taken from William Lawson, *A New Orchard and Garden (with) The Country Housewifes Garden* (London, 1618).
23. Bea Howe, *Lady with Green Fingers: The Life of Jane Loudon* (Country Life, 1961), Introduction.

24. Tusser, *Five Hundred Points*, p. 179. In order to make this particular doggerel rhyme one must try pronouncing plough as pluff or enough as enow, but then pronunciation was different in the sixteenth century, as was the criteria for a good rhyme!
25. Mclean, *Medieval English Gardens*, p. 182.
26. *Gerard's Herbal or General History of Plants*, ed. Marcus Woodward (Senate, 1994), p. xvi.
27. Mary Rose Blacker, *Flora Domestica: A History of Flower Arranging 1500–1930* (National Trust, 2000), p. 15.
28. From the Introduction to 'A Description of a Journey Undertaken for the Discovery of Plants into the County of Kent' (1632) in *Thomas Johnson: Journeys in Kent and Hampstead*, ed. J.S.L. Gilmour (Pittsburgh, 1972). Quoted in Anna Pavord, *The Naming of Names: The Search for Order in the World of Plants* (Bloomsbury Publishing, 2005), pp. 5–6.
29. John Parkinson, *Paradisi in sole Paradisus Terrestris* (London, Humfrey Lownes and Robert Young, 1629), p. 65.
30. Jonathan Goddard, *The Unhappy Condition of the Practice of Physick in London* (London, 1670). Quoted in Sue Bennett, *Five Centuries of Women and Gardens* (National Portrait Gallery, 2000), p. 18.
31. Parkinson, *Paradisi in sole Paradisus Terrestris*, p. 11.
32. John Rea, *Flora; seu de Florum Cultura or a Complete Florilege* (London, Richard Marriott, 1665), dedicatory pages.
33. *Diary of John Evelyn (1620–1706)*, ed. Guy de la Bédoyère (The Boydell Press, 1995), p. 294.
34. Stephen Switzer, *The Nobleman, Gentleman, and Gard'ners Recreation* (1715), quoted in Bennett, *Women and Gardens*, p. 37.
35. *Oxford Dictionary of National Biography* (Oxford, Oxford University Press, 2004–5), accessed at www.oxford.dnb.
36. Molly McClain, *Beaufort: The Duke and his Duchess 1657–1715*, (New Haven, CT, Yale University Press, 2001), pp. 211–15.
37. Eleanor Coade, the phenomenally successful eighteenth-century purveyor of artificial stone statues and vases, was to remain single for that very reason, having seen her father bankrupt the family earlier in her life.
38. Harvey, *Early Nurserymen.*
39. Quoted in Harvey, *Early Nurserymen*, p. 43.
40. Moses Cook worked at one time as head gardener to Arthur Capel at Hadham Hall, and would thus have known, at least by sight, Arthur's daughter Mary Capel who was to become the famed plant collector the Duchess of Beaufort.
41. Harvey, *Early Nurserymen*, plate 9.
42. A later series of lists indicates that there were about 150 principal firms throughout England by 1839. Harvey, *Early Nurserymen.*

Chapter Two

1. John Davies, *Hymnes to Astraea*, No. IX 'To Flora' (1600) in Roy Strong, *The Renaissance Garden in England* (2nd edn, Thames &

Hudson, 1998), p. 48. Astraea (the Just Virgin of Virgil's IVth Eclogue) was one of the symbolic identities of Queen Elizabeth.

2. Liberate Roll, 34 Hen. III. m. 6, quoted in Eleanour Sinclair Rohde, *The Story of the Garden* (Medici Society, 1932), p. 39.
3. Maggie Campbell-Culver, *The Origin of Plants: The People and Plants that have shaped Britain's Garden History since the Year 1000* (London, Headline, 2001), p. 62.
4. *Ibid.*, p. 63. The poetic nature of the 'golden love apple' is perhaps lessened when one learns that quince is popularly supposed to smell of a loved woman and have the same hardness of heart'.
5. Jane Fearnley-Whittingstall, *The Garden: An English Love Affair: One Thousand Years of Gardening* (Ted Smart Pub, 2003), p. 29.
6. John Harvey, *Early Nurserymen: with Reprints of Documents and Lists* (Phillimore, 1974), p. 34.
7. John Carmi Parsons, 'Eleanor (1241–90), in *Oxford Dictionary of National Biography* (Oxford, Oxford University Press, 2004), assessed at www.oxforddnb.com Jan 2006.
8. The rosemary's qualities are described in a treatise on plants transcribed and reproduced by John Harvey in *Early Nurserymen*. Queen Philippa's role in its introduction is also discussed in Eleanour Sinclair Rohde, *The Story of the Garden* (Medici Society, 1932), p. 45.
9. Dawn MacLeod, *Down-to-Earth Women: Those who Care for the Soil* (Blackwood, 1982). Nearly 400 years later similar creatures were created to celebrate the Coronation of Queen Elizabeth II, stone copies of which were later gifted to Kew Gardens and survive in front of the Palm House.
10. British Museum, Elizabeth I as 'Rosa Electa' flanked by Tudor roses and eglantine. Engraving by William Rogers, *c.* 1590–1600.
11. Roy Strong, *The Renaissance Garden in England* (2nd edn, Thames & Hudson, 1998), p. 47.
12. Quoted in *ibid.*, p. 45. As described in an entertainment put on for Elizabeth I on her visit to Lord Burghley at Theobalds.
13. William Shakespeare, *A Midsummer Night's Dream* Act II Scene i.
14. Edmund Spenser, *The Shepherds Calender*, April Eclogue, 1579.
15. James I obviously agreed with the general opinion, to the extent that he forced Cecil into giving up his palace in exchange for Hatfield, Elizabeth's childhood home.
16. Information on the Cecil gardens taken from Strong, *Renaissance Garden*, pp. 45–60.
17. *Ibid.*, p. 45.
18. Louisa Johnson, *Every Lady Her Own Flower Gardener* (London, Wm S. Orr & Co., 1839/40).
19. Strong, *The Renaissance Garden*, pp. 93–7.
20. Somerset House history – www.somerset-house.org.uk.
21. Mary Rose Blacker, *Flora Domestica: A History of Flower Arranging 1500–1930* (National Trust, 2000), p. 21.
22. Daniel Defoe quoted in Mavis Batey and Jan Woudstra, *The Story of the*

Privy Garden at Hampton Court (Barn Elms, 1995), pp. 8, 12.

23. Queen Mary's love of flowers is discussed in Blacker, *Flora Domestica*, pp. 37–9.
24. Charles Hatton quoted in Batey and Woudstra, *Story of the Privy Garden*, p. 12.
25. Batey and Woudstra, *Story of the Privy Garden.*
26. National Portrait Gallery 5227. I am indebted to the Archives Office at the NPG for this information. Unfortunately they could not make a secure identification of the statue, although it is possibly military.
27. Daniel Defoe quoted in Ray Desmond, *The History of the Royal Botanic Gardens, Kew* (Harvill, 1995), p. 1.
28. A wonderful phrase coined by Stephen Switzer while grappling with the new informality.
29. National Trust, *Stowe Landscape Gardens* (National Trust, 1997).
30. G. Sherburn, *Correspondence of Alexander Pope* (1956), vol. 2, p. 14, quoted in Desmond, *History of the Royal Botanic Gardens*, pp. 3–5.
31. Details and descriptions taken from Desmond, *History of the Royal Botanic Gardens*, pp. 12–19.
32. *Fog's Weekly Journal*, 6 December 1735, quoted in Desmond, *History of the Royal Botanic Gardens*, p. 18.
33. Quoted in Sue Bennett, *Five Centuries of Women and Gardens* (National Portrait Gallery, 2000), p. 51.
34. Lady Hill quoted in Desmond, *History of the Royal Botanic Gardens*, p. 38.
35. Peter Collinson, quoted in *ibid.*, p. 69.
36. Joseph Banks quoted in *ibid.*, p. 79.
37. See Chapter 4.

Chapter Three

1. *Letters Written by The Late Honourable Lady Luxborough to William Shenstone Esq*. ed. J. Dodsley (London, 1775), pp. 144–5.
2. I am grateful to Dr Stephen Bending for sharing his thoughts and research into women, gardens and retirement in eighteenth-century society with me at an early stage in my writing. His own academic research, funded by a Leverhulme Grant, will be available in 2006. Another study of the romantic aspect of female gardening is J.M. Labbe, 'Cultivating One's Understanding: the Female Romantic Garden' in *Women's Writing*, vol. 4, no. 1 (1997), pp. 37–57.
3. Information on Lady Coke and her gardens has been provided by Tim Knox in 'Lady Mary Coke's Garden at Notting Hill House' in *The London Gardener*, vol. 4 (1999), pp. 52–63.
4. As can be seen in a picture of 1766 by Joshua Rhodes in his *A Topographical Survey of the Parish of Kensington* (1766) noted in Knox, 'Lady Mary Coke's Garden', pp. 52–63.
5. All quotes from Lady Mary Coke taken from Knox, 'Lady Mary Coke's Garden', pp. 52–63.

6. Distantly related (by marriage) to Mary Duchess of Beaufort (the seventeenth-century plant collector) and the Sackvilles of Knole, who were one day going to include (obliquely) Vita Sackville-West.
7. In common with Lady Luxborough and the Ladies of Llangollen, Lady Mary also kept sheep, ducks and chickens in the style of an 'ornamented farm'.
8. Information on Lady Luxborough and quotes from *Letters Written by The Late Honourable Lady Luxborough*, which were published shortly after her death by J. Dodsley (1775), and an article by Joan Percy, 'Lady Luxborough (1700?–56): Farmeress, and her Lost Ferme Ornée' in *Hortus*, vol. 4, no. 2 (1990), pp. 90–8. In addition, Andrew Craythorn has recently completed a short history, *Barrells Hall: from Riches to Ruins* (Private pub., 2003). Jane Brown has also discussed Lady Luxborough in her chapter on 'Emancipated Gardeners' in *The Pursuit of Paradise: A Social History of Gardens and Gardening* (HarperCollins, 1999). Jane Brown's book *My Darling Heriott: Henrietta Luxborough, Poetic Gardener and Irrepressible Exile* (HarperCollins, 2006) was published as this book went to press.
9. *Letters Written by The Late Honourable Lady Luxborough*, p. 90.
10. *Ibid.*, p. 126–7.
11. Elizabeth Mavor has written a biography of this romantic friendship which includes considerable material on the gardening activities at Plas Newydd. Elizabeth Mavor, *The Ladies of Llangollen* (Penguin, 1973).
12. Although their biographer refers to their relationship as a 'marriage' in all other respects, there is no direct evidence of any physical relationship nor any contemporary record of one. Descriptions of the ladies themselves, and their letters to each other, do however indicate the type of romantic attachment that might be expected to have a physical expression.
13. Even their gardener added to the air of the picturesque, rejoicing in the name of Moses Jones. Frequently fired by the impetuous Eleanor, he was as frequently reinstated by the forgiving Sarah.
14. Joseph Addison, *The Spectator*, Saturday 17 March 1711, kindly provided by Stephen Bending from his draft article 'Mrs Montagu's Contemplative Bench: Bluestocking Gardens and Female Retirement' (no pagination).
15. All quotes from letters of Elizabeth Montagu quoted in Bending, 'Mrs Montagu's Contemplative Bench: Bluestocking Gardens and Female Retirement'.
16. *Ibid.*
17. James Collett-White, 'Yorke, Jemima, *suo jure* Marchioness Grey (1722–1797)' in *Oxford Dictionary of National Biography* (Oxford, Oxford University Press, 2004), accessed at www.oxforddnb.com/view/article/68351

18. Her entry in the *Oxford Dictionary of National Biography* is categorised 'letter-writer'.
19. The letters of Jemima, Marchioness Grey are preserved in the Bedfordshire Record Office. A study of Jemima's life has been undertaken by Joyce Godber and published as *The Marchioness Grey of Wrest Park* (Bedfordshire Historical Record Society, 1968), vol. XLVII. This particular letter is dated 18 August 1740.
20. Bedfordshire Record Office BRO L30, Letters of Jemima Marchioness Grey, various dates, quoted in Land Use Consultants, 'Historical Survey of Wrest Park' (1993; unpublished report for private client).
21. Amabel Hume-Campbell was widowed in 1787. She was to inherit Wrest Park from her mother and in turn to love its gardens. She was also a great intellectual writing and publishing on history and politics including an examination of the French Revolution.
22. BRO L30, Letters of Jemima Marchioness Grey, quoted in Land Use Consultants, 'Historical Survey of Wrest Park'.
23. English Heritage, *The Gardens of Audley End* (English Heritage, 1995), pp. 30–2.
24. I am indebted to Steffie Shields of the Lincolnshire Gardens Trust for alerting me to Lady Elizabeth Pope, and the provision of information and quotes about her garden work.
25. Ronald Fletcher, *The Parkers at Saltram 1769–1789* (BBC, 1970), p. 15.
26. David Allen, *The Naturalist in Britain: A Social History* (Allen Lane, 1976), p. 28.
For a fascinating insight into the role played by women in late eighteenth and nineteenth centuries see also Ann Shteir, *Cultivating Women, Cultivating Science: Flora's Daughters and Botany in England 1760 to 1860* (John Hopkins University Press, 1996).
27. Ruth Hayden, *Mrs Delany and Her Flower Collages* (British Museum Press, 1980; 3rd edn, 1992), pp. 131–2.
28. One of the most important items was the so-called Portland Vase purchased at the sale by the British Museum.
29. Ellen Willmott of Warley Place, Essex, is discussed in more detail in Chapter 8.
30. Joanna Martin, *Wives and Daughters: Women and Children in the Georgian Country House* (Hambledon and London, 2004). I am grateful to Joanna for conversations on the involvement of the Fox Strangways in gardening, and also her enthusiasm for my own project. In the space available I cannot possibly do justice to her thorough and painstaking research and recommend that anyone interested in this fascinating family, or women's lives more generally in the eighteenth century, read her work.
31. Martin, *Wives and Daughters*, p. 264.
32. *Ibid*., p. 267.
33. Charles Hamilton also knew Henry Fox (1st Baron Holland) at Holland House and appears to

have also given advice there (Martin, *Ibid.*, p. 268). Henry had eloped with Caroline Lennox. He also advised Lady Ilchester in her gardens at Abbotsbury.

34. Martin, *Wives and Daughters*, p. 276.
35. *Ibid.*, p. 281, Louisa Petty to Mary Talbot, 1808.
36. At the other end of life, we know that Jane Austen's mother gardened into her seventies, wearing a labourer's green smock in their kitchen garden at Small House, Chawton. See Dawn MacLeod, *Down-to-Earth Women: Those who Care for the Soil* (Blackwood & Sons, 1982), p. 13.
37. Kay Sanecki, 'Charlotte and her Garden at Ashridge', in *Hortus*, vol. 1, no. 4 (1987), pp. 55. For background material on Ashridge and Charlotte's gardens see Kay Sanecki, *Ashridge: A Living History* (Phillimore, 1996).
38. Quoted in Kay Sanecki, 'Charlotte and her Garden at Ashridge' (in *Hortus*, vol. 1, no. 4 (1987), pp. 54–63.

Chapter Four

1. John Rea, *Flora; seu de Florum Cultura or a Complete Florilege* (London, Richard Marriott, 1665), dedicatory pages.
2. John Loudon, *Gardener's Magazine*, quoted in *A Vision of Eden: The Life and Work of Marianne North*, ed. Holt Rinehart Wilson (Webb & Bower, Royal Botanic Gardens, Kew, 1980), p. 9.
3. This quote, and much of the information for the history of embroidery was taken from Thomasina Beck, *Gardening with Silk and Gold: A History of Gardens in Embroidery* (David & Charles, 1997). This was a revision of the same author's *Embroidered Gardens* (1979). Thomasina Beck appears to be one of very few authors to have tackled this subject; see also her books on *The Embroiderer's Garden* (1988), *The Embroiderer's Flowers* (1992) and *The Embroiderer's Story* (1995), all published by David and Charles.
4. John Gerard, *Herball or General Historie of Plants* (1597; Thomas Johnson, 1633), dedicated to Lord Burghley.
5. Roy Strong, *The Spirit of Britain: A Narrative History of the Arts* (Hutchinson, 1999), pp. 169–201.
6. Roy Strong, *The Artist and the Garden* (Yale University Press, 2000), 'Lady of the Hampden Family', p. 84. (Original in Museum of Art, Rhode Island School of Design, Providence, Rhode Island, gift of Miss Lucy T. Aldrich)
7. Flanked by Wisdom on her left and Folly on her right. See Beck, *Gardening with Silk and Gold*, p. 44.
8. In his picture of the 'Spring' garden a lady inspects her tulip collection. This engraving was later used as a backdrop for a portrait of Charles I and Henrietta Maria (*c.* 1637, British Museum Collection).
9. Mrs Theresa Earle and her 'Pot-Pourri' appear in Chapter 7. This is from her March entry in *Pot-Pourri from a Surrey Garden* (Macmillan & Co., 1897).

10. Illustrated in Beck, *Gardening with Silk and Gold*, p. 54. A similar box is owned by the Fitzwilliam Museum, but held in store. These cabinets or boxes are surprisingly common and merit a separate study by a garden historian.
11. See Chapter 1 for a description of Lucy's gardens at Moor Park and Twickenham.
12. Tim Knox, 'The Artificial Grotto in Britain' in *Magazine Antiques*, June 2002, accessed at http://findarticles.com/p/articles/mi_m1026/is_6_161/ai_87130288
13. *Ibid.*
14. Deryn Lake, *Death in the Setting Sun* (Allison & Busby Ltd, 2005).
15. Mary Delany (private correspondence 1992) quoted in Ruth Hayden, *Mrs Delany and Her Flower Collages* (British Museum Press, 1992), p. 24. Ruth Hayden (a descendant of Mary Delany's sister Anne) is an expert on Mary and her works and has compiled as complete a list as possible as a supplement to her biography.
16. *Ibid.*
17. *Ibid.*, pp. 85–6.
18. *Ibid.*, pp. 44–5.
19. It is possible that the original black backgrounds for Mrs Delany's flower collages were based on the botanical artwork of the sisters Barbara and Margereta Deitzsch. Although it is interesting to note that Mary Moser's flower paintings (fl. 1769–83) were also often on dark backgrounds. Ehret, who was working at Bulstrode at the time, seems always to have painted on white or cream backgrounds.
20. Quoted in Anne Shteir, *Cultivating Women, Cultivating Science: Flora's Daughters and Botany in England 1760 to 1860* (John Hopkins University Press, 1996), pp. 43–4.
21. John Loudon, *The Suburban Gardener and Villa Companion* (Longman, Orme, Brown, Green, and Longmans, 1838), p. 6.
22. Gertude Jekyll will be discussed more fully in her role as garden designer and plantswoman in Chapter 8.
23. Christine de Pizan (also spelt Pisan) was the author of the fourteenth century *Cité des Dames*. A full-length English translation and discussion is available as E.J. Richards, *Livre de la Cité des Dames* (Persea Books, 1982).
24. A modern edition of her *New Book of Flowers* was published in 1999 by Prestel Books, with a biography by Thomas Burger.
25. Her plant-collecting sister Mary, Duchess of Beaufort, employed a Dutch artist named Everard Kik to record her collections of flowers and butterflies, and also to train a particularly talented under-footman who was to take over the great work of recording and cataloguing when Kik left. She does not appear to have undertaken paintings herself.
26. National Portrait Gallery, London (NPG 1437). See also Sue Bennett, *Five Centuries of Women and Gardens* (National Portrait Gallery, 2000).
27. Much of the following information is taken from David Scrace, *Flower Drawings*, Fitzwilliam Museum

Handbooks (Cambridge University Press, 1997). Although few of these paintings are on permanent exhibition, a small temporary exhibition of female water-colourists was mounted in 2005 entitled 'A Pleasing Occupation'.

28. Quoted in Bennett, *Five Centuries of Women and Gardens*, p. 89.
29. A page is devoted to Margaret Meen on Kew's website of people and artists associated with the gardens and collection. See www.kew.org/heritage/people/meen.html. She is also discussed in William Blunt and Wilfred Stearn's magisterial *The Art of Botanical Illustration*, rev. edn (Antique Collectors' Club, 1994).
30. Brent Elliott (RHS Librarian and Archivist), 'The First Lady of Botanical Art' in *The Garden*, December (2004), p. 932.
31. Marianne North wrote an autobiography towards the end of her life entitled *Recollections of a Happy Life* (1893). This has been abridged and republished as *A Vision of Eden: The Life and Work of Marianne North*, Holt Rinehart Wilson, ed. (Webb & Bower/Royal Botanic Gardens, Kew 1980). Lavishly illustrated, it combines a brief overview of her life and the importance of her work with Marianne's own words.
32. Wilfrid Blunt, *The Art of Botanical Illustration* (1950), quoted in *A Vision of Eden*, p. 13.
33. Published as *Margaret Mee's Amazon: the Diaries of an Artist Explorer* (Antique Collectors' Club, 2004). A short but excellent biography is also given by Anita McConnell, 'Mee, Margaret Ursula (1909–1988)', *Oxford Dictionary of National Biography* (Oxford University Press, 2004), accessed at www.oxforddnb.com/view/article/60330. For another version of her journals see Tony Morrison (ed.), *Margaret Mee in Search of Flowers of the Amazon Forests* (Nonesuch Expeditions, 1988).
34. The association between female botanic artists and Kew has been continued into the twentieth and twenty-first centuries by women such as Stella Ross-Craig (1906–), Christabel King (1950–) and Lucy Smith (1968–). A fascinating overview into the collection of botanical illustrations in the Kew Archives is given by Marilyn Ward and John Flanagan in 'Portraying Plants: Illustrating Collections at the Royal Botanic Gardens, Kew' in *Art Libraries Journal*, vol. 28, no. 2 (2003), pp. 22–8.
35. Married women authors at this period would usually publish under their husband's name (the name which they would formally be known by). This can make it frustratingly difficult to find their works in libraries or trace their own names. Theresa Earle, author of *Pot-Pourri from a Surrey Garden* (Macmillan & Co., 1897) was published under the title 'Mrs C.W. Earle'. This was particularly ironic given that Charles (C.W.) Earle, scandalised by the thought of his wife as a published writer, is rumoured to have offered her £100 not to publish.
36. See the detailed history of her life and influence in Ina Taylor, *Helen*

Allingham's England: an Idyllic View of Rural Life (Webb & Bower, 1990), pp. 104–7.

37. Quoted in Andrew Clayton-Payne and Brent Elliott, *Victorian Flower Gardens* (Weidenfeld and Nicolson, 1988).
38. *Ibid.*, p. 63.
39. Penelope Hobhouse and Christopher Wood, *Painted Gardens: English Watercolours 1850–1914* (Pavilion, 1988).
40. *Ibid.*
41. Alison Kelly, *Mrs Coade's Stone* (Alison Kelly/Self-Publishing Association, 1990).

Chapter Five

1. Or as he put it in a later edition of *Systema Naturae: Creationis telluris est gloria Dei ex opere Naturae per Hominem solum* – The Earth's creation is the glory of God, as seen from the works of Nature by Man alone.
2. These are mainly the conifers.
3. Ray Desmond, *The History of the Royal Botanic Gardens, Kew* (Harvill Press, 1995), p. 79.
4. Quoted in Ann Shteir, *Cultivating Women, Cultivating Science: Flora's Daughters and Botany in England 1760 to 1860* (Johns Hopkins University Press, 1996), pp. 27–8.
5. The sexual parts of flowers such as the lily were still being removed prior to the flowers being brought into the house well into the twentieth century.
6. Quoted in David Stuart, *The Garden Triumphant: A Victorian Legacy* (Viking, 1988), p. 20.
7. For a superb discussion of the impact of Linnaeus on botanical studies and women in the eighteenth century see the fascinating work of Ann Shteir, *Cultivating Women, Cultivating Science*. The ramifications of the introduction of sex into botany were far wider ranging than can even be hinted at here. The difficulties women such as Agnes Ibbetson had to be recognised for their scientific work also highlights the double discrimination encountered by the few female scientists. Agnes had a plant named after her by the editor of *Curtis's Botanical Magazine* in 1810. Cruelly the *Ibbetsonia genistoides* was later changed to *Cyclopia genistoides*.
8. Shirley Hibberd, *The Fern Garden: How to Make, Keep and Enjoy It, or Fern Culture Made Easy* (Groombridge & Sons, 1869), p. 34.
9. An excellent social history of the growth of fern mania is David Elliston Allen, *The Naturalist in Britain: A Social History* (Allen Lane, 1976).
10. Charles Druery, *Choice British Ferns: Their Varieties and Culture* (Upcott Gill, 1888), p. 10.
11. Quoted in Shteir, *Cultivating Women, Cultivating Science* (1996), p. 1.
12. Jane Loudon, *The Lady's Country Companion*, ed. Nicolas Barker (1845; The National Trust, 1984), pp. 5 and 200. Published privately for members of The National Trust.

13. On her tombstone in St John's, Hampstead she is merely described as 'wife of Edwin Lankester'.
14. Interestingly, Charles Druery also apologised for the introduction of technical terms and stated that his work would avoid 'scientific terms . . . as much as possible'. Druery, *Choice British Ferns*, p. 10.
15. Both quotes taken from Nona Bellairs, *Hardy Ferns: How I Collected and Cultivated Them* (Smith, Elder & Co., 1865).
16. This contains a particularly fine collection of fern books which was invaluable in the writing of this chapter.
17. Hibberd, *The Fern Garden* (Preface). This may have been a not very subtle dig at Jane Loudon herself who had published just a few years earlier and whose work was still very popular. Ironically Mrs Theresa Earle was to choose the very title *Gardening for the Ignorant* for her 1912 publication, breaking away from her usual 'Pot-Pourri' theme.
18. Quoted in David Elliston Allen, *The Victorian Fern Craze: A History of Pteridomania* (Hutchinson & Co., 1969), p. 56.
19. George Francis Heath, *The Fern World* (5th edn, Sampson Low, 1878), p. 109.
20. There is some disagreement as to whether it was seeds or tubers that were sent.
21. This and further information on the family, including a connection with Caroline Lamb, from www.pellow.com.
22. Maggie Campbell-Culver, *The Origin of Plants: The People and Plants that have shaped Britain's Garden History since the Year 1000* (Headline, 2001), pp. 200–1.
23. *Ibid.*, p. 170.
24. Actually discovered in 1818, but brought into cultivation by Lady Amherst in 1831.
25. Campbell-Culver, *The Origin of Plants*, p. 190. Now *Anemone tomentosa*.
26. She had by then moved from her 28 acres at Drayton Green described below to her subsequent gardens in Ealing.
27. Edinburgh Botanic Gardens has been claimed to have the oldest Tree Peony in the United Kingdom. The plant originally grew in the gardens of a house in Arbroath, the former home of John Alexander Duncan who was responsible for collecting the first Tree Peony to reach the Western world in 1787. A plant that he donated to Kew did not survive (hence the need for reintroduction).
28. She is referred to as 'Christina' by Maggie Campbell-Culver (*The Origin of Plants*, p. 192) but as Christian in the *Oxford Dictionary of National Biography*.
29. Some of these survive in the collections of the Centre for South Asian Studies, Cambridge, others in the Dalhousie Papers in the Nova Scotia Museum.
30. J. Archibald, 'Dalhousie Castle and Garden' in *Gardener's Magazine*, 1 (1826), pp. 251–8, quoted in Janet Browne, 'Ramsay, Christian, Countess of Dalhousie (1786–1839)', *Oxford Dictionary*

of *National Biography* (Oxford University Press, 2004, accessed at www.oxforddnb.com/view/article/57840

31. D. Dewing (ed.), *Home and Garden: Paintings and Drawings of English Middle-class Urban Domestic Spaces 1675–1914* (Geffrye Museum, 2003), illustrates many examples of this genre and gives a full critique of each picture.
32. John Loudon, *The Suburban Gardener and Villa Companion* (Longman, 1838), p. 574.
33. A 'rustic basket' would have been a woven (usually) wooden-basket shaped frame with plants inserted. Not, as might be assumed, a portable basket.
34. John Loudon would have greatly appreciated the presence of the cows, as he specifically recommended the keeping of one or two decorative cows in his *Suburban Gardener.*
35. Quoted in David Stuart, *The Garden Triumphant: A Victorian Legacy* (Viking, 1988), p. 26.
36. He had an affair (1840–3) with the Countess of Tankerville, thirty-five years his senior; he philandered (1843) with Eugénie Mayer, step-daughter of Wellington's aide John Gurwood; he embarked on, but shirked (1844), courtships of two heiresses to the bank, Coutts and Drummond; he contracted liaisons and venereal disease. His one genuine romance (1843–4), with the 17-year-old daughter of the Russian ambassador to France, Count Stackelberg, was broken off by her parents (unsurprisingly in the circumstances). Mary S. Millar, 'Smythe, George Augustus Frederick Percy Sydney, seventh Viscount Strangford (1818–57)', *Oxford Dictionary of National Biography* (Oxford University Press, 2004), accessed at www.oxforddnb.com/view/article/25964
37. All plant names taken from W.R. Trotter, 'The Glasshouses at Dangstein and their Contents' in Journal of *Garden History*, vol. 16, no. 1, pp. 71–89.
38. Owners of particularly impressive gardens or plant collections might expect to be approached for visits by editors of the many and various gardening and horticultural magazines of the period and lists would be compiled to assist them; in addition, fellow enthusiasts would exchange visits.
39. Reproduced in Trotter, 'The Glasshouses at Dangstein and their Contents', pp. 71–89.
40. They had moved from Biddulph in the late 1860s, however, and spent their last decades living and gardening in Worthing.
41. Kathryn Bradley-Hole, *Lost Gardens of England* (Country Life, 2004).
42. Quotes from *The Garden Notebook*, and details of Caroline Hamilton's life have been taken from Dawn Macleod, *Down-to-Earth Women: Those who Care for the Soil* (Blackwood & Sons, 1982), pp. 24–7.
43. See Chapter 3.
44. Joseph Hooker in *Curtis's Botanical Magazine* (1847), quoted in Desmond, *The History of the Royal Botanic Gardens, Kew*, pp. 184–5.

45. Sue Bennett, *Five Centuries of Women and Gardens* (National Portrait Gallery, 2000), p. 107.

Chapter Six

1. Jane Loudon, *Instructions in Gardening for Ladies* (John Murray, 1840), p. vi.
2. June Taboroff, '"Wife, Unto Thy Garden": The First Gardening Books for Women' in *Journal of Garden History*, vol. 11, no. 1, Spring (1983), pp. 1–5.
3. Quoted in Ann Shteir, *Cultivating Women, Cultivating Science: Flora's Daughters and Botany in England 1760 to 1860* (Johns Hopkins University Press, 1996), p. 40.
4. This seems variously to be spelt Jackson or Jacson. I have used Jacson as that is, the spelling preferred by Joan Percy in her 'Maria Elizabetha Jacson and Her Florist's Manual' in *Journal Garden History*, vol. 20, no. 1 (1992). Quotes from Jacson are taken from this article.
5. Rosa was featured by David Stuart in his *The Garden Triumphant: A Victorian Legacy* (Viking, 1988), pp. 86–94.
6. Louisa Johnson, *Every Lady Her Own Flower Gardener* (Wm S. Orr & Co., 1839/40), p. 4.
7. The first publication date of *Every Lady Her Own Flower Gardener* is greatly disputed. Sue Bennett (*Five Centuries of Women and Gardens*) records it variously as 1837 or 1843, while Dawn MacLeod (*Down-to-Earth Women*) states that it appeared 'the same year as Jane Loudon's' (i.e. 1840). A copy survives in the British Library dated 1839, but appears to be a second edition. Certainly an introduction to the 1840 edition records that additions have been made to 'earlier edition'. A third edition was reviewed by Loudon's *Gardener's Magazine* in 1840. The RHS Lindley Library holds an 1844 6th edition. The book achieved nine editions in ten years, and was still being produced in 1852, but editions earlier than 1840 are rare. All quotes here are taken from the 1840 and 1851 editions.
8. Also spelt 'averruncator' by John Loudon, this was a long-handled pruner reaching to a height of 15ft.
9. Louisa Johnson, *Every Lady's Guide to Her Own Greenhouse* (Wm S. Orr & Co., 1851), quoted in Sue Bennett, *Five Centuries of Women and Gardens* (National Portrait Gallery, 2000), p. 96.
10. Elizabeth von Arnim, *Elizabeth and Her German Garden* (1898; Virago, 1985), p. 53.
11. Gladys Rawson, *Eve's Garden* (W.H.&L. Collingridge, 1940), p. 1.
12. Several writers have given accounts of Jane Loudon's life (including herself). The most accessible is that of Bea Howe, *Lady with Green Fingers: The Life of Jane Loudon* (Country Life, 1961). A few details are added by Ann Shteir in her biography in the *Oxford Dictionary of National Biography* (OUP, 2004). The life of John and Jane together is charted by Priscilla Boniface in *In Search of English*

Gardens: The Travels of John Claudius Loudon and his Wife Jane (Lennard Publishing, 1987). An academic critique of her role in middle-class female society is presented by Heath Schenker, 'Women, Gardens, and the English Middle Class in the Early Nineteenth Century' in Michael Conan (ed.), *Bourgeois and Aristocratic Cultural Encounters in Garden Art, 1550–1850*, Dumbarton Oaks Library Research and Collection vol. 23, pp. 336–71.

13. Reprinted in 1994 by the University of Michegan Press and still available.
14. Particularly given their age differences: he was some twenty-four years older than her and very well established in his career.
15. Jane Loudon, *Botany for Ladies* (London, 1842), Preface.
16. Loudon, *Instructions in Gardening*, p. 392.
17. Some years ago I was responsible for instructing a party of volunteers on the correct use of a shovel, and could only long for the equivalent of a Jane Loudon for prospective shovel users.
18. Gertrude Jekyll, 1896, quoted in Cherry Lewis, *The Making of a Garden, Gertrude Jekyll: An Anthology of her writings, illustrated with her own photographs and drawings, and watercolours by contemporary artists* (Antique Collectors' Club, 1984), p. 14.
19. Loudon, *Instructions in Gardening*, pp. 7–8.
20. von Arnim, *Elizabeth and Her German Garden*, pp. 25–6.
21. Deborah Jaffe, *Ingenious Women* (Stroud, Sutton Publishing, 2003), chapter 3.
22. This picture may well be supposed to be Jane and Agnes, although one suspects she had little time left for practical gardening.
23. Oscar Wilde, *The Importance of Being Earnest* (1895).
24. Jane Loudon, *The Lady's Country Companion* (Longmans, 1845), p. 290.
25. Perhaps due to declining sales of the publication, the publishers dismissed her from the post in 1850 and replaced her with a male editor. Whether this resulted in increased sales is unknown. Certainly the summary dismissal did nothing for Jane's own self-esteem or financial situation.
26. Jane Loudon, *The Ladies' Companion at Home and Abroad* (1850) quoted in Dawn MacLeod, *Down-to-Earth Women: Those who Care for the Soil* (Blackwood, 1982) p. 23.
27. Quoted in Martin Hoyles, *Bread and Roses: Gardening Books from 1560 to 1960* (Pluto Press, 1995), p. 83.
28. After 70 years of neglect a BBC Radio 4 feature on Mrs Earle's Surrey Garden was broadcast in 1981 and repeated in 1982, leading to the publication of *Mrs Earle's Pot-Pourri* by Anne Jones, one of the presenters (BBC, 1982). It is to Anne Jones' work that I owe much of the biographical material on Mrs Earle and the quotes from some of her less available work. In addition *Pot-Pourri from A Surrey Garden* has been reprinted as a facsimile by Summersdale Press (2004).

29. The very first entry in Mrs Earle's *Pot-Pourri from a Surrey Garden* (1897) claims that 'I merely wish to talk to you on paper about several subjects as they occur to me throughout one year; and if such desultory notes prove to be of any use to you or others, so much the better'.
30. Excerpts are reproduced by Anne Jones in *Mrs Earle's Pot-Pourri* (BBC, 1982).
31. Although much later in the book Earle does mention Mrs Loudon's *Gardening for Ladies* when referring to instructions on the growing of bulbs in pots.
32. Mrs C.W. Earle, *Pot-Pourri From a Surrey Garden*, facsimile edition (Summersdale, 2004), pp. 30–1.
33. The anonymous author of *The Garden that Paid the Rent* (Chapman and Hall, 1860) would have disagreed strongly with this statement. But then the author 'knows one lady who alone keeps in order a garden of a quarter of an acre, and two greenhouses. She also attends entirely to her poultry.' Quoted in Hoyles, *Bread and Roses*, p. 82.
34. Quoted in Lewis, *The Making of a Garden*, p. 62.
35. Gertrude Jekyll is discussed in more detail in Chapter 8 as her influence extends more properly through the twentieth century.
36. It is interesting to note that *The Secret Garden* (1888) came out just ten years before *Elizabeth and Her German Garden*. One is of course a fictional work for children while the other a biographical work, but there are many coincidences between them. Both deal with the transforming nature of the garden and the emotional responses to growth and seasons.
37. Quoted as a review comment in von Arnim, *Elizabeth and Her German Garden* (Virago, 2003), rear cover.
38. Von Arnim, *Elizabeth and Her German Garden* (Virago, 1985), review quoted in the Introduction by Elizabeth Jane Howard.
39. *Ibid.*, E.M. Forster's and Hugh Walpole's comments in the Introduction.
40. Vita Sackville-West coined this memorable phrase in a reply to a man who 'writes to me quite often from a Priory in Sussex'. Vita Sackville-West, *Even More For Your Garden* (Michael Joseph, 1958), quoted in Deborah Kellway (ed.), *The Virago Book of Women Gardeners* (Virago, 1996), p. 21.
41. Published under the pseudonym Barbara Campbell.
42. Lady Martineau also wrote *The Herbaceous Border* (1913) for those left behind in the gloom of England. The book must have been horticulturally accurate (and in the latest wild style) as it had an introduction by William Robinson.
43. The genre appears to have lost popularity with the rise of the television and radio gardeners in the 1960s and 1970s.
44. An incitement that he managed with aplomb. His arch rival William Robinson responded with some of the most vitriolic arguments that have ever graced gardening magazines!
45. Later Hon. Mrs Evelyn Cecil, under which name she wrote *London*

Parks and Gardens (Macmillan, 1907) and *Children's Gardens* (Macmillan, 1902). To avoid confusion I have continued to refer to her as Alicia Amherst.

46. Alicia Amherst, 1935 in Hoyles, *Bread and Roses*, p. 10.
47. In the first years of the twentieth century both Jekyll and Willmott would publish their own books, as would Frances Wolseley, but they will be dealt with in Chapters 7 and 8.
48. Quoted in the Foreword by Judith Tankard in Rose Standish Nichols, *English Pleasure Gardens* (1902; David R. Godine Publications, 2003).
49. Quoted in Yvonne Cuthbertson, *Women Gardeners: A History* (Arden Press, 1998), p. 172.
50. Eleanour Sinclair Rohde, *The Story of the Garden* (Medici Society, 1932), p. 137.
51. For example Lady Charlotte Murray, *The British Garden* (London, 1799), and a book on greenhouse plants by a Mrs Henrietta Moriarty, neither of which are referenced elsewhere.
52. Rohde, *The Story of the Garden*, p. 184.
53. Alicia Amherst, Lady Cecil, apparently published this in *Archaeologia* LIV, quoted in Rohde, *Story of the Garden*, p. 47.
54. For more on the work of Maud Messell at Nymans (and the source of the above quotes) see Shirley Nicholson, *Nymans: The Story of a Sussex Garden* (Sutton Publishing/ The National Trust, 1992/2001).
55. Quoted in Shteir, *Cultivating Women, Cultivating Science*, p. 50 (noted as being cited in Wilfrid Blunt, *The Compleat Naturalist: A Life of Linnaeus* (Collins, 1971).

Chapter Seven

1. Hon. Frances Wolseley, *Gardening for Women* (Cassell and Co., 1908), p. 5.
2. In 1899 Daisy, Countess of Warwick published an article highlighting the plight of what she termed The Surplus Million of Women in the *Women's Agricultural Times*, vol. 1, no. 1, July (1899).
3. Capable of being re-sharpened these wedge-shaped 'thimbles' of metal were popular with both men and women weeders probably since the medieval period.
4. Pamela Horn, *The Rise and Fall of the Victorian Servant* (Alan Sutton,1996), p. 105.
5. The 1899 meeting of women's employment in horticulture was held as part of The International Congress of Women. The quotes come from Kay Sanecki, 'The Ladies and The Gentleman' in *Hortus*, vol. 8, no. 4 (1994), pp. 63–72.
6. Information on these schools is available from the detailed work of Anne Meredith. Anne Meredith, 'Horticultural Education in England, 1900–40: Middle-Class Women and Private Gardening Schools' in *Journal of Garden History*, vol. 31, no. 1 (2003); Anne Meredith, 'Middle-Class Women and Horticultural Education, 1890–1939', unpublished Ph.D. thesis, University of Brighton,

2001. The article necessarily contains only a very small part of the material covered in the thesis. Anne Meredith's work has been fundamental in correcting the perception in garden history that the Glynde College had been of greater impact than many others. It also re-examined our understanding of the social make-up of the pupils at the various colleges, and the role of the lower-middle-class daughters, as well as daughters of 'professionals'.

The details and history of many of these is taken from Wolseley, *Gardening for Women*, where she gives details of other gardening schools, including syllabuses, fees, etc. both in England and abroad; in addition, material has been taken from Anne Meredith's more recent work on the histories of the schools. See Meredith, 'Horticultural Education in England, 1900–40'; Meredith, 'Middle-Class Women and Horticultural Education'.

7. Although the school opened in 1906 it was not enrolled with the RHS until 1909.
8. She became Viscountess on the death of her father in 1913. Jane Brown includes a chapter on Frances Wolseley in her book *Eminent Gardeners: Some People of Influence and their Gardens 1880–1980* (Viking, 1990). In addition, a biography of Frances Wolseley was written by Marjory Pegram entitled *The Wolseley Heritage, The Story of Frances Viscountess Wolseley and Her Parents* (John Murray, 1939).
9. Wolseley, *Gardening for Women*, p. 5.
10. *Ibid.*, p. 120.
11. Wolseley, *Gardening for Women.*
12. It is interesting to note the dual terminologies that exist at this period. Although Wolseley's books used the term 'women/woman' in their titles and text, her school and many of the other private schools were usually named as schools for 'lady' gardeners.
13. Published in 1916, and with a foreword dated 1914, the statement by Viscountess Wolseley that the gardens were by then fifteen years old stands at odds with the evidence elsewhere that the school was founded on her thirtieth birthday. Perhaps she had been mentally planning the school and gardens from 1900 – although certainly the move to Ragged Lands did not occur in that year.
14. William Robinson, *The Wild Garden* (John Murray, 1870).
15. Both Frances Wolseley's *Gardening for Women* and her later book, *In a College Garden* (John Murray, 1916) are well provided with photographs. This despite the difficult period in which the latter was published. Interestingly, the military nature of the uniform at Glynde School appears accentuated in the latter book; there is also a reference to the giving of small flower-shaped medals for particularly good and diligent work (p. 55).
16. Le Lièvre, *Miss Willmott of Warley Place: Her Life and Her Gardens* (Faber and Faber, 1980), p. 209.
17. Wolseley, *In a College Garden.*

18. Earle, *Pot-Pourri from a Surrey Garden* (1897; Summersdale, 2004), p. 55.
19. *Ibid.*
20. *Ibid.* Frances Wolseley also expressed the same opinion in her own various publications, and preferred women to wait until they were 18 or even 20 before embarking on training for a gardening career. She also felt that they should commit themselves, rather than having the decision made by their parents, as the training involved long and arduous years of study.
21. Chrystabel Proctor's papers are held at Girton College, Cambridge.
22. The following quotes on the role of women gardeners in the colonies are taken from Wolseley, *Gardening for Women*, pp. 89–97.
23. *Ibid.*, p. 110.
24. Books by women describing the making and management of their own gardens comment with considerable frequency on the drunkenness and on occasions, even insanity, of their gardeners (see Chapter 6). The issue of drunkenness was frequently addressed in Victorian magazines on the household and garden. For a fascinating discussion see David Stuart, *The Garden Triumphant: A Victorian Legacy* (Viking, 1988), pp. 229–36. In his wonderful phraseology, he records that 'Rosa' (the anonymous writer in the *Cottage Gardener*, 'saw alcohol everywhere, and especially in the garden'.
25. Wolseley, *Gardening for Women*, pp. 113–14.
26. See Note 6.
27. Ursula Maddy, *Waterperry: A Dream Fulfilled* (Merlin Books, 1990). Apparently Beatrix did mellow slightly when Bridget brought her children to the school on a visit.
28. Quoted in Maddy, *Waterperry*, p. 15.
29. Sue Bennett, *Five Centuries of Women and Gardens* (National Portrait Gallery, 2000), p. 128.
30. Information on life at Waterperry taken from Maddy, *Waterperry*.
31. Undertaking research on the Lost Gardens of Wandlebury, Cambridgeshire, I was delighted to come across a cutting of the advertisement, and correspondence about the possibility of Schwerdt and Kreutzberger taking on the derelict kitchen gardens there. Alas for Wandlebury they chose Sissinghurst instead.
32. Photograph by Valerie Finnis held at the Royal Horticultural Society, Lindley Library.
33. Countess of Warwick also appears in her role as a garden creator in Chapter 8.
34. Peter King, *Women Rule the Plot* (Duckworth, 1999), pp. 8–9.
35. Lord Willoughby de Broke, *Land Magazine*, Spring 1898. Quoted in M. Blunden, *The Countess of Warwick: A Biography* (Cassell, 1967), p. 121.
36. See Kay Sanecki, *A Short History of Studley College* (Privately published, 1990); E. Morrow, 'History of Swanley, Wye', in *Journal of the Agricola Club and Swanley Guild*, XII (1984/5), pp. 61–142.

37. Information taken from website on Violet Firth, writer and psychic, who trained at Studley.
38. The school and nursery later moved to Aldersey Hall, Cheshire. See Meredith, 'Horticultural Education in England, 1900–40'.
39. Maggie Campbell-Culver, *The Origin of Plants: The People and Plants that have shaped Britain's Garden History since the Year 1000* (Headline, 2001), p. 224.
40. Wolseley, *Gardening for Women.*
41. Frances Wolseley discusses schools and women's education movements abroad in both *Gardening for Women* and *Women and the Land* (Chatto & Windus, 1916), often contrasting England's poor record with that of other European countries.
42. Wolseley, *In a College Garden*, p. 105.
43. Wolseley, *Gardening for Women*, p. 222.
44. By 1899 the fashion for children's gardens was such that even the Revd Samuel Reynolds Hole (a respected rosarian and plantsman) had added a chapter on Children's Gardens to his book *Our Gardens* (Dent & Co., 1899).
45. Lucy Latter, *School Gardening for Little Children* (Swan Sonnenschein & Co., 1906), pp. xviii, 35.
46. Essex Gardens Trust for example run schemes in association with local schools to promote school gardening.
47. Wolseley, *Gardening for Women*, p. 29.
48. *Ibid.*, p. 33.

Chapter Eight

1. Quoted in Sylvia Kent, 'Wonderful Winter at Warley', in *Essex Countryside*, December 1999, p.19.
2. Louisa Johnson, *Every Lady Her Own Flower Gardener* (Wm S. Orr & Co., 1839/40), p. 4.
3. Dates for Norah's birth have been revised from those normally given in the light of research being undertaken by her biographer Allyson Hayward. Allyson has also revised much of the material on Norah and emphasises the mature age and approach that Norah had attained by the time of her gardening career. Information from this research, to be published in America *c.* 2007 was kindly shared by Ms Hayward at a conference given by the Garden History Society in November 2005.
4. In fact the Manor House itself had been given to the couple by Lord Wantage, a Lindsay family friend, who had also given Norah a cheque for £5,000 on her wedding day.
5. Christopher Hussey, 'The Manor House Sutton Courtenay, Berkshire', *Country Life*, 16 May (1931), pp. 646–52.
6. Norah Lindsay 'The Manor House Sutton Courtenay' in *Country Life*, 23 May (1931); also quoted in Jane Brown, *Eminent Gardeners: Some People of Influence and their Gardens 1880–1980* (Viking, 1990), p. 65.
7. Lindsay, 'The Manor House, Sutton Courtenay, in *Country Life*, 23 May.

8. Brown, *Eminent Gardeners*, p. 63.
9. These three names are themselves representatives of the eccentric genius of the country house circles of the period. Nancy Astor was the first female to take a seat in Parliament, and Cliveden country house parties were unequalled for the number and range of political and social figures who would gather there, particularly in Ascot week. Lady Sibyl Colefax, wife of Sir Arthur Colefax, was a society hostess who went on to found the interior design firm of Colefax and Fowler with John Fowler. Lady Emerald Cunard was a reputed drug addict, an American who moved in the highest circles of society and was later to be party to the affair between Mrs Simpson and Edward VII. Her daughter Nancy Cunard had connections with the Charleston set through Duncan Grant.
10. A 'lolloping bush' of Phlomis appears labelled as such in a photograph of the garden in Lindsay, 'The Manor House, Sutton Courtenay', in *Country Life*, 23 May (1931), p. 615.
11. *Ibid*. pp. 610–16.
12. Quoted in Brown, *Eminent Gardeners*, Chapter 3.
13. I have to thank Allyson Hayward (Norah Lindsay's biographer) for this wonderful quote shared at a conference given by the Garden History Society in November 2005.
14. Edith Wharton was later to be Johnston's neighbour in France during the 1920s.
15. Vita Sackville-West, 'Hidcote Manor' in *Journal of the Royal Horticultural Society*, vol. lxxiv, part 11, November (1949), pp. 476–81.
16. Brown, *Eminent Gardeners*, p.72.
17. In a rather complicated negotiation Johnston gifted Hidcote to The National Trust, but unfortunately did not specify the exact involvement of the Lindsays in its future management.
18. James Lees-Milne Diaries (27 August 1948) quoted in Anna Pavord, *Hidcote Manor Garden* (National Trust, 1993; 2004) p. 25.
19. Letter from Lord Esher (Gardens Committee) to James Lees-Milne, quoted in Pavord, *Hidcote Manor Garden*, p. 27.
20. In her article on Lawrence Johnston, Alvide Lees-Milne gives Norah a passing mention as being one of several friends who 'perhaps contributed an idea here or there'. See Alvide Lees-Milne, 'Lawrence Johnston, Creator of Hidcote Garden', in *Hortus*, vol. 1, no. 2 (1987), pp. 75–83. The latest guidebook by the garden historian Anna Pavord gives prominence to the role of Norah in the later relaxed style of the garden planting (Anna Pavord, *Hidcote Manor Garden* (National Trust 2004) as does Jane Brown in her discussion of Hidcote (Brown, *Eminent Gardeners*).
21. A memorial fund set up in her name exists to 'assist women in the study of botany and in particular in the collection of plants and seeds of possible horticultural value'.
22. Quoted in David Buttery, *Portrait of a Lady: The Illustrated Life of*

Frances, Countess of Warwick (Brewin Books, 1988) p. 18.

23. Gertrude Jekyll quoted in Cherry Lewis, *The Making of a Garden, Gertrude Jekyll: An Anthology of her writings, illustrated with her own photographs and drawings, and watercolours by contemporary artists* (Antique Collectors' Club, 1984) p. 13.
24. Gertrude Jekyll, *Children and Gardens* (1908; Antique Collectors' Club, 1982) p. 9.
25. Quoted in Primrose Arnander, 'Jekyll Family History' in Michael Tooley and Primrose Arnander (eds), *Gertrude Jekyll: Essays on the Life of a Working Amateur* (Michaelmas Books, 1995).
26. Joan Edwards 'Gertrude Jekyll: Prelude and Fugue', in Tooley and Arnander (eds), *Gertrude Jekyll*: Essays, p. 48.
27. Her books also inspired Constance Spry, the famous flower arranger of the early to mid-twentieth century.
28. Gertrude Jekyll and Lawrence Weaver, *Gardens for Small Country Houses* (Country Life, 1914), p. 36. The chapter entitled 'A Garden in West Surrey' is about Munstead Wood, but the garden is never identified by name, nor is the fact that it is owned by one of the authors.
29. Folly Farm currently hosts a Women Returners to Amenity Gardening Scheme (WRAG) trainee, something of which Gertrude would have fully approved.
30. Quoted in Lewis, *The Making of a Garden*, p. 22.
31. Quoted in Judith Tankard and Martin Wood, *Gertrude Jekyll at Mustead Wood: Writing, Horticulture, Photography, Homebuilding*, (Bramley Books, 1998), p. 108.
32. Helen Allingham lived near Godalming and recorded in watercolour some of the villages that Jekyll photographed. Allingham's watercolour of the South Border at Munstead Wood was recently acquired by the Godalming Museum with assistance from the National Art Collections Fund.
33. Quoted in Lewis, *The Making of a Garden*, p. 31.
34. *Ibid.*
35. *Ibid.*
36. Gertrude Jekyll, *Children and Gardens* (1908; Antique Collectors' Club, 1982), p.62.
37. Jekyll, *Children and Gardens*, p. 9.
38. On Jekyll's death Ellen Willmott wrote that Gertrude Jekyll 'was a sensitive and great personality . . . In her were all the qualities I most admire, for apart from being a great gardener and lover of plants, her sense of beauty and the picturesque in a garden combined with horticulture and cultivation at its best is rarely found.' With rather more bias she added, 'In fact I have never known it except in the case of my sister, Mrs Berkley, at Spetchley.' Ellen Willmott letter to Mr H. Cowley quoted in Betty Massingham, *Miss Jekyll: Portrait of a Great Gardener* (David & Charles, 1973), pp. 171–2.
39. Ellen Willmott, *The Genus Rosa*, 2 vols (John Murray, 1910, 1914).

40. Avray Tipping writing in *Country Life*, May 1915, quoted in Bea Howe, 'Rosarian of Essex: Ellen Willmott (1858–1934)' in *Essex Countryside*, June (1959) pp. 236–7.
41. Much of the information on Miss Willmott and Warley Place is taken from her biography by Audrey le Lièvre, *Miss Willmott of Warley Place: Her Life and Her Gardens* (Faber and Faber, 1980).
42. Helen Tasker was herself a somewhat unusual woman of the period. Devoutly Catholic, her charity and generosity to the Catholic Church resulted in her being created a Countess of the Holy Roman States.
43. Mrs C.W. Earle and Ethel Case, *Gardening for the Ignorant* (Macmillan & Co., 1912), p. xiv.
44. Le Lièvre, *Miss Willmott of Warley Place*, p. 48.
45. *Ibid.* It is possible that she was already working on daffodils before she joined the RHS and the membership was an initial stage to her planned eventual election.
46. *Ibid.*
47. Jekyll, *Children and Gardens*, pp. 24, 27.
48. Le Lièvre, *Miss Willmott of Warley Place*, p.117.
49. *Ibid.*, p. 140.
50. Major sources for this section have been Anne Scott-James, *Sissinghurst: the Making of a Garden* (Michael Joseph, 1974) and Jane Brown, *Vita's Other World* (Viking, 1985).
51. Vita Sackville-West writing in *The Observer* quoted in Scott-James, *Sissinghurst*, p. 121.

Chapter Nine

1. Mary Hampden, *Every Woman's Flower Garden* (Herbert Jenkins, 1915) quoted in Martin Hoyles, *Bread and Roses: Gardening Books from 1560 to 1960* (Pluto, 1995), p.75.
2. Ray Desmond, *The History of the Royal Botanic Gardens, Kew* (Harvill, 1995), p. 306.
3. *Ibid.*, p. 376.
4. Quoted in Viscountess Frances Wolseley, *Women and the Land* (Chatto & Windus, 1916), p. 211.
5. Although Frances Wolseley was optimistically confident that the war was coming to a close in 1916, she was realistic about the number of men that would be lost and its impact on economy and society.
6. Internal reorganisation in *c.* 1915 led to a name change, becoming the Women's Farm and Garden Union (WFGU), as used by Viscountess Wolseley in her writings of 1916. After the First World War the name changed again to the Women's Farm and Garden Association (WFGA), when the WFGU and the Women's National Land Service Corps (WNLSC) were combined. The WNLSC had been formed prior to the war and assisted the government in the setting up of the Women's Land Army (WLA).
7. Dawn MacLeod, *Down-to-Earth Women: Those who Care for the Soil* (Blackwood, 1982).
8. Anne Meredith, 'Horticultural education in England, 1900–40: Middle-Class Women and Private Gardening Schools in *Journal of*

Garden History, vol. 31, no.1, Spring (2003), p. 67–79.

9. Daphne Byrne quoted in Ursula Maddy, *Waterperry: A Dream Fulfilled* (Merlin Books, 1990), p. 46–7. This rate is queried by Ursula Maddy, who suggests that the soldiers were actually paid one shilling a day.
10. There is no date printed in the book but the text makes it clear that it was published at the outbreak of war.
11. Richard Suddell, *Practical Gardening and Food Production in Pictures*, Odhams Press (*c.* 1940).
12. Buckner Hollingsworth, *Her Garden was Her Delight: Famous Women Gardeners* (New York, Macmillan 1962), Dedication.
13. Edward Brown, *Make Your Garden Feed You: a concise practical book on gardening, poultry, rabbit breeding and bee-keeping in war-time conditions* (Literary Press, *c.* 1940).
14. In fact the slightly odd shape of both the shaft and the metal 'plate' makes positive identification as either a shovel or a spade difficult.
15. All quotes from Marjorie Williams taken from her private journal by very kind permission of her granddaughter Cassandra Phillips. This fascinating and poignant journal is to be published by Truran Press in 2007.
16. A phrase used extensively by Mr Bristow in his book on *How to Run an Allotment*, (Nelson & Sons Ltd, 1940) specifically for novices to the allotment world. This book is a wonderful insight into the allotment in wartime. However, at this early stage in the war the effect of conscription had obviously not hit home, as he still addresses 'the average man with a normal job of work to do'.
17. Society for the Diffusion of Useful Knowledge, *The Penny Magazine*, 1845, pp. 87–9.
18. David Crouch and Colin Ward, *The Allotment: Its Landscape and Culture* (Five Leaves, 1997), pp. 71–3.
19. *Ibid.*, pp. 74–5.
20. Allotments are still set out as 10 poles (or occasionally rods). This is approximately 275 sq metres.
21. Although by the time *Gardening for the Ignorant*, was published in 1912, Mrs Earle's attitude was beginning to change to one of active hands-on management in all spheres of the garden. By then, too, Mrs Earle had also begun to abandon her London house and live permanently in the 'suburban' house to be nearer the garden at all seasons.
22. Flora Thompson, *Lark Rise to Candleford* (Penguin, 1939), pp. 62–3.
23. Martyn Hall, *Allotment Gardening* (Ward, Lock & Co., 1951), Preface. Why weeding should always be associated with the term 'light' when women are involved is a mystery.
24. Yvonne Cuthbertson, *Women Gardeners: A History* (Arden Press, 1998), p. 188.
25. Website of Culpeper accessed in 2004 at www.culpepper.co.uk
26. As well as material taken from her own books, biographical detail presented here was supplemented

in particular from Joan Thirsk, 'Rohde, Eleanour Sophy Sinclair (1881–1950)', *Oxford Dictionary of National Biography*, Oxford University Press, 2004) accessed at www.oxforddnb.com/view/article/38541

27. Beatrix Potter, *The Tale of Tom Kitten* (Frederick Warne & Co., (1907).
28. Rabbits do not like box plants and the characteristic smell will also mask the scent of anything more to their taste on the other side. Like all rabbit deterrents this is not, however, rabbit proof or foolproof. Mr McGregor's neat kitchen garden was also based on a real garden at Lingholm, near Keswick and stands as a monument to many an Edwardian kitchen garden. A re-creation of Mr McGregor's Garden won a gold medal at Chelsea Flower Show in 1999.
29. It is interesting to note that Gertrude Jekyll, Ellen Willmott, Norah Lindsay and Theresa Earle all recorded that they favoured William Robinson's style of gardening as outlined in his book *The Wild Garden*, (John Murray, 1870) and *The English Flower Garden* (John Murray, 1883).
30. Quoted in *The Times*, Obituary, 22 January 2005.
31. With its organic principles, Highgrove also pays tribute to Lady Eve Balfour (1898–1990), author of *The Living Soil* (Faber & Faber, 1943) and early promoter of the holistic approach of the Soil Association.
32. Beth Chatto and Christopher Lloyd, *Dear Friend and Gardener: Letters on Life and Gardening* (Frances Lincoln, 1998).
33. The making of Barnsley House garden is documented in Rosemary Verey, *The Making of a Garden* (Frances Lincoln, 2001).
34. *Report of the Departmental Committee of Inquiry into Allotments*, Cmnd 4166 (HMSO, 1969) ('Thorpe Report'). Quoted in Crouch and Ward, *The Allotment*, p. 91.
35. Geraldine Kilbride, *One Woman's Plot: A Year in the Life of a Suburban Allotment* (Five Leaves, 1997), gives a fascinating insight into the interactions of the male and female plotholders around her, and the skirmishes of the modern allotment army.
36. Vita Sackville-West, *Even More for Your Garden* (Michael Joseph, 1958), quoted in Deborah Kellaway (ed.), *The Virago Book of Women Gardeners* (Virago Press, 1996), p. 21.

Bibliography

PUBLICATIONS PRE-1957

Abercrombie, J. *Every Man His Own Gardener*, W. Griffin, 1767
Amherst, Hon. A. (Cecil, Lady Evelyn), *Children's Gardens*, Macmillan, 1902
——. *London Parks and Gardens*, Constable & Co., 1907
——. *A History of Gardening in England*, Bernard Quaritch, 1896
——. *Historic Gardens of England*, Country Life, 1938
Anon., *The Garden that Paid the Rent*, Chapman and Hall, 1860
Anon. 'The Manor House, Sutton-Courtenay, Berks', *Country Life*, 6 February (1904) pp. 198–204
Arnim, Elizabeth, Countess von, *Elizabeth and her German Garden*, 1898; Virago, 1985
——. *The Solitary Summer*, Macmillan, 1899
——. *The April Baby's Book of Tunes*, Macmillan, 1900
——. *The Adventures of Elizabeth in Rügen*, Macmillan, 1904
Austen, J. *Pride and Prejudice*, Penguin, 1972 edn (orig. pub. 1813)
Austen, R. *A Treatise of Fruit Trees with the Spirituall Use of the Orchard*, London, 1653
Balfour, Lady Eve. *The Living Soil*, Faber & Faber, 1943
Bateman, J. *Orchidaceae of Mexico and Guatemala*, London, 1837–43
Beaufort, H. *Dialogues on Botany: for the use of young persons explaining the structure of plants and the progress of vegetation*, R. Hunter, 1819
Bellairs, N. *Going Abroad*, London, 1857
Bellairs, N. *Hardy Ferns: How I Collected and Cultivated Them*, Smith, Elder & Co., 1865
Bellairs, N. *Wayside Flowers: or Gleanings from Rock and Field towards Rome*, Smith, Elder & Co., 1866
Blackwell, E. *A Curious Herball*, London, 1737–9
Blomfield, Sir R. *The Formal Garden in England*, Macmillan & Co., 1892
Boyle, E.V. (Hon.). *Days and Hours in the Garden*, Elliot Stock, 1884
——. *A Garden of Pleasure*, Elliot Stock, 1895
——. *Gardens in Summer*, Elliot Stock, 1905
Brewer, J.A. *A New Flora of the Neighbourhood of Reigate, Surrey*, Pamplin, 1856

Bristow, M. *How to Run an Allotment*, Nelson & Sons Ltd, 1940
Brookshaw, G. *A New Treatise on Flower Painting or Every Lady her own Drawing Master*, William Stockdale, 1816
Brown, E.T. *Make Your Garden Feed You: a concise practical book on gardening, poultry, rabbit breeding and bee-keeping in war-time conditions*, The Literary Press Ltd, *c*. 1940
Butler, C. *Feminnene Monarchie*, London, 1623
Campbell, Barbara (pseudonym M.A. Wright). *The Garden of a Commuter's Wife*, Macmillan & Co., 1911
Chamberlain, E.L. with Douglas, F. *The Gentlewoman's Book of Gardening*, Henry and Co., 1892
Chanter, C. *Ferny Combes: A Ramble after Ferns in the Glens of Devonshire*, Lovell Reed, 1856
Cook, E.T. and Parsons, B. *Gardens of England*, A. & C. Black, 1908
Druery, C. *Choice British Ferns: Their Varieties and Culture*, Upcott Gill, 1888
Earle, C.W. *Pot-Pourri from a Surrey Garden*, Macmillan & Co., 1897
——. *More Pot-Pourri from a Surrey Garden*, Macmillan & Co., 1899
——. *Old Time Gardens*, Macmillan & Co., 1901
——. *A Third Pot-Pourri*, Macmillan & Co., 1903
——. *Memoirs and Memories*, Smith, Elder & Co., 1911
——. and Case, E. *Gardening for the Ignorant*, Macmillan & Co., 1912
——. *Pot-Pourri Mixed by Two*, Smith, Elder & Co., 1914
Edgeworth, M. *The Parent's Assistant, or, Stories for Children*, 2nd edn, J. Johnson, 1796
——. *Early Lessons for Children on Moral and Religious Duties* Enforced by Scripture Examples, J. Johnson, 1801
Elgood, G.S. (with text notes by G. Jekyll). *Some English Gardens*, Longmans & Co., 1914
Ely, H.R. *A Woman's Hardy Garden*, New York, Macmillan & Co., 1903
Evelyn, C. *The Lady's Recreation* (Republished in 1718 as *Being a Third Part of the Art of Gardening Improv'd*), London 1717
Ewing, J.H. *Letters From a Little Garden*, Society for Promoting Christian Knowledge, 1886
——. *Mary's Meadow*, Society for Promoting Christian Knowledge, 1886
Fairbrother, N. *Men and Gardens: England and its Gardens from the Anglo-Saxons to the Modern Age*, Hogarth Press, 1956
Fiennes, C. *Through England on a Side Saddle in the Time of William and Mary*, 1697–8; Leadenhall Press, 1888
Fish, M. *We Made a Garden*, W.H. & L. Collingridge, 1956; Modern Library Gardening, 2002
Fitton, S.M. (with E. Fitton). *Conversations on Botany*, Longman, 1817
Fitzherbert, Sir A. *Book of Husbandry*, London, 1523
Francis, G.H. *The Fern World*, London, 1877
——. *Fern Paradise: a Plea for the Culture of Ferns*, London, 1878

Francis, G.W. *An Analysis of the British Ferns and their Allies*, London, 1837

Gerard, J. *Herball or General Historie of Plants*, London 1597; Thomas Johnson, 1633

Gothein, M.L. *A History of Garden Art*, Germany 1913; Dent & Sons, 1928

——. *Indian Gardens*, Germany, 1926

Grey, E. *A Choice Manuel of Rare and Select Secrets in Physic and Chyrurgy*, London, *c.* 1630

Hale, T. *Eden: or a Compleat Body of Gardening, compiled and digested from the papers of the late Mr Hale*, London, 1757

Hall, M. *Allotment Gardening*, Ward, Lock & Co., 1951

Hampden, M. *Every Woman's Flower Garden*, Herbert Jenkins, 1915

Hassard, A. *Floral Decorations for the Dwelling House*, Macmillan & Co., 1875

Hibberd, S. *Brambles and Bay Leaves: Essays on the Homely and Beautiful*, London, 1855

——. *Rustic Adornments for Homes of Taste: and Recreations for Townfolk in the Study and Imitation of Nature*, Driffield, 1856

——. *The Fern Garden: How to Make, Keep and Enjoy It, or Fern Culture Made Easy*, Groombridge & Sons, 1869

Hill, J. *The Gardener's New Kalendar*, London, 1758

——. *The Vegetable System*, London, 1759

Hole, S. Reynolds. *Our Gardens*, Dent & Co., 1899

Hope, F. *Notes and Thoughts on Gardens and Woodlands*, Macmillan & Co., 1881

Hughes, W. *The Flower Garden; or how most flowers are ordered, increased etc*, London, 1672

Hussey, Christopher. 'The Manor House, Sutton Courtenay, Berkshire', *Country Life*, 16 May (1931), pp. 646–52

Ibbetson, Agnes. 'On the Sturcture and Growth of Seeds', *Journal of Natural Philosophy, Chemistry and the Arts*, vol. xxvii, no. 121, September 1810

Jacson, M. *Botanical Dialogues between Hortensia and Her Four Children*, London, 1797

——. *Florist's Manual*, Henry Colburn, 1816

Jekyll, G. *Wood and Garden: Notes and Thoughts, Practical and Critical, of a Working Amateur*, Longmans, 1899

——. *Homes and Gardens: Notes and Thoughts, Practical and Critical, of a Worker in Both*, Longmans, 1900

——. *Lilies for English Gardens: A Guide for Amateurs*, Country Life, 1901

——. *Wall and Water Gardens*, Country Life, 1901

——. *Roses for English Gardens*, Country Life, 1902

——. *Old West Surrey: Some Notes and Memories*, Longmans, 1904

——. *Children and Gardens*, Country Life, 1908; Antique Collectors' Club, 1982

——. *Colour in the Flower Garden*, Country Life, 1908

——. *Garden Ornament*, Country Life, 1918

——. *Old English Household Life: Some Account of Cottage Objects and Country Folk*, B.T. Batsford, 1925

—— and Weaver, L. *Gardens for Small Country Houses*, Country Life, 1914

Johnson, C. *The Ferns of Great Britain*, London, 1855

Johnson, L. *Every Lady Her Own Flower Gardener*, Wm S. Orr & Co., 1839/40

——. *Every Ladies' Guide to Her Own Greenhouse*, Wm S. Orr & Co., 1851

Kent, E. *Flora Domestica: or the Portable Flower Garden*, Whittaker, Treacher & Co., 1823

——. *Sylvan Sketches: or a companion to the park and shrubbery: with illustrations from the works of the poets*, Whittaker, Treacher & Co., 1825

——. 'An Introductory View of the Linneaean System of Plants', *Magazine of Natural History* (in 9 instalments) (1830)

King, Mrs F. *The Well-Considered Garden*, Charles Scribner's Sons, 1915

——. *The Beginner's Garden*, Charles Scribner's Sons, 1921

Knight, R.P. *The Landscape: A Didactic Poem, in Three Books Addressed to Uvedale Price etc.*, W. Bulmer & Co. for G. Nichol, 1794

——. *An Analytical Enquiry into the Principles of Taste*, London, (T. Payne and J. White), 1805

Lankester, P. *A Plain and Easy Account of the British Ferns: together with their classification, arrangement of genera, structure and functions and a glossary of technical and other terms*, Robert Hardwicke, 1860

——. *Wild Flowers Worthy of Notice*, W.H. Allen, *c.* 1870

Latter, L. *School Gardening for Little Children*, Swan Sonnenschein & Co., 1906

Lawson, W. *A New Orchard and Garden (with) The Country Housewifes Garden*, Roger Jackson, 1618

Lee, J. *Introduction to Botany: Extracted from the Works of Dr Linnaeus*, London, 1760

Leyel, Mrs C.F. (Hilda). *The Magic of Herbs: A Modern Book of Secrets*, Jonathan Cape, 1927

——. *Picnics for Motorists*, G. Routledge & Sons, 1936

——. *Compassionate Herbs*, Faber & Faber, 1946

——. *Elixirs of Life*, Culpeper House, 1948

——. (ed.) and Grieve, M. *A Modern Herbal. The medicinal, culinary, cosmetic and economic properties, cultivation and folk-lore of herbs, grasses, fungi, shrubs & trees . . .*, Jonathan Cape, 1931

Lindsay, N. 'The Manor House, Sutton Courtenay', *Country Life*, 23 May 1931, pp. 610–16

Linnaeus, C. *Systema Naturae*, Lugduni Batavorum, 1736

Linton, W.J. *The Ferns of the English Lake Country: with a List of Varieties*, Hamilton, Adams & Co., 1865

Llanover, Lady. *The Autobiography and Correspondence of Mary Granville, Mrs Delany*, (6 vols), London, 1861–2

Loudon, J. (Jane). *The Mummy! A Tale of the Twenty-Second Century*, Henry Colburn Pub., 1827

——. *Stories of a Bride*, London, 1829

——. *Conversations on Chronology*, London, 1830

——. *Agnes, or the Little Girl who could keep a Promise*, London, 1839

——. *Instructions in Gardening for Ladies*, John Murray, 1840
——. *The Ladies' Flower-Garden of Ornamental Annuals*, Smith, 1840
——. *The Young Naturalist's Journey: or the Travels of Agnes Merton and her Mama*, 1840; Routledge, 1863
——. *The Ladies' Flower-Garden of Ornamental Bulbous Plants*, London, 1841
——. *The Ladies' Companion to the Flower Garden. Being an alphabetical arrangement of all the ornamental plants usually grown in gardens and shrubberies*, London, 1841
——. *The First Book of Botany . . . for Schools and Young Persons*, London, 1841
——. *Botany for Ladies, or, a Popular Introduction to the Natural System of Plants*, London, 1842
——. *The Ladies' Magazine of Gardening*, London, 1842
——. *The Year-Book of Natural History, for Young Persons*, London, 1841
——. *The Lady's Country Companion*, Longmans, 1845
——. *The Amateur Gardener's Calendar*, London, 1847
——. *The Ladies' Flower-Garden of Ornamental Greenhouse Plants*, London, 1848
Loudon, J.C. *The Villa Gardener: comprising the choice of a suburban village residence, the layout out, planting and culture of the garden . . . more particularly for the use of ladies*, ed. Jane Loudon, William Orr & Co., London, 1850 (first published as *The Suburban Gardener*)
——. *The Suburban Gardener and Villa Companion*, Longman, Orme, Brown, Green, and Longmans, 1838
——. *Arboretum et Fruticetum Britannicum*, Longman, 1838 (later editions published as the *Encyclopedia of Trees and Shrubs*)
Luxborough, H. *Letters Written by The Late Honourable Lady Luxborough to William Shenstone Esq*, ed. J. Dodsley, London, 1775
MacGregor, J. *Gardens of Celebrities and Celebrated Gardens in and around London*, Hutchinson, 1919
Maling, E.A. *The Indoor Gardener*, Longmans, 1860
Markham, G. *The English Housewife*, Roger Jackson, 1615
Martineau, Lady A.M. *The Herbaceous Border*, Williams and Norgate, 1913
——. *Gardening in Sunny Lands*, Richard Gobden-Sanderson, 1924
Meen, M. *Exotic Plants from the Royal Gardens at Kew*, RHS, 1790
Merian, M(aria). *Metamorphosis Insectorum Surinamensium*, 1705
Middleton, Mr. *Mr Middleton's Garden Book*, Daily Express Publications, *c.* 1940
Miller, P. *The Gardener's Dictionary*, London, 1731
Milton, J. *Paradise Lost*, London, 1667
Moore, T. *A Handbook of British Ferns: Intended as a guide and companion in fern culture and comprising scientific and popular descriptions . . .*, London, 1848
Moriarty, H. *Viridarium: or Greenhouse Plants*, London, 1806
Gathorne-Hardy, R. (ed.), *The Amateur Gardener's Calendar*, Faber and Faber, 1918; 1974
Murray, Lady C. *The British Garden, A Descriptive Catalogue of Hardy Plants, Indigenous or Cultivated*, London, 1799

Murray, K. *The Ladies' Flower-Garden of Ornamental Greenhouse Plants*, Thacker, Spink & Co., 1913

——. *My Garden in the Wilderness*, Thacker, Spink & Co., 1915

Nichols, R. Standish. *English Pleasure Gardens*, New York, Macmillan, 1902; David R. Godine Pub., 2003

North, M. *Recollections of a Happy Life*, ed. Mrs John Addington, Macmillan and Co., 1893

Passe, Crispin de. *Hortus Floridus* [Ultrajecti], 1614

Parkinson, J. *Paradisi in sole Paradisus Terrestris. Or A Garden of all sorts of pleasant flowers which our English ayre permitt to be noursed up: with A Kitchen garden of all manner of herbes, rootes, & fruites, for meate or sauce used with us, and An Orchard of the right orderinge planting & preserving of them and their uses & all sorte of fruit bearing Trees and shrubbes fit for our Land together with vertues*, London, Humfrey Lownes and Robert Young, 1629

Pegram, M. *The Wolseley Heritage: the Story of Frances Viscountess Wolseley and Her Parents*, John Murray, 1939

Perry, F. *Water Gardening*, Country Life, 1938

Phillips, H. *Sylva Florifera: The Shrubbery historically and botanically treated; with observations on the formation of ornamental plantation and picturesque scenery*, Longmans, 1823

Plues, M. *Rambles in Search of Mosses*, London, 1861

——. *Rambles in Search of Ferns*, London, 1861

——. *Rambles in Search of Wild Flowers*, George Bell & Sons, 1863

——. *Rambles in Search of Flowerless Plants*, Journal of Horticulture & Cottage Garden Office, 1864

Potter, B. *The Tale of Peter Rabbit*, Frederick Warne & Co., 1902

——. *The Tale of Benjamin Bunny*, Frederick Warne & Co., 1904

——. *The Tale of Tom Kitten*, Frederick Warne & Co., 1907

——. *The Tale of the Flopsy Bunnies*, Frederick Warne & Co., 1909

Pratt, A. *The Ferns of Great Britain and their Allies the Club Mosses, Pepperworts and Horsetails*, Society for Promotion of Christian Knowledge, 1855

——. *The Flowering Plants, Grasses, Sedges and Ferns of Great Britain*, Frederick Warne & Co., 1889

Price, U. *An Essay on the Picturesque*, J. Robson, 1794

Rawson, G. *Eve's Garden*, W.H.&L. Collingridge, 1940

Rea, J. *Flora; seu de Florum Cultura or a Complete Florilege*, London, Richard Marriott, 1665

Roberts, M. *Wonders of the Vegetable Kingdom Displayed: In a Series of Letters*, W.B. Whittaker, 1822

Robinson, W. *The Wild Garden*, John Murray, 1870

——. *The English Flower Garden*, John Murray, 1883

Rohde, E., Sinclair. *The Old English Herbals*, Longmans & Co., 1922

——. *The Story of the Garden*, Medici Society, 1932

——. *Shakespeare's Wild Flowers, Fairy Lore, Gardens, Herbs, Gatherers of Simples and Bee Lore*, Medici Society, 1935

——. *Herbs and Herb Gardening*, Medici Society, 1936
——. *The War-time Vegetable Garden*, Medici Society, 1940
—— and Parker, E. *The Gardener's Weekend Book*, Seeley, 1939
Roupell, A. *Flora of South Africa by a Lady*, South African Natural History Publication Co., 1850
Royal Horticultural Society. *The Vegetable Garden Displayed*, 2nd edn, Royal Horticultural Society, 1941
Sackville-West, V. 'The Land' (a poem), 1926; Webb & Bower, 1989
——. 'The Garden' (a poem), 1946; Webb & Bower, 1989
——. 'Hidcote Manor', *Journal of the Royal Horticultural Society*, vol. lxxiv, part 11, November (1949), pp. 476–81
Seton, Lady Frances Eveleen. *My Town Garden*, Nisbet & Co., 1927
Shakespeare, W. *A Midsummer Night's Dream*, London, 1595
Shenstone, W. *Unconnected Thoughts on Gardening in The Works in Verse and Prose of William Shenstone Esq*, ed. R. Dodsley, London, 1764
Sidgwick, A. and Paynter, Mrs. *Children's Book of Gardening*, Adam & Charles Black, 1909
Skene, M. *Flower Book for the Pocket*, Oxford University Press, Oxford, 1935
Society for the Diffusion of Useful Knowledge. 'The Allotment System', *The Penny Magazine*, No. 14 (1845)
Stuart, M. *Fool's Garden*, Jonathan Cape, 1936
Suddell, R. *Practical Gardening and Food Production in Pictures*, Odhams Press Ltd, *c.* 1940
Switzer, S. *The Nobleman, Gentleman, and Gard'ners Recreation*, 1715
Thompson, F. *Lark Rise to Candleford*, 1939; Penguin, 1982
Thompson, R. *The Gardener's Assistant*, Blackie & Son, 1859
Tusser, T. *Five Hundred Points of Good Husbandry*, 1573; Oxford, Oxford University Press, 1984
Wakefield, P. *An Introduction to Botany: In a Series of Familiar Letters with Illustrative Engravngs*, Newberry et al., 1796
Walpole, H. *An Essay on Modern Gardening*, Strawberry Hill Press, 1780; New York, Urses Press, 1995
Warwick, F., Countess of. *An Old English Garden*, A.L. Humphries, 1898
——. 'The Surplus Millions of Women', *Women's Agricultural Times*, vol. 1, no. 1, July (1899)
——. *Life's Ebb and Flow*, Hutchinson & Co., 1929
Waterfield, M. *Garden Colour*, Dent, 1905
Wharton, E. *Italian Villas and their Gardens*, New York, The Century Co., 1904
Wilder, L.B. *Adventures in my Garden and Rock Garden*, Doubleday Page & Co., 1928; Dyer Publications, 1976
Williams, L. *A Garden in the Suburbs*, John Lane and Bodley Head, 1901
Willmott, E. *Warley Garden in Spring and Summer*, 1909; 2nd edn, Wheldon & Wesley, 1924
——. *The Genus Rosa*, 2 vols, John Murray, 1910, 1914
Wolley, H. *The Gentlewoman's Companion . . .*, London, *c.* 1673

——. *The Queen-like Closet or Rich Cabinet*, London, 1675
——. *The Accomplish'd Ladies Delight . . .*, London, 1677
Wolseley, F. *Gardening for Women*, Cassell and Co., 1908
——. *In a College Garden*, John Murray, 1916
——. *Women and the Land*, Chatto & Windus, 1916
——. *Gardens: Their Form and Design*, Edward Arnold, 1919
Yonge, C. *Heartsease*, 2nd edn, John W. Parker & Son, *c.* 1854
——. *The Instructive Picture Book: or Letters from the Vegetable World*, Edinburgh, 1858

BOOKS PUBLISHED POST-1957

Allen, D.E. *The Victorian Fern Craze: A History of Pteridomania*, Hutchinson, 1969
——. *The Naturalist in Britain: A Social History*, Allen Lane, 1976
Baird, R. 'The Queen of the Bluestockings': Mrs Montagu's House at 23 Hill Street Rediscovered', *Apollo*, August, 2003, accessed at http//findarticles.com/p/articles/mi_mOPAL/is_498_158/ai_106652584
Batey, M. and Woudstra, J. *The Story of the Privy Garden at Hampton Court*, Barn Elms, 1995
Beck, T. *Embroidered Gardens*, David & Charles, 1979
——. *The Embroiderer's Garden*, David & Charles, 1988
——. *The Embroiderer's Flowers*, David & Charles, 1992
——. *The Embroiderer's Story*, David & Charles, 1995
——. *Gardening with Silk and Gold: A History of Gardens in Embroidery*, David & Charles, 1997
Bédoyère, G. de la (ed.). *Diary of John Evelyn (1620–1706)*, The Boydell Press, 1995
Bending, S. 'Mrs Montagu's Contemplative Bench: Bluestocking Gardens and Female Retirement', draft of article provided by the author, 2005
Bennett, S. *Five Centuries of Women and Gardens*, National Portrait Gallery, 2000
Blacker, M.R. *Flora Domestica: A History of Flower Arranging 1500–1930*, National Trust, 2000
Blunden, M. *The Countess of Warwick: A Biography*, Cassell, 1967
Blunt, W. and Stearn, W. *The Art of Botanical Illustration*, rev. edn, Antique Collectors' Club, 1994
Boniface, P. (ed.). *In Search of English Gardens: The Travels of John Claudius Loudon and his Wife Jane*, Lennard Publishing, 1987
Bradley-Hole, K. *Lost Gardens of England*, Country Life, 2004
Brown, J. *Vita's Other World*, Viking, 1985
——. *Eminent Gardeners: Some People of Influence and their Gardens 1880–1980*, Viking, 1990
——. *The Pursuit of Paradise: A Social History of Gardens and Gardening*, Harper Collins, 1999

——. *My Darling Heriott: Henrietta Luxborough, Poetic Gardener and Irrepressible Exile*, HarperCollins, 2006

Browne, J. 'Ramsay, Christian, Countess of Dalhousie (1786–1839)', *Oxford Dictionary of National Biography*, Oxford University Press, 2004. Accessed on line at www.oxforddnb.com/view/articles/57840

Burger, T. *Maria Sibylla Merian's 'A New Book of Flowers'*, Prestel Books, 1999

Buttery, D. *Portrait of a Lady: The Illustrated Life of Frances, Countess of Warwick*, Brewin Books, 1988

Campbell-Culver, M. *The Origin of Plants: The People and Plants that have shaped Britain's Garden History since the Year 1000*, Headline, 2001

Carson, R. *Silent Spring*, Riverside Press, 1962

Chatto, B. *The Dry Garden*, J.M. Dent, 1978

——. *The Damp Garden, J.M. Dent, 1982*

——. *and Lloyd, C.* Dear Friend and Gardener: Letters on Life and Gardening, *Frances Lincoln, 1998*

Christianson, C. 'Herbwomen in London 1660–1836', *The London Gardener*, vol. 6 (2001), 22–31

Clayton-Payne, A. and Elliott, B. *Victorian Flower Gardens*, Weidenfeld and Nicolson, 1988

Colborn, N. 'Dr Miriam Rothschild', *Hortus*, vol. 9. 1989, pp. 56–63

Collett-White, J. 'Yorke, Jemima, suo jure Marchioness Grey (1722–1797)', *Oxford Dictionary of National Biography*, Oxford, Oxford University Press, 2004. Accessed on line at www.oxforddnb.com/view/article/68351

Craythorn, A. *Barrells Hall: from Riches to Ruins*, privately published, 2003

Crouch, D. and Ward, C. *The Allotment: Its Landscape and Culture*, Five Leaves, 1997

Cuthbertson, Y. *Women Gardeners: A History*, Arden Press, 1998

Desmond, R. *Dictionary of British and Irish Botanists and Horticulturalists including Plant Collectors, Flower Painters and Garden Designers*, Taylor & Francis/Natural History Museum, 1994

——. The *History of the Royal Botanic Gardens, Kew*, Harvill, 1995

Dewing, D. (ed.). *Home and Garden: Paintings and Drawings of English Middle-class, Urban Domestic Spaces 1675–1914*, Geffrye Museum, 2003

Earle, C.W. *Pot-Pourri from a Surrey Garden*, Macmillan & Co., 1897; Summersdale, 2004 (facsimile edn)

Eastwood, D. *The Story of Our Gardens*, Gordon Fraser, 1958

Elliott, B. 'The First Lady of Botanical Art', *The Garden*, December 2004, 932

Fearnley-Whittingstall, J. *The Garden: An English Love Affair: One Thousand Years of Gardening*, Ted Smart, 2003

Fisher, C. *Flowers in Medieval Manuscripts*, British Library, 2004

Fleming, L. and Gore, A. *The English Garden*, Michael Joseph, 1979; Mermaid Press, 1982

Fletcher, R. *The Parkers at Saltram 1769–1789*, BBC, 1970

Foley, C. *Practical Allotment Gardening: A Guide to Growing Fruit, Vegetables and Herbs on your Plot*, New Holland, 2002

Fox, S. (ed.). *The Medieval Woman: An Illuminated Book of Days*, Cambridge, Galileo, 1999

Godber, J. *The Marchioness Grey of Wrest Park*, Bedfordshire Historical Record Society, vol. XLVII, 1968

Hall, M. *Allotment Gardening*, Ward, Lock & Co., 1951

Harvey, J. *Early Nurserymen: with Reprints of Documents and Lists*, Phillimore, 1974

——. *Medieval Gardens*, Batsford, 1981

Hayden, R. 1988/1992, *Mrs Delany and her Flower Collages*, British Museum Press 1992

Hobhouse, P. *Plants in Garden History: An Illustrated History of Plants and Their Influence on Garden Styles – from Ancient Eygpt to the Present Day*, pbk edn., Pavilion, 1997

——. *The Story of Gardening*, Dorling Kindersley, 2002

——. and Wood, C. *Painted Gardens: English Watercolours 1850–1914*, Pavilion Books, 1988

Hollingsworth, B. *Her Garden was Her Delight: Famous Women Gardeners*, New York, Macmillan, 1962

Holmes, C. (ed.). *Icons of Garden Design*, Prestel, 2001

Horn, P. *The Rise and Fall of the Victorian Servant*, Alan Sutton Publishing, 1996

Howe, B. *Lady with Green Fingers: The Life of Jane Loudon*, Country Life, 1961

Hoyles, M. *Bread and Roses: Gardening Books from 1560 to 1960*, Pluto Press, 1995

Innes, M. and Perry, C. *Medieval Flowers*, Kyle Cathie Ltd, 2002

Jaffe, D. *Ingenious Women*, Sutton, 2003

Jones, A. *Mrs Earle's Pot-Pourri*, BBC, 1982

Kellway, D. (ed.). *The Virago Book of Women Gardeners*, Virago, 1996

Kelly, A. *Mrs Coade's Stone*, Alison Kelly/Self-Publishing Association, 1990

——. 'Coade Stone in Georgian Gardens', *Journal of Garden History*, vol. 16, no. 2 (1999), 109

Kilbride, G. *One Woman's Plot*, Five Leaves, 1997

King, P. *Women Rule the Plot*, Duckworth, 1999

Knox, T. 'Lady Mary Coke's Garden at Notting Hill House', *The London Gardener*, vol. 4 (1999), pp. 52–63

——. 'The Artificial Grotto in Britain', *Magazine Antiques*, June 2002, accessed December 2005 at http://findarticles.com/p/articles/mi_m1026/is_6_161/ai_87130288.

Labbe, J.M. 'Cultivating One's Understanding: the Female Romantic Garden', *Women's Writing*, vol. 4, no. 1 (1997), 39–57

Lake, D. *Death in the Setting Sun*, Allison & Busby, 2005

Lees-Milne, A. 'Lawrence Johnston, Creator of Hidcote Garden', *Hortus*, vol. 1, no. 2 (1987), 75–83

Leslie, M. and Raylor, T. *Culture and Cultivation in Early Modern England: Writing and the Land*, Continuum International Publishing, 1992

Lewis, C. *The Making of a Garden, Gertrude Jekyll: An Anthology of her writings, illustrated with her own photographs and drawings, and watercolours by contemporary artists*, Antique Collectors' Club, 1984

Lièvre, A. le. *Miss Willmott of Warley Place: Her Life and Her Gardens*, Faber and Faber, 1980

Land Use Consultants. *Historical Survey of Wrest Park*, privately printed for English Heritage, 1983

MacLeod, D. *Down-to-Earth Women: Those who Care for the Soil*, Blackwood & Sons, 1982

Maddy, U. *Waterperry: A Dream Fulfilled*, Merlin Books, 1990

Martin, J. *Wives and Daughters: Women and Children in the Georgian Country House*, Hambledon and London, 2004

Massingham, B. *Miss Jekyll: Portrait of a Great Gardener*, Country Life, 1966; David & Charles, 1973

Mavor, E. *The Ladies of Llangollen: A Study in a Romantic Friendship*, Penguin Books, 1971 (pbk 1973)

McClain, M. *Beaufort: The Duke and his Duchess 1657–1715*, New Haven, CT, Yale University Press, 2001

McConnell, A. 'Mee, Margaret Ursula (1909–1988)', *Oxford Dictionary of National Biography*, Oxford, Oxford University Press, 2004

McLean, T. *Medieval English Gardens*, Collins, 1981

Meredith, A. 'Middle-Class Women and Horticultural Education, 1890–1939', unpublished Ph.D. thesis, University of Brighton, 2001

——. 'Horticultural Education in England, 1900–40: Middle-Class Women and Private Gardening Schools', *Journal of Garden History*, vol. 31, no. 1, Spring (2003), 67–79

Miller, M.S. 'Smyth, George Augustus Frederick Percy Sydney, seventh Viscount Strangford', *Oxford Dictionary of National Biography*, Oxford, Oxford University Press, 2004, accessed at www.oxforddnb.com/view/article/25964

Morrell, Lady Ottoline, V. *Ottoline at Garsington: Memoirs of Lady Ottoline Morrell 1915–18*, ed. R. Gathorne-Hardy, Faber, 1974

Morrison, T. (ed). *Margaret Mee in Search of Flowers of the Amazon Forests*, Nonesuch Expeditions, 1988

Morrow, E. 'History of Swanley, Wye', *Journal of the Agricola Club and Swanley Guild*, XII (1984/5), 61–142

Nicholson, S. *Nymans: The Story of a Sussex Garden*, Sutton Publishing/The National Trust, 1992, 2001

Parker, P. 'Gardens in Fiction: The Gardens of Beatrix Potter', *Hortus*, vol. 30 (1994), 106–15

Parker, R. 'Unnatural History: Women, Gardening and Femininity' in Kingsbury, N. and Richardson, T. (eds), *The Culture and Politics of Gardens*, Frances Lincoln, 2005

Pavord, A. *Hidcote Manor Garden*, The National Trust, 1993, 2004

——. *The Naming of Names: The Search for Order in the World of Plants*, Bloomsbury Publishing, 2005

Percy, J. 'Lady Luxburough Farmeress (1700–56): and her Lost Ferme Ornée',

Hortus, vol. 4, no. 2, Summer (1990), 90–8
——. 'Maria Elizabeth Jacson and her Florist's Manual', *Journal of Garden History*, vol. 20, no. 1, Spring (1992)
——. 'The Villa Garden', *Journal of Garden History*, vol. 20, no. 1, Spring (1992) 45–56
Richards, E.J. *Livre de la Cité des Dames*, Persea Books, 1982
Rothschild, Dame M. *The Butterfly Gardener*, Michael Joseph, 1983
Roupell, A. *More Cape Flowers by a Lady: The Paintings of Arabella Roupell*, South African Natural History Publication Co., 1964
Sanecki, K. 'Charlotte and her Garden at Ashridge', *Hortus*, vol. 1, no. 4 (1987), pp. 54–63
——. 'Hard Work in High Society', *Hortus*, vol. 1, (1987), pp. 64–75
——. K. *A Short History of Studley College*, privately published, 1990
——. 'The Ladies and The Gentlemen', *Hortus*, vol. 8, no. 4 (1994), pp. 63–72
——. *Ashridge: A Living History*, Phillimore, 1996
Schenker, H. 'Women, Gardens, and the English Middle Class in the Early Nineteenth Century', *Bourgeois and Aristocratic Cultural Encounters in Garden Art, 1550–1850*, ed. Michael Conan, vol. 23, 336–71, Dumbarton Oaks Research Library and Collection, 2002
Scott-James, A. *Sissinghurst: The Making of a Garden*, Michael Joseph, 1974
Scrace, D. *Flower Drawings*, Fitzwilliam Museum Handbooks, Cambridge, Cambridge University Press, 1997
Seymour, M. *Lady Ottoline Morrell: Life on a Grand Scale*, Sceptre, 1998
Shteir, A. *Cultivating Women, Cultivating Science: Flora's Daughters and Botany in England 1760 to 1860*, John Hopkins University Press, 1996
——. 'Loudon, Jane (1807–1858)', *Oxford Dictionary of National Biography*, Oxford, Oxford University Press, 2004
Stearn, W. 'Mrs Robb and "Mrs Robb's Bonnet" (*Euphorbia robbiae*)', *Journal of the Royal Horticultural Society*, vol. xcviii, part 6, June (1973), pp. 306–10
Strong, R. *The Renaissance Garden in England*, 2nd edn, Thames & Hudson, 1998
——. *The Spirit of Britain: A Narrative History of the Arts*, Hutchinson, 1999
——. *The Artist and the Garden,* New Haven, CT, Yale University Press, 2000
Stuart, D. *The Garden Triumphant: A Victorian Legacy*, Viking, 1988
——. Gardening with Antique Plants, Conran Octopus, 1997
Taboroff, J. '"Wife, Unto They Garden": The First Gardening Books for Women', *Journal of Garden History*, vol. 11, no. 1, Spring (1983), pp. 1–5
Tankard, J. and Wood, M. *Gertrude Jekyll at Munstead Wood: Writing, Horticulture, Photography, Homebuilding*, Bramley Books, 1998
Taylor, I. *Helen Allingham's England: An Idyllic View of Rural Life*, Webb & Bower, 1990
Taylor, J. *Beatrix Potter's Letters*, Warne, 1989
Thacker, C. *The Genius of Gardening: The History of Gardens in Britain and Ireland*, Weidenfeld and Nicolson, 1994
The National Trust. *Stowe Landscape Gardens*, The National Trust, 1997
——. *Biddulph Grange Garden Guide*, The National Trust, n.d.

Thomas, G.S. *Old Shrub Roses*, Phoenix House, 1955

Titchmarsh, A. *Royal Gardeners: The History of Britain's Royal Gardens*, BBC Books, 2003

Tooley, M. and Arnander, P. (eds). *Gertrude Jekyll: Essays on the Life of a Working Amateur*, Michaelmas Books, 1995

Trotter, W.R. 'The Glasshouses at Dangstein and their Contents', *Journal of Garden History*, vol. 16, no. 1 (1983), pp. 71–89

Verey, R. *The Making of a Garden*, Frances Lincoln, 2001

——. *The Scented Garden*, Frances Lincoln, 2002

Ward, M. and Flanagan, J. 'Portraying Plants: Illustrating Collections at the Royal Botanic Gardens, Kew', *Art Libraries Journal*, vol. 28, no. 2 (2003), pp. 22–8

Wilson, H.R. *A Vision of Eden: The Life and Work of Marianne North*, Royal Botanic Gardens Kew, 1980

Woodward, M. (ed.). *Gerard's Herbal or General History of Plants*, Senate, 1994

Index